Heresy Disguised as Tradition

Pedro Gabriel

En Route Books and Media, LLC
Saint Louis, MO

En Route Books and Media, LLC
5705 Rhodes Avenue
St. Louis, MO 63109

Contact us at contact@enroutebooksandmedia.com

Cover Credit: "The Temptation of St Anthony,"
Hieronymus Bosch (manner of) c. 1550 - c. 1600

ISBN: 979-8-88870-032-7
Library of Congress Control Number: 2023932110

For information contact: pedrogabrielbooks@gmail.com

Dedication

I dedicate this book to St. Peter, my namesake and saint of my devotion, that he may be the rock, the firm ground where this book stands.

I also dedicate this book to my dear Pope Benedict XVI, recently departed from our presence, that this work may be a defense of true tradition through an exercise of the hermeneutic of continuity he so steadfastly advocated.

Finally, I ask for the intercession of St. Linus, St. Pius, St. Anicetus, St. Victor, St. Callixtus, St. Dionysius, St. Sylvester, St. Celestine, St. Sixtus III, St. Leo the Great, St. Gelasius, St. Hormisdas, St. Gregory the Great, St. Agatho, St. Leo II, St. Gregory VII, St. Pius V, Bld. Innocent XI, Bld. Pius IX, St. Pius X, Vb. Pius XII, St. John XXIII, St. Paul VI, and St. John Paul II.

May God, through the intercession of these saintly pontiffs, show me the path to truth and help me assist the Church in this time of need. May I never fall into error, but rather help bring clarity where there is confusion, and unity where there is disunity. May I, useless servant, always be an instrument of His will, and never of my own. Amen.

Acknowledgments

I wish to thank my beautiful wife Claire Navarro Domingues for all her support throughout the drafting, editing, and querying for this book. I could not have done it without her invaluable assistance.

I thank Prof. Robert Fastiggi as well, for all his support and kind words, for reviewing my book, and for accepting to write the preface.

I would also like to thank Mark Hausam for reviewing chapter 13, and for sharing his expertise on apologetics about the allegedly heretical popes.

Finally, I thank Mike Lewis, Prof. Rocco Buttiglione, and Prof. Rodrigo Guerra Lopez for beta-reading and for graciously providing blurbs for my book.

Testimonials

"Pedro Gabriel displays the same admirable qualities found in his other writings, viz., careful research, clear argumentation, and charitable but cogent refutations of the false claims made by papal critics. Although Dr. Gabriel is very well-versed in theology, he is a medical doctor … by training and profession. In Heresy Disguised as Tradition, his medical training is apparent. He is able to diagnose the cancer of false theology disguised as tradition and expose its pathological qualities." **— Dr. Robert Fastiggi, Professor of Systematic Theology, Sacred Heart Major Seminary, Detroit, Michigan**

"Pedro Gabriel has succeeded in articulating an impassioned Catholic defense of the true Tradition against its pseudo-traditionalist deformations. Nothing could be more timely to understand – once and for all – that the Holy Spirit has not gone on vacation and constantly assists all successors of Peter in leading and governing the Church." **— Rodrigo Guerra Lopez, Secretary of the Pontifical Commission for Latin America.**

"Pedro Gabriel has the gift of giving transparent and honest answers to intricate questions. Now in this book he explains what Catholic Tradition is. One of the plagues of the current discussion on the Pontificate of Pope Francis are the traditionalists who do not know the tradition of the Church. To propose the same truth in a different context, in front of a different culture and of different challenges, it is not enough to repeat the same words. The words are always interpreted in a context. It seems that there is only the choice between severing ourselves from the culture we live in in order to become men of the culture in which the Tradition (that encompasses the Scripture) was originally formulated (but then we lose the capacity of enlightening with the words of the Scripture the dilemmas of the world of today) or to read the Scripture in the light of the Spirit of Our Time (but then we lose the capacity of affirming those truths that our time is unwilling to accept and instead of transforming ourselves according to the Spirit of Jesus we transform Jesus according to our Mind). The Catholic answer is that God has instituted through the sacrament of order and the Primate of Peter the appropriate context for the interpretation of his Message. This context is at the same time in time and out of time. Without the assistance of the Holy Spirit there can be no Tradition, or at least no Catholic Tradition. This is the reason why it is not possible to oppose the catholic Tradition to the Primate of Peter. *Simul stabunt, simul cadent* (together they stay or together they fall). The reader will find clear answers in a language that is easy to understand and in which a fervent love to Tradition and to the body of Christ incarnate shines through." — **Rocco Buttiglione, Member of the Pontifical Academy of Social Sciences and of the Pontifical Academy of St. Thomas.**

"Pedro Gabriel offers a well-written and deeply researched defense of Catholic teaching in response to the errors of contemporary Catholic traditionalism. Dr. Gabriel engages directly with the arguments of radical traditionalists and offers a thorough response, leaving no stone unturned. The book emphasizes the Church's doctrines regarding the papacy, especially the crucial role of the pope in maintaining the Church's unity and as the guarantor of orthodoxy. I highly recommend this book to anyone interested in Catholic ecclesiology who wants to understand the ongoing debates about authority and tradition in the Church." — **Mike Lewis, Co-Founder and Editor of the website Where Peter Is.**

Table of Contents

List of Abbreviations

Biblical Abbreviations:

1 Cor—First Epistle of the Apostle St. Paul to the Corinthians
1 John—First Epistle of the Apostle St. John
1 Sam—First Book of Prophet Samuel
1 Tim—First Epistle of the Apostle St. Paul to Timothy
2 Chron—Second Book of Chronicles
2 Macc—The Second Book of Maccabees
2 Tess—Second Epistle of the Apostle St. Paul to the Thessalonians
2 Tim—Second Epistle of the Apostle St. Paul to Timothy
Acts—Book of the Acts of the Apostles
Col—Epistle of the Apostle St. Paul to the Colossians
Deut—Book of Deuteronomy
Exod—Book of Exodus
Ezek—Book of Prophet Ezekiel
Gal—Epistle of the Apostle St. Paul to the Galatians
Gen—Book of Genesis
Heb—Epistle to the Hebrews
Hos—Book of Prophet Hoseah
Is—Book of Prophet Isaiah
Jer—Book of Prophet Jeremiah
John—Gospel according to St. John
Lev—Book of Leviticus
Luke—Gospel according to St. Luke
Mark—Gospel according to St. Mark
Mic—Book of Prophet Micah
Mt—Gospel according to St. Matthew
Pr—Book of Proverbs
Ps—Book of Psalms
Rev—Book of Revelation
Rom—Epistle of the Apostle St. Paul to the Romans
Zech—Book of Prophet Zechariah

(Note: All of the biblical quotes were taken from the Douay-Rheims, except in the cases where they were quoted as embedded in other documents, in which case the version of said document was followed.)

Non-biblical Abbreviations:

AAS—*Acta Apostolicae Sedes*
CCC—Catechism of the Catholic Church
CDF—Congregation for the Doctrine of the Faith
EN—*Evangelii Nuntiandi*
PDG—*Pascendi Dominici Gregis*
SSPX—International Priestly Society of St. Pius X
TLM—Traditional Latin Mass

Preface

I first came to know the name of Pedro Gabriel from the website *Where Peter Is* in the fall of 2019. Some people I knew were disturbed by an alleged pagan ceremony that took place in the Vatican Gardens on October 4, 2019, with Pope Francis present. As I was searching online for information about this supposed idol worship, I came across an article by Pedro Gabriel entitled "Paganism in the Vatican? Hermeneutic of Suspicion at its Peak." This was the first of a series of insightful articles by Pedro Gabriel debunking the pagan worship narrative being put forward by so many papal critics. Subsequently, I read other articles of Dr. Gabriel defending Pope Francis's apostolic exhortation *Amoris Laetitia* as well as the Holy Father's stance on the death penalty. I came to admire Pedro Gabriel even more when I read his 2022 book *The Orthodoxy of Amoris Laetitia*, and I later had the pleasure and honor of discussing this book with him in a podcast.

In the present work, *Heresy Disguised as Tradition*, Pedro Gabriel displays the same admirable qualities found in his other writings, viz., careful research, clear argumentation, and charitable but cogent refutations of the false claims made by papal critics. Although Dr. Gabriel is very well-versed in theology, he is a medical doctor—an oncologist—by training and profession. In *Heresy Disguised as Tradition,* his medical training is apparent. He is able to diagnose the cancer of false theology disguised as tradition and expose its pathological qualities. He is able to examine the false premises of various traditionalist authors and show how they contradict the very Catholic tradition that they claim to defend.

Heresy Disguised as Tradition is impressive in its Scriptural and historical analyses. For example, Dr. Gabriel explains that Paul's rebuke of Peter in Gal 2:11–14 was not a challenge to Peter's doctrinal authority. Instead, it concerned Peter's hypocrisy and inconsistency on one occasion. In no way does Gal 2: 11–14 justify the rejection of the teachings of Pope Francis or any other pope. Dr. Gabriel likewise shows how many contemporary traditionalists resemble Luther and other Protestants in their claim to be restoring the Church to her original pristine life.

This present volume is impressive with its historical analysis of the alleged heretical lapses of popes such as Liberius, Vigilius, Honorius I, and John XXII. As Dr. Gabriel shows, none of these popes can be justly charged with formal heresy, which is the obstinate post-baptismal denial or doubt of a truth which must be believed with divine and Catholic faith (cf. *Catechism of the Catholic Church*, 2089). Dr. Gabriel likewise explains the true nature of doctrinal development as taught by the 5th-century theologian St. Vincent of Lérins and the 19th-century theologian St. John Henry Newman. Doctrinal development allows for maturation and expansion over time without contradicting the deposit of faith. Pope Francis understands the true nature of doctrinal development, but many of his critics do not.

How, though, is heresy disguised as tradition? Many papal critics of today claim to hold to tradition, but in reality they distort and contradict it. This is especially the case with their disregard or opposition to legitimate exercises of papal jurisdiction and teaching. The irony is that many traditionalists of today fail to understand how deeply rooted papal authority is in Catholic tradition. They appeal to St. Pius X as their hero, but they do not look upon the Roman Pontiff in the way St. Pius X did. In his 1905 *Major Catechism* (*Catechismo Maggiore*) no. 204, the saintly Pontiff raised this question: "How should each Catholic behave towards the Pope?" The reply was: "Each Catholic should recognize the Pope as Father, Shepherd, and universal Teacher and be united with him in mind and heart."

Unfortunately, some traditionalists of today do not unite themselves in mind and heart with the Roman Pontiff. Instead, they look for every possible occasion to attack or criticize him. Some go so far as to claim that Vatican II (or even Vatican I) taught error; or they claim that the present Church has been infiltrated by diabolical forces. Such attitudes are indeed heretical, for they challenge the indefectibility of the Church in general and the indefectibility of the Apostolic See of Rome in particular. We have the sad phenomenon of many authors writing on allegedly Catholic sites who constantly criticize Vatican II and the popes who defend it. Dr. Gabriel is aware that not all traditionalists are the same. Not all go to the extreme of heresy. Unfortunately, a good number of them do go to this extreme. They present themselves as the guardians of tradition and the supporters of the "true Church" while at the same time undermining the authority of the Roman Pontiff who is the divinely appointed Vicar of Christ and guardian of tradition.

I have been teaching Catholic ecclesiology at the university or seminary level for over 35 years. I always defend the authority of popes and ecumenical councils because I know how essential this authority is for the maintenance of Catholic tradition. I also know that this authority has been solemnly taught by Vatican I and affirmed at Vatican II. Upholding Catholic tradition must involve upholding the authority of the Roman Pontiff and the authority of ecumenical councils such as Vatican II. To resist this authority in the name of tradition is to disguise heresy as tradition. Dr. Pedro Gabriel has diagnosed this present cancer, and we owe him much gratitude for this present work.

— Robert L. Fastiggi, Ph.D.
Bishop Kevin M. Britt Chair,
Dogmatic Theology and Christology,
Sacred Heart Major Seminary,
Detroit, Michigan USA

"Like all the fomenters of heresy and schism, they make false boast of having kept the ancient Catholic faith while they are overturning the principal foundation of the Faith and of Catholic doctrine. They certainly recognize in Scripture and Tradition the source of Divine Revelation, but they refuse to listen to the ever-living magisterium of the Church."

— Pius IX, *Inter gravissimas*

Introduction

There is a famous allegorical tale entitled "The Naked Truth and the Lie dressed up as Truth." This legend probably originated in the nineteenth century, inspired by a series of paintings from the French artist Jean-Léon Gérôme.[1] According to this story, there were two women: one named Truth and the other named Lie.[2] I will now make a slight twist to the story. Instead of calling one woman Truth, let us call her Tradition. Likewise, let us call the other woman Heresy, instead of Lie. Since this book is aimed at a Catholic audience, I do not think the reader will mind this modification.

Now, Heresy was a very beautiful and well-mannered woman. Her features were attractive, her voice velvety, her words pleasant. Everyone sought her company, for anyone who would sit by her side would delight in her erudite speeches. But, for all her sweet talk and seductive charms, Heresy's successes were hindered by her raggedy, uncouth vestments. Many people, looking at her, felt repulsed and went away.

As for Tradition, she was as astonishing as Heresy. Though she was older than Heresy, she did not look her age, so that one could believe them to be perfect twins. However, that was not the case. Unlike Heresy, Tradition was the daughter of a king, and she dressed for that part. She always wore an immaculately white tunic, covered by a mantle of purple. Her diadem was made of pure gold, inlaid with the most precious gems. Her sandals were cobbled by the finest artisans in the country. Wherever she went, all eyes were drawn to her, and everyone bowed at her majesty as she passed.

Of course, Heresy grew jealous of Tradition's luxurious attire. So, she concocted a plan. One hot summer day, Heresy asked Tradition to accompany her for a walk. Though of royal lineage, Tradition liked to indulge her subjects, so she accepted. Heresy brought Tradition outside the city walls, till they arrived at a lagoon. There, Heresy brought attention to the scorching sun and how refreshing it would be to bathe in those waters. She disrobed herself and dipped into the lake. Tradition was hesitant to join her,

---

[1] Hoakley. "Too Real: the narrative paintings of Jean-Léon Gérôme, 7."

[2] A version of the original story can be read in Henderson. "According to a 19th century legend."

but seeing how Heresy was enjoying herself, she eventually gave in. The princess removed all her precious clothes and dove into the cool lacustrine waters.

Heresy then dared Tradition for a swimming competition. Tradition accepted, confident as she was in her athletic skills, despite her more advanced years. When the race began, Tradition soon took the lead. She had left Heresy so far behind that she could no longer hear her strokes in the tranquil lagoon waters. When Tradition noticed the deceit, it was already too late. Heresy had jumped out of the lake and stolen all of Tradition's treasured garments.

Heresy then went into the city, parading herself in her new clothes. Everyone kept asking: "Who is this gracious lady?" To which Heresy replied: "I am Tradition, the daughter of the king." Through her cunning, Heresy tricked many people who sought to curry favor with the king by entertaining her. She was invited inside the people's homes, where she feasted and was showered with gifts, emptying both pantries and coffers.

At that moment, Tradition returned. Since she was wearing nothing but her birthday suit, the people confused her with an innovation. No matter how much the princess would cry: "I am Tradition, the daughter of the king," she was met with derision. "Tradition is a guest in our house,"— people would say— "and we know how she looks like, and you are obviously not her. A daughter of a king would never display herself in such a shameless manner."

But there were some sensible individuals in the village who thought to themselves: "To insult the daughter of the king would be most unwise. And certainly, appearances can be deceiving. It is not the dress that makes the princess, but the blood running through her veins. How can we know who the real Tradition is? How can we know the truth?"

***

Let us now move away from the allegory and into the material world. The date: July 16, 2021. The news spread through social media like wildfire. Several Catholics were clicking through articles of Catholic news sites and even running to the Vatican official website to see it with their own eyes. There had been rumors since a few weeks before, but there are always rumors involving the Holy See. So, these Catholics were praying and hoping that those would be just that: rumors. Yet, to their dismay, it had now become true. A new *motu proprio*[3] stood there, bearing the signature of Pope Francis, its words clearly drawn against the distinctive parchment background of the Vatican website. The title of the document was *Traditionis Custodes.*

Why was this significant? *Traditionis Custodes* severely restricted the use of the 1962 edition of the Roman missal in the liturgical celebrations of the Roman rite. For someone unacquainted with the inner workings of the Church, this might seem like a mere footnote, without any significance. However, for a certain group of Catholics, the impact of this decision was enormous. The 1962 edition was the last version of the Roman missal issued before the liturgical reform that took place in the wake of the Second Vatican Council (1962-1965). This meant that this missal was still much used and beloved by Catholics known as "traditionalists."

It is not surprising, therefore, that this decision generated a wave of indignation among traditionalist Catholics, who decried the document as "an attack on them and the ancient liturgy."[4] Rorate Caeli, a popular traditionalist blog, tweeted the following (emphasis as in the original tweet): "Francis HATES US. Francis HATES Tradition. Francis HATES all that is good and beautiful. Francis is an Anti-Christical figure for this age."[5] Barely three months after *Traditionis Custodes*, Peter Kwasniewski, a traditionalist theologian, published an anthology of no less than seventy essays and articles by cardinals, bishops, prelates, theologians, canonists, and philosophers, all critical of the *motu proprio.*[6]

It is quite remarkable how the document at the epicenter of this controversy has such an appropriate name: *Traditionis Custodes* means

---

[3] *Motu proprio* is "the name given to certain papal rescripts on account of the clause *motu proprio* (*of his own accord*) used in the document. The words signify that the provisions of the rescript were decided on by the pope personally, that is, not on the advice of the cardinals or others, but for reasons which he himself deemed sufficient. The document has generally the form of a decree" (MacErlean, "Motu Proprio").

[4] Winfield. "Pope reverses Benedict, reimposes restrictions on Latin Mass."

[5] @RorateCaeli's tweet from July 16, 2021.

[6] Kwasniewski. *From Benedict's Peace to Francis's War.*

"Custodians of Tradition"[7] (or "Guardians of Tradition"[8]) in Latin.[9] Herein lies the crux of the whole matter, and the source of the dispute.[10] In the very first sentence of the *motu proprio*, Pope Francis explains (emphasis from now on is always mine, unless stated otherwise):

> Guardians of the tradition, *the bishops in communion with the Bishop of Rome constitute the visible principle and foundation of the unity* of their particular Churches. Under the guidance of the Holy Spirit, through the proclamation of the Gospel and by means of the celebration of the Eucharist, they govern the particular Churches entrusted to them.[11]

Those who are critical of *Traditionis Custodes* do not seem to disagree with the substance of this paragraph. It is a quite traditional statement. However, they would argue that the current circumstances change the way it must be received. According to them, the Bishop of Rome and the bishops in communion with him have fallen short of this holy task. Pope and bishops—so these Catholics say—have not been friendly towards tradition,

---

[7] This is how it was translated in the Italian and Spanish versions of the *motu proprio.*

[8] Official English translation.

[9] Even before Francis, Pope St. Paul VI uses the term *depositum custodi* ("custodian of the deposit" [of the faith]) to refer to the hierarchical Catholic Church, citing 1 Tim 6:20 and 2 Tim 1:14 for this effect (see Paul VI. "General Audience," January 19, 1972)

[10] The irony of this title was not lost on the author of an article for LifeSiteNews: "Taking into account this clearly expressed aim to obliterate the Traditional Roman Rite, let's ponder a moment over the title given to the motu proprio, which is an example of what one might call Orwellian antiphrasis. Antiphrasis is the rhetorical device that consists in sarcastically saying the opposite of what is actually meant in such a way that one's true intention is made manifest and obvious. Pope Francis clearly announces his determined will to eliminate the Traditional Mass of the Ages, and yet the decree is sarcastically entitled: '*Traditionis Custodes*,' meaning 'Guardians of Tradition.' No theological studies are required to see the obvious: this is sheer sneering sarcasm that, presupposing the best intentions on the part of the Holy Father, is a trickery of the devil, who has so cleverly managed to disorient his mind and his heart." (Darantière. "*Traditionis Custodes*: Guardians of tradition or betrayers of tradition?").

[11] Francis. *Traditionis Custodes.*

consistently failing to uphold and safeguard it.[12] Sometimes—so it is argued—the hierarchy has even been actively antagonistic towards tradition.[13] Since no one is effectively defending tradition against a hostile world riddled with anti-traditional modernism, it befalls these Catholics to pick up the slack and protect tradition—sometimes from the very pope himself.[14] These Catholics then become, in their own eyes, and in practice, the true guardians and custodians of tradition.

How do they reconcile this dissonance between acknowledging the Pope and bishops as "guardians of tradition" while assuming this role themselves in opposition to the official guardians? There are several approaches. For some, the problem started with the Second Vatican Council and its promulgation of several erroneous teachings that contradicted traditional Catholic doctrine in matters of religious freedom, ecumenism, interreligious dialogue, Church-state relations, and the style of the Church's dialogue with the modern world.[15] This was further aggravated by the post-conciliar liturgical reforms that effectively replaced the Roman missal promulgated by St. Pius V in 1570, and last revised by St. John XXIII in 1962, by a new missal issued by St. Paul VI in 1970.

Among these critics of the council, some believe that the post-conciliar popes, by promulgating error, have *de facto* excommunicated themselves,

---

[12] See Pelletier. "Self-described Catholics abandoning true teachings": "The Catholic bishops over the last 50 or so years have largely failed. They failed to promote good liturgy, they failed to preach the gospel in its fullness and they failed to protect the souls entrusted to them."

[13] See Skojec. "Smashing Traditions: The Vatican War Machine is Back.": "This theme — *that those who follow Church teaching and tradition are the bad guys* — is one he [Pope Francis] reiterated just this week . . . You see, the Lives of the Saints are filled with stories of men and women, boys and girls, who all shared one thing in common: they were obstinate in their adherence to Catholic truth, even to the point of cruel and ignominious death. Pope Francis either does not understand this or refuses to accept it, either of which *make it impossible for him to be a friend of Catholic tradition*"

[14] See van den Aardweg et al. "*Correctio Filialis de Haeresibus Propagatis.*"

[15] A superb collection of refutations of most anti-Vatican II arguments can be seen, in Portuguese, on the website *Apologistas Católicos* (http://apologistascatolicos.com.br/index.php/vaticano-ii). Also recommended: Guarino, *The Disputed Teachings of Vatican II.*

being therefore unable to hold office in the Catholic Church. For these believers, the Holy See is vacant (*sede vacante*) and the official magisterial acts of the post-conciliar popes are null, as they are void of authority.[16] These are called sedevacantists.

Some others have followed in the footsteps of Marcel Lefebvre, a French archbishop who became the most visible face of the opposition to Vatican II.[17] In 1970, Archbishop Lefebvre founded the International Priestly Society of St. Pius X (SSPX), a fraternal order of priests devoted to preserving Catholicism as it was practiced before the council. The SSPX was canonically suppressed in 1975, and the archbishop suspended *a divinis.*[18] Yet, Lefebvre kept the society functioning, in open rebellion with the pope's stipulations. Despite decades of dialogue, the SSPX retains an irregular status with the Holy See to this day.[19] Several Catholics, however, continue to attend SSPX masses.

These Lefebvrian Catholics do *recognize* the authority of the Pope, but they do not submit to his teachings, as they believe they must *resist* erroneous doctrines and unjust orders that contradict tradition.[20] For this reason, their position has been labeled "recognize and resist." Others would eventually adopt their own version of the "recognize and resist" stance as well, as we shall see.

A more recent group started to gestate in 2007, when Pope Benedict XVI issued his own *motu proprio*: *Summorum Pontificum*. This document allowed many concessions to the celebration of the 1962 Roman missal,

---

[16] Derksen. "White Smoke, Anti-Pope: A Response to Rev. Brian Harrison."

[17] Vere. "A Canonical History of the Lefebvrite Schism."

[18] "A Beautiful Mystery: The History of the Society of St. Pius X" *General House*; see also Vere. "A Canonical History of the Lefebvrite Schism."

[19] Benedict XVI. "Letter to the Bishops of the Catholic Church concerning the remission of the excommunication": "There needs to be a distinction, then, between the disciplinary level, which deals with individuals as such, and the doctrinal level, at which ministry and institution are involved. In order to make this clear once again: until the doctrinal questions are clarified, the Society has no canonical status in the Church, and its ministers – even though they have been freed of the ecclesiastical penalty – do not legitimately exercise any ministry in the Church."

[20] See Gleize. "The State of Necessity": "We do indeed recognize the pope's authority, but when he makes use of it to do the opposite of that for which it was given him, it is obvious that we cannot follow him."

making it an extraordinary form of the Roman rite[21] (the ordinary form being the one promulgated after Vatican II). From that point onward, there was a propagation of parishes and priests celebrating this extraordinary form. As many Catholics rediscovered the beauty of the ancient liturgy, they unfortunately felt like they had been deprived of a heritage that was rightfully theirs. Some of them started to grow skeptical of and even hostile towards the council. Already during Francis's papacy, the latter became a major bulwark of the "recognize and resist" bloc.[22] It is quite plausible that the harsh restrictions set forth in *Traditionis Custodes* were meant to quell this movement[23].

Lastly, there are those who never viewed Vatican II with suspicion until Pope Francis was elected in 2013—and possibly not even after that. These Catholics thrived during the pontificates of St. John Paul II and Benedict XVI. However, they found it difficult to reconcile Francis's teachings with the ones from his two immediate predecessors,[24] namely regarding communion for the divorced and remarried,[25] and the admissibility of the death penalty.[26] Also, they began to view Francis's papacy with increasing

---

[21] Benedict XVI. *Summorum Pontificum*, Art. 1.

[22] See Sammons, Eric. "Can Catholics 'Recognize and Resist'?": "We recognize that Francis is the legitimate pope and that as pope he is our Holy Father who deserves our obedience. Yet at the same time we resist all aspects of his work that are contrary to apostolic tradition."

[23] See Francis, "Letter to the Holy Father Francis to the Bishops of the whole world that accompanies the Apostolic Letter Motu Proprio Data '*Traditionis Custodes*.'": "With the passage of thirteen years, I instructed the Congregation for the Doctrine of the Faith to circulate a questionnaire to the bishops regarding the implementation of the Motu proprio Summorum Pontificum. The responses reveal a situation that preoccupies and saddens me, and persuades me of the need to intervene . . . An opportunity offered by St. John Paul II and, with even greater magnanimity, by Benedict XVI, intended to recover the unity of an ecclesial body with diverse liturgical sensibilities, was exploited to widen the gaps, reinforce the divergences, and encourage disagreements that injure the Church, block her path, and expose her to the peril of division."

[24] Lawler. "This Disastrous Papacy."

[25] To understand how Francis's teachings on this topic can be reconciled with tradition, see Gabriel. *The Orthodoxy of Amoris Laetitia.*

[26] For my take on this issue, see Gabriel. "Death Penalty – continuity or hardness of heart?."

suspicion, as controversies kept pilling up: the diplomatic deal between the Vatican and communist China;[27] the signing of the *Interreligious Declaration on Human and Religious Freedom*, purportedly affirming that God willed other religions besides the Catholic one;[28] the supposed pagan ceremony at the Vatican gardens, allegedly worshipping the goddess Pachamama during the opening of the synod for the Amazon;[29] the homily where Francis said that apostates belong to the communion of saints;[30] etc.

Some of these critics of Francis's pontificate adopted their own brand of "recognize and resist." Those who did not take this opportunity to reevaluate their stance towards Vatican II became at least somewhat empathetic towards the plight of their fellow traditionalists.[31]

Finally, some went so far as denying the validity of Benedict XVI's resignation—and therefore, the validity of Pope Francis's election.[32] The latter would become known as benevacantists, at least while Benedict was alive.

Of course, it is impossible to describe all varieties of such a heterogeneous group.[33] Nor can we say that these factions are completely airtight: some Catholics may have positions that are hybrid of several of these parties.[34] However, I believe I accurately and fairly described the major outlines of the most important types of traditionalism in the contemporary Catholic Church.

---

[27] For a contextualization on this issue from someone loyal to the pope, see Lewis. "Perspective on the China / Vatican deal."

[28] My take on this can be seen here: Gabriel. "Pluralism and the will of God… is there another way to look at it?"

[29] I have researched this topic extensively and thoroughly debunked this claim. A summary of my conclusions can be seen here: Gabriel. "Our Lady of the Amazon: solving the contradictions."

[30] See my explanation in Gabriel. "Pope Francis and apostates: is this the communion of saints?"

[31] Lawler. "The Liturgical Edsel."

[32] I refute this claim in my 3-part series: Gabriel. "Was Pope Benedict Forced to Resign?"

[33] There are some who, for example, follow antipopes "elected" on the grounds of the supposed *sede vacante.*

[34] For example, a Catholic may have been critical of Francis and never attended a pre-Vatican II mass, and then may have felt inclined to join the SSPX in the wake of *Traditionis Custodes.*

Is there anything tying such a diverse group together? Even among such an array of different positions (sometimes quarrelling intensely against each other),[35] they have at least two things in common: their views on what constitutes Catholic tradition, and their idea that either Pope or Council (or both) has not been faithful to this same tradition. In this sense, I think a good summary of their common ground can be found in this definition, taken from a traditionalist article:

> Traditionalist: One who challenges the novel practices and teachings of Catholics (including bishops and priests) which *appear to contradict the prior teaching* of the Church. A traditionalist questions the prudence of new pastoral approaches and holds the belief that *those things generally deemed objectively good or evil several decades ago remain so today.*[36]

For a Catholic, this way of thinking seems logical. After all, we believe that God guides His Church into the truth, and that truth does not change. Therefore, if the Church deemed a certain belief or practice correct in the past, then those who believed or did such things were not led into error. Conversely, people who believe or do the exact same thing today should not be in error either.

If the Church changes her stance and seems to contradict herself, then Catholics are faced with a dilemma: should they submit to the present teaching or to the past teaching? If Catholics must choose, they would be in more solid ground if they kept believing or doing the same as their forebears, since what was not wrong then, cannot be wrong now.

Seems like a fail-safe strategy, but there is a catch. It assumes that the Church is wrong today. Traditionalists will have no problem admitting to this. But if we believe that God guides His Church into the truth, then this

---

[35] For a sedevacantist takedown of the "recognize and resist" position, see Derksen. "No, Catholics Can't 'Recognize and Resist': Response to One Peter Five." For a refutation of sedevacantism from a leading "recognize and resist" website, see Massey. "Sedevacantism is Modern Day Luciferianism." See also Lewis. "Getting it Half-right: Sedes and SSPX.."

[36] Miller, Peter. "A Brief Defense of Traditionalism."

must hold as true now as it did in the past. If the Church taught truthfully yesterday, why is she not doing so today?

Traditionalists will argue that "while the Church has gone through crises in its past, the *current crisis is nearly unprecedented* in its desolation and heterodoxy."[37] They will say that, "*for the first time*, we have seen the widespread acceptance of an interpretation of Catholicism that is anti-traditional, free to reshape itself according to indeterminate 'modern needs.'"[38] The current situation is out of the ordinary, even unparalleled in Church history. Therefore, this "state of emergency"[39] (or "state of necessity")[40] justifies the current resistance.

Nevertheless, is this situation as unprecedented as traditionalists claim it to be? In this book, I will argue otherwise. However, I will not do so on the traditionalists' terms. I will not set out to prove that there have been times in history when the Church has failed to uphold tradition as it is supposedly doing today. Rather, I am going to focus on historical precedent for this kind of reasoning:

> The Supreme Pontiff is indeed deserving of the benefit of the doubt and his teachings deserving of "internal assent" (*except* in cases where there is nothing towards which to assent or *an apparent contradiction with previous teaching*).[41]

Can a Catholic withhold assent from a magisterial teaching that *apparently* contradicts previous teaching? Though this claim is widespread in traditionalist circles,[42] I have yet to see a magisterial document allowing this

---

[37] Dobbs. "Taking the Tradpill."

[38] Kwasniewski. "What does it mean to be a 'traditional Catholic? Aren't all Catholics traditional?"

[39] Dobbs. "Taking the Tradpill."

[40] Gleize. "The State of Necessity."

[41] Miller. "A Brief Defense of Traditionalism."

[42] See, for instance, Ferrara. "*Amoris Laetitia*: Anatomy of a Pontifical Debacle": "Just as God cannot contradict Himself, the Magisterium cannot contradict itself. For the Magisterium is the teaching office of the Church; it presents what the Church teaches, which is not determined by the latest utterance of the current Pope. Therefore, whatever contradicts the constant prior teaching of the Church cannot possibly belong to the Magisterium . . . Nor can it be argued that the faithful have no capacity to recognize these contradictions but rather must blindly presume

course of action. It is highly concerning that the mere *appearance* of contradiction seems to be sufficient grounds for dissent since, as we shall see later, appearances can be deceiving. However, also concerning is the amount of traditionalists who seem to confuse appearance of contradiction with a *de facto* contradiction.[43]

This mindset is not innocuous. As I said before, we believe that the Holy Spirit guides His Church, now as always. If the Church can be wrong today, then it could also have been wrong in the past. A mere appeal to tradition as a reliable guide for what is true today does not stand on its own, because it is grounded on the reliability of the Church in the past, which in turn is grounded on the reliability of the Church herself, at all times. Ironically, traditionalists are undermining the foundations of tradition under the pretense of defending them. Tradition will not survive this brand of traditionalism.

The only way to solve this conundrum is to accept that the apparent contradictions with previous doctrine are merely apparent, not true contradictions. For this reason, many Catholics have followed on the footsteps of Benedict XVI and tried to read the current magisterium through a "hermeneutic of continuity." Many authors (myself included) have written articles, books, and essays trying to solve the apparent contradictions between Vatican II and the pre-conciliar Church, or between Pope Francis and his predecessors.

Unfortunately, traditionalists will often dismiss these efforts as mere mental gymnastics: Continuists would be twisting themselves into pretzels to justify the unjustifiable.[44] In this sense, rehashing continuist arguments

---

that somehow they do not exist. This is the Catholic Church, whose deposit of Faith is objectively knowable, not a gnostic sect headed by the Oracle of Rome, who announces what 'Jesus wants' today."

[43] See McCusker. "Key doctrinal errors and ambiguities of Amoris Laetitia": "It is *quite clear* then that the Apostolic Exhortation *Amoris Laetitia* of Pope Francis *directly contradicts* the teaching and practice of the Catholic Church on the question of the admission of 'divorced and remarried Catholics' to Holy Communion." To understand why this is not true, see Gabriel. *The Orthodoxy of Amoris Laetitia*, 135-233.

[44] Skojec. "The Hermeneutic of Ambiguity."

in favor of Vatican II or Francis will not produce the desired effect. It is not sufficient for these arguments to be correct—for them to be accepted, they must be considered more plausible than the simpler, more appealing explanation: "there *seems* to be a contradiction, because there *really is* a contradiction." Unfortunately, this is not so much a matter of debating minutiae, as of a greater worldview—how a Catholic will respond, will ultimately depend on how much confidence he has in the current magisterium to begin with. The less trustful he is, the more likely he is to accept that there is a contradiction, and therefore the less likely he is to accept continuist arguments.

For this reason, I decided to try something different in this book. Traditionalists have trust in the pre-conciliar magisterium. That much is a given. So, I invite them to consider a thought experiment. What if Catholics resisted this pre-conciliar magisterium on the grounds that it did not uphold tradition?

Unlikely? It is true; there are very few traditionalists today who would question the reliability of the pre-conciliar magisterium. But I am not talking about contemporary traditionalists. I am talking about "traditionalists" from ages long past.

The reason why we do not call them traditionalists, is because Catholic orthodoxy came to be identified as the opposite of what they defended. Nowadays, they are viewed as heretics, or at least heterodox. History judged them as being on the wrong side of the doctrinal debate.

Why did I call them "traditionalists," then? Is it not true that heresy always constitutes a departure from the deposit of the faith handed down since apostolic times (i.e., tradition)? In other words, is it not true that heresy always constitutes a *novelty*? Catholics would be protected from heresy if they eschewed novelty in favor of tradition. How can someone, therefore, claim that the heretics of yore were "traditionalists"?

It is true that heterodoxy is always a novelty, a departure from tradition. However, it is also true that Catholics who subscribed to these heterodoxies never considered themselves as departing from tradition. Rather, they often (if not always) viewed themselves as restoring Christianity to a sort of original purity, before it was corrupted by alien ideas from Church authorities. They simply disagreed among themselves about the timing of when this corruption took place. Whether explicitly or implicitly, the heretic was always, in his own mind, a guardian of tradition against the Pope and the bishops in communion with him at the time. *These historical precedents are what this book intends to explore.*

Let us take a look at Protestantism, for instance. Protestants read the Holy Bible and find some teachings there that seem, on the surface, to contradict Catholic doctrine and praxis (e.g.: venerating images) or that do not seem to have any scriptural basis (e.g.: praying for the intercession of the saints). For them, these Catholic teachings and practices contradict a most venerable tradition inscribed in scripture. They will solve this tension by claiming that scripture alone (*sola scriptura*) is exempt from the possibility of teaching error. Consequently, when the Protestant senses a conflict between scripture and the authoritative teachings of the Church, he feels a moral obligation to go with (his interpretation of) scripture.[45] *Sola scriptura* is the way to access what Jesus Christ taught, and what early Christians believed, before a general apostasy took over the hierarchy.

However, *sola scriptura* is itself a novelty.[46] Christianity evolved from temple Judaism, which was a very priestly religion, centered on the performance of rituals at the temple by a priestly class. Even scripture confirms this repeatedly, from Leviticus to the Epistle to the Hebrews.[47] The most ancient branches of Christianity (Catholic, Eastern Orthodox, Coptic, etc.) are priestly in nature, with a hierarchy of priests tasked to interpret scripture and tradition, tracing their succession line to the apostles themselves. As the Catechism of the Catholic Church (CCC) points out, Christianity was not considered a Religion of the Book[48] (like, say, Islam) until Luther formulated the concept of *sola scriptura*, a millennium and a half after Jesus ascended into heaven. On the contrary, early Christianity always revolved around worship at the Holy Mass.[49]

This may be obvious for traditionalists today. After all, the Church has condemned *sola scriptura* for centuries now,[50] and continues to do so

---

[45] Hay. "Did the Early Christians subscribe to Sola Scriptura?"
[46] Hay. "Did the Early Christians subscribe to Sola Scriptura?"
[47] See, for example, Lev 21:10 and Heb 7.
[48] CCC 108.
[49] Barbour. "We're not a 'Religion of the Book.'"
[50] Trent, 4th Session.

today.[51] The condemnation of *sola scriptura* is very traditional. In like manner, traditionalists will acquiesce to the Church's condemnations of all the heresies of the past and consider these anathemas traditional. But I want to point out that they seem obvious *now* because we have assimilated centuries of theological explanations that preceded us, so that they seem perfectly natural to us. However, at the time of the controversy, you would have two factions, each one claiming to be the true guardian of tradition, with the interpretation favored by the Church sometimes being the one that seemed, on the surface, to have less traditional roots.

In other words, adhering to the seemingly traditional position against the official interpretation given by the Church does not necessarily prevent one from falling into heterodoxy. Demonstrating this thesis is the main goal of this book.

To achieve this purpose, I have decided to structure the book according to three sections, inspired by the allegorical tale with which we started. In the first section, we will see how it was possible for the townspeople to look at Tradition, naked as a baby, and confuse her with innovation. In the second section, we are going to glance at Heresy wearing Tradition's garments and how she deceived the city folk. In the third section, we are going to help the wise people identify who the real Tradition is. So, this book will be divided the following way:

❖ First Section: A few introductory remarks, where some important concepts are defined, which will help illustrate the historical precedents laid out in the following sections.

  - Chapter 1: Definition of tradition.
  - Chapter 2: The concept of "*ressourcement*".
  - Chapter 3: Why a legitimate doctrinal development may sometimes seem contradictory with previous teachings.
  - Chapter 4: How the Church often discerns a synthesis between two opposing statements, and how failing to do so can lead to heresy.

[51] *CCC* 82.

❖ Second Section: An evaluation of several historical precedents where the heterodox position was viewed as a defense of a more traditional understanding of Christianity.

- Chapter 5: The correction of St. Peter by St. Paul in light of the Judaizer controversy.
- Chapter 6: The *Commonitorium* of St. Vincent of Lèrins in the context of the ecumenical councils that defined the creed.
- Chapter 7: Liturgical controversies throughout the centuries, where the Church suppressed practices once deemed sacred.
- Chapter 8: The Reformation, especially regarding Protestant attitudes towards scripture.
- Chapter 9: The Traditionalist and Gallican movements of the nineteenth century, in light of the First Vatican Council.
- Chapter 10: Modernism and Postmodern Liberalism's views on Jesus and the Church.

❖ Third Section: A demonstration of how a Catholic can discern where true tradition lies, when such is not clear.

- Chapter 11: The precedent set by Jesus Christ Himself.
- Chapter 12: The magisterium as the authoritative interpreter of tradition.
- Chapter 13: Answer to a common objection to the magisterium's reliability—the existence of bad popes in the past.

Before we proceed with the substance of the book, I would like to provide a full disclosure. I am a practicing Catholic, and I proclaim my fidelity to every single doctrine of the Church, in every single matter. I have been faithful to every teaching of Pope Benedict XVI—the pope that helped me convert to the fullness of the Catholic faith—and my fidelity to Francis is a simple extension of what I did during the previous pontificate. I also take the authority of *every* successor of Peter seriously, both pre- and post-conciliar. I have no ideology nor political party. I am neither liberal nor conservative.

Furthermore, it is not out of distaste for tradition that I write this book. On the contrary, it is out of love for tradition that I endeavored to do it. Tradition is one of the deposits of the Word of God, and one of the pillars of truth. It has a structural and foundational role in the Church in general and for each faithful in particular. It is a treasure of priceless value that I wish to see appreciated in its unadulterated entirety—including the traditions of papal primacy and Church indefectibility, so attacked during recent years.

In addition, *I would like to clarify three points*. First, it would be fruitless for a person who seeks to refute my book to argue something like "Current day traditionalists are not like past heretics because they do not believe X or Y." My point is not to establish a perfect parallel between traditionalists and, say, Arians or Protestants. I know their tenets are not the same. The only point that I seek to prove is whether Arians or Protestants fought the Church of their time because they thought they were defending some sort of tradition. This attitude, and this attitude *alone*, is the sole focus of this book.

Second, I want to clarify an ambiguity that may arise from my use of the word "traditionalist." Sometimes, the word "traditionalist" is employed simply to denote a Catholic who likes to attend an older form of the Roman rite. Such a Catholic is not necessarily against the current magisterium and may be faithfully obedient to the specifications laid out by the present pope. Therefore, I have made a distinction between "traditionalists" and "*radical* traditionalists" elsewhere.[52] Other authors have made similar distinctions.[53] The former would be Catholics who exercise their liturgical preferences in perfect harmony with Pope and Council. The latter would be the Catholics who reject, in some way or another, the current pope or Vatican II.

I have nothing but sympathy for the legitimate traditionalists in communion with the Church who, through no fault of their own, are suffering

---

[52] Gabriel. "Showing mercy towards traditionalists."

[53] See, for instance, Armstrong. "Definitions: Radical Catholic Reactionaries vs. Mainstream 'Traditionalists.'"

because of *Traditionis Custodes*' harsh restrictions.[54] However, this book does not address their particular kind of traditionalism. My book is concerned solely with so-called radical traditionalists. Therefore, for brevity and simplicity's sake, I will henceforth use the word "traditionalist" to signify only those who do not assent, in some way, to the conciliar and/or post-conciliar magisterium. In short, I will employ the term "traditionalist" according to the definition that I quoted before in this introduction. This means that "traditionalist" can even refer to someone who never once attended a liturgy according to the 1962 missal, but who dissents from magisterial acts of Pope Francis on the basis that they contradict his predecessors.

Third—and lastly—I wish to explain something about how I structured this book. At the beginning of each chapter, I am going to make a small introduction where I tell part of the story of a traditionalist Catholic. This is meant to better exemplify how the historical parallels work in real life. This traditionalist Catholic character is not meant to be a strawman or a caricature, but an archetype. He was pieced together based on my interactions with real life traditionalists in social media and does not seek to represent any individual in particular, but the movement itself. Of course, not all traditionalists will have the same opinions or wield the same arguments as this ideal version that I created. But I believe it is a fair representation of the overall traditionalist worldview.

In fact, while I tell this story, I will also use the archetype of an apologist who is faithful to Pope Francis, and even of a secularized, progressive Catholic. For these characters, the same logic applies. Hopefully, this will make the book more interesting and help humanize the people involved in these polemics, so that we may grow in mutual understanding and respect for each other's positions, disagreements notwithstanding.

So, without further ado, let us begin.

---

[54] In this sense, I enthusiastically welcome initiatives like "*The Manifesto of the New Traditionalism*," which seeks to promote a new kind of traditionalism while retaining the fidelity owed to the council. See Chapp et al. "*The Manifesto of the New Traditionalism*."

Section I

Tradition confused with innovation

Chapter 1

What is Tradition?

Indeed, "the history of the Church shows that Christianity does not have simply one cultural expression, but rather, 'remaining completely true to itself, with unswerving fidelity to the proclamation of the Gospel and the tradition of the Church, it will also reflect the different faces of the cultures and peoples in which it is received and takes root'. In the diversity of peoples who experience the gift of God, each in accordance with its own culture, the Church expresses her genuine catholicity and shows forth 'the beauty of her varied face.'"

—Francis, *Veritatis Gaudium*

Our story begins in 2011, with a young man in his 20s called Thomas Lawson. Since an early age, Thomas was blessed with an intellect reminiscent of an Aquinas. Unfortunately, this gift would also curse him, in much later years, to foster the struggles of a Doubting Thomas.

Tom was raised as a Protestant Evangelical in the bosom of a very conservative American family. His Christian faith played a major role in his life. So, Tom decided he could not just keep to himself the joy of the gospel he had received. He needed to preach it. He saw the internet as a major venue for this preaching—after all, as a millennial, he was savvy enough to use it to this end. He searched for online spots where he could find virtual ears for his proselytism. Eventually, he stumbled upon Catholic apologetics forums. There he would unleash all his rhetorical acumen, provoking fierce debates in every post he visited.

As a Protestant, Thomas was particularly adamant about the doctrine of *sola scriptura*. He would quote 2 Tim 3:16-17 about how "all scripture, inspired of God, is profitable to teach, to reprove, to correct, to instruct in justice." He thought he had a foolproof argument right there. To his surprise, Catholics in the forum began to push back . . . by using the Bible itself. They correctly made the distinction between "*all* scripture" and "*only* scripture" and then proceeded to quote St. Paul when he said: "Therefore, brethren, stand fast; and hold the *traditions* which you have learned, whether *by word*, or by our epistle" (2 Thess 2:14). In other words, the apostle admitted that not all tradition had been written down—some had been passed down orally.

Slowly, Tom was exposed to the Catholic concept of tradition. Many of the Catholic doctrines that Tom believed, at face value, to be unscriptural, began to make sense. Gradually, Tom's adversarial posture gave way to genuine curiosity.

He could no longer contain this pull towards Catholicism. As much as he prayed, it seemed like it was the Holy Spirit nudging him in that direction. Eventually, he decided to attend a Catholic mass. The impact on his soul was unimaginable! The liturgy had nothing to do with the Protestant services he was so accustomed to since childhood. The solemnity of the consecration, in particular, brought his eyes to tears—he could sense Jesus's real presence in the Eucharist. When the priest said: "The Mass is ended," Thomas Lawson was already firm in his decision to become Catholic. He could hardly wait to tell this joyful news to his online friends at the Catholic forums that had helped him convert!

Of course, this was met with much elation. Tom was congratulated left and right for his decision to cross the Tiber. But amid the congratulations, something caught Tom's eyes. Some commenters were saying words to the effect of: "If you feel like this with a *Novus Ordo*[1] Mass, just wait till you attend a Traditional Latin Mass (TLM)."[2]

"Traditional." There was that word again! Thomas had come to love that word. It had been the word that had guided him away of his Protestantism and into the fulness of truth contained in the Catholic faith. Certainly, having more of it could be nothing but beneficial. Coincidentally, his parish had a mass in the extraordinary form in its schedule. After all, Benedict XVI's *Summorum Pontificum* was, at the time, in full force.

If the ordinary form of the mass had such a deep impact on Tom, the extraordinary form just blew him away! Never, in his days as a Protestant, had he experienced such a sense of reverence. He could not yet figure out what the Latin words meant, but they seemed to heighten the sacredness and purpose of every of the priest's gestures. When the priest said "*Ite missa*

---

[1] Short for *Novus Ordo Missae*, literally meaning "new order of the Mass" in Latin. Usually used in a derogatory way by traditionalists to refer to St. Paul VI's new Roman Missal.

[2] Term often used online to refer to the extraordinary form of the Mass, i.e., the one celebrated according with the 1962 Roman Missal.

est," Tom was already firm in his decision to always attend the extraordinary form from that point onward.

He messaged his online traditionalist friends, relaying what had happened. They told him that his experience mirrored their own and expressed sadness for the fact that the extraordinary form was not more disseminated. Some of them had to drive a long time just to find a parish that could fulfill their liturgical yearnings. Thomas was scandalized! Why was that? They then told him about the Second Vatican Council and the "protestantization" of the mass by "Bugnini and his accomplices."[3] They told him about how modernism had infiltrated the highest spheres of the Church and had tried to crush the "mass of the ages," depriving them of a heritage that, as Catholics, was rightfully theirs. But fortunately, Benedict had implemented *Summorum Pontificum* some years earlier, allowing for the celebration of the old liturgy as an extraordinary form—soon, the TLM would outgrow the *Novus Ordo.* Tradition would, one day, be restored.

From this, we can see how "tradition" deeply shaped Thomas Lawson's faith journey. However, Tom's understanding of tradition was acquired through a kind of osmosis during the course of his theological discussions online. Tom could certainly identify what "tradition" means, in generic and intuitive terms. But he would probably have some difficulty defining this word with more theological precision than "what the Church has always taught, at least until Vatican II."

This is dangerous since, as we have seen, Tom is on his way to becoming not only a Catholic, but a "traditionalist" as well. In other words, he is about to embrace a movement that attaches an "ism" to a concept he cannot properly characterize. Others have defined this word for him—and they are at the same time sowing mistrust for the hierarchy. In other words, the traditionalists have claimed the word "tradition" for themselves and labeled any disagreement with them as "anti-traditional," even if it comes from a priest or bishop. Therefore, Tom's rightful love for tradition, while

[3] Archbishop Annibale Bugnini, the secretary of the commission that worked in the reform of Catholic liturgy after the Second Vatican Council. There is a traditionalist talking point that Bugnini's reforms were meant to appease Protestants at the expense of Tradition.

commendable, is making him vulnerable to accept non-authoritative, reductive, and/or inaccurate definitions of tradition from Catholics he now considers more trustworthy than the successors of the apostles.

So, before we proceed with our story, it is important to define what "tradition" is, exactly. Only then will we be able to find where tradition lies amidst a sea of divergent interpretations.

Tradition in common parlance

Though "tradition" has a more expansive and deep meaning in Catholic theology, I believe we can gain some insights by first taking a glance at its meaning in everyday language. The definition from the *Merriam-Webster Dictionary* seems to be a particularly valuable starting point:

Tradition (noun) . . .

1. an inherited, established, or customary pattern of thought, action, or behavior (such as a religious practice or a social custom) . . .
2. the handing down of information, beliefs, and customs by word of mouth or by example from one generation to another without written instruction . . .
3. cultural continuity in social attitudes, customs, and institutions.[4]

Tradition means the *transmission* of a certain information or *content*. In this sense, tradition can be considered both in its *object* (objective tradition) and according to its *act* (active tradition.) "Objective tradition" means the content being transmitted, whereas "active tradition" means the way through which this content is transmitted. In other words, objective tradition is the "what is being transmitted," and active tradition is the "how it is being transmitted."

Active tradition includes the object, but we cannot know the object without knowing the source, the act, the way, and the means through which it has reached the present day. Therefore, to have a complete picture, we

---

[4] *Merriam-Webster.com*. "Tradition."

must take tradition in its *composite* sense, as made up of two parts—the act of transmission and the thing being transmitted.[5] To put it simply, we must always consider the "process of tradition," not only its contents.[6]

According to the social sciences, "tradition" means the ensemble of attitudes and values that identify the culture of a given human group and which are taught to the next generations and are modified by these according to the needs and survival of the group.[7] It is, therefore, a characteristically human trait. Cardinal Joseph Ratzinger—future Pope Benedict XVI—would go so far as calling tradition a "prerequisite of humanity."[8]

Ratzinger draws this conclusion from experiments with a chimpanzee who, though able to invent new kinds of tools, was unable to convey this ability to future generations. According to Ratzinger, "the fact that animals have no intellect is revealed in their inability to transform invention into tradition and so into a historical context. In other words, invention acquires meaning only if it can create tradition, for only thus can history be generated."[9] Tradition is constitutive of a humanity that is truly human.[10]

Being both human and divine, the Church obviously partakes of this human dimension of tradition. However, the theological and Catholic notion of tradition is much broader and fundamental.

---

[5] Agius, *Tradition and the Church*, 1-2. See also Bainvel, "Tradition and Living Magisterium": "The word tradition . . . refers sometimes to the thing (doctrine, account, or custom) transmitted from one generation to another; sometimes to the organ or mode of the transmission."

[6] Bearing this in mind will be important in future chapters, namely when we are dealing with the concepts of doctrinal development and living magisterium.

[7] Martins, *Introdução à Teologia*, 107 (my translation from the original Portuguese).

[8] Ratzinger, *Principles of Catholic Theology*, 86.

[9] Ratzinger, *Principles of Catholic Theology*, 86-87. Today, we know that this might not be entirely true, since some studies have shown that chimpanzees can indeed pass on knowledge by means of imitation. See, for example, Vale, "Acquisition of a socially learned tool use sequence in chimpanzees: Implications for cumulative culture." However, it is undeniable that this trait is much more sophisticated in humans than in any other species, so calling it a characteristically human trait is not inaccurate.

[10] Ratzinger, *Principles of Catholic Theology*, 87.

Tradition as transmission of the mystery of salvation

Tradition in the Catholic sense goes beyond the sociological notion. It is the mystery of salvation passed down by God the Father to the Son, and by the Son to the apostles, and by the apostles to the whole Church.[11] Tradition is like a "communication that descends, as in a cascade, from God, through Christ and the apostles,"[12] so that what God "revealed for the salvation of all nations would abide perpetually in its full integrity and be handed on to all generations."[13] The Second Vatican Council teaches that sacred tradition is "like a mirror in which the pilgrim Church on earth looks at God, from whom she has received everything, until she is brought finally to see Him as He is, face to face."[14] Since the Father handed out this mystery of salvation to the Son, the act of tradition has its origins in the person of Jesus Christ.[15] This tradition consists in everything that we learned through the words, actions, and attitudes of Jesus.[16]

Does this mean that the Old Testament is not a part of tradition, as it precedes the earthly existence of Jesus? Not at all. There was tradition in the Old Testament because there was a sense of history—the biblical concept of "memory."[17] So, for example, Israel would celebrate Passover as a *memorial* of the night when the angel of death passed by Egypt, breaking Pharaoh's resistance to set the Hebrew people free.[18] Later, the prophets would interpret each new event in the history of Israel in light of God's covenant and also of other salvific events in the past.[19]

---

[11] Martins, *Introdução à Teologia*, 107.

[12] Congar, *La Tradition et la vie de l'Eglise*, 16.

[13] Vatican II. *Dei Verbum*, 7. See also Benedict XVI, "General Audience": "The Church transmits all that she is and believes, she hands it down through worship, life and doctrine. So it is that Tradition is the living Gospel, proclaimed by the Apostles in its integrity on the basis of the fullness of their unique and unrepeatable experience: through their activity the faith is communicated to others, even down to us, until the end of the world."

[14] Vatican II. *Dei Verbum*, 7.

[15] Martins, *Introdução à Teologia*, 107.

[16] Martins, *Introdução à Teologia*, 108.

[17] Martins, *Introdução à Teologia*, 106.

[18] Exod 12:14

[19] Martins, *Introdução à Teologia*, 106.

However, for us Christians, the Old Testament must also be read in light of Jesus Christ.[20] After all, the prophets of the Old Testament did not merely interpret the events of their time through the lens of Israel's historical memory. They also foretold of a messiah that would usher in a new kingdom of God, no longer limited to the people of Israel, but encompassing all peoples.[21] We also believe that the sacrificial lamb whose blood marked the Hebrew houses, so that the angel of death would spare them, was a prefiguration of Jesus's sacrifice on the cross, redeeming us from our sins.[22] Christ was the fulfilment of the law of the Old Testament (see chapter 11).[23]

Conversely, Jesus often quoted the Old Testament in His own teachings. Tradition means we must follow His example in this regard. So, even though the act of tradition started with Jesus, the Old Testament is part of this tradition as well.

When teaching what God wanted to reveal to humankind, Jesus did not write these truths down. He only preached.[24] Therefore, the disciples absorbed God's revelation by learning from Jesus's teachings and by following His example. However, not all revelation was completed by Christ while He dwelt on earth. As He said: "I have yet many things to say to you: but you cannot bear them now. But when he, the Spirit of truth, is come, he will teach you all truth. For he shall not speak of himself; but what things soever he shall hear, he shall speak; and the things that are to come, he shall shew you."[25]

At the day of Pentecost, the Holy Spirit descended upon the apostles and instructed them on truths they had not heard before, or truths they could not understand while they lived with Christ.[26] This instruction—and

---

[20] Martins, *Introdução à Teologia*, 112.

[21] Ott, *Fundamentals of Catholic Dogma*, 292-93.

[22] 1 Cor 5:7

[23] Ott, *Fundamentals of Catholic Dogma*, 8.

[24] Bainvel, "Tradition and Living Magisterium"

[25] John 16:12-13

[26] Agius, *Tradition and the Church*, 6. The same author makes a distinction between Dominical tradition—from the Latin word *Dominus*, or Lord—and Divine-Apostolic tradition. The former was revealed by Christ Himself, whereas the latter

consequently, God's revelation—was completed when the last apostle died.[27]

Just like Jesus did not write, He also did not command the apostles to write, but to teach. It was through oral teaching that the apostles preached the gospel to the nations.[28] In order to preserve and safely pass down the deposit of faith from generation to generation, even after their death, the apostles instructed and enjoined their own disciples—people who heard and saw how the apostles practiced their faith, learning from them[29]—to teach everything that they themselves taught. Thus, the process of tradition was set in motion.

But some apostles and their disciples did this also by writing down these divine truths, along with other laws and precepts.[30] These would become the part of scripture we call the New Testament. But this was not the only way. The apostles, handing on what they themselves received, warned the faithful to hold fast to the traditions learned from them either by word of mouth or by letter.[31] This is the reason behind the passage of 2 Tess 2:15 that we discussed earlier.

For the gospel to be kept forever whole and alive within the Church, scripture alone would not suffice. The apostles left bishops (a word that means "overseer" in Greek)[32] as their successors, handing over to them

---

was revealed by the Holy Spirit through the apostles. Together, these two kinds of tradition constitute the Divine traditions, concerning truths of faith, which are to be distinguished from Ecclesiastical traditions, pertaining to Church discipline (see Agius, *Tradition and the Church*, 5). We will see later in this chapter how the distinction between Divine and Ecclesiastical traditions is important.

[27] Agius, *Tradition and the Church*, 5. See also Ott, *Fundamentals of Catholic Dogma*, 8.

[28] Bainvel, "Tradition and Living Magisterium."

[29] Agius, *Tradition and the Church*, 11.

[30] Agius, *Tradition and the Church*, 7, 11. See also Vatican II, *Dei Verbum*, 7: "this commission was faithfully fulfilled by the Apostles who, by their oral preaching, by example, and by observances handed on what they had received from the lips of Christ, from living with Him, and from what He did, or what they had learned through the prompting of the Holy Spirit. The commission was fulfilled, too, by those Apostles and apostolic men who under the inspiration of the same Holy Spirit committed the message of salvation to writing."

[31] Vatican II. *Dei Verbum*, 8.

[32] Mullin, *A Short World History of Christianity*, 23. See also O'Malley, *Vatican I*, 7.

the authority to teach in their own place.[33] As St. Paul said to Timothy: "Thou has fully known my doctrine . . . but continue thou in those things which thou hast learned, and which have been committed to thee: knowing of whom thou hast learned them."[34]

These bishops, in turn, had their own successors, who became bishops as well. Thus, an unbroken apostolic succession brought the deposit of the faith to our present day.

Tradition in the broad and strict senses

From what was said above, we can understand that there is an intricate closeness between scripture and the apostles' oral teaching. Both come from God, through Jesus and the Holy Spirit. Both were relayed to the next generations by the apostles and their immediate disciples. The only difference is the means of transmission: one in writing and the other orally. As the Catechism describes, there is one *common source*, but two different *modes of transmission.*[35]

In this sense, if we consider tradition as everything handed down by God for the salvation of humankind, regardless of mode of transmission, then scripture must *also* be considered tradition.[36] As the Second Vatican Council beautifully puts it:

> Hence there exists a close connection and communication between [oral] sacred tradition and Sacred Scripture. For both of them, flowing from the *same divine wellspring*, in a certain way merge into a unity and tend toward the same end . . . Sacred tradition and Sacred Scripture *form one sacred deposit* of the word of God, committed to the Church.[37]

---

[33] Vatican II. *Dei Verbum*, 7.

[34] 2 Tim. 3:10,14

[35] CCC, 80-81.

[36] Agius, *Tradition and the Church*, 10. See also Martins, *Introdução à Teologia*, 108.

[37] Vatican II. *Dei Verbum*, 9. See also Vatican I, *Dei Filius*, Chapter 2, 5: "Now this supernatural revelation, according to the belief of the universal church, as declared by the sacred council of Trent, is contained in written books and unwritten

In other words, the whole of tradition constitutes a single deposit of faith entrusted to the Church. This tradition was relayed through two modes of transmission: by oral word and by writing. If we want to have access to the fullness of the deposit of the faith, we must consider both.[38]

However, when we talk about tradition, we usually refer only to what has been handed down *orally*. Again, as the Second Vatican Council teaches in the very same paragraph:

> For Sacred Scripture is the word of God inasmuch as it is consigned to writing under the inspiration of the divine Spirit, while sacred tradition takes the word of God entrusted by Christ the Lord and the Holy Spirit to the Apostles, and hands it on to their successors in its full purity, so that led by the light of the Spirit of truth, they may in proclaiming it preserve this word of God faithfully, explain it, and make it more widely known.[39]

Consequently, there are two senses for the word "tradition": a *broad* sense and a *strict* sense. The broad sense includes *all* that was revealed by God, including scripture. The strict sense, more often used, refers to what was transmitted through *other means besides writing*, therefore excluding scripture.[40] During the course of this book, I will use the strict sense, except when dealing with heresies that take advantage of scripture to appear more traditional (e.g., chapters 5, 8, and 10).

This strict sense of the word "tradition," however, does not include only the repetition of the words of Jesus and the apostles, but also the life and concrete experiences the Church has lived throughout her history, even to this day.[41] Again, we must remember that tradition refers not only to the

---

traditions, which were received by the apostles from the lips of Christ himself, or came to the apostles by the dictation of the holy Spirit, and were passed on as it were from hand to hand until they reached us."

[38] See Vatican II. *Dei Verbum*, 9: "Consequently it is not from Sacred Scripture *alone* that the Church draws her certainty about everything which has been revealed. Therefore both sacred tradition and Sacred Scripture are to be accepted and venerated with the same sense of loyalty and reverence."

[39] Vatican II. *Dei Verbum*, 9.

[40] Agius, *Tradition and the Church*, 10. See also Martins, *Introdução à Teologia*, 108.

[41] Martins, *Introdução à Teologia*, 108-09.

content (objective tradition), but also to the act of transmission of this content (active tradition),[42] i.e., the "process of tradition."[43] Therefore, tradition is a *living reality*.[44] Traditionalists often have trouble understanding this,[45] and thus endanger tradition under the pretext of defending it, since they are putting the very "process of tradition" in jeopardy.

The peril of tradition

Pope Francis, alongside his predecessors, alludes often to this concept of "living tradition." One of his most famous interventions is this:

> Tradition is the guarantee of the future, not the guardian of ashes. It is not a museum . . . The nostalgia of fundamentalists, return to the ashes, no. Tradition is the root that allows the tree to grow, flourish, and bear fruit . . . Every single one of the tree's flowers comes from what is buried.[46]

Cardinal Joseph Ratzinger agreed with this proposition, for he himself said that "the past can be discovered as something to be preserved only if the

---

[42] Agius, *Tradition and the Church*, 1-2.

[43] Martins, *Introdução à Teologia*, 122.

[44] See Vatican II. *Dei Verbum*, 8: "The words of the holy fathers witness to the presence of this *living tradition*, whose wealth is poured into the practice and life of the believing and praying Church."

[45] See, for example, Vennari, "Modernism in a Nutshell": "'Tradition' for the modernist, is nothing more than the former expressions of the collective feelings of a religious group throughout the ages. But the modernist will insist on a 'living tradition' that casts aside old dogmas and practices if they are not considered relevant to modern man . . . If dogma is to be 'living' it must be subjected to the 'new insights' of modern theologians. 'Outdated' Catholic Tradition must be replaced by 'Living Tradition.' Thus, the ideal modern Catholic religion, one that shows that it is alive, must have a New Theology, New Mass, New Code of Canon Law, New Catechism, and New Evangelization. And every one of these 'new' items will contain aspects that in some way or another, contradict the traditional ('static') Catholic teaching and practice."

[46] Francis, "Press Conference during the flight of return to Rome from Romania" (my translation from the original Italian).

future is regarded as a duty; discovery of the future and discovery of the past are inseparably connected, and it is this discovery of the indivisibility of time that actually makes tradition."[47] Ratzinger would go on to say:

> We were able to affirm that true tradition is by no means concerned only with the past but is intimately connected also with the future. We come now to a further point. *Tradition, which is by nature the foundation of man's humanness, is everywhere mingled with those things that deprive him of his humanity*. The basis of man's humanness—tradition—is contaminated. It bears simultaneously within itself both itself and, for this very reason, the seeds of antihumanism. Its source and its destruction are inextricably intermingled—that is the real tragedy of mankind. Man must hold fast to tradition if he is to hold fast to his humanness, but in doing so, he inevitably holds fast also to the forces of alienation. The simple statement with which we began acquires thereby a strange ambiguity, for we must expand it into the statement: Tradition is the precondition of man's humanness*, but it is also its peril.* Whoever destroys tradition destroys man . . . *But even he who would preserve tradition falls likewise into the danger of destroying it.*[48]

A somber warning indeed for those who claim to be traditionalists. As everything good that God has given us, tradition can be perverted, especially if we attach an "ism" to it. And lest anyone might think that Ratzinger is talking here merely about human traditions and not Church traditions, he quickly adds: "a nation must be assiduous in purifying its own traditions; the Church must do likewise."[49]

But, if sacred tradition came from God Himself, how can we dare to purify this tradition or believe that it can be dangerous? The answer lies in a very important distinction, which Ratzinger also makes:

> We must consequently, analyze tradition from two very different perspectives. From the theological point of view, it is necessary

[47] Ratzinger, *Principles of Catholic Theology*, 87.
[48] Ratzinger, *Principles of Catholic Theology*, 89-90.
[49] Ratzinger, *Principles of Catholic Theology*, 90.

first of all to *guard tradition against traditions*; that is, we must not let ourselves be suffocated by the luxuriant growth of individual traditions but must be assiduous in cutting away what is accidental and temporary, and keeping it within bounds in order to make room for what is fundamental.[50]

Tradition and traditions

What is the difference, then, between "tradition" and "traditions"? What does it mean to say that some traditions are "accidental or temporary"? Ratzinger is alluding to the distinction between *apostolic* tradition and *ecclesial* tradition.[51] The apostles were promulgators of the truths revealed to them by God, but they were also legislators and pastors of the churches they founded. Likewise, bishops and popes along history to this very day were not only teachers, but also lawmakers and policymakers.

What the apostles preached and wrote regarding revelation constitutes the apostolic tradition and cannot be changed, because it is what God relayed to them in an unrepeatable way. However, as legislators and pastors, they also established certain laws and rules which they deemed necessary or useful in the particular churches they founded. These ecclesial traditions are subject to revision, dispensation or even abrogation, namely by the pope, successor of St. Peter. This is especially true for ecclesial traditions in post-apostolic times.[52] So, the Catechism teaches that:

Tradition is to be distinguished from the various theological, disciplinary, liturgical or devotional traditions, born in the local churches over time. These are the *particular forms*, adapted to different places and times, in which the great Tradition is *expressed.* In the light of Tradition,

---

[50] Ratzinger, *Principles of Catholic Theology*, 90.

[51] Or between Divine tradition and Ecclesiastical tradition, according to the terminology employed by Agius, *Tradition and the Church*, 9.

[52] Agius, *Tradition and the Church*, 6-9.

> these traditions can be retained, modified or even abandoned under the guidance of the Church's Magisterium.[53]

Therefore, at each given moment, we must verify whether any ecclesial tradition is binding on the faith of the Church or not.[54] Often, the error of the traditionalist is to fail to understand how this is possible. For him, abandoning traditions is the same as abandoning tradition. The traditionalist will confuse this with modernism. But there is a crucial difference. Modernism affirms that parts of divine tradition must be abandoned to fit with modern times. On the contrary, Catholicism says that tradition must remain unchanged, but the way tradition is *expressed* can change. Modernism postulates that we must get on with the times because nothing is eternal. Catholicism firmly asserts that there are eternal realities, but they must be conveyed in a way the temporal will understand.

It is true that the gospel must remain untouched, but its universality (i.e., "catholicity") demands that its *expressions* adapt to the several existential and cultural situations around the world and across history. It is within these "traditions," and never without them, that the gospel is preached.[55] It is folly to presume that we have access to tradition in its pure form without the "traditions" enveloping it.

Furthermore, the traditions that, throughout the centuries, expressed the salvific event of Jesus Christ are no mere "external coatings," but significantly enrich the unique message of the gospel, allowing it to reach all parts of the world.[56] God, who gave up His Son to the world so that it would have life in abundance, always wants to be present at each moment in history and each different culture, so that *all* humans may have access to His salvation.[57]

According to the Second Vatican Council, finding solutions to human problems means that we have to discern the best way to apply the eternal truths of revelation to the changeable conditions of human affairs.[58] To carry out such a task, the Church has always had the duty of scrutinizing

---

[53] CCC, 83.
[54] Martins, *Introdução à Teologia*, 110.
[55] Martins, *Introdução à Teologia*, 110.
[56] Martins, *Introdução à Teologia*, 111.
[57] Martins, *Introdução à Teologia*, 122.
[58] Vatican II. *Optatam totius*, 16.

the "signs of the times" and of interpreting them in the light of the gospel. Thus, in language intelligible to each generation, the Church can respond to the perennial questions which men ask about this present life and the life to come, and about the relationship of the one to the other.[59] As Pope St. John XXIII explained during the opening of the council: "One thing is the substance of the '*depositum fidei*,' that is, the truths contained in our doctrine, and another thing is the formulation with which they are expressed, conserving, however, the same sense and the same reach."[60] This is the basis of a concept that played a big part in Vatican II, called *aggiornamento*—meaning "bringing up to date" in Italian. This *aggiornamento* is not an invention from John XXIII, but it was already formulated before Vatican II by Pope Benedict XV. In his first encyclical, Benedict wrote that in matters "subject to change" the rule should be "old things, but in a new way" (*non nova, sed noviter*).[61]

For the "process of tradition" to take place, the Church must purify herself from ecclesial, non-binding traditions that do not speak to—or even hinder the dialogue with—the culture they are trying to engage at that specific moment, even if they were adequate in other times and places. When the Church does so, she is actually allowing the eternal, apostolic tradition to come forth and be communicated to a new generation and culture, as is proper of tradition. But retrieving tradition from the midst of traditions, while being the truly traditional action, may create the illusion of anti-traditionalism. We are going to explore this illusion in the next chapter.

---

[59] Vatican II. *Gaudium et Spes*, 4.

[60] John XXIII, "Discorso del Santo Padre" (my translation from the original Italian).

[61] Benedict XV. *Ad Beatissimi Apostolorum*, 25.

Chapter 2

"Back to the Sources"

Brothers and sisters, let us return to the Council, which rediscovered the living river of Tradition without remaining mired in traditions. The Council rediscovered the source of love, not to remain on mountain heights, but to cascade downwards as a channel of mercy for all.

—Francis,
Homily on the 60th Anniversary of the Second Vatican Council

On February 10, 2013, Thomas Lawson woke up to a bitter surprise. His alarm clock rang, as usual. He turned it off, as usual. He got up, brushed his teeth, got dressed, and prepared his breakfast, as usual. And he checked the early news, as usual. But something unusual was afoot. Something so unusual, it had not happened for 718 years.[1] The pope had voluntarily renounced the ministry of bishop of Rome.[2]

Tom was taken by a great sadness. He deeply loved Benedict XVI, the pope who had seen him convert. Why, of all the popes that ever were in centuries, did it have to be Benedict to resign? This question churned on Tom's head and heart throughout the whole day, the whole week, the whole month. With teary eyes, he saw the live footage of Benedict taking a helicopter to Castel-Gandolfo on February 28, never to be seen again as ruling pontiff. It was not just Benedict who was flying away; it was his whole pontificate.

Thomas's sadness was somewhat attenuated in the following days. The Vatican was bustling with activity, preparing to receive the cardinals for the next conclave. Sorrow gave way to curiosity. Who would be the next pope? Every news channel was making predictions, all the while explaining the details about how the conclave was going to be held.

Our young friend heard all of this with interest. He had lived through Benedict's election, but as a Protestant, he did not pay much attention to it. This was the first conclave he would actually follow. On March 12, Tom

---

[1] de Sousa. "Father Raymond J. de Souza on the Pope: The Holy Father takes his leave."

[2] Benedict XVI, *Declaratio.*

was glued to his TV set. All the pomp and ceremony surrounding the preparation and the opening of the conclave certainly appealed to Tom's traditionalist proclivities. But all of it would soon be taken away from his senses, as the Sistine Chapel's doors were shut close and locked. They would only open when the see was no longer vacant.

There was black smoke coming from the Vatican's chimney that day, announcing that the first ballot had not gathered enough votes to elect the pontiff. There would be black smoke again three more times the next day. But at 7 pm CET on March 13, there was white smoke. Good news! *Habemus Papam*! [3]

The bells were chiming. People at St. Peter's Square were rejoicing. Tom's heart was pounding. Who would be the next pope? The Cardinal Protodeacon came to the balcony of St. Peter's Basilica. All eyes, all cameras, all the attention of the world were focused on him. Then, he announced the name:

> *Dominum* Georgium Marium *Sanctae Romanae Ecclesiae Cardinalem* Bergoglio*, qui sibi nomen imposuit* Franciscum. [4]

Tom saw the new pope come out to the balcony. He was wearing a white cassock and matching pellegrina. As someone who had never seen an announcement like this, Tom did not notice that Francis had eschewed the papal regalia characteristic of such a solemn occasion. By foregoing the red, white ermine trimmed mozzetta and the gold embroidered papal stole, Francis was breaking with a sartorial tradition in place since at least Pius XI's 1922 election. [5] However, this signaled that Francis wanted to return

---

[3] "We have a pope" in Latin—traditional saying uttered when a new pontiff is elected.

[4] "Lord *Jorge Mario*, Cardinal of the Holy Roman Church, *Bergoglio*, who takes to himself the name *Francis*." (translated from the Latin).

[5] See Urbano, "Clothes and the Man: How popes communicate through clothing."

to a simpler church, a Church "that is poor and for the poor"[6]—an older and more venerable tradition than any papal dress code.[7]

Not knowing of this coded message, Tom was fascinated by the new pope's smile and authenticity, especially when he greeted the crowd with a simple "*Buona sera.*"[8] When the pope asked all Catholics watching to pray for him,[9] Tom kneeled and asked God to bless Francis's pontificate.

After the papal blessing, Tom rushed to his computer. He wanted to know more about this Jorge Mario Bergoglio. Unfortunately, Bergoglio's page on Wikipedia was crashing due to the overflow of traffic. Since the most usual sources were unavailable, Tom would take recourse to the traditionalist blogs he had learned to follow. And he would indeed find new information. Thirty minutes after the papal blessing, the well-known traditionalist website Rorate Caeli had already published an article titled "The Horror," describing Bergoglio as a "sworn enemy of the Traditional Mass."[10]

Thomas Lawson's joy was shattered. His bliss gave way to dread. Could it be? Had God abandoned His Church to the hands of an anti-traditionalist modernist? Unfortunately for him, the next couple of years would not help allay his concerns.

It is true, at that time no one would say that any of Francis's teachings were heretical or heterodox. After all, they could all be traced back to social encyclicals from Benedict XVI, John Paul II, or even from before them. But his overemphasis on social justice seemed to show a liberal streak. Francis's predecessors also taught about social justice, but Tom had learned that those teachings were merely the prudential judgments of the popes,

---

[6] Davies, "Pope Francis declares: 'I would like to see a church that is poor and is for the poor.'"

[7] One can recall the famous apocryphal story of St. Thomas Aquinas visiting the pope and finding him counting a large sum of money. Referring to the episode of Acts 3:6, the pope would have said: "Ah Thomas, Peter can no longer say 'silver and gold have I none,'" to which Aquinas would have replied: "True, Your Holiness, but then neither can Peter now say 'Arise and walk.'" See Chesterton. *St. Thomas Aquinas*, 18.

[8] Italian for "good evening."

[9] Francis, "First Greeting of the Holy Father Pope Francis"

[10] New Catholic [pseudo.], "The Horror."

that is, not-binding on the faithful.[11] The Catholic magisterium on political matters had parts that could be underlined with a gold marker (the ones to be followed by all the faithful, without exception) and others that could be underlined with a red marker (and could be ignored).[12] The truly non-negotiable issues were abortion and other matters directly connected with Catholic bioethics and sexual anthropology.[13]

As someone raised in the bosom of a conservative Evangelical family, one of the things that had attracted Tom to the Catholic faith was her firm defense of truth on those topics. The West in general, and the USA in particular, were locked in a culture war where liberals used social justice to undermine the Church's stance on life and family. Now Francis was giving fodder to the Church's political enemies. Sure, Francis still defended the Church's doctrine on abortion and other such life issues.[14] But for some reason, his emphasis on social justice was harder to ignore than with his predecessors. Why was Francis so keen on bringing up those previously forgotten teachings to the forefront of his pontificate? Why not let sleeping doctrines lie?

Yet, Francis knew that his focus on the poor was not as radical as some things proposed by the gospel[15] or many Fathers of the Church.[16] All of his actions and all his discourses were not motivated by a hatred of tradition. Quite the contrary, the new pontiff sought to return to a deeper, more fundamental tradition, that had been de-emphasized before—sometimes not even by his predecessors, but by those media interpreting them for the Catholic masses. In other words, Francis wanted Catholics to "return to the source."

---

[11] See Horn, "'Prudential Judgment,' and Voting Q+A."

[12] See Weigel. "Caritas in Veritate in Gold and Red."

[13] See *Voter's Guide for Serious Catholics*, 2006.

[14] I collected many of Francis' pro-life interventions on a 3-part series: Gabriel, "Pope Francis, Pro-Life Champion."

[15] As a non-exhaustive example, see Mark 10:21: "And Jesus looking on him, loved him, and said to him: One thing is wanting unto thee: go, sell whatsoever thou hast, and give to the poor"

[16] Again, as a non-exhaustive example, see St. John Chrysostom, as cited by Francis, *Fratelli tutti*, 119: "Not to share our wealth with the poor is to rob them and take away their livelihood. The riches we possess are not our own, but theirs as well."

Back to the source or new theology?

For us to know whether there has been historical precedent for a "traditionalist" resistance to pre-conciliar magisterium, we must first understand how the conciliar and post-conciliar magisterium came to be seen as anti-traditional. In his fundamental work about the history of Vatican II, the renowned historian John O'Malley explains that to truly grasp the council's reforms, we need to understand three concepts: 1) *aggiornamento*, 2) doctrinal development, and 3) *ressourcement*. All three assume that Catholic tradition is "richer, broader, and more malleable"[17] than the way it is sometimes presented. I already touched on the concept of *aggionarmento* on my last chapter. Regarding doctrinal development, I am going to explore it with more detail on my next chapter. So, let us now look into *ressourcement*, the most traditional of the three—and paradoxically, the most potentially radical.[18]

Ressourcement means "back to the sources" in French.[19] This word was originally coined by the great French Catholic thinker Charles Péguy in the wake of the twentieth century.[20] It is, therefore, hardly surprising that the French would be the ones more familiar with this term—and the ones who would develop it to its furthest expression.

Péguy would die in 1914, in the battlefields of World War One, but his intellectual legacy endured. Two decades later, the teeming theological milieu of 1930s France would pick up this concept and apply it to its theological works. This would happen mainly in two hotspots.

The first of these was the Jesuit Faculty of Lyon-Fourvière. Among the masters of this school, Henri de Lubac is regarded as the *ressourcement* theologian par excellence.[21] To better explain de Lubac's thought, we must

---

[17] O'Malley. *What Happened at Vatican II*, 37. See also Guarino, *The Disputed Teachings of Vatican II*, 55-56.

[18] O'Malley. *What Happened at Vatican II*, 301.

[19] O'Malley. *What Happened at Vatican II*, 40.

[20] Flynn and Murray. *Ressourcement, a Movement for Renewal*, 4.

[21] Guarino. *The Disputed Teachings*, 60.

look at a distinction he made between two kinds of theologians, as Msgr. Thomas Guarino explains in his seminal work on Vatican II:

> On the one hand are those who do not wish to "correct even a word" of papal teaching *from the last century*. . . In other words, *recent* ecclesial teaching is taken as the preeminent guide for all theological investigation. On the other hand are the *ressourcement* theologians . . . who wish to reread Scripture and the Fathers, the Eastern writers, and the entire *living tradition* of the church and bring these to bear on contemporary problems. De Lubac's simple point is that the ordinary magisterium of the past hundred years cannot be equated with the great theological tradition of Christianity. It is the broader and deeper tradition that must be mined for resources as the church faces new challenges.[22]

The second pole blossomed in a Dominican-founded faculty in Le Saulchoir, Belgium, which would be transferred to Paris in 1937 (though retaining the name Le Saulchoir.) The most influential of the theologians of this school was Yves Congar, whose work was also dedicated to a recovery of Christian tradition beyond recent papal and magisterial teachings.[23] He would write, in his book "True and False Reform":

> Many would receive the faith fairly easily if it were offered to them in the form that it receives from its *sources* (the Bible and early tradition.) But they have trouble recognizing the Gospel beneath the historical baggage that hides its living reality and that seems foreign to it . . . To "go back to the sources," as we say now, means to rethink the situation in which we find ourselves in the light and in the spirit of everything that the integrity of tradition teaches us about the meaning of the church.[24]

In other words, *ressourcement* advocated bypassing the present to access the past, thus retrieving from Church history something more spiritually

---

[22] Guarino. *The Disputed Teachings*, 60.
[23] Guarino. *The Disputed Teachings*, 61.
[24] Congar. True and False Reform, 50, 295.

enriching.[25] *Ressourcement* scholars were skeptical of the present,[26] so they would never set out to create a "revolution." Rather, they wanted to move towards a deeper tradition.[27] For these theologians, tradition was not about a mere repetition of the *recent* past, but about the unity of *ever-living* tradition.[28] They had a "dynamic view of tradition"[29]—which, as we have seen in the last chapter, is the proper way to understand it. As de Lubac would say, what he most regretted in the theological milieu of his time was not so much the "lack of openness to the problems and currents of contemporary thought," but the "lack of a truly traditional mind."[30]

In practice though, this movement was a reaction against the Catholic mainstream of their day. This mainstream, in turn, was grounded on Neo-Scholasticism, based on Thomistic theology. Paradoxically, this neo-scholastic movement was also very vibrant in France. One of the most influential neo-scholastics of this period was Fr. Garrigou-Lagrange, a Dominican and former student and teacher of Le Saulchoir.

A clash was imminent. The *ressourcement* thinkers disliked the Thomistic dryness of the neo-scholastics, seeking instead a more ancient and spiritually nourishing tradition,[31] more influenced by scripture and the Church Fathers of the first centuries.

Interestingly, though their aim was to uncover a more profound and primordial tradition, these theologians were accused of the exact opposite. Since they were a recent movement railing against the mainstream, they were considered a "new theology." Here, we can already take a glimpse at a recurring theme in Church history, the major premise of this book: those who seek a more profound tradition are often seen as being anti-tradition.

---

[25] O'Malley. *What Happened at Vatican II*, 300-301.

[26] O'Malley. *What Happened at Vatican II*, 40.

[27] Congar, "The Brother I have known", as quoted by Flynn and Murray. *Ressourcement, a Movement for Renewal*, 4.

[28] Flynn and Murray. *Ressourcement, a Movement for Renewal*, 5.

[29] Flynn and Murray. *Ressourcement, a Movement for Renewal*, 8.

[30] De Lubac, *At the Service of the Church*, as quoted by Flynn and Murray. *Ressourcement, a Movement for Renewal*, 8.

[31] O'Malley. *What Happened at Vatican II*, 41, 75.

Not surprisingly, the greatest resistance to the *ressourcement* movement came from the neo-scholastics they opposed. To this end, the neo-Thomists referred to it with the pejorative term "*la nouvelle théologie*" i.e., "the new theology."[32] The term originated in 1942, with Pietro Parente, an assessor of the Holy Office,[33] but became more widespread when Fr. Garrigou-Lagrange wrote an article in 1946, asking in the title: "Where is the new theology leading us?" He replied: "To modernism."[34]

Obviously, the *ressourcement* theologians vehemently rejected the "*nouvelle théologie*" label. De Lubac detested the expression.[35] How could they be proposing a new theology, when their main concern was to recover a deeper tradition?

Maybe we can answer this question if we look at it from another angle. It is true that *ressourcement* theologians tried to dig up a more profound tradition from the past and apply it to the present. However, is this practice itself traditional? In other words, is there tradition for using *ressourcement*?

Ad fontes: the tradition behind ressourcement

Though *ressourcement* was a neologism coined by Charles Péguy in the twentieth century, its practice was a part of a more venerable tradition. The historian John O'Malley goes so far as saying that "some form of *ressourcement* lay behind every reform movement in Western Christianity . . . at least up to the Enlightenment."[36]

A preliminary form of *ressourcement* could be seen in the eleventh century, during the so-called Gregorian reforms. These comprised a religious reform movement, whose name was taken from its most forceful advocate: Pope St. Gregory VII. This pontiff was adamant about reigning in on the clerical immorality of his day, namely by pushing back against simony (i.e., the purchase of ecclesiastical offices,) and sexual immorality. To this end, Gregory prohibited the "traditional" investiture of bishops and abbots, which until then could be done by lay rulers and kings—an obvious source

---

[32] O'Malley. *What Happened at Vatican II*, 41.

[33] O'Malley. *What Happened at Vatican II*, 75.

[34] Flynn and Murray. *Ressourcement, a Movement for Renewal*, 36. See also O'Malley. *What Happened at Vatican II*, 86.

[35] Flynn and Murray. *Ressourcement, a Movement for Renewal*, 6.

[36] O'Malley. *What Happened at Vatican II*, 41.

of political corruption. Instead, Gregory insisted that these members of the clergy should be canonically elected. The pontiff believed that the Church had lost the original purity of apostolic times and would frequently cite John 10:1-18 as his ideal for the priesthood.[37]

Some decades later, this Gregorian reform would be condensed into laws on canonical episcopal elections and clerical celibacy promulgated by the First and Second Lateran Councils. As O'Malley says: "The reformers understood their position on these two matters as reassertions of the normative practice of an earlier era, which implied a mandate to reinstate the older practice."[38]

Some centuries afterwards, the Renaissance saw the rebirth of classicism, with its fascination and adoption of ancient Greek and Latin forms of art, architecture, literature, and philosophy.[39] In fact, one can argue that Renaissance and *ressourcement* are almost synonyms.[40]

It was also during the Renaissance that the concept of *ressourcement* was first named. *Ad fontes!*—Latin for "to the sources!"—would be the motto of the great humanist movement of this period. Just like the later *ressourcement* theologians, Erasmus of Rotterdam sought to displace medieval scholasticism and return to the sources, notably the Bible and the Fathers of the Church.[41]

Already during the twentieth century, Pope St. Pius X's liturgical reforms would also be considered a kind of *ressourcement.*[42] Curiously, Pius would use the expression "*Revertimini ad fontes*" ("let us return to the sources") to designate the sort of theological, pastoral, and liturgical renewal he envisioned.[43]

But the more interesting example of *ressourcement* can be found a bit earlier. In 1879, Pope Leo XIII published his encyclical *Aeterni Patris*,

---

[37] Blumenthal. "Gregorian Reform."
[38] O'Malley. *What Happened at Vatican II*, 41.
[39] Davis. "Classicism and the Renaissance."
[40] O'Malley. *What Happened at Vatican II*, 300.
[41] O'Malley. *What Happened at Vatican II*, 41.
[42] Flynn and Murray. *Ressourcement, a Movement for Renewal*, 4.
[43] Congar. *Chrétien en dialogue.*

urging the revival of the study of St. Thomas Aquinas and of the scholastic method.[44]

> Later on, the doctors of the middle ages, *who are called Scholastics*, addressed themselves to a great work—that of diligently collecting, and sifting, and storing up, as it were, in one place, for the use and convenience of posterity the rich and fertile harvests of *Christian learning scattered abroad in the voluminous works of the holy Fathers.* And with regard, venerable brethren, to the origin, drift, and excellence of this scholastic learning, it may be well here to speak more fully in the words of one of the wisest of Our predecessors, Sixtus V: "By the divine favor of Him who alone gives the spirit of science wisdom, and understanding, and who thou ages, as there may be need, *enriches His Church with new blessings and strengthens it with safeguards*, there was founded by Our fathers, men of eminent wisdom, *the scholastic theology*, which two glorious doctors in particular angelic St. Thomas and the seraphic St. Bonaventure, illustrious teachers of this faculty, . . . skillfully arranged and clearly explained in a variety of ways, *handed down to posterity*."[45]

Thus, by trying to retrieve medieval Thomistic theology from the shelves of history, Leo XIII planted the seeds of the neo-scholastic movement—the same movement that would later on oppose de Lubac and his companions. This raises the question: if both are based on a kind of *ressourcement*, which one is more traditional?

Vatican II weighs in: The true *ressourcement*

Leo XIII's Thomistic revival was enthusiastically supported by Pius X and subsequent popes. Therefore, it was only a matter of time until the *ressourcement* theologians' opposition to neo-scholasticism would set them in a collision course with the Vatican's vision. In 1950, Pope Pius XII published the encyclical *Humani Generis.* Though Pius would not name those he condemned in this document, the implications seemed obvious:

---

[44] O'Malley. *What Happened at Vatican II*, 41.

[45] Leo XIII. *Aeterni Patris*, 14.

> *The contempt for terms and notions habitually used by scholastic theologians* leads of itself to the weakening of what they call speculative theology, a discipline which these men consider devoid of true certitude because it is based on theological reasoning. Unfortunately these advocates of novelty easily pass from despising scholastic theology to the neglect of and even *contempt for the Teaching Authority of the Church itself, which gives such authoritative approval to scholastic theology* . . . What is expounded in the Encyclical Letters of the Roman Pontiffs concerning the nature and constitution of the Church, is deliberately and habitually neglected by some with the idea of giving force to *a certain vague notion which they profess to have found in the ancient Fathers*, especially the Greeks. The Popes, they assert, do not wish to pass judgment on what is a matter of dispute among theologians, so *recourse must be had to the early sources, and the recent constitutions and decrees of the Teaching Church must be explained from the writings of the ancients.*[46]

Even though de Lubac and Congar did not think that Pius XII's criticisms were an accurate portrayal of their theology, the truth is that *Humani Generis* led to their dismissal—along with many other *ressourcement* theologians—from their teaching posts.[47] However, it has been argued that Pius XII did not have de Lubac in mind when his encyclical, for eight years later the pontiff sent a letter to de Lubac's confessor, expressing gratitude for de Lubac's works, blessing him and encouraging him to proceed with his studies.[48] Also, it is very important to highlight that Pius XII did not exclude the possibility of a certain kind of *ressourcement.* In typical Catholic fashion, the pontiff sifted through the theology he condemned, allowing what was compatible with the faith to shine through:

> It is also true that theologians must always *return to the sources* of divine revelation: for it belongs to them to point out how the

---

[46] Pius XII. *Humani Generis*, 17-18.

[47] Flynn and Murray. *Ressourcement, a Movement for Renewal*, 6-7.

[48] Kirby. "Seven Persistent Myths."

> doctrine of the living Teaching Authority is to be found either explicitly or implicitly in the Scriptures and in Tradition. Besides, each source of divinely revealed doctrine contains so many rich treasures of truth, that they can really never be exhausted. Hence it is that *theology through the study of its sacred sources remains ever fresh*; on the other hand, speculation which neglects a deeper search into the deposit of faith, proves sterile, as we know from experience.[49]

By reading the encyclical carefully, we can sense that what ultimately upset Pius XII was not so much *ressourcement* itself, but rather a certain cavalier attitude towards scholasticism and, by extension, towards the magisterial authority promoting it. Could *ressourcement* be salvaged still?

De Lubac meditated this criticism for several years. Did his theology give the impression of a refusal of the whole theological development successive to the Fathers—and therefore also of the theology of St. Thomas Aquinas? De Lubac was not against Thomism, but only against a certain modern interpretation of Thomism, concocted from the sixteenth century onward. To highlight this nuance, the Jesuit priest rewrote, in a certain sense, his earlier book *Surnaturel*, naming it *Augustinisme et theologie moderne*. Here, he convincingly shows how the whole work of St. Thomas is fully inserted in the Patristic tradition. The main thesis of the two books of de Lubac is the same. However, the second book is more mature and takes in due account the formidable contribution of St. Thomas Aquinas.[50]

Later, the previously sanctioned theologians would be rehabilitated during the Second Vatican Council. Both de Lubac and Congar would be invited to be *periti*[51] during the council's proceedings. Nevertheless, it is also true that the Second Vatican Council still placed Aquinas's work in high regard.[52] The council, therefore, absorbed the two kinds of *ressourcement* and, though favoring the one from de Lubac and Congar (just like Leo XIII had favored neo-scholasticism,) achieved a balanced synthesis between the two. This kind of dialectics is extremely characteristic of Catholic

---

[49] Pius XII. *Humani Generis*, 21.

[50] I thank Prof. Rocco Buttiglione for bringing these points to my consideration.

[51] Expert advisors.

[52] See, for example, Vatican II. *Optatam totius*, 16, and *Gravissimum educationis*, 10.

tradition, as we shall see in chapter 4. The fact that Vatican II's preference for *ressourcement* led to a withering of neo-scholasticism does not mean that the council did not have a more moderate position than the extremes of the contending parties.

This synthesis was better expressed by Gérard Philips, a Belgian priest who, as adjunct secretary of the council's theological commission, played a pivotal role in many episodes of Vatican II. As Thomas Guarino explains, for Philips we should not conceive of *ressourcement* as a return to a source which has been for a long time abandoned and now finally recovered, but rather as a matter of looking at the Divine Word of God as preached and committed to writing and transmitted in a *living tradition*. This tradition was like a chain coming down from the apostles, through the Fathers, the councils, and the acts of the magisterium. Scholasticism was *also* a part of this chain of tradition—as Catholics concerned with tradition, we should not skip a single link of this chain.[53]

In other words, according to Philips, *ressourcement* must take into account the *whole* tradition of the Church, including scripture and the Fathers on one side, and Thomism and post-Tridentine theologians on the other.[54] In this sense, *ressourcement* means *supplementing*, rather than *supplanting*.[55] A synthesis was achieved here, in which *ressourcement* became truly traditional, without forgetting any part of our Catholic history.[56]

If we want to uphold tradition today, we must "go back to the sources." This includes the venerable tradition of *ressourcement*, in its true sense. This means that we cannot merely dismiss the Church as it was

[53] Guarino. *The Disputed Teachings*, 59.

[54] In fact, the *ressourcement* theologians themselves did not oppose Aquinas's theology, but only his modern interpreters' neo-Thomism. See Flynn and Murray. *Ressourcement, a Movement for Renewal*, 355-358.

[55] Guarino. *The Disputed Teachings*, 61.

[56] See also "*Manifesto of the New Traditionalism*": "*Ressourcement* theology, which is at the heart of the Second Vatican Council, was the first of many theological approaches which *developed* the Sacred Tradition, in a way entirely compatible with the foundations of Saint Thomas . . . While all of these new theologies have, at times, been dismissive of other traditions or even promoted by heretics, we, grounded in the solid rock of orthodoxy, have no fear of fruitful dialogue as we seek 'the harmony which exists between elements of the faith' (*DV* 12).'"

before the council. This is the reason why Joseph Ratzinger—himself a second generation *ressourcement* theologian and a *peritus* during Vatican II—would emphasize the need for a "hermeneutic of continuity" in the way we should implement the council.[57] However, it would be equally anti-traditional to discard the Second Vatican Council's developments, for these too belong to the entirety of tradition. We are not allowed to skip over the conciliar and post-conciliar magisterium, for these too are a part of the unbroken chain of living tradition going back to the apostles.

However, it is important to note that, as we have seen, exercises of *ressourcement*, though more traditional, can create the illusion of anti-traditionalism. This is especially true if *ressourcement* is coupled with *aggiornamento* and doctrinal development. We will talk about the latter in the next chapter.

---

[57] Flynn and Murray. *Ressourcement, a Movement for Renewal*, 19, 429. See also Benedict XVI. "Address to the General Assembly," and also Ratzinger, Joseph. "Mass '*Pro Eligendo Romano Pontifice*'"

Chapter 3

"Great outward changes"

The word of God cannot be moth-balled like some old blanket in an attempt to keep insects at bay! No. The word of God is a dynamic and living reality that develops and grows because it is aimed at a fulfilment that none can halt. This law of progress, in the happy formulation of Saint Vincent of Lérins, "consolidated by years, enlarged by time, refined by age," is a distinguishing mark of revealed truth as it is handed down by the Church, and in no way represents a change in doctrine.

—Francis,
Address to the Pontifical Council for the New Evangelization

As years passed, and as traditionalist articles accumulated, Thomas Lawson's distrust for Pope Francis only increased. However, at the time, only a fringe would say that his magisterium was heterodox or heretical. After all, every single one of his teachings could be traced to his immediate predecessors. But all of that was about to change.

As part of his endeavors for a more synodal Church, Francis called for two synods to be held, one in 2014 and another in 2015, about a pressing matter in Western society today: the crisis of the family—a concern that Tom certainly shared.

This did not please Tom, however. Conservative and traditionalist commentators kept raising concerns about certain movements within the synods. Liberal bishops were pushing for a greater opening towards giving communion to the divorced and civilly remarried that kept having sexual intercourse[1]—a possibility ruled out by St. John Paul II's *Familiaris Consortio.*[2] Tom was particularly alarmed when Francis called Cardinal Walter Kasper—the spearhead figure of the liberal wing on this issue—to deliver an address about it to a consistory of cardinals called to prepare the synod.[3]

But as papal biographer Austen Ivereigh explains, saying that Francis was siding with the liberals was to misread him. Francis's aim, especially in this pre-synod stage, was to create the conditions for an authentic

[1] As an example, see Douthat. "The Plot to Change Catholicism."
[2] John Paul II. *Familiaris Consortio*, 84.
[3] McCusker. "The almost unbelievable account."

discernment. Francis did not want to take the permissive route. However, he also noted the problems the current sacramental discipline posed to the pastoral care of many divorced and remarried people. Most delegates agreed—a solution was needed that would retain the general norm but allow greater pastoral flexibility in its application. A middle way was needed.[4]

In 2016, after a two-year discussion among the bishops, Francis finally published his post-synodal apostolic exhortation *Amoris Laetitia.* In this document, Francis did indeed implement a new sacramental discipline, but based on the traditional teaching of mitigating circumstances,[5] thereby eschewing both the laxist and rigorist approaches.[6]

However, this balance was severely misconstrued by the traditionalists, who saw *Amoris Laetitia* as a full-blown capitulation to the liberal faction. Worse, it had allegedly changed perennial Church teaching.[7] Francis was—so the traditionalists were saying—heterodox after all, as they had suspected all along.

Tom was distraught. The Holy Spirit had seemingly failed in protecting the Church from heresy. The pope was now not merely, through cunning or negligence, allowing the spread of liberalism in the Church, under a veneer of orthodoxy. The Holy Father was now—so he thought—using magisterial channels to actively promote heterodoxy. How to respond to this? How to submit to the teachings of a pope that is actively spouting heresy?

Tom kept following the controversy with much anxiety. As time went on, the critics of the pope kept finding supposed contradictions between *Amoris Laetitia* and previous magisterial pronouncements, namely *Familiaris Consortio*, *Veritatis Splendor*, the Council of Trent, Canon Law, etc.[8] Some defenders of the pope insisted that this was a case of doctrinal development, a valid mechanism for Church teaching. However, Tom did not buy that explanation. He had learned that doctrine could *develop*, but not

---

[4] Ivereigh. *The Wounded Shepherd,* 252-53, 272.

[5] Francis. *Amoris Laetitia*, 300-305, n351.

[6] See Gabriel. *The Orthodoxy of Amoris Laetitia*, 31-42.

[7] Ferrara, "*Amoris Laetitia*: Anatomy of a Pontifical Debacle": "Every Catholic worthy of the name has a duty to resist this attempted overthrow of the *perennial Magisterium* by a wayward Pope who clearly has no respect for the teaching of his own predecessors."

[8] I explain the continuity between *Amoris Laetitia* and all of these in Gabriel. *The Orthodoxy of Amoris Laetitia*, 152-201.

contradict itself. *Amoris Laetitia*, however, was clearly contradictory with previous tradition. Anyone could see that. How could it be, then, a legitimate development?

The rules of St. Vincent

As was pointed out in the last chapter, one of the three main concepts necessary to understand the council (and the post-conciliar Church) is "doctrinal development." According to the definition provided by Thomas Guarino, development means a progressive and proportional expansion of an idea, with that idea's fundamental nature remaining intact.[9] If this fundamental nature is altered, we do not have a proper development, but a perversion. Therefore, when faced with a doctrinal change, we must distinguish between a true, legitimate development (*profectus fidei*,) and an illicit corruption (*permutatio fidei*.)[10]

Often, there is disagreement between the magisterium and traditionalists on what constitutes development and corruption. It is very common for traditionalists to believe that recent magisterial teachings constitute *permutationes fidei*, whereas the magisterium denies it. Who is right? To help us answer this question, we must take recourse to the insights of the two greatest theologians on doctrinal development: St. Vincent of Lérins and St. Cardinal Henry Newman.

Let us start with the earliest one: St. Vincent, a fifth-century monk. In his fundamental work *Commonitorium*, St. Vincent establishes two rules that help us distinguish between a legitimate and an illegitimate development. These are:

- "*id teneamus Quod ubique, quod semper, quod ab omnibus creditum est*": i.e., that we hold that faith which has been believed everywhere, always, by all.[11]

---

[9] Guarino. *The Disputed Teachings*, 59.
[10] Guarino, *The Disputed Teachings*, 12–15.
[11] Vincent of Lérins, *Commonitorium*, chap. 2.

- "*in eodem sensu eadamque sententia*": i.e., the doctrine of the church should develop only in its own kind, that is to say, in the same doctrine, in the same sense, and in the same meaning.[12]

At face value, these two rules seem to exclude any and all kind of doctrinal development. Yet, this is not the case. The chapter in the *Commonitorium* where St. Vincent of Lérins expounds on "*in eodem* . . ." is titled "On Development in Religious Knowledge."[13] The saint notes:

> But some one will say, perhaps, Shall there, then, be no progress in Christ's Church? *Certainly; all possible progress.* For what being is there, so envious of men, so full of hatred to God, who would seek to forbid it? *Yet on condition that it be real progress, not alteration of the faith.* For progress requires that the subject be enlarged in itself, alteration, that it be transformed into something else. The intelligence, then, the knowledge, the wisdom, as well of individuals as of all, as well of one man as of the whole Church, ought, in the course of ages and centuries, to increase and make much and vigorous progress; but yet only in its own kind; that is to say, *in the same doctrine, in the same sense, and in the same meaning.*[14]

In other words, St. Vincent does allow doctrinal development, as long as it fulfills the two rules I laid out before. However, what does it mean to teach a doctrine "in the same sense and in the same meaning"? And what does it mean to hold a faith that has been "believed everywhere, always, by all"?[15] Many of today's traditionalists will simply point out the alleged contradictions between Francis and his predecessors, or between conciliar documents and pre-conciliar pronouncements, and use this mere appearance of

---

[12] Vincent of Lérins, *Commonitorium*, chap. 23.

[13] Vincent of Lérins, *Commonitorium*, chap. 23.

[14] Vincent of Lérins, *Commonitorium*, chap. 23.

[15] See Martins, *Introdução à Teologia*, 115: "We must recognize that it is difficult to find a statement that has been believed always, explicitly, and by everyone . . . However, even if it is true that, if taken to the letter, the canon of St. Vincent of Lérin does not produce satisfactory results, the fact is that it provides important elements for the discernment of Tradition"

contradiction as proof that recent doctrinal developments are an illegitimate *permutatio fidei.*[16]

Nevertheless, just because there *appears* to be a contradiction, it does not mean that such contradiction actually exists. Arguing so would, in fact, go against what St. Vincent wrote about doctrinal development. After all, Vincent warned that "*There may supervene shape, form, variation in outward appearance*, but the nature of each kind must remain the same."[17]

I will look more deeply into the Vincentian rules and their relation with pseudo-traditionalist heresies in chapter 6 of this book. But for now, we must ask the question: if the mere appearance of contradiction does not suffice to violate the Vincentian rules, then how can we distinguish between a development and a corruption? Here, we will have to ask for the assistance of the second great Catholic theologian on doctrinal development: St. Henry Newman, a nineteenth century English cardinal.

The "doctrinal butterfly" effect[18]

To make the bridge between the theologies of St. Vincent and St. Newman, we must pay attention to a metaphor that they both use, albeit with different emphases. They both compare doctrinal development to the growth of a living being. Once again, we can see how a proper understanding of tradition sees it as "living." As St. Vincent explains:

> There is a wide difference between the flower of youth and the maturity of age; yet they who were once young are still the same now that they have become old, insomuch that though the stature

[16] See, for example Ferrara, "*Amoris Laetitia*: Anatomy of a Pontifical Debacle": "Nor can it be argued that the faithful have no capacity to recognize these contradictions but rather must blindly presume that somehow they do not exist. This is the Catholic Church, whose deposit of Faith is objectively knowable, not a gnostic sect headed by the Oracle of Rome, who announces what 'Jesus wants' today."

[17] Vincent of Lérins, *Commonitorium*, chap. 23.

[18] This chapter was based on my article: Gabriel. "The Flight of the Doctrinal Butterfly."

> and outward form of the individual are changed, yet his nature is one and the same, his person is one and the same. An infant's limbs are small, a young man's large, yet the infant and the young man are the same.[19]

Cardinal Newman also picks up this analogy of doctrinal development as a growing, living body, in his seminal *Essay on the Development of Christian Doctrine.* However, he does not merely repeat it, but builds upon it. One can even say that Cardinal Newman developed the concept of doctrinal development, but in a way that allows much more outward variation. The difference: he compares doctrinal development, not so much with the growth of a human body, but with the metamorphosis of a caterpillar:

> *This is readily suggested by the analogy of physical growth.* . . . The adult animal has the same make as it had on its birth; young birds do not grow into fishes, nor does the child degenerate into the brute, wild or domestic. . . . However, as the last instances suggest to us, this unity of type, characteristic as it is of faithful developments, *must not be pressed to the extent of denying all variation, nay, considerable alteration of proportion and relation,* as time goes by, in the parts or aspects of an idea. *Great changes in outward appearance and internal harmony occur in the instance of the animal creation itself. The fledged bird differs much from its rudimental form in the egg. The butterfly is the development, but not in any sense the image, of the grub.*[20]

Externally, a butterfly is much different from a caterpillar. Yet one cannot deny that a butterfly was once a caterpillar, and that a caterpillar will

---

[19] Vincent de Lérins, *Commonitorium,* chap. 23.

[20] Newman, *Development of Christian Doctrine,* 171-172, 175. It is important to note that Newman was writing his essay mainly as a response against Protestant objections that the Catholic Church does not correspond to the Church of the early centuries (see chapter 8). See also Benedict XVI. "Farewell Address" (citing Romano Guardini): "The Church is not an institution conceived and built in theory... but a living reality.... She lives through the course of time, in becoming, like every living being, in undergoing change.... And yet in her nature she remains ever the same and her heart is Christ. Tradition is a living reality and only a partial vision regards the "deposit of faith" as something static."

naturally develop into a butterfly. Butterfly and caterpillar are one and the same creature, albeit in different stages of development.

Catholics are not unfamiliar with this type of reasoning. For example, we acknowledge this type of natural continuity and development when we advocate for the intrinsic human dignity of the unborn child. One common pro-choice talking point is the assertion that an acorn is not a tree.[21] The pro-life response is that a tree and an acorn are indeed the same organism, but in different stages of development.[22] The Catholic position is that fetuses, embryos, and zygotes are human persons in the early stages of life, whereas pro-choice advocates will insist that these are mere "clumps of cells."[23]

The miracle of the human body's development from its beginning as a single-cell zygote to a fully formed adult attests to how development can occur in surprising, sometimes even seemingly impossible ways. The Catholic Church teaches that throughout all these stages of life, a human person is endowed with a soul, personhood, and inviolable human dignity.[24] Despite dramatic physical changes, the human being retains what Newman calls "unity of type,"[25] (the first of seven notes characterizing a true doctrinal development.)

---

[21] This argument was classically established in Thomson. "A Defense of Abortion": "We are asked to notice that the development of a human being from conception through birth into childhood is continuous; then it is said that to draw a line, to choose a point in this development and say 'before this point the thing is not a person, after this point it is a person' is to make an arbitrary choice, a choice for which in the nature of things no good reason can be given. It is concluded that the fetus is or anyway that we had better say it is, a person from the moment of conception. But this conclusion does not follow. Similar things might be said about the development of an acorn into an oak tree, and it does not follow that acorns are oak trees . . . A newly fertilized ovum, a newly implanted clump of cells, is no more a person than an acorn is an oak tree."

[22] See, for example, van der Breggen. "Acorns and oak trees . . . and abortion."

[23] White. "A clump of cells."

[24] CCC, 2270: "From the first moment of his existence, a human being must be recognized as having the rights of a person - among which is the inviolable right of every innocent being to life."

[25] Newman, *Development of Christian Doctrine*, 171.

We can explore the analogy even further and apply it to today's traditionalists. Their approach is analogous to someone who looks at the butterfly and—remembering the caterpillar from which they are told it came—assumes it is impossible that one developed into the other. A person that would think like that could, for example, point to a worm and argue that the caterpillar developed into that.

Caterpillars and worms are certainly much more alike at first glance. Instinctively, one might find the idea of a caterpillar developing into a worm more intuitive than a caterpillar becoming a butterfly. However, a closer inspection dashes those expectations. Scientists involved in the fields of genetics, taxonomy, and histology will find that the external similarities mask extreme discontinuities. A nematode or an annelid (i.e., worm) has nothing to do with an insect (i.e., caterpillar.)

In an analogous way, traditionalists who disregard the post-conciliar magisterium are rejecting the official explanations of those who have the authority to make such determinations, because they cannot square these conclusions with their knowledge and comprehension. They will postulate that their claims are "self-evident," which gives them permission to reject legitimate authority, as if a mathematician had just told them to believe that 2+2=5.[26]

Of course, this is not what the authorities are telling them. They are not being told to accept something contradictory, but rather the truth, which is stranger and greater than anything they can fathom. Otherwise, one risks becoming imprisoned in a world of outward appearances, refusing to be formed by those who have the competence to do so.

The worm, just like a traditionalism detached from a living tradition, has no connection with the caterpillar whatsoever, despite appearances. It is bound to crawl on the surface of the earth and feed on dead matter from ages long past. But the butterfly is much freer, much more beautiful than a worm. The caterpillar, who was once bound to the ground, is teleologically determined to develop into a flying organism, soaring to the heights for which it was created. The butterfly, and the miracle that created it, is a witness to God's power, creativity, and wisdom. We would do well to simply appreciate the flight of the doctrinal butterfly, as it will guide our gaze up on high, where God dwells.

---

[26] Gabriel. "2+2=5?"

The "airplane" objection

When faced with Newman's analogy, a traditionalist might argue: "What, then, is to stop an authority from proclaiming that a butterfly can develop into, say, an airplane?" On the one hand, this objection seems reasonable. The doctrinal butterfly effect would seem to mandate that we never trust our senses, so an authority must always interpret reality for us. This seems cultist and fideistic, and therefore, profoundly anti-Catholic.

On the other hand, has any scientist ever argued that a butterfly could develop into an airplane? Not at all. That would be absurd. The absurdity of the scenario is intended, for this is a *reductio ad absurdum* kind of argument. But the absurdity of the scenario also makes the analogy falter. A scientist would never make such an outlandish claim. The proof in the pudding is that none has done so.

But is it not true that scientists have indeed failed in the past and proposed things that turned out to be untrue? Correct. Yet, we usually do not discard anti-intuitive scientific truths because of that. We usually do not say: "I believe the sun revolves around the earth, because my senses see the sun move in the firmament throughout the day; scientists may say otherwise, but they have already failed in the past when they promoted tobacco as medicinal, so what's to stop them from being wrong now?" If scientific authorities are fallible, an unformed opinion based on external appearances is even more so.

I am reminded of some classical Protestant arguments against transubstantiation. According to this most traditional Catholic doctrine—which I believe no contemporary traditionalist disputes—the host and the wine in the chalice become the body and blood of Christ during the consecration at mass.[27] How then, do we still see and taste them as if they were bread

---

[27] CCC 1376: "The Council of Trent summarizes the Catholic faith by declaring: 'Because Christ our Redeemer said that it was truly his body that he was offering under the species of bread, it has always been the conviction of the Church of God, and this holy Council now declares again, that by the consecration of the bread and wine there takes place a change of the whole substance of the bread into the substance of the body of Christ our Lord and of the whole substance of the

and wine? Because, according to Catholic doctrine, there is a distinction between "substance" and "accidents." The "accidents" are the qualities, properties, and attributes the senses can perceive. However, the senses cannot perceive the thing itself that bears these qualities—i.e., its substance. Our senses perceive accidents, but only the mind can know the substance. Usually, the mind safely assumes that substance and accidents are not separable, correlating a given substance to the set of accidents the senses perceive when dealing with that particular thing. But in the instance of the Eucharist, the substance of the bread and wine is changed into the substance of the body and blood of Christ, while retaining the accidents of bread and wine.[28]

To this, the Protestant argues: if substance and accidents are separable, then what is to stop me from arguing that this bible in my hand is not actually the pope and all the bishops in the world sitting together in council?[29] The *reductio ad absurdum* is strikingly similar. What both objections have in common is a mistrust for the authority promulgating the teaching, so they would think that it is possible for the magisterium to define a bible as a pope and council—or conversely, to define a butterfly as developing into an airplane.

At face value, the doctrine of transubstantiation seems irrational. However, traditionalist Catholics often find the Thomistic-Aristotelian explanations for this doctrine to be satisfactory. There is indeed an intellectual and theological substrate for this doctrine, a substrate that does not exist for the belief of a bible turning into a pope and bishops. Likewise, there is a scientific and empirical basis for the fact that a caterpillar turns into a butterfly, whereas a butterfly never turns into an airplane.

The same can be said of legitimate doctrinal developments that appear contradictory. The Church does not require us to accept these things on faith. The magisterium usually provides an explanation for those developments. If that does not happen, usually it will be easy to find scholars and apologists who will step up and provide such an explanation.

---

wine into the substance of his blood. This change the holy Catholic Church has fittingly and properly called transubstantiation. '"

[28] Sheed. *Theology for Beginners*, 162.

[29] Johnson. *The Absolute Impossibility of Transubstantiation*, 2.

But all of this requires that one keeps the mind open to accept those explanations, and not discard them as inherently irrational just because they appear so, and especially because one fosters an attitude of distrust towards authorities who know the substance of things, regardless of outward appearances. Only if one does not immediately reject the apparently bizarre notion of transubstantiation, is one able to receive the sublime explanations that Thomistic-Aristotelian philosophy provides.

Similarly, one can only accept Vatican II or Francis's magisterium as legitimate developments if one does not deride this idea to begin with. This will only bear fruit, however, if the traditionalist will forego his lack of trust in the modern Church. By trusting the conciliar and post-conciliar magisterium the same way he trusts the pre-conciliar one, the traditionalist would never entertain the notion that ecclesiastical authorities could ask Catholics to believe that a butterfly can develop into an airplane. Hence, the purpose of my book. By unearthing examples of pre-conciliar doctrinal developments that seem contradictory, I wish to bring the traditionalist to face two possible conclusions: either 1) there is a possibility of extreme outward variation in doctrine, and this is true now as it was before the council; or 2) the Church has taught that butterflies are airplanes many times even before Vatican II. What is implausible is to believe that the Church taught that caterpillars develop into butterflies for 1960 years of history and then suddenly started teaching that butterflies develop into airplanes.

Chapter 4

"Tensions with the flavor of the Gospel"

This requires acknowledging a principle indispensable to the building of friendship in society: namely, that unity is greater than conflict. Solidarity, in its deepest and most challenging sense, thus becomes a way of making history in a life setting where conflicts, tensions and oppositions can achieve a diversified and life-giving unity. This is not to opt for a kind of syncretism, or for the absorption of one into the other, but rather for a resolution which takes place on a higher plane and preserves what is valid and useful on both sides.

—Pope Francis, *Evangelii Gaudium*

Thomas Lawson's anxiety kept building up. For a while, he tried to give Francis the benefit of the doubt. After all, some apologists were saying that *Amoris Laetitia* could be interpreted in an "orthodox way"—meaning, as if the sacramental discipline had not changed since *Familiaris Consortio.*[1] This was, in his mind, the only way to achieve continuity without contradiction.

But soon, Francis would publish a letter saying that "there are no other interpretations"[2] of the document besides the one given by the bishops of the Buenos Aires Pastoral Region. These Argentinian guidelines allowed communion for divorced and remarried people who had mitigating circumstances diminishing their subjective culpability. This possibility was not contemplated by *Familiaris Consortio.*[3] Francis then elevated both his letter and the Buenos Aires guidelines to "authentic magisterium."[4]

Tom did not know how to solve this tension.

Again, he turned to his trustworthy Catholic forums. He found them in an uproar. Even Catholics who had, until then, refrained from openly criticizing the pope, were venting about this "disastrous papacy." Tom felt a certain relief, a relaxation of accumulated tensions, for he was now reassured that his misgivings were not irrational and that he needed not

[1] See, for example Gagliarducci, "Interpreting Amoris Laetitia"

[2] *Acta Apostolicae Sedes* (*AAS*) 108 (2016), no. 10, 1071-1072.

[3] Bishops of the Pastoral Region of Buenos Aires, "Carta del Santo Padre Francisco."

[4] *AAS* 108 (2016), no. 10, 1074.

continue to search for ways to reconcile the irreconcilable.[5] Soon, Tom was joining his voice to the virtual choir of lamentations against Francis.

One of Tom's online friends noticed his distress. This friend's name was Justin Peterson. He was a young man, about the same age as Tom. Since the early 2000's, Justin had been inspired by his first-century namesake Justin Martyr to be a comment section apologist. He had witnessed Tom's conversion back in 2011. In fact, Justin had contributed to this conversion, through intense prayer and patient email exchanges.

For months, Justin had been pointing out that *Amoris Laetitia* had indeed changed the sacramental discipline, while remaining orthodox. No one listened to him then. Now that the Buenos Aires guidelines had been validated, thereby proving Justin right . . . no one was listening again. He was also one of those who had tried to explain to Tom that this was a legitimate doctrinal development. To no avail.

Occasionally, Justin would message Tom for old times' sake, sharing with him some of Pope Francis's pro-life or pro-family quotes, or some of the Holy Father's spiritual—and obviously traditional—reflections. By doing so, he hoped to allay Tom's concerns that the pope was heterodox. Maybe then his friend would start reading the pontiff's words for himself and not rely on the distorted interpretations coming from pundits from the Catholicosphere. Again, to no avail.

Tom knew that Pope Francis would say something orthodox once in a while. His traditionalist friends had explained that this was all a part of Bergoglio's strategy. By being ambiguous, Francis could allow his liberal friends to wreak havoc on the Church, while maintaining a certain plausible deniability that he had ever said anything heterodox.[6] A diabolical strategy! —so Tom would say. Soon, his traditionalist friends were telling him that a similar strategy of weaponized ambiguity had also been employed during

---

[5] This is how the feeling was described by Lawler, "This Disastrous Papacy."

[6] Chapman, "Catholic Scholar: 'Pope Francis Has Created Enough Confusion'": "Why would you not want clarity unless your intent was to provide that fuzzy space in which people can maneuver around church teaching? . . . Pope Francis has created enough confusion so that there is a huge space for maneuver, for people who want to, one way or another, take an end run around Church moral teachings"

Vatican II to promote modernist teachings that went against the perennial teaching of the Church.[7]

However, as we have seen in the last chapter, this is a way to misread Francis. The Holy Father did not seek to promote a liberal agenda. In fact, both he and the synod fathers rejected such an approach. But Francis did indeed apprehend that there was a tension at play. On the one hand, the proposal for a more expansive approach to the issue of communion was heterodox; on the other hand, the previous paradigm posed serious pastoral difficulties for the divorced and remarried. The pontiff then solved this tension through an extremely elegant solution: by taking recourse to an orthodox and traditional doctrine—the teaching of mitigating circumstances—and applying to the divorced and remarried the general rule that was previously applied to all other penitents.[8]

This is a *modus operandi* often employed by Pope Francis: the *complexio oppositorum* (Latin for "complex of opposites.") This gets confused with ambiguity, since it makes it impossible to square his thought into hermetic camps, like the ones waging a dichotomic culture war from across polar opposites of the ideological divide. Nevertheless, as I wish to explain in this chapter and in the rest of this book, the *complexio oppositorum* is both a very traditional operation in Church history, and also a reason why tradition sometimes gets confused with anti-traditional statements.

---

[7] Alexander, "Vatican II Cannot Be Separated from Its 'Spirit'": "First off, Monsignor Pope has explained the phenomenon of the Spirit of Vatican II as 'Weaponized Ambiguity'. He argues that the council fathers of Vatican II wrote the documents with purposely ambiguous phrases so that unsuspecting orthodox believers of the Faith could read the documents without being scandalized." I refute this idea in Gabriel, "Vatican II and 'Weaponized Ambiguity.'"

[8] Buttiglione, *Risposte amichevoli*, 37, 68, 146. See also pp. 144–45: "Before, the divorced and remarried were sinners of a particular kind, almost excommunicated (even if not formally excommunicated, they could not partake of Communion unless they lived 'as brothers and sisters'). Now, they have become ordinary sinners." (my translation from the original Italian).

Crucified Christ, tensioned Church[9]

The Church is the Body of Christ.[10] Since no disciple is above his master,[11] Christians are called to imitate Christ. Namely, the Church is called to complete those things that are still wanting of the sufferings of Christ.[12]

One of the most characteristic and poignant images of Christ is the image of His crucifixion. Therefore, the Church has been challenged throughout all her existence to be this image of the crucified Christ. Not just, mind you, in everyday sufferings and sacrifices, but also in the tension between competing (and seemingly contradictory) values.

The Christian, just like Christ, must present himself to the world with two outstretched arms. On one hand, this Christian holds the truth of the Church, while the other hand is reaching out, not to a religion or ideology, but to an individual. In this way, the Christian becomes a living bridge between the Church and another person. Someone with both arms outstretched is an image of someone crucified. People on one side will say, "You're compromising too much! You're being too generous to these heretics and sinners!" On the other side you will hear cries of, "You're being rigid and intolerant!"[13]

Any tension between two extremes in the Christian faith invokes the outstretched arms of the crucified Jesus. Humanly speaking, the crucifixion is a scandal. That is the reason why the impenitent thief asks Jesus to free him from the cross.[14] It is a very human reaction. Whenever we feel extended beyond our limitations, our self-preservation instincts kick in: a crucified person, spread with his arms open, almost to the point of rupturing muscle and sinew, tries to free himself, and thus to find a way to escape the torture he is forced to endure. If that crucified person would be able to free only one arm, then the tension would be somewhat solved and he would

---

[9] This part of the chapter is based on my article Gabriel. "The Crucified Church: Tensions with the flavor of the Gospel."

[10] 1 Cor 12:12-14

[11] Mt 10:24

[12] Col 1:24

[13] This metaphor was how Paul Fahey, co-founder of the website *Where Peter Is*, recounted a talk he heard from Dr. Mary Healy, professor of Sacred Scripture at Sacred Heart Major Seminary, at the 2020 Encounter Conference. See Fahey. "The Living Bridge to LGBT Catholics."

[14] Luke 23:39

feel a bit of relief. But as we shall see, relieving tension by freeing oneself from one of the competing values is not a proper solution.

That is not the way of the Church, because that is not the way of Christ. Jesus endured His cross, for that was His Father's will. Therefore, the Church, as the Body of Christ, has withstood these tensions as well, even if its human members did so imperfectly at times. Pope Francis, then, considers the Church a *coincidentia oppositorum*[15] (meaning, "coincidence of opposites" in Latin):

> What's at the root of this temptation is to think that, given so many problems and deficiencies, the best answer would be to reorganize things, make changes and especially "patches", that would order and synchronize the life of the Church by adapting it to the logic of a particular group. Through this path, it would seem that everything would be solved if the ecclesial life would acquire a predetermined order, new or old, *that would end the tensions proper to our being human*, and even those that the Gospel seeks to provoke.
>
> This path would eliminate tensions, by being "in order and line," but with time, it would only put to sleep and domesticate our people's hearts, and weaken the vital and evangelic strength that the Spirit wants to give us . . . Today, we are called to gestate imbalance. We cannot do something good and evangelical if we are afraid of imbalance. We cannot forget that *there are tensions and imbalances that have the flavor of the Gospel.*[16]

This notion permeates Francis's pontificate and helps clarify much of his detractors' confusion. To understand it, we must explore Jorge Bergoglio's intellectual formation.

---

[15] See Borghesi, *The Mind of Pope Francis*, 300

[16] Francis, "Letter to the People of God peregrinating in Germany."

Francis and the theology of polar opposition

There is a prevalent belief among his critics that Francis is theologically unsophisticated.[17] His supposed lack of theological savviness is contrasted with his predecessor's theological acumen. Nothing could be further from the truth.[18] Bergoglio's theological formation is extremely rich. His roots, however, are not well-known in the Anglo-Catholicosphere, the place where these prejudicial ideas come from. To know more about these roots, I advise the reading of Prof. Massimo Borghesi's excellent intellectual biography of the current pontiff.[19]

Let us start with the pope's seminar years. During his studies, the young Jorge Bergoglio came into contact with the work of Gaston Fessard,[20] a French Jesuit and personal friend of Henri de Lubac (see chapter 2). One of Fessard's greatest contributions was to form Bergoglio's thought in a *dialectic way*.[21] "Dialectic" means "opposition of contraries." It is a very useful tool, both in theology and philosophy, as we shall soon see.

As a Jesuit, Fessard applied this dialectic thinking especially to the spirituality of St. Ignatius of Loyola, the order's founder. In his so-called epitaph, Ignatius wrote the following sentence: "*non coerceri a maximo, contineri a minimo, divinum est*". Roughly, this translates as: "not to be limited by the greatest and yet to be contained in the tiniest, this is divine."[22] In this motto, we can see an opposition between the concepts of "greatest" and "tiniest." To analyze this opposition in a dialectical way was one of the achievements of Fessard's theology.

---

[17] See, for example, Dougherty, "Pope Francis is a humble man, but a terrible choice."

[18] Conversely, Benedict is viewed as an impractical man when compared with Francis's pastoral approach. The pope emeritus rejected both these ideas in *The Italian Insider*. "Ratzinger comes to defence of Pope Francis." See also Aucone, "Tomismo dialettico."

[19] Borghesi, *The Mind of Pope Francis*.

[20] Borghesi, "I Maestri di Papa Francesco"

[21] See Borghesi, "I Maestri di Papa Francesco": "But the writer . . . that had a great influence on me [Pope Francis] was Gaston Fessard. I have read *The Dialectic of the 'Spiritual exercises of Saint Ignatius of Loyola'* several times, and other works from him. There he gave me so many elements that were then mixed." (my translation from the original Italian).

[22] Borghesi, *The Mind of Pope Francis*, 5-6

Later, when Bergoglio was already a provincial of the Argentine Jesuits, he was shaped by the violent dialectic opposition dividing the Argentinian church and society during the 1970s.[23] In 1975, he would also be deeply influenced by Pope St. Paul VI's exhortation *Evangelii Nuntiandi* (EN), about evangelization in our times. In this papal document, Paul VI mentions several dichotomies presented to the Church as a false choice, namely: between God and the Church,[24] between the gospel and human development,[25] and between personal conversion and structural change.[26] For all of these dichotomies, Paul VI's answer is: do not choose between one or the other, do not divide what God has united.[27] According to Paul VI, the power of evangelization is considerably diminished if the gospel is rent by doctrinal disputes and ideological polarizations.[28] This had a significant impact on Bergoglio's ideas, still resonating to this day on his concept of evangelization.

In 1986, Bergoglio traveled to Germany to work on his doctoral thesis, about another great twentieth century theologian: Romano Guardini.[29] He never finished, nor published this thesis, but the knowledge he acquired therein would be foundational after his papal election, namely in outlining the principles laid out in his programmatic apostolic exhortation *Evangelii Gaudium*.[30]

Much of Guardini's theology was grounded on the concept of *opposizione polare* (Italian for "polar opposition.") As Bergoglio would explain in an interview:

> [Romano Guardini] spoke of a polar opposition in which *the two opposites are not annulled.* One pole does not destroy the other. *There is no contradiction* and no identity. For him, opposition is resolved at

---

[23] Borghesi, *The Mind of Pope Francis*, 57

[24] EN 16.

[25] EN 31-34.

[26] EN 36.

[27] Borghesi, *The Mind of Pope Francis*, 67

[28] EN 77.

[29] Borghesi, "I Maestri di Papa Francesco"

[30] Borghesi, *The Mind of Pope Francis*, 103

> a higher level. In such a solution, however, the polar tension remains. *The tension remains; it is not cancelled out.* The limits are overcome, not negated. Oppositions are helpful. Human life is structured in an oppositional form. And we see this happening now in the church as well. The tensions are not necessarily resolved and ironed out; *they are not like contradictions.*[31]

Though neither pole is annulled, Guardini postulates that at any given time, one pole is dominant.[32] I have written elsewhere how a shift of emphasis (i.e., from one pole to the other) in magisterial pronouncements can be confused with contradiction.[33] The two poles, however, are not contradictory—they are merely at both ends of a continuum. If there were a contradiction between the poles, a continuum between them would not be possible.

Yet, the dominance of one pole over the other cannot be sustained for long. For Guardini, an equilibrium is a situation of exception, possible only temporarily. A system of living opposites, fixed in constant equilibrium, where all opposing forces are balanced and all tensions stabilized is either: 1) self-sufficient (which is only possible for an absolute being, not finite beings such as us,) or 2) simply dead.[34] Human life, therefore, must always exist in this polar opposition.

As Prof. Stefano Martini beautifully said in a lecture, "the *opposizione polare* expresses the guardinian vision of existence as polarity, as a method to embrace reality in all its complexity, through the tension of opposites that one cannot eliminate, nor manipulate, nor subjectivize, nor partialize, but which one must recognize and hold together."[35]

The specter of Hegel

It is easy to confuse the dialectics of Fessard or Guardini with the dialectics of Hegel. The latter was a nineteenth century German philosopher, who popularized a dialectic method consisting of three steps: 1) a

---

[31] Borghesi, *The Mind of Pope Francis*, 105

[32] Borghesi, *The Mind of Pope Francis*, 120

[33] Gabriel, *The Orthodoxy of Amoris Laetitia*, 140-141.

[34] Borghesi, *The Mind of Pope Francis*, 120

[35] Martini, "La malinconia." (my translation from the original Italian).

beginning proposition called "thesis", 2) a negation of that thesis called "antithesis", and 3) a proposition reconciling the two conflicting ideas, called "synthesis."[36] Then, the synthesis would become a thesis in the next step and so on. By repeating this method infinitely, Hegel sought to rationally explain all of reality.

Pre-conciliar Catholicism was very wary of Hegelianism. As we shall see, however, this has less to do with Hegel's dialectic method in itself and more to do with the rest of his philosophy, wherein he tried to achieve a complete synthesis of reality in terms of reason—a Gnostic worldview where all of reality can be expressed in rational categories.[37] Also, Hegelianism had a decisive influence in certain schools of materialism, pantheism, and Marxism,[38] which came to oppose the Church in modern times. Traditionalists picked up on this traditional Catholic mistrust for Hegel and extrapolated it to everything pertaining to this philosopher, casting doubt on Francis and the post-conciliar Church whenever they attempted some kind of dialectical synthesis.[39]

However, even if Hegel's dialectic is the most famous one, there are other kinds of dialectical thinking. Some are actually quite Catholic and traditional, as we shall soon see. For now, it suffices to examine how Fessard, Guardini, and Bergoglio's *opposizione polare* differs from Hegel's dialectical method. These Catholic thinkers are not Hegelian—at most, they use Hegel in order to transcend him.[40] As Bergoglio would say:

> It is necessary to strip the term "dialectic" of every Hegelian resonance, and to understand it simply as the expression of a reciprocal interaction of reality . . . It could be called *sineidetic thought*, in which the particulars must be considered as a function of the whole.[41]

---

[36] Schnitker, Sarah, and Robert Emmons "Hegel's Thesis-Antithesis-Synthesis Model."

[37] Modello, "Hegelianism."

[38] Modello, "Hegelianism."

[39] Milles, "A Hegelian papacy?." See also Derksen. "Ratzinger, Hegel, and 'Summorum Pontificum.'"

[40] Borghesi, *The Mind of Pope Francis*, 81

[41] Borghesi, *The Mind of Pope Francis*, 128

Here lies the crucial difference. The sineidetic thought alluded to by Bergoglio sees the whole as in relation to the parts, and the parts as in relation to the whole, without separating the whole from the parts.[42] In Hegel, by contrast, the particular is only apparently "conserved" in the universal. This is, for example, at the root of Marxism's collectivism, where the reality of the individual is dissolved in the collective.[43]

But Catholicism is, by definition, "universal" (i.e., *katholikos* in Greek.) The difference is that in Catholicism *the universal calls for the care of the particular.*[44] This is the meaning of St. Ignatius's epitaph: "not to be confined to what is greater, but to be concerned with what is smaller: this is divine." As I said before, Fessard's dialectic takes this Ignatian motto as its starting point.

One of Hegel's dialectics was the dichotomy between master and servant. This dichotomy was at the basis of two opposing atheist ideologies of modern times: Marxism and National Socialism (the latter, inspired by Nietzsche.)[45] Nietzsche depicted the world as seen from the master's point of view and Marx from the servant's.[46] But Fessard complemented Hegel with the dialectics of the apostle St. Paul: the dialectic master/servant, yes, but also man/woman and Jew/Greek.[47] Fessard's dialectic is, therefore, not based on a master/servant relationship, but based on "friendship" or even the love between a man and a woman.[48]

For Guardini, there is only *opposizione polare* when the poles are not absolute. In other words, one pole does not exclude the other, but presupposes it.[49] There is a confrontation, but not as a struggle against an enemy, but as a tension that bears fruits.[50] Authentic totality (i.e., "Catholicism") is not totalitarianism. It does not sacrifice the particular, as Hegel's philosophy proposed.[51]

---

[42] Borghesi, *The Mind of Pope Francis*, 128.
[43] Borghesi, *The Mind of Pope Francis*, 91.
[44] Borghesi, *The Mind of Pope Francis*, 65.
[45] Borghesi, *The Mind of Pope Francis*, 81.
[46] Borghesi, *The Mind of Pope Francis*, 97.
[47] Gal 3:28. Borghesi, *The Mind of Pope Francis*, 92.
[48] Borghesi, *The Mind of Pope Francis*, 96.
[49] Borghesi, *The Mind of Pope Francis*, 107.
[50] Borghesi, *The Mind of Pope Francis*, 107.
[51] Borghesi, *The Mind of Pope Francis*, 65.

Thomist dialectical tradition

Traditionalists may also criticize the concept of *opposizione polare* on the grounds that it is not a traditional kind of thinking, or that it may lead to syncretism. As proof of this, they may point to a Thomist-Aristotelian axiom: the law of non-contradiction. So, for example, an object cannot exist and not exist simultaneously. One cannot believe in two contradictory statements at once. If that would be so, all opinions would be true,[52] a notion condemned by the Church (namely by Benedict XVI) as the error of relativism.[53]

Thomism's opposition to this kind of relativism has been superbly described by the great writer and apologist G.K. Chesterton in his description of the debate between St. Thomas Aquinas and his contemporary Siger of Brabant:

> And Siger of Brabant, following on some of the Arabian Aristotelians, advanced a theory, which most modern newspaper readers would instantly have declared to be the same as the theory of St. Thomas. That was what finally roused St. Thomas to his last and most emphatic protest . . . Siger of Brabant said this: the Church must be right theologically, but she can be wrong scientifically. There are two truths, the truth of the supernatural world, and the truth of the natural world, which contradicts the supernatural world . . . In other words, Siger of Brabant split the human head in two, like the blow in an old legend of battle; and declared that a man has two minds, with one of which he must entirely believe and with the other may utterly disbelieve. To many this would at least seem a parody of Thomism. As a fact, it was an assassination of Thomism. It was not two ways of finding the same truth, it was an untruthful way of pretending that there are two truths . . . St.

---

[52] Aristotle, *Metaphysics*, 67.

[53] See Ratzinger, "Relativism: The Central Problem.": Relativism is defined as the philosophy where the "existence of one valid truth for all" cannot be affirmed."

> Thomas was willing to allow the one truth to be approached by two paths, precisely because he was sure there was only one truth.[54]

But is this what we are talking about when we are discussing *complexio oppositorum*? Is Bergoglio more akin to Aquinas or Brabant? Please note that Chesterton mentions how Siger's philosophy could easily be confused with Thomism, hence Aquinas's passionate defense. How could it be possible to confuse one with the other? Simply put because scholastic philosophy in general—and Aquinas's philosophy in particular—is profoundly dialectical.

Those who have taken a cursory look at the *Summa Theologiae*, Aquinas's greatest work, can appreciate how it is structured in the following way: "*It seems that . . .*" (thesis), "*On the contrary . . .* " (antithesis), "*I answer that . . .* " (synthesis).[55] The scholastic method consisted in thoroughly reading the works of a certain author, critically learning his theories, evaluating the points of disagreement and contention with other sources, and then trying to reconcile the two sides of the argument through dialectics.[56] Therefore, the distinguishing mark of scholasticism in the age of its highest development is its use of the dialectical method.[57]

These Thomist dialectics also had a profound impact on Jorge Bergoglio. In 1978, Bergoglio had lunch with several theologians, as a run-up to a conference of the Catholic bishops of Latin America. One of the theologians he met during that lunch was Alberto Methol-Ferré, the greatest Latin American lay Catholic thinker of the second half of the twentieth century.[58]

---

[54] Chesterton, *St. Thomas Aquinas*, 53-54.

[55] See also Turner, "Scholasticism": "There is a good deal of divergence among the principal Scholastics in the details of arrangement, as well as in the relative values of the sub-titles, 'part', 'question', 'disputation', 'article', etc. All, however, adopt the manner of treatment by which thesis, objections, and solutions of objections stand out distinctly in the discussion of each problem."

[56] New World Encyclopedia contributors. "Scholasticism."

[57] Turner. "Scholasticism."

[58] Borghesi, "I Maestri di Papa Francesco." See also Borghesi, *The Mind of Pope Francis*, p. 89: "It is by reading Methol-Ferré and Podetti that I [Francis] took something of the dialectic."

Methol-Ferré, on his end, based his own dialectics on a very important idea from St. Thomas Aquinas's theology: the concept of "hylomorphism." This means that there is an inseparable unity between "matter" and "form". In our material world, there is no form without matter and no matter without form:[59]

> It would be superhuman to fully understand the *coincidentia oppositorum* that the church is. Some real dimensions always remain in the shadows or are forgotten. The church has essentially two poles, born of the Spirit of God and of Jesus Christ in the Apostles. It is visible and invisible, in a single, indissoluble breath. Ecclesiologies tend to emphasize one or the other of the poles: at certain times they lean toward "spiritualization," at other times toward "incarnation." . . . One's hold on neither of the two poles can be released, yet it is humanly impossible not to give a certain supremacy to one of them. The balance is always unstable, moving, being restored. If allowed to break, the church cannot "breathe" and then either dissolves into abstract mysticism or gets bogged down in institutional forms. Spirit without institution or institution without Spirit—both are false oppositions that destroy the church. An ever-present risk.[60]

Just like Fessard before him transcended Hegel's master/slave dialectics by superimposing the Pauline pairs (namely man/woman), so did Methol-Ferré do the same, by employing the matter/form dichotomy from Aquinas's hylomorphism.[61]

In other words, the *complexio oppositorum* advocated by Bergoglio's teachers was not a law of contradiction, like Siger of Brabant's philosophy.

---

[59] Borghesi, *The Mind of Pope Francis*, 91.

[60] Ferré, "La Chiesa, popolo tra i popoli," as quoted by Borghesi, *The Mind of Pope Francis*, 88-89.

[61] Borghesi, *The Mind of Pope Francis*, 92.

If there was contradiction, the dialectic would cease, since one of the terms would have to be excluded.[62]

We are also not talking about syncretism either. The *complexio oppositorum* is not about finding an easy middle ground,[63] nor a mixture or some sort of compromise. What emerges from this process is something completely distinct and original.[64] The two poles are not absorbed into one another—rather, there is a resolution taking place on a higher plane which preserves what is valid and useful on both sides.[65] A conciliatory syncretism is, according to Bergoglio, a veiled form of modern totalitarianism, trying to reconcile without regard for the values at hand. In fact, this kind of totalitarian syncretism always generates fundamentalism—people will react against it, by searching for a misguided "purity."[66]

Nor can we say that this kind of dialectic is not traditional. As we have seen, it dips its roots, through Methol-Ferré, on the dialectics of Aquinas and the scholastics. Also, this kind of dialectic also existed in the Fathers of the Church.[67] After all, the Council of Chalcedon describes Christ in the following way:

> Therefore, following the holy fathers, we all with one accord teach men to acknowledge one and the same Son, our Lord Jesus Christ . . . recognized in two natures, *without confusion, without change, without division, without separation*; the distinction of natures being in *no way annulled by the union*, but rather the characteristics of *each nature being preserved and coming together to form one* person and subsistence, not as parted or separated into two persons, but one and the same Son and Only-begotten God the Word, Lord Jesus Christ.[68]

This is the kind of tension between opposite principles that we have been describing until now.

---

[62] Borghesi, *The Mind of Pope Francis*, 95.

[63] Borghesi, *The Mind of Pope Francis*, 57.

[64] Borghesi, *The Mind of Pope Francis*, 114.

[65] Borghesi, *The Mind of Pope Francis*, 115.

[66] Borghesi, *The Mind of Pope Francis*, 127.

[67] Aucone. "Tomismo dialettico."

[68] The Formula of Chalcedon, as translated in Bettenson, *Documents of the Christian Church*, 51-52.

Heresy as relaxation of tension

As we have seen, at the center of the *complexio oppositorum* lies the idea of a unity that does not annul differences or reduce conflict. It is a *unity in tension* that recognizes the value of polarity, rejecting resolution through contradiction.[69]

Let us return to the metaphor of the crucified Christ with which we started this chapter. Again: On one hand, the Christian holds the truth of the Church, while the other hand is reaching out to an individual, thereby forming a bridge between Church and individual. As an institution of divine origin, the Church is called to gestate the same tension of the crucified Christ. Humanly speaking, however, the elements composing the Church tend to flee the discomfort of tension. There is always a temptation to try to dissolve the tension, or at least reduce tension by choosing one of the poles to the detriment of the other.[70] This is, as we have seen, the temptation to alleviate the tension of the crucifixion by releasing one of the arms from the cross.

But to do so endangers tradition itself, because it disconnects tradition from the practical reality of the individual we are trying to reach out to. Breaking this tensional bridge inevitably leads to theology becoming an ideology.[71] This is, as Guardini points out, a breeding ground for heresy. Historically, heresies happened when one of the poles "grew too luxuriant," almost to the point of dominating the Church. Though these heresies were not able to overpower the Church, they certainly narrowed and impoverished her.[72] As the famous writer Hillaire Belloc so aptly puts it:

> Heresy is the dislocation of some complete and self-supporting scheme by the introduction of a novel denial of some essential part therein. . . . Heresy means, then, the warping of a system by "Exception": by "Picking out" one part of the structure, it implies that

[69] Borghesi, *The Mind of Pope Francis*, 61.
[70] Borghesi, *The Mind of Pope Francis*, 123-124.
[71] Borghesi, *The Mind of Pope Francis*, 118.
[72] Borghesi, *The Mind of Pope Francis*, 70.

> the scheme is marred by taking away one part of it, denying one part of it, and either leaving the void unfilled or filling it with some new affirmation.[73]

This is what is truly diabolical. After all, the Greek word "diabolus" means precisely "to divide," being directly opposed to "symbol" (Greek "symbolus")—here meaning a creed, like the Nicene symbol.[74]

Let us look at some historical examples. Right at the beginning, in the apostolic age, the baptized Gentiles posed a problem: how to receive these new Christians? On the one hand, it was argued that they should not be tormented by being required to follow the entire Mosaic law. They were Gentiles, not Jews. On the other hand, the faith they were being baptized into could not deny its Jewish roots, for Jesus was indeed an observant Jew, and many of the prophecies regarding the Messiah could only be understood by being familiar with the Old Testament. We are going to explore this situation in the next chapter.

Later on, as the Church emerged from the catacombs, she needed to find herself among the shards left scattered by the chaos of Roman persecutions. The Church needed to do this, by clearly defining who was this person she worshipped. On the one hand, Jesus was a man. On the other hand, Christ was God (see chapter 6). Would it be possible to solve all these tensions?

These are just two examples. They are certainly not exhaustive, but they are instructive. In all of them, we find tensions that, at first sight, seem irreconcilable. Judaizers dealt with the tension by doing away with the freedom the gospel had afforded the Gentiles. Marcionists dealt with the same tension by doing away with the Old Testament. Arians dealt with their tension by downplaying Jesus's divinity. Monophysites did the same by downplaying Christ's humanity.

So, when Judaizers and Marcionists told the Church: "you have to choose," the Church said: "I choose both the New Testament and the Old. I will part with neither." The Church chose tension, to the scandal of both

---

[73] Belloc, *The Great Heresies*, 7-8.

[74] Joseph Ratzinger has a beautiful explanation on the original definition of the word "symbol" as an object split in half, in which two people (each with a half) could recognize each other if their halves matched (see Benedict XVI, *Introduction to Christianity*, 97).

Greeks and Jews. In the same way, when Arians and Monophysites told the Church: "you have to choose," the Church said: "Jesus is both fully human and fully divine."

The present is not devoid of the same kind of tensions. In a highly secularized and hedonistic society, the greatest tension is how to balance the love for sinners with the hate for sin. The tension between orthodoxy and pastoral care. Please, bear in mind, they are not contradictory: the opposite of orthodoxy is heterodoxy, not pastoral care. However, many people today have difficulty grasping this. Secularists will evaluate this tension as too hard to bear and will demand that the Church discard orthodoxy.

There is a mirror image of this: those who, without any authority to do so, will appoint themselves as guardians of orthodoxy and tear down the notion of pastoral care. They will demand that the Church must choose between the pureness of the faith and the messiness of reality.

Here, as in past centuries, the Church continues to manifest her divine nature and mandate by not giving in to tension, but by embracing it. People may cry: "You must choose! You must choose between Benedict XVI and Francis! You must choose between *Amoris Laetitia* and *Veritatis Splendor*! You must choose between pre-Vatican II and post-Vatican II!"

And the Church will look upon these demands and will simply pass through them, drifting away from these false dichotomies, and choosing neither extreme. The Church can, in fact, do nothing else, for she is configured to the crucified Christ, with His arms extended to the point of disarticulation, embracing all of humanity and the entirety of creation.

In summary:

By the end of this section, we have established that there are three theological concepts which are fundamental to understand the Second Vatican Council: 1) *aggiornamento*, 2) *ressourcement*, and 3) doctrinal development. To these, we must add a fourth concept to have a better grasp of Pope Francis's magisterium: 4) *complexio oppositorum*. As we have seen, all of these four concepts are perfectly traditional, but can at the same time create the illusion of anti-tradition:

1) *Aggiornamento*: while retaining the *substance* of tradition, this process seeks better ways to *express* it, allowing this tradition to be passed down to every age and culture. By doing this, *aggiornamento* may purify the Church of non-binding ecclesial "traditions" (see chapter 1). This may look anti-traditional to someone who does not know the difference between tradition and traditions.
2) *Ressourcement*: by going back to the source, the Church may retrieve a more profound tradition. Those who confuse the *status quo* with the only possible tradition may see this as a new theology (see chapter 2).
3) Doctrinal development: even if doctrine does not contradict itself, it may develop in surprising ways, with extreme outward variation, while preserving a unity of type (chapter 3). Traditionalists may mistake this for an illegitimate permutation in the faith.
4) *Complexio oppositorum*: the Church embraces the unity in tension between polar opposites without doing away with either pole, but rather by solving these tensions in a higher plane, preserving what is valid and useful on both sides. People may be tempted to alleviate this tension by choosing one pole to the detriment of the other, identifying the former with tradition and the latter with anti-tradition.

Having mastered these four concepts, we are better equipped to critically evaluate the historical precedents of the pseudo-traditionalist heresies we are going to explore in the following section.

Section II

Heresy wearing Tradition's garments

Chapter 5

"But Paul corrected Peter"

Indeed, some Christians who had come from Judaism had infiltrated, and began to sow theories contrary to the Apostle's teaching, even going so far as to denigrate him. They began with doctrine — "No to this, yes to that", and then they denigrated the Apostle. It is the usual method: undermining the authority of the Apostle . . . These opponents of Paul argued that even the Gentiles had to be circumcised and live according to the rules of Mosaic Law. They went back to the previous observances, those that had been superseded by the Gospel.

—Francis, General Audience

Thomas Lawson kept following the controversy around *Amoris Laetitia* with much apprehension. A beam of hopeful light was beginning to emerge, though. A few days after the publication of the controversial apostolic exhortation, Cardinal Raymond Burke, a conservative cleric, gave an interview to the National Catholic Register. In this interview, the cardinal explained how *Amoris Laetitia* was just the pope's personal opinion, not magisterial teaching, so the faithful needed not assent to it.[1] Soon after, Cardinal Burke would join three other cardinals and submit five *dubia* ("questions") to the Holy Father, asking clarification about the meaning of the document. These cardinals then made these *dubia* public, along with some notes that seemed to cast doubt on the orthodoxy of the pope's preferred interpretation.[2]

On the day after making the *dubia* public, Cardinal Burke gave another interview to the National Catholic Register, where he said that if the Holy Father failed to give the clarification of the Church's teaching he hoped to achieve, he would trigger a formal act of correction.[3] Francis never answered the *dubia*, and Cardinal Burke's correction never came.

---

[1] Burke, "'*Amoris Laetitia*' and the Constant Teaching and Practice of the Church." I refute these arguments in Gabriel. *The Orthodoxy of Amoris Laetitia*, 4-8.

[2] Pentin, "Full Text and Explanatory Notes of Cardinals' Questions on '*Amoris Laetitia*.'" I explain why this was not appropriate in Gabriel. *The Orthodoxy of Amoris Laetitia*, 117-122.

[3] Pentin, "Cardinal Burke on *Amoris Laetitia Dubia*."

However, the idea of a "correction" kept floating in the air, and that genie could not go back into the bottle. A few months later, sixty-two clergy and lay scholars would indeed issue a formal act of correction—the so-called "filial correction."[4]

Justin Peterson was appalled by this. How dared these theologians correct the pope? By what authority did they claim to do so? But he was alone in his complaints. On Catholic social media, it seemed like everyone else was cheering for the correctors—including Tom. Finally, someone had done what the pope should have done long ago! —so they would say— Someone had corrected the errors and heresies of the document, so the confusion could begin to dissipate. Why would it matter whether those scholars had authority or not? The truth was on their side, so they could (or rather, they *had to*) correct a wrong pope.

Nevertheless, Justin kept pressing forward. Of course, the question of authority mattered! The Church was not a democracy! The Pope was the successor of St. Peter, who had received that authority from Jesus Christ Himself! His authority could not simply be hijacked by any Catholic, no matter how learned or prominent!

Tom intervened. He had read the whole *Correctio filialis*, from beginning to end, nodding approvingly from the first to the last word. He knew the correctors had preemptively defended themselves against Justin's objections. They had laid out the precedents for this course of action. Almost reflexively, Tom replied:

"But Paul also corrected Peter!"[5]

Thomas shuddered. It had been a while since he had typed these words in a keyboard. In fact, not since his conversion to Catholicism. Before that conversion though, during his Protestant years, he had indeed typed these

---

[4] van den Aardweg et al. *Correctio filialis.*

[5] See van den Aardweg et al. *Correctio filialis*, 1: "We are permitted to issue this correction . . . by the law of Christ: for His Spirit inspired the apostle Paul to rebuke Peter in public when the latter did not act according to the truth of the gospel (Gal. 2). St Thomas Aquinas notes that this public rebuke from a subject to a superior was licit on account of the imminent danger of scandal concerning the faith (Summa Theologiae 2a 2ae, 33, 4 ad 2), and 'the gloss of St Augustine' adds that on this occasion, 'Peter gave an example to superiors, that if at any time they should happen to stray from the straight path, they should not disdain to be reproved by their subjects' (ibid.)"

words several times. It was one of his handiest arguments, whenever Catholics would claim that the pope was infallible.[6]

Usually, Catholic apologists worked tirelessly to debunk that Protestant claim.[7] Now, however, in a stroke of irony, Catholics were the ones propagating this argument. "But now it's different!"—so Tom thought to himself— "*Now* this precedent is truly applicable!"

This raises the question: is this precedent applicable to Pope Francis (or, for that matter, to the post-conciliar popes)? Why would Protestants be wrong, and traditionalists correct in invoking the same historical episode? To answer these questions, we must learn more about Paul's correction to Peter. What happened then, and why? But we cannot really understand Paul's correction without a proper context. To grasp this context, we will need to go back to the beginning. Not just any beginning, but the *actual beginning of everything.*

"In your flesh, a perpetual covenant"

In the very first chapter of the Bible, we learn that God created everything that exists, and that everything He created was good.[8] This includes humankind, created in God's image and likeness.[9] However, scripture goes on to describe how evil entered the world when humans turned away from their creator. The next ten chapters of the book of Genesis depict a downward spiral, where humans stray further and further from God: from Adam's primordial act of disobedience in the garden of Eden[10] to the murder of Abel by his brother Cain,[11] to the depravity that brought forth the

---

[6] Baker. *Exodus from Rome*, 103: "If Peter was infallible, this severe correction by Paul was unnecessary, and worse yet—an act of infidelity, if as the Roman Catholic Church claims, Peter is the infallible teacher of faith and morals, like all the Popes that followed after him."

[7] See, for example, Broussard, "Paul's Rebuke and Peter's Infallibility." See also Armstrong, "Does Paul's Rebuke of Peter Disprove Papal Infallibility?"

[8] Gen 1:31

[9] Gen 1:27

[10] Gen 3

[11] Gen 4

deluge,[12] to the incident of the tower of Babel and the subsequent scattering of the nations,[13] we witness a progressive deterioration of the relationship between humanity and God.

This downward spiral is only momentarily interrupted by Noah's fidelity[14] during the episode of the deluge. For this reason, God spared Noah and his family, alongside His creation, by ordering Noah to build a floating ark containing a pair of each kind of animal.[15] When the flood ended, God established a covenant with Noah[16]—the *Noahide covenant.*

The terms of this covenant were as follows: God promised to never again destroy the earth through a universal flood.[17] On his end, Noah—and, by extension, all humanity descended from him—would have to submit to certain universal precepts. For the purpose of this chapter, let us only highlight one of those precepts:

> And every thing that moveth and liveth shall be meat for you . . .
> Saving that flesh with *blood you shall not eat.*[18]

Unfortunately, this period of peace was short lived. In the very same chapter where God establishes the Noahide covenant, Noah gets drunk, and his son Ham performs a heinous act,[19] leading him to be cursed by his father.[20] Evil had once again entered the world.

It is only in the twelfth chapter of Genesis that we see a reversal of this negative trajectory. This upward movement, no longer *away* from God but *towards* God, would become constant from that point onward—though, granted, always shaky and with no few detours.

This restoration of humankind started when God set His eyes on a simple Mesopotamian sheep herder, son of an idol-maker. The name of

---

[12] Gen 6:1-7

[13] Gen 11

[14] Gen 6:8

[15] Gen 6:11-8:19

[16] Gen 9

[17] Gen 8:21

[18] Gen 9:3-4

[19] The exact nature of this sinful act is still debated among scholars. A good summary of the several hypotheses can be seen in Bergsman, "Noah's nakedness."

[20] Gen 9:21-25

this man was Abram. God ordered Abram to go out of his father's house and follow Him to wherever He commanded. In turn, God promised to make a great nation out of Abram and to bless all the earth through him.[21]

Just like with Noah, God established a covenant with Abram. This covenant was so significant, it changed Abram's name, transforming his whole identity and essence. Abram would henceforth be called Abraham, and the covenant would be the *Abrahamic covenant.*[22] As an external sign of this covenant, God asked all Jewish males to undergo circumcision:

> And you shall circumcise the flesh of your foreskin, that it may be for *a sign of the covenant* between me and you. An infant of eight days old shall be circumcised among you, every man child in your generations: he that is born in the house, as well as the bought servant shall be circumcised, and whosoever is not of your stock: And my covenant shall be *in your flesh* for a *perpetual covenant.*[23]

Later, Abraham's numerous descendants would become the Hebrew people and be enslaved in Egypt.[24] Once again, God took the initiative by calling Moses[25] to go to Egypt and bring the Hebrews out of their captors' land.[26] Once free, the Hebrews set camp at the mount Sinai, where God established another covenant, this time with Moses—the *Mosaic covenant.*[27]

---

[21] Gen 12:1-3

[22] Gen 17

[23] Gen 17:11-13. Circumcision was so important in the Old Testament, that it is considered a prefiguration of the sacrament of baptism. See, for example, Col 2:11-12: "In whom also you are circumcised with circumcision not made by hand, in despoiling of the body of the flesh, but in the circumcision of Christ: Buried with him in baptism, in whom also you are risen again by the faith of the operation of God, who hath raised him up from the dead."

[24] Exod 1:8-15

[25] As an interesting aside, it is worth noting that Moses neglected to circumcise his young son and, for that reason, was almost punished by God with death (Exod 4:24-26). This once again shows the importance of circumcision, that even Moses could not disobey without peril for his own life.

[26] Exod 3

[27] Exod 6-8

Also at Sinai, Moses received the tablets containing the ten commandments, the touchstone from which the rest of Jewish law is derived.[28]

The rest of the Torah—the first five books of scripture—intersperses the narrative of the Hebrews' journey through the desert with God laying down several other laws: criminal, civil, and religious.[29] Among the latter are ritual purity laws, namely concerning what animals one could eat. The Hebrews were to abstain from the meat of animals deemed "unclean."[30] When the Hebrews settled in the promised land, they founded the nation of Israel, and the Mosaic laws became their legal system.[31]

Before we proceed, it is important to understand exactly what a covenant is, and how significant these acts were. In ancient Near Eastern culture, a covenant is better rendered as a "treaty." Kings used the enter into treaties with their subjects in the following way: first, there would be a historical prologue where the king reminded the subjects of the beneficial actions he had performed on behalf of the vassals; afterwards the king presented the law he expected his subjects to obey; finally, the king enunciated sanctions, blessings, and curses that followed the obedience or disobedience to said laws.[32]

In this sense, God, the supreme king, enters into a treaty with His people, first by reminding them of all the good things He has previously done for them, then by establishing the laws that they are to obey, and finally laying out the blessings and curses that come from obeying or disobeying His laws. Through Noah, God enters into a covenant with all humankind—since all are Noah's descendants—and through Moses, He enters into a covenant with Israel.

Naturally, this placed a big responsibility on the Israelites, that they should not disobey God's law, lest they break this covenant. Doing so would result in terrible penalties, namely that God would "scatter you [Israel] among the nations," and "unsheathe the sword after you," so that "your land shall be a desolation, and your cities shall be a waste."[33] The

[28] Skeel, "The Mosaic Law in Christian Perspective", 9.
[29] Skeel, "The Mosaic Law in Christian Perspective", 9.
[30] Lev 11
[31] Skeel, "The Mosaic Law in Christian Perspective", 3.
[32] Skeel, "The Mosaic Law in Christian Perspective", 2.
[33] Skeel, "The Mosaic Law in Christian Perspective", 4.

Jewish religion, therefore, highlighted the importance of "righteousness" i.e., of following the law.

The law was at the center of Israel's national and religious identity: as in other ancient civilizations, ethnicity defined cult and cult defined ethnicity.[34] In the following centuries, however, Israel would lose its independence several times to foreign conquerors, dispersing many Jews around the Mediterranean world. This would present challenges to the way Jews were to follow the law of their forefathers and their religion, both at their homeland and at the diaspora.

Particularly important for the present chapter was the Greek rule. In the fourth century BC, Alexander the Great conquered a vast empire, including the territories of Judea. Many of the Jewish diaspora also came to fall under Alexander's rule. Greek culture rested upon cosmopolitanism and philosophy, notions seemingly in tension with Judaism's emphasis on a "people set apart" and monotheistic faith. How to respond to the Hellenization (i.e., "Greekification") of their ancient customs became a question that divided Judaism to its core.[35]

The Jews of the diaspora, living in foreign lands under Greek rule, soon adopted the Greek language, the *lingua franca* of that time. Others, like Philo of Alexandria, became philosophers and tried to explain their scriptures in more Greek-friendly terms, through allegory.[36]

At home, in conquered Judea, the divisions were more profound. As the historian Robert Mullin aptly puts it: "The gymnasium, symbol of the Hellenistic world, where naked young men exercised their bodies, and the Jewish Temple, where pious men in long robes prayed to the God of Israel, seemed like different worlds."[37] Since athletes participated naked in their games and sports, some Hellenized Jews tried to erase their distinctive sign and reverse their circumcision through a procedure called "epispasm." Circumcision became then, not only an external sign of the covenant God had

---

[34] Fredricksen, "Judaizing the Nations", 234.
[35] Mullin, *A Short World History of Christianity*, 4.
[36] Mullin, *A Short World History of Christianity*, 4-5.
[37] Mullin, *A Short World History of Christianity*, 5.

established with His people, but also a statement of Jewish national loyalty.[38]

The frictions became more pronounced during the time of the King Antiochus IV Epiphanes in 160 BC. Antiochus tried to force the Jews to Hellenize their customs. He forbade circumcision and desecrated the Jewish temple with a syncretic pagan-Jewish cult.[39] A particularly poignant episode depicts a mother and her seven sons being martyred for refusing to eat pork, an unclean meat.[40] This religious persecution eventually resulted in the revolt of the Maccabees and the reinstitution of an autonomous Jewish state until the Roman conquest of the first century BC.

The Greek rule, however, did not just bring a rift between Hellenized and zealous Jews. It also brought many Gentiles (i.e., non-Jews) into contact with Judaism. Debates sprung about how proselytes (i.e., Gentile converts to the Jewish faith) should be integrated. Should they undergo circumcision or not? The zealous faction answered in the affirmative, but Hellenized Jews of the diaspora tended to believe that proselytes required no other initiation besides a purification bath.[41] The idea for this bath (*tevilah* in Hebrew) came from various ceremonial washings and absolutions prescribed by the Mosaic law, signifying inward spiritual cleansing and renewal. Therefore, the *tevilah* could also be a sign of conversion. This is, in fact, the meaning behind St. John the Baptist's actions in the desert.[42] The astute reader may have already intuited that the Jewish *tevilah* would become a prefiguration of the Christian baptism.

In this debate, however, the rigorous position tended to prevail over the liberal one, with many Gentiles undergoing circumcision[43]—sometimes even being put to death by their pagan peers for that action.[44] It was

---

[38] Hirsch, "Circumcision", 93.

[39] Mullin, *A Short World History of Christianity*, 5.

[40] 2 Macc 7

[41] Hirsch, "Circumcision", 94-95.

[42] Marshall. *The Crucified Rabbi*, 71-76.

[43] The *Jewish Encyclopedia* (Hirsch, "Circumcision", 95) mentions, among others, the Parthian King Izates II. For more about this concrete case, see also Rosner, "Paul and the Law", 33-34.

[44] Once again, the *Jewish Encyclopedia* (Hirsch, "Circumcision", 95) mentions the case of Flavius Clemens, a nephew of the Roman emperors Titus and Domitian.

in the midst of this historical context that Christianity emerged and gave its contribution to the ongoing debate.

Paul's new theology

After Jesus ascended to heaven, a pressing question imposed itself with the full weight of a new reality: who would now lead the new church, namely at Jerusalem? After all, no one could fill up Jesus's sandals. Nowadays, we may think that the answer is obvious, but the early Christians had nothing but tradition to guide them. And traditionally, the succession of the high priest's office was according to bloodline. So, it was James, Jesus's half-brother, who assumed the headship of the church at Jerusalem.

It is also not strange that St. James would follow not only the traditional forms of leadership, but also the traditional forms of devotion. After all, the church of Jerusalem was mostly composed of devout Jews, who kept following the Mosaic law and attending the temple.[45] However, there were also some Hellenized Jews there, who became extremely active in preaching the gospel to the Gentiles.[46] Once again, the question would eventually arise: should these Gentile Christians be circumcised or not? Should they follow the whole of Mosaic law or not?

A key player in this debate was St. Paul. Paul was not his birthname though, but a Latinization of his original name. He was born as Saul, the name of the first king of Israel. Paul was not just Jewish by name, but by conviction—a very strong conviction. He was a disciple of Gamaliel, the great doctor of the law. Eventually, he ended up in the party of the Pharisees, one of the strictest Jewish currents of the day. According to his own testimony: "I made progress in the Jewish religion above many of my equals in my own nation, being more abundantly zealous for the traditions of my fathers."[47]

Paul was probably present when Stephen, a Hellenized Jewish Christian, was judged for allegedly saying that "Jesus of Nazareth . . . shall change

---

[45] Mullin, *A Short World History of Christianity*, 14.
[46] Mullin, *A Short World History of Christianity*, 15.
[47] Gal 1:14

the traditions which Moses delivered unto us."[48] Stephen would be found guilty and stoned, becoming the first Christian martyr.[49]

Paul became a fierce persecutor of the early Church. One day, as he was travelling to Damascus to hunt more Christians there, Jesus appeared to him in a flash of light, blinding him. After being miraculously cured of his blindness, Paul converted to Christianity and began preaching the gospel alongside his newfound friend, St. Barnabas.[50]

Paradoxically, and despite his religious past, Paul focused this preaching mostly on the Gentiles, not his fellow Jews. He founded and safeguarded several churches in modern day Greece and Turkey—a mostly Hellenized area at the time. For this indefatigable missionary work, Paul would become known as the "Apostle of the Gentiles."

However, the doctrine Paul was teaching to the new converts had completely novel elements. As historian Robert Mullin once again says, he "boldly reinterpreted the history of Israel."[51] The traditional interpretation was that the Abrahamic covenant had set Abraham's descendants apart from the rest of humanity, circumcision being the seal of this covenant. But Paul taught instead that God's covenant was based on Abraham's *faith*, not Abraham's *actions*.[52] Therefore, the covenant was not tied to circumcision or bloodline; rather it was open to all believers.[53] By completely reinterpreting the Abrahamic covenant, Paul in effect "invented" the Old Testament, because ancient scripture could now only be properly understood when read through the lens of Jesus Christ[54] (see chapter 1). Also, as a corollary of his views on circumcision, Paul exhorted his Gentile converts not to undergo the ritual.

Now, let us engage in a thought experiment. Let us think of ourselves as first century Christians, converting from a Jewish setting. Let us remind

---

[48] Acts 6:15

[49] Acts 7:57-59

[50] Acts 9:1-27

[51] Mullin, *A Short World History of Christianity*, 17.

[52] See Rom 4:2-3: "For if Abraham were justified by works, he hath whereof to glory, but not before God. For what saith the scripture? Abraham believed God, and it was reputed to him unto justice."

[53] See Rom 4:23-24: "Now it is not written only for him, that it was reputed to him unto justice, But also for us, to whom it shall be reputed, if we believe in him, that raised up Jesus Christ, our Lord, from the dead"

[54] Mullin, *A Short World History of Christianity*, 17.

ourselves of everything that was said before about circumcision and Mosaic law. Let us remember all those who were persecuted and martyred for not daring to deviate an inch from the law. Let us remember the venerable antiquity of those traditions, and how they were inextricably linked to national, cultural, and religious identity. And let us now imagine how we would react to Paul coming along and uttering these words:

> Is any man called, being circumcised? Let him not procure uncircumcision. Is any man called in uncircumcision? Let him not be circumcised. *Circumcision is nothing, and uncircumcision is nothing*: but the observance of the commandments of God.[55]

However, Paul's eccentric teachings did not stop here. Even as Paul spoke favorably about the "observance of the commandments of God," he also seemed to repudiate the law, or speak about it in negative terms. Here are some examples:

> *For not through the law was the promise to Abraham*, or to his seed, that he should be heir of the world; *but through the justice of faith.* For if they who are of the law be heirs, faith is made void, the promise is made of no effect. *For the law worketh wrath. For where there is no law, neither is there transgression.* Therefore is it of faith, that according to grace the promise might be firm to all the seed; not to that *only which is of the law, but to that also which is of the faith* of Abraham, who is the father of us all.[56]

And also:

> *For if there had been a law given which could give life*, verily justice should have been by the law. But the scripture hath concluded all under sin, that the promise, by the faith of Jesus Christ, might be given to them that believe. *But before the faith came, we were kept under the law*

[55] 1 Cor 7:18-19.
[56] Rom 4:13-16.

> *shut up*, unto that faith which was to be revealed. Wherefore the law was our pedagogue in Christ, that we might be justified by faith. *But after the faith is come, we are no longer under a pedagogue.*[57]

Finally, about unclean meats, Paul had this to say:

> Now him that is weak in faith, take unto you: not in disputes about thoughts. For one believeth that he may eat all things: but he that is weak, let him eat herbs. Let not him that eateth, despise him that eateth not: *and he that eateth not, let him not judge him that eateth.*[58]

For anyone remotely familiar with the Old Testament, this theology seems a novelty, a blatant contradiction of the constant traditions handed over to Abraham and Moses and practiced for centuries before Paul. Also, if justification was not done by the works of the law, this could only, by definition, lead to license and lawlessness.[59] This was, at least, the belief of a party within the primitive church who became known as "the Judaizers."

So, when Paul went to Jerusalem to discuss the question of the Gentiles, one would think that the apostles' job would be an easy one: They would have to unequivocally condemn Paul and urge all converts, Jewish and Gentiles alike, to undergo circumcision and follow the precepts of the Mosaic law. This would be what tradition would seem to demand.[60] However, there was more at play here than meets the eye.

Paul's hermeneutic of continuity

---

[57] Gal 3:21-25.

[58] Rom 14:1-3.

[59] Rosner, "Paul and the Law", 21.

[60] See Mathews, "The Council at Jerusalem", 338: "Nothing could be more natural than the position of the Jerusalem Christians at this point. Jesus was a Jew; they were Jews; the gospel was Jewish . . . It was natural for these primitive Christians to feel that it would always be so limited . . . The call, therefore, to the Gentile community at Antioch to be circumcised and obey the Torah if its members wished to enjoy the messianic salvation is not to be taken in the spirit of proselytism, but rather as a conscious effort to establish the new converts of Christianity in an assured relationship with the coming kingdom."

Despite the apparent and seemingly unsolvable contradictions, there was indeed a continuity between Paul and the law, though it required a proper hermeneutic. As New Testament scholar Brian Rosner points out, this continuity hinges on this fact: the law is not considered as a legal demand, but as a *new righteousness that only Jesus Christ was able to accomplish.*[61] According to Paul, Christians not as much *keep* the commandments, as they *fulfill* them, in an obedience far more radical than the observance of any legalistic code.[62] For Paul, the question is not *what bits* of the law are to be followed, but in *what sense* they are to be followed.[63]

To make this continuity more apparent, we must "go back to the source." We must retrieve some aspects of the law that, though traditional, might not have been as evident to Paul's contemporaries as a literal observance of the Mosaic precepts. I will enumerate three of those aspects which highlight the traditional elements of Paul's theology.

Firstly, we need to go back to ancient Near Eastern covenantal culture. As was said before, a covenant obeyed the following structure: the king would first remind the subjects of the beneficial actions he had performed on their behalf and only then present the law he expected them to obey. This means that, as law professor David Skeel puts it: *law does not create the relationship, but rather the law is a response to the previous actions of the sovereign.*[64] Likewise, with regards to God's covenants, His grace precedes the law. Paul tries to remind us that the *law does not establish relationship with God but is a way of expressing gratitude to God for His gracious redemption.*[65]

Secondly, we must remember that, throughout the history of Israel, the Old Testament itself had undergone some doctrinal development.[66]

---

[61] Rosner, "Paul and the Law", 29.

[62] Rosner, "Paul and the Law", 38.

[63] Rosner, "Paul and the Law", 41.

[64] Skeel, "The Mosaic Law in Christian Perspective", 2.

[65] Skeel, "The Mosaic Law in Christian Perspective", 2.

[66] This was confirmed even by the pre-conciliar Church. In 1906, the Biblical Commission recognized that "no one today doubts the existence of these [posterior modifications and additions to Moses] or does not admit a progressive accretion of the Mosaic laws due to the social and religious conditions of later times, a progression which also manifests itself in the historical records." (my translation

Namely, we notice a shift of emphasis away from a mere external observance of the law to a more innermost predisposition. Still in the Torah, in the book of Deuteronomy, we read that God would "*circumcise thy heart*, and the heart of thy seed: that then mayest love the Lord thy God with all thy heart and with all thy soul."[67] This theme of the "circumcision of the heart" would be expanded in prophetic times, with both Jeremiah and Ezekiel admonishing those who had "uncircumcised hearts."[68]

Later, this internalization of the law would become a hallmark of Jesus Christ's teaching (see chapter 11). In a clear reference to ritual purity laws about clean and unclean meats, Jesus would say: "Not that which goeth into the mouth defileth a man: but what cometh out of the mouth, this defileth a man."[69] This idea would be further developed during the Sermon of the Mount:

> "You have heard that it was said to them of old: Thou shalt not kill. And whosoever shall kill shall be in danger of the judgment. But I say to you, that *whosoever is angry with his brother*, shall be in danger of the judgment. And whosoever shall say to his brother, *Raca*,[70] shall be in danger of the council. *And whosoever shall say, Thou Fool*, shall be in danger of hell fire . . . You have heard that it was said to them of old: Thou shalt not commit adultery. But I say to you, that *whosoever shall look on a woman to lust after her*, hath already committed adultery with her in his heart"[71]

St. Paul's theology seems to be an extension of this doctrinal development, a logical step forward in this reasoning. The law is not a mere adherence to a legal code external to us, but a radical adherence to a new kind of righteousness, coming from each person's heart.

---

from the original French). This statement was later enshrined in the *Acta Apostolicae Sedes*, where the official acts of the Holy See are published. See *AAS* 40, (1948).

[67] Deut 30:6

[68] Jer 9:26, Ezek 44:7,9. It is interesting that, during his trial, St. Stephen also called his accusers "uncircumcised in heart and ears" (Acts 7:51).

[69] Mt 15:11

[70] An expression of contempt and reproach in Aramaic.

[71] Mt 5:21-22,27-28.

Lastly, the Mosaic law was given to Israel as a nation, whereas the Church was composed of people from many nations.[72] This is especially important if we notice that, in the Torah, there are laws that are specifically addressed not only to Jews, but to the "foreigner living among you"[73] i.e., Gentile immigrants into the land of Israel. This would imply that the rest of the law was not applicable to the Gentiles, only the Israelites.

Here, we must make an important distinction between two different dichotomies which may not be obvious to modern-day readers of the Bible: 1) *pure/impure* and 2) *holy/profane.* These are not the same thing, and this is reflected in the way the law is to be received. "Holy" can be rendered as "set apart", or "separated from." In this sense, Israel was a holy nation because it was "set apart" from the other nations by being chosen by God. "Impurity," on the other hand, was a ritual condition that was a consequence of certain natural bodily processes (e.g., menstruation) or of contact with those processes (e.g., touching blood).

As regards to impurity, we must make another distinction between purely *ritual* impurity (e.g., when a person touched blood) and *moral* impurity (e.g., when one would commit adultery or incest). *Ritual* impurity was contagious, but it was neither a moral condition, nor a state of sinfulness. Rather, it was a virtually unavoidable, albeit temporary, state, which could be reversed through proper ritualistic practices. In contrast, *moral* impurity was not contagious, but voluntary and avoidable.[74]

Ritual purity legislation was applicable only to Israel, not to the Gentiles. Since ritual impurity was unavoidable, pagans would be, not *intrinsically impure*, but *functionally impure.*[75] However, even if Gentiles were not inherently impure, they were *inherently profane*, in that they did not belong to the holy nation of Israel, which had been set apart by God from the other nations.[76]

---

[72] Skeel, "The Mosaic Law in Christian Perspective", 3. See also Matthews, "The Council at Jerusalem", 337: "The gospel is an ethicalized and denationalized messianic hope."

[73] Savelle, "A Reexamination of the Prohibitions", 460.

[74] Fredricksen, "Judaizing the Nations", 245.

[75] Fredricksen, "Judaizing the Nations", 246.

[76] Fredricksen, "Judaizing the Nations", 246.

Moral impurity, though, presented the possibility of another kind of division. Unlike ritual purity, Gentiles were indeed asked to follow the law as regards to moral purity. Therefore, Christian Gentiles, by separating themselves from their pagan counterparts through their chastity, could be said to have been "set apart" from the rest of the world as well.[77] So, even if the Israelites conceived of only two categories of people—the holy Israelites and the profane Gentiles—Paul solved these opposites in a higher plane: by also dividing the Gentiles between the holy believers of God and the rest of the world.[78]

In summary, when Paul went to Jerusalem to meet the other apostles, there were two distinct and irreconcilable views on how the Gentiles should uphold the law. On the one hand, there was the Judaizer party—which enjoyed St. James's sympathy—that believed that Gentiles should be circumcised and submit to the whole Mosaic law, as would seem obvious from a plain reading of scripture. On the other hand, there was the Pauline party, that had a more nuanced view on the subject which—as we have seen—was no less traditional than the Judaizer's view, although less evidently so.

First dispute, first council, first pope

The book of the Acts of the Apostles explains how some Christians from Judea came to meet Paul's thriving church at Antioch, in Asia Minor. There, they starting instructing the Gentiles to be circumcised, otherwise they could not be saved. What ensued next is depicted in a way that can only be defined as euphemistic: "Paul and Barnabas had no small contest with them." The final verdict: Paul and Barnabas would have to go to Jerusalem to discuss the question with the apostles and presbyters there.[79]

Unbeknownst to Paul and the other apostles, they were about to start a tradition of their own, a tradition that would be a part of the Church for the next 2,000 years. From that point onward, whenever there would be significant disputes involving the Church, those would be settled by means of a council. The Bible reports that "the apostles and ancients assembled

[77] Fredricksen, "Judaizing the Nations", 247.

[78] Rosner, "Paul and the Law", 32.

[79] Acts 15:1-2

to consider of this matter,"[80] as would later bishops do whenever some important conflict arose in matters of doctrine or discipline. This council in particular would come to be known as the Council of Jerusalem (ca. 49 AD).

Though Paul's theology seemed like an innovation, or even a break with tradition, the council allowed free discussion on this matter.[81] This does not mean that the discussion was not heated ("there had been much disputing.")[82] However, in an approach that seems to mirror Pope Francis's much maligned synodality, they allowed all parties involved to express their opinions on the controversy.

First, Paul and Barnabas talked about the massive Christian booming in Hellenized territories. The previous chapters of Acts, in fact, relay Paul's exploits throughout the Gentile world, and the surprising reception of the gospel in these unexpected soils. It is noted that these news created "great joy among the brethren."[83] The wondrous conversion of the Gentiles to the gospel was indeed good news, that much was undisputed. The problem was: at what cost did it come? Should their most sacred traditions be sacrificed in the altar of expediency?

The Judaizers counter-argued. It is all well and good that the Gentiles are converting in droves. But they must be circumcised and be commanded to follow the laws of Moses,[84] just like Jews have been doing for centuries. Paul's theology denied that this was necessary, as we have seen. Furthermore, doing so would endanger this Gentile wave, for many Gentiles would not be amenable to obey so many prescriptions, especially circumcision. The ideals of both poles seemed not to be reconcilable. . .

Who could untie the knots of this impasse? Who would have the authority to make such an important and hard decision, when the debate was already exhausted? One would feel tempted to look up to James, the bishop of Jerusalem, the overseer with jurisdiction over the meeting's location, and

---

[80] Acts 15:6
[81] Mathews, "The Council at Jerusalem", 340.
[82] Acts 15:7
[83] Acts 15:3
[84] Acts 15:5

also Jesus's own brother and successor as high priest. However, when everyone present looked up, it was not James who stood, but the towering presence of another character, that we have not considered until now: St. Peter.

Tradition considers Peter the first pope. How this came to be is going to be explored later in this book, in chapter 12. For now, it suffices to say that Peter was not exactly inexperienced on the matter of Gentile converts.[85] It all had started a few years before, when Peter was stricken by a puzzling vision: a big sheet came down from heaven by being let down to earth by its four corners. On top of this sheet every kind of animal was displayed: fowl and sheep, of course; but also pigs and even reptiles. As Peter was very hungry, he heard a voice come from above, telling him to "kill and eat." Peter was, of course, scandalized by this command, because there were unclean animals there, which Mosaic law forbid to eat. The voice, however, replied: "That which God hath cleansed, do not thou call common." But Peter would not relent. As an observant Jew, he would rather die than break the law of Moses. The voice would insist three times before taking the sheet and the animals back to heaven again, leaving Peter behind, utterly bewildered.[86] Had God just put him to the test? And most importantly: had he passed the test or not? Human logic would dictate that yes, Peter had done good. He had not broken the law. But then, why did this vision keep churning inside his brain?

As Peter kept pondering, he received the visit of three men. They had been sent by Cornelius, a Roman centurion—in other words, a Gentile. The envoys spoke of Cornelius as a just and God-fearing man. He too had received a vision, telling him to send for Peter and meet him. Peter, upon receiving confirmation from the Holy Spirit that this was God's will, followed the messengers back to Cornelius's house.[87]

Cornelius had gathered all his family and close, faithful friends. When Peter crossed the threshold of the house, the good Gentile rushed to the holy apostle and threw himself at his feet—an outrageous act, certainly, for a Roman centurion to grovel before a conquered Jew. Peter, on his end,

---

[85] And not just Peter, for that matter. Acts 8:26-39 tells of the episode of the baptizing of an Ethiopian eunuch by the apostle St. Philip.

[86] Acts 10:11-16

[87] Acts 10:19-23

was also uncomfortable. After all, it was "abominable" for a "Jew to keep company or to come unto one of another nation." Cornelius, however, was undeterred by all these human considerations. The centurion explained his vision to Peter, and how God had told him: "thy prayer is heard, and thy alms are had in remembrance in the sight of God." Now that Peter was there, Cornelius would do all things whatsoever commanded by the Lord through the first pope. Peter marveled. All his human ideas and prejudices had been shattered. God was not "a respecter of persons," after all. Quite the contrary, everyone who feared God and who worked towards justice was acceptable to Him, regardless of nation.[88]

After Peter finished preaching the gospel, everyone present began speaking in tongues, a sure sign the Holy Spirit had descended upon them. The Bible tells us "The faithful of the circumcision, who came with Peter, were astonished." But Peter knew he could not deny the waters of baptism to those who had received the Holy Spirit. So was Cornelius and all his household baptized.[89]

Later, other "faithful of the circumcision" in Judea caught word of what happened and "contended" with Peter. The first pope then recounted everything that had transpired, from his vision to Cornelius's baptism. As they heard, the Jewish Christians "held their peace, and glorified God, saying: God then hath also to the Gentiles given repentance unto life."[90]

Now, years later, as all the apostles were gathered in Jerusalem to discuss the situation of the Gentiles, it was Peter's time to speak his mind. He stood up at the council, his past experiences informing his words, the Holy Spirit guiding his resolve. This is what he said:

> Men, brethren, you know, that in former days God made choice among us, that by my mouth the Gentiles should hear the word of the gospel, and believe. And God, who knoweth the hearts, gave testimony, giving unto them the Holy Ghost, as well as to us; *And put no difference between us and them, purifying their hearts by faith.* Now

---

[88] Acts 10:24-35
[89] Acts 10:44-48
[90] Acts 11:1-18

> therefore, *why tempt you God to put a yoke upon the necks of the disciples,* which neither our fathers nor we have been able to bear? But *by the grace of the Lord Jesus Christ, we believe to be saved, in like manner as they also.*[91]

In other words, there would be no difference between Jewish and Gentile Christians, even if the latter purified their hearts through faith. They could be saved by the grace of Jesus, so they needed not any additional yoke placed upon them. Peter had taken the side of Paul. Before this authoritative decision, there were no cries of "we must follow tradition, not Peter." On the contrary, the Bible says, once again, that those present "held their peace."[92] On that day, Petrine authority was heeded, starting a venerable tradition that would become a constant throughout history and throughout this book.

However, we must still bear in mind that this council sat in St. James's jurisdiction. The last word, therefore, went to the head of the church of Jerusalem. James acquiesced to Peter's decision, but sought to add a few conditions, as a way of concession to the Judaizer party. Proselytes were not to be disquieted but should nonetheless refrain from four things: 1) pollution of idols, 2) fornication, 3) meat of strangled animals, and 4) *blood.*[93] Thus were the proceedings of the Council of Jerusalem closed, and letters sent to Antioch with all these decisions. Paul and Barnabas respected this ruling scrupulously. The first controversy in Christian history had been successfully resolved . . . or so it seemed.

Paul stands to Peter's face

Since Peter validated the Pauline party at the Council of Jerusalem, one is tempted to ask: Why then, did Paul correct Peter? The problem that would cause Paul's drastic measures was not a result of the council, but of its aftermath. The Council of Jerusalem, as definitive as it seemed, did not completely quell the controversy, as often happens with the Church, today as yesterday. The Judaizer party was still around and tried to either oppose

---

[91] Acts 15:7-11.

[92] Acts 15:12

[93] Acts 15:19-20

the council's decisions or interpret them in a way that would be favorable to their worldview.

After the closing of the Council of Jerusalem, Peter came to visit Antioch[94] to check that wondrous Gentile miracle—a church made up almost exclusively of proselytes! This visit became the background of what would later be called: "The Incident at Antioch." In the beginning, everything seemed to go along just fine. Peter would eat with the Gentiles, just like he had done before with Cornelius. But then, an entourage came from Jerusalem, sent from James's part, and started sowing confusion. From that moment on, Peter "withdrew and separated himself, fearing them who were of the circumcision."[95] In other words, he would no longer eat with the Gentiles to avoid ritual impurity. In his epistle to the Galatians, Paul laments that even his good friend Barnabas eventually did the same.[96] It seemed that, for the Gentiles to be fully accepted to the tables of their fellow Jewish Christians, they would have to submit to the Mosaic purity and dietary laws, negating in practice what the council had previously decided in theory. Paul would have none of it. This is the context in which the apostle says he went up to Cephas ("rock / Peter" in the original Aramaic) and "withstood him to the face, because he was to be blamed."[97] This is Paul's famous correction to Peter.

Throughout the centuries, Catholic apologists and exegetes understood the seriousness of this biblical passage. It is not used solely by traditionalists or Protestants today, but was used by pagans even in Patristic times, to question the reliability of the papacy and the Church.[98] For this reason, many Fathers of the Church tried to find ways to justify this blatant inversion of Church hierarchy, whereby a bishop could correct the pope himself. Some, like St. Clement of Alexandria, would postulate that Cephas

---

[94] Gal 2:11

[95] Gal 2:12

[96] Gal 2:13

[97] Gal 2:11

[98] See Griffith, "Apostolic Authority and the 'Incident at Antioch,'" 120: "The challenge of pagan anti-Christian rhetoric provides the other main exegetical context. Origen and Jerome were aware that this passage in Galatians provided fodder for pagan critiques"

was another person besides St. Peter, though "Cephas" was the name Jesus used in Mt 16:18. Others, like St. Jerome or Origen, would claim that the correction was a deception concocted by Peter and Paul as a teaching moment. Even others, like Tertullian, would accuse Paul of overreacting. And still others, like St. Augustine, simply dismissed those kinds of apologetics and agreed that Peter was indeed to blame, and that no leader is above correction.[99]

I believe it is not necessary to go to such lengths to make sense of what happened. Peter was not acting magisterially when he stopped eating with the Gentiles. Rather, he was acting in his private capacity.[100] Though the Church asks submission of mind and will to *magisterial teachings* (as we shall see in chapter 12), it is not true that any bishop's or pope's *private actions* are above reproach. This is especially important, because Peter's behavior was being used to undermine his own magisterial decision at the Council of Jerusalem.[101]

So, let us return to the *Correctio filialis*. Its signatories affirm that they can use the Pauline reproach as a precedent for their own correction of *Amoris Laetitia*, sustaining that this magisterial document contains seven heretical propositions. However, this is not what happened in the first century. The authors of the *Correctio filialis* would indeed have a point if, after Peter's intervention at the Council of Jerusalem, James would have withstood the pope to his face, saying that he had just taught heresy and that Gentile converts should indeed submit to the venerable Mosaic tradition of their forebears. But this is not the case. *Paul did not accuse Peter of heresy, but of hypocrisy.*

In this sense, a better parallel would be if Pope Francis, after consulting the Synod of Bishops on this topic, and after promulgating *Amoris Laetitia*, would have cowered at the criticisms from traditionalist quarters and would have personally refused to give communion to divorced and remarried couples who would seek him, even if they had mitigating circumstances

---

[99] Griffith, "Apostolic Authority and the 'Incident at Antioch'", 118.

[100] This interpretation is shared by Broussard, "Paul's Rebuke and Peter's Infallibility", and also by Akin, "Peter in Galatians."

[101] Some scholars believe that Paul's correction happened *before* the Council of Jerusalem. Be that as it may, it still does not change the distinction that was made here, between Peter's magisterial teaching at the Council (whether before or after the correction) and Peter's behavior (which was indeed reproachable).

diminishing their subjective culpability so that they were not in mortal sin. This would mean that, even if he had magisterially published his decision on the matter, he would be casting doubts on the legitimacy of his own decision, out of fear of scandalizing traditionalists. In this situation, a bishop with a pastoral mind set on accompanying the divorced and remarried in his diocese would do well to criticize the Holy Father for his double standard and for undercutting his own magisterium. This would be the perfect parallel if it actually existed. However, I do not believe such a precedent would please the authors of the *Correctio filialis.*

Eating blood: A final aftershock

Paul's correction to Peter seems to have closed the Judaizer controversy for good. We do not have an account of Peter's side, but it is safe to assume that Peter accepted the reproach and returned to the table of his Gentile brethren. Nowadays, the idea that Christians need not undergo circumcision or follow every single precept of Mosaic law is relatively incontrovertible. However, an astute reader might have noticed a certain discrepancy between the praxis of early and of modern Church.

As was mentioned before, St. James introduced four prohibitions at the end of the Council of Jerusalem. Amongst these was a ban on eating blood or meat from strangled animals. However, it is well known that this ban is not enforced in Christian countries. My own country of Portugal is traditionally very Catholic,[102] and yet also has some traditional dishes prepared with blood. Among these I would like to highlight *morcela*—a typical blood sausage[103]—and *cabidela*—a kind of rice cooked on chicken's blood.[104] However, I have never heard any priest condemning these

[102] In a 2011 census, eighty-one percent of the total population identified as Catholic. See Instituto Nacional de Estatística, *Censos 2011 Resultados Definitivos—Portugal*, 530.

[103] A recipe of *morcela* can be found at "Portuguese Black Pudding (Morcela) Recipe", *Portuguese Recipes.*

[104] A recipe of *cabidela* can be found at "A Portuguese favorite: Arroz de cabidela recipe", *Taste Porto.*

gastronomical delicacies from the pulpit even once. So, what is the reason for this?

To understand why eating blood is acceptable for Catholics in spite of the apostolic ban, we must also comprehend the reason behind this ban. What is the meaning of the four prohibitions? Why did St. James insist upon them, even after St. Peter's discourse? We do know that James was trying to appease the Jewish Christians somehow. But why he proposed these specific prohibitions and not others, we do not know for sure. Scholars propose three main theories for the origin of these injunctions.

The first theory is that James was basing himself on the rabbinical wisdom of his day, wherein Jews were allowed, during times of persecution, to compromise in every custom of the law, except idolatry, incest, and shedding of blood. The second theory is that James was referencing the Noahidic covenant, since this covenant was applicable to all humankind descended from Noah, unlike the Mosaic covenant celebrated only with Israel. Among the Noahidic prohibitions was the command to never eat blood.[105] The third theory is that James was thinking about Lev 17-18, the parts of the Mosaic law that applied, not only to the Israelites, but also to "the foreigner living among you." None of these three theories explains the four prohibitions in their entirety or in a way that is completely textually congruent with what we read in the book of the Acts of the Apostles. So, the most likely explanation is that all three justifications contribute in a way to explain St. James's thought process.[106]

Whatever the theoretical basis for the four prohibitions, they had a single practical purpose: to improve the relationship between Jewish and Gentile Christians, by allowing them to sit at the same table and share the same meals (especially in the context of communion,) without eliciting scruples among the Jewish Christians as to whether they were becoming ritually impure by doing so. Furthermore, it helped avoid scandal, since all the activities prohibited by the Council of Jerusalem could be associated with pagan practices.[107] In this sense, it is easy to understand St. Paul's frustration with Peter's hypocrisy, since the first pope's reluctance to eat with Gentiles was undermining even the very practical foundation for the

---

[105] Gen 9:3-4

[106] Savelle, "A Reexamination of the Prohibitions", 457-461.

[107] Savelle, "A Reexamination of the Prohibitions", 463-464.

Council of Jerusalem's prohibitions. If these injunctions were not mitigating scandal and bringing Jewish and Gentile Christians together, what was their purpose after all?

However, we must ask ourselves: are these prohibitions applicable to us today? After all, the Church nowadays is composed mostly of Gentiles, so the problem of sharing meals no longer applies. Also, the pagan practices associated with eating blood are no longer common. This is the reason why the Church does not enforce the apostolic ban anymore. In 1442 AD, the Council of Florence would promulgate the following:

> "[The Holy Roman Church] firmly believes, professes and teaches that every creature of God is good and nothing is to be rejected if it is received with thanksgiving, because according to the word of the Lord not what goes into the mouth defiles a person, and because the difference in the Mosaic law between clean and unclean foods belongs to ceremonial practices, *which have passed away* and lost their efficacy with the coming of the gospel. It also declares that the apostolic prohibition, to abstain from what has been sacrificed to idols and from blood and from what is strangled, *was suited to that time* when a single church was rising from Jews and gentiles, who previously lived with different ceremonies and customs. This was so that the gentiles should have some observances in common with Jews, and occasion would be offered of coming together in one worship and faith of God and a cause of dissension might be removed, since by ancient custom blood and strangled things seemed abominable to Jews, and gentiles could be thought to be returning to idolatry if they ate sacrificial food. In places, however, where the Christian religion has been promulgated to such an extent that no Jew is to be met with and all have joined the church, uniformly practising the same rites and ceremonies of the gospel and believing that to the clean all things are clean, *since the cause of that apostolic prohibition has ceased, so its effect has ceased.* It condemns, then, no kind of food that human society accepts and

> nobody at all neither man nor woman, should make a distinction between animals, no matter how they died."[108]

If we are going to say that a council has introduced novelties in doctrine, so that the Church contradicted herself, then we must acknowledge that the same happened many centuries before Vatican II. The biblical prescriptions (including the Noahidic laws) were "suited to that time" but have in effect "ceased" and "'passed away." Some distracted traditionalist might confuse this wording with modernism, if uttered by the Church today. However, the Church has indeed authoritatively allowed something that seemed perpetually forbidden, even by the Noahidic covenant. The Church made such an allowance by authoritatively interpreting these prohibitions, using their proper historical and religious context. By doing so, the Church re-centered this biblical passage in what is truly important.

In an ancient mindset, blood symbolized a life force that should be offered to the gods. Therefore, it had an enormous religious significance and was inextricably tied to idolatry. Modern day society simply does not attribute to blood the same religious and ritualistic value that ancient pagan and Jewish societies gave to it (even in apostolic times.) So, forbidding the eating of blood does not add anything of value to our faith anymore. In fact, by defending a literalist interpretation of Gen 9:4, we risk interpreting it in anachronistic and life-threatening ways, like Jehovah's Witnesses do regarding blood transfusions. Focusing too much on the blood part might distract us from dealing with idolatry, which is the main theme of the biblical passage in question, and which manifests in completely different ways nowadays.[109] This is why *living tradition* is so important.

---

[108] Florence. "Session 11."

[109] Gabriel, "Death penalty—the Gen 9:6 objection."

Chapter 6

"In the same sense, in the same meaning"

Some may wonder . . . if these Gentiles were sinners and were damned and then they changed, then does faith change? No. Faith never changes. Faith is the same, but it moves; it grows; it broadens . . . Saint Vincent of Lérins, an elderly monk from the 5th century, said these words: 'the truths of the Church go forward'; 'ut annis consolidetur, dilatetur tempore sublimetur aetate' . . . *That is, they become stronger with time, with the years; they broaden with time and grow with the age of the Church.*

—Francis, Dio Delle Sorprese

It was October 11, 2017. Thomas Lawson prepared for his regular prayers. He took his trusted rosary out of a drawer of his study. Then, with great devotion, he held the rosary's cross firmly in his hand, so tight it imprinted creases on his palm. "Please, Holy Spirit, guide Pope Francis so he will stop leading the Church astray." He started praying, in Latin: "*Credo in unum Deum, Patrem omnipotentem. . .*"[1]

Tom felt a sense of relief. In these prayers, he could feel the uninterrupted 2,000-year-old tradition of the Church coursing through his soul: ". . . *genitum, non factum, consubstantialem Patri. . .*"[2] In these millennial verses, there was no trace of ambiguity whatsoever, only words withstanding the test of time: ". . . *qui ex Patre Filioque procedit. . .*"[3] No innovations hammered into the formulas by papal *fiat*, an exercise of sheer authority. After finishing the creed, Tom moved to the Our Father, and finally to the Hail Mary: "*Sancta Maria, Mater Dei. . .*"[4]

When Tom pronounced the last "Amen," he was confident that his prayers had been received by the ears of the Almighty. Imagine his horror when he logged into his Catholic news websites! Pope Francis had just celebrated the twenty-fifth anniversary of the apostolic constitution *Fidei Depositum*, by which John Paul II had promulgated the Catechism of the Catholic Church. During his speech, Francis manifested his intention to

---

[1] "I believe in one God, the Father, the Almighty."

[2] "Begotten, not made, consubstantial to the Father"

[3] "Who proceeds from the Father and the Son"

[4] "Holy Mary, Mother of God"

change the Catechism's teaching on the death penalty. Namely, the death penalty should now be viewed as "*inadmissible.*"[5]

Tom was once again distraught. This was a major reversal of Church teaching! Traditionally, even up to the pontificate of Pius XII (the last of the pre-conciliar popes,) the Church had allowed the death penalty as a means to exercise justice.[6] Granted, that had changed since St. John Paul II. The Polish pontiff had taught that the death penalty was "both cruel and unnecessary,"[7] and had publicly and forcefully called for its abolition worldwide. However, John Paul II had been careful not to allow his abolitionist stance to cast a shadow on the Church's trustworthiness. He knew that the Church could not declare as "intrinsically evil" (i.e., not morally justifiable in any circumstance) something that she had declared acceptable in previous times. Otherwise people could say that the Church was not a reliable teacher on faith and morals. John Paul II had arrived at a very elegant solution for this: to allow the death penalty in theory, while claiming that the practical instances where such a punishment was morally applicable today were so rare, they were "practically non-existent," thereby allowing for its total abolition.[8] This is why the version of the Catechism, promulgated by John Paul II, taught the following:

---

[5] Francis, "To Participants in the Meeting."

[6] See Pius XII, "A los participantes en el I Congreso Internacional de Histopatología", #28 (in Spanish).

[7] John Paul II, "Eucharistic Celebration." This call for abolition was continued by John Paul II's immediate successor. See Benedict XVI, *Africae Munus*, #83: "I draw the attention of society's leaders to the need to make every effort to eliminate the death penalty and to reform the penal system in a way that ensures respect for the prisoners' human dignity"

[8] John Paul II, Evangelium Vitae, #56: "This is the context in which to place the problem of the death penalty. On this matter there is a growing tendency, both in the Church and in civil society, to demand that it be applied in a very limited way or even that *it be abolished completely*. The problem must be viewed in the context of a system of penal justice ever *more in line with human dignity* and thus, in the end, with God's plan for man and society. . . It is clear that, for these purposes to be achieved, the nature and extent of the punishment must be carefully evaluated and decided upon, and ought not go to the extreme of executing the offender *except in cases of absolute necessity*: in other words, when it would not be possible otherwise to defend society. Today however, as a result of steady improvements in the organization of the penal system, *such cases are very rare*, if not *practically non-existent*."

> *The traditional teaching of the Church does not exclude*, presupposing full ascertainment of the identity and responsibility of the offender, recourse to the death penalty, *when this is the only practicable way to defend the lives of human beings effectively* against the aggressor. If, instead, *bloodless means are sufficient* to defend against the aggressor and to protect the safety of persons, *public authority should limit itself to such means* . . . Today, in fact, given the means at the State's disposal to effectively repress crime by rendering inoffensive the one who has committed it, without depriving him definitively of the possibility of redeeming himself, cases of absolute necessity for suppression of the offender "*today ... are very rare, if not practically non-existent.*"[9]

However, many Catholic commentators, especially in the US, took this theoretical concession—fashioned specifically to safeguard the integrity of the Church's past magisterium—and used it as a loophole to ignore the pope's clear calls for abolition and defend the *status quo* instead.[10] This was compounded by the leak of a private letter by then prefect of the Congregation for the Doctrine of the Faith (CDF) Joseph Ratzinger to the American Cardinal McCarrick, in which he said: "There may be a legitimate diversity of opinion even among Catholics about waging war and applying the death penalty, but not however with regard to abortion and euthanasia."[11] This letter was private and not released with the papal approval that would make

---

[9] CCC 2267 (2nd edition, 1997 version).
[10] See Ferrara, "Can the Church ban Capital Punishment?"
[11] Ratzinger, "Worthiness to receive Holy Communion."

it magisterial.[12] Still, these same Catholic commentators took hold of this quote to justify their position.[13]

As a conservative American Catholic, Tom's opinion on this topic was molded by these commentators. So, Tom would appeal to his prudential judgment to dismiss the pope's call for an abolition of the death penalty, while claiming to be faithful to the "perennial teaching of the Church" on that matter. But now, Pope Francis was threatening to disrupt this careful balance.

In 2018, Pope Francis's so awaited (or dreaded) Catechism revision was finally promulgated. It now read:

> Recourse to the death penalty on the part of legitimate authority, following a fair trial, *was long considered an appropriate response* to the gravity of certain crimes and an acceptable, albeit extreme, means of safeguarding the common good. Today, however, there is *an increasing awareness that the dignity of the person is not lost even after the commission of very serious crimes*. . . Consequently, the Church teaches, in the light of the Gospel, that "the death penalty is *inadmissible* because it is an attack on the inviolability and dignity of the person", and she works with determination for its abolition worldwide.[14]

Tom was utterly disoriented. Pope Francis had, again, overstepped the limits of his authority to teach something contrary to the tradition of the

---

[12] See CDF, *Donum Veritatis*, 18: "Consequently, the documents issued by this Congregation [of the Doctrine of the Faith] *expressly approved* by the Pope participate in the ordinary magisterium of the successor of Peter." This is not the case, as explained by a later prefect of the CDF, Cardinal Luís Ladaria: "Regarding Cardinal Ratzinger's 2004 letter to Cardinal McCarrick, this Congregation respects Cardinal Ratzinger's stipulations that '*these principles were not intended for publication*.' The letter was in the form of a *private communication* addressed to the bishops." (see Crary, "Vatican warns US Bishops").

[13] See, for example, Feser. "Capital punishment should not end (UPDATED)": "One might suppose from the statement that all faithful Catholics agree. But that is not the case. As then-Cardinal Ratzinger famously affirmed in 2004, a Catholic may be 'at odds with the Holy Father' on the subject of capital punishment and 'there may be a legitimate diversity of opinion even among Catholics about… applying the death penalty.'"

[14] CCC 2267 (2nd edition, 2018 version).

Church! As usual, Tom ran to his Catholic online forums to vent. Justin Peterson, our fellow apologist, was there and noted Tom's distress. In a private message, Justin explained that Francis had not contradicted his predecessors, quite the contrary. He had said exactly the same as John Paul II and Benedict XVI, all the while closing the loophole by declaring the death penalty "inadmissible" in practice.

"Inadmissible?"—Tom asked in a loud voice, as if people could hear him from behind the screen—"That won't do!" The Church had traditionally taught that states could take recourse to the death penalty! How could she now be declaring that the death penalty was intrinsically evil?

Justin very calmly pointed out that "intrinsically evil" and "inadmissible" were not synonymous. The former referred to an act that could never be morally justified, not even in principle, whereas the latter referred to all its practical applications at a given time. This was, in fact, what John Paul II had tried to do. Francis had simply moved from "practically non-existent" to "non-existent in practice."[15] There should be a reason why Francis had used "inadmissible" and not "intrinsically evil."

Unfortunately, this did not convince Tom. If "inadmissible" did not mean intrinsically evil, it was still a confusing term, prone to misinterpretation.[16] Furthermore, it was a novel word, with no precedent in tradition.[17] It was an innovation from Pope Francis, and therefore anti-traditional.[18]

---

[15] For more of my apologetical reasoning on this topic, see Gabriel. "Death Penalty – continuity or hardness of heart?"

[16] See Rutler. "Pope Francis' new comments": "Pope Francis uses the term 'inadmissible' to describe the death penalty, although it has no theological substance, and by avoiding words such as 'immoral' or 'wrong' inflicts on discourse an ambiguity similar to parts of *Amoris Laetitia*. The obvious meaning is that capital punishment is intrinsically evil, but to say so outright would be too blatant."

[17] See Pakaluk. "Cardinal Dulles's Dubia": "Everyone has pointed to the strangeness of the word 'inadmissible' in the new teaching. . . the word 'inadmissible' occurs nowhere else in the Catechism. It is almost a solecism in moral theology."

[18] This claim is false since there is abundant precedent for the use of this word in magisterial pronouncements. A recollection of several such instances can be found in Lewis. "Simply Inadmissible."

Justin tried to explain that, even if the word "inadmissible" was new, it was not necessarily anti-traditional or even untraditional. Rather, it was new because it was a development in doctrine.[19] But Tom countered: it could not be a legitimate development, because it contradicted what came before it. Quoting St. Vincent of Lérins, Tom argued that doctrine should develop only in its own kind, that is to say, "in the same sense, and in the same meaning" (see chapter 3). Therefore, this Catechism revision was not a true development, but a corruption of the faith.

Interestingly, Pope Francis had *also* quoted St. Vincent of Lérins in his much-maligned speech, where he expressed his intention to revise the Catechism on the death penalty. The Holy Father had said:

> Tradition is a living reality and only a partial vision regards the "deposit of faith" as something static . . . The word of God is a dynamic and living reality that develops and grows because it is aimed at a fulfilment that none can halt. This law of progress, in the happy formulation of Saint Vincent of Lérins, "*consolidated by years, enlarged by time, refined by age*", is a distinguishing mark of revealed truth as it is handed down by the Church, and in no way represents a change in doctrine.[20]

So, who adequately interpreted St. Vincent's canon? Thomas Lawson or Pope Francis?[21] What is more important? The part where Vincent

---

[19] See CDF, "Letter to the Bishops", 7: "The new revision of number 2267 of the Catechism of the Catholic Church, approved by Pope Francis, situates itself in *continuity* with the preceding Magisterium while bringing forth a *coherent development* of Catholic doctrine."

[20] Francis, "To Participants in the Meeting."

[21] It is worth noting that Thomas Guarino, the respected scholar of Vatican II that I have quoted extensively in the first section of this book, believes that Pope Francis is incorrect in applying the Vincentian quote of "consolidated by years. . ." to the case of the death penalty, because St. Vincent would only apply such a logic to a development, not to a reversal. See Guarino. "Pope Francis and St. Vincent of Lérins": "Note that St. Vincent never speaks positively about reversals. A reversal, for Vincent, is not an advance in the Church's understanding of truth; it is not an instance of a teaching 'enlarged by time.'" However, this presupposes that there was a reversal, not a proper development, as I have explained throughout this chapter by the mouth of Justin Peterson, and also in Gabriel. "Death Penalty – continuity or hardness of heart?"

postulates: "consolidated by years, enlarged by time," as the pontiff claims? Or is it, as the pope's critics affirm, the part where Vincent posits: "same sense, same meaning"?

We cannot answer these questions without knowing why St. Vincent formulated his famous rules. And we cannot know this without diving into the historical context shaping this fifth-century theologian's ideas of tradition, innovation, and doctrinal development. So, let us start by turning our eyes to the Church of the earliest centuries.

The wheat of tradition, the chaff of heresy

It was 100 AD, and St. John the Apostle was on his deathbed. Since he ended up being the only apostle to die of old age, he was the only of the Twelve alive at that time. All others had been martyred, persecuted by their faith. St. James, bishop of Jerusalem, had been stoned to death at around 60 AD.[22] St. Paul followed, beheaded outside Rome's walls. As for St. Peter, he had been condemned to die as the Lord. Feeling unworthy of such an honor, Peter asked to be crucified upside down.[23]

But now that John was exhaling his final breath, the Church faced another dilemma. Gone was the last person to receive the Holy Spirit at the day of Pentecost. There were no more apostles to preach the tradition, either in writing or by word of mouth. Divine revelation had come to an end. How could the barge of the Church sail through the stormy seas of new challenges? Granted, the apostles had left "overseers" to tend to the flock in their stead. St. Linus had become St. Peter's successor as bishop of Rome. But would this be enough? And what did this entail, exactly?

The Roman Empire did not stop at killing the apostles. Christian persecutions kept popping up sporadically in the following two centuries. Emperors tried to crush this Christian movement, for it endangered—so they thought—the very fabric of society.[24] This, in turn, drove the Church

[22] Nash. "Who are the Twelve Apostles?"

[23] Curtis. "Whatever Happened to the Twelve Apostles?"

[24] See Fredricksen, "Judaizing the Nations", 240: "Worse than turning their backs on their human kin, however, was the fact that such people also turned their

underground, a situation that also made it more difficult for the various churches to communicate freely and, therefore, fully synchronize their beliefs amongst themselves. This was very important, since Christians were grappling with a three-headed *complexio oppositorum.* They were to hold three claims at the same time, all seemingly in tension with one another: 1) There was only one God; 2) Christ was God; and 3) the Father and the Son were distinct.[25] Failing to maintain this delicate balance could lead to heresy.

This is, in fact, what happened. The first four centuries of the Church's history saw a proliferation of heresies, namely as regards to Christ's nature. At the earliest, we had two diametrically opposed heresies. On one side, there were the Ebionites, who clung to the observance of the Jewish law and who denied Christ's divinity.[26] For them, Jesus was merely a human messiah. On the other side, there were the Docetists, who claimed that Jesus only *appeared* or *seemed* to be a man, to have been born, to have lived and suffered.[27]

Against both extremes stood a bishop, St. Ignatius of Antioch, one of St. John's disciples.[28] As the historian Robert Mullin explains: "Against the Ebionites, he [Ignatius] declared that Christ was born of a *virgin.* Against the Docetists he declared that Christ was *born* of a virgin."[29]

In other words, the orthodox position was the one espoused by the bishop. Here, we can see a progressive crystallization of certain typically Catholic overtones that would become fully developed only later on. The Church was the bulwark against heresy, and the center of the Church was

---

backs to the gods who were theirs by birth and blood. They thereby disrupted the fundamental relationship between gods and their humans. Such behavior not only insulted the pagan community: It endangered the pagan community, because it insulted that community's gods, and angry gods made for sorry humans." See also Mullin, *A Short World History of Christianity*, 42-43.

25 Mullin, *A Short World History of Christianity*, 64. See also Bickerton. "The Development of a Theology of Tradition," 11: "All sides agreed on these Christian tenets: it was monotheistic; Jesus was not simply an ordinary human; through Christ salvation had come to mankind; the Scriptures were God's word . . . While differences appear in the interpretation of all four of these fundamental tenets, the root of the 'Arian' controversy is how to resolve the paradox of the first two. How is Christianity monotheistic, yet Jesus Christ is no mere human?"

26 Arendzen. "Ebionites."

27 Arendzen. "Docetae."

28 Bennett. *Four Witnesses*, 104.

29 Mullin, *A Short World History of Christianity*, 27.

the bishop.[30] As St. Ignatius would preach: "You must all follow the lead of the bishop, as Jesus Christ followed that of the Father. . . Where the bishop appears, there let the people be, just as where Jesus Christ is, there is the Catholic Church."[31] This was, in fact, the first known instance of the word "Catholic" ever used in history.

Another prevailing heresy was Gnosticism. Though Gnostics constitute a very heterogeneous group, they held a common belief: the idea that salvation comes from knowledge (*gnosis* in Greek). They can be defined as: "A collective name for a large number of greatly-varying and pantheistic-idealistic sects, which flourished from some time before the Christian Era down to the fifth century, and which, while borrowing the phraseology and some of the tenets of the chief religions of the day, and especially of Christianity, held matter to be a deterioration of spirit, and the whole universe a depravation of the Deity, and taught the ultimate end of all being to be the overcoming of the grossness of matter and the return to the Parent-Spirit, which return they held to be inaugurated and facilitated by the appearance of some God-sent Saviour."[32]

Against the Gnostics stood another bishop, St. Irenaeus of Lyon. As Robert Mullin once again explains, Irenaeus made two assertions that helped distinguish between the true Christian faith and the Gnostic depravations: 1) this faith was *Catholic* (i.e., universal, whereas the gnostic teachings were local); and 2) it was *apostolic* (linked by strong traditions to the apostles themselves.)[33] Once again, we see an embryonic concept of tradition taking form (see chapter 1). Tradition was paramount: it was what kept the connection between the Church of the time and the teachings of the recently deceased apostles.[34] So, it was important to recognize, amidst a vortex of conflicting interpretations, where the true doctrine and tradition would lie: with the Church. This would be especially relevant once the Church would leave the anonymity of its condition of persecuted.

---

30 Mullin, *A Short World History of Christianity*, 27.

31 Ignatius. "Epistle to the Smyrnaeans", 8.

32 Arendzen. "Gnosticism."

33 Mullin, *A Short World History of Christianity*, 28. See also Bennett. *Four Witnesses*, 249-252.

34 Price. *Chalcedon in Context*, 9.

Eventually, that is exactly what happened. When Diocletian—the Roman emperor who most severely persecuted the Christians—relinquished his power in 305 AD, he triggered a succession crisis. One of the contenders for the throne was an ambitious upstart named Constantine. To achieve his goal, however, Constantine would have to defeat his rival Maxentius, who at the time controlled the Roman capitol. Both armies eventually faced each other near the Milvian bridge, by the river Tiber.[35]

The Church historian Eusebius of Caesarea recounts that, on the eve of the battle, Constantine had a vision. A burning cross came down from heaven, with the following inscription: "*in hoc signo vinces*" (Latin for "under this sign, you shall be victorious.") For this reason, Constantine ordered his soldiers to paint the Christian *chi-rho* symbol on their shields. During the battle, Constantine routed his rival's forces, pushing them to a chaotic retreat over the Milvian bridge. The bridge collapsed under the weight of men and armor and Maxentius drowned on the Tiber. A few years later, Constantine would be the sole candidate for the title of Roman emperor.[36]

Constantine never forgot the religious significance of his victory. He converted to Christianity and issued the Edict of Milan in 313 AD, granting religious tolerance across the empire, namely to Christians. The Church could now emerge from the catacombs. But the tension between the three seemingly contradictory Christological statements was still left mostly unresolved. The Church was now free, but not free from the heresies plaguing her. One heresy in particular would become prevalent and spread like wildfire: Arianism.

A (con)substantial confusion

Arius was a presbyter in Alexandria and a bold adversary of the Sabellians,[37] the disciples of a Roman priest named Sabellius. According to Sabellius, the Godhead is a unit, expressing itself in three *operations* (not *persons*): the Father, for creation; the Son, for redemption; and the Holy Spirit for sanctification.[38] Arius fought against this error, and rightfully so. But by doing so—and as is usually the case—he fell in the opposite extreme.

[35] "How Constantine's Victory at The Milvian Bridge." *History Hit.*
[36] "How Constantine's Victory at The Milvian Bridge." *History Hit.*
[37] Barry. "Arianism."
[38] The Editors of Encyclopaedia Britannica. "Sabellianism."

For Arius, the Son was also a creature (i.e., created) and could not, therefore, be coeternal with the Father.[39] For Arius, to say that Father and Son were coeternal, meant that there were two gods, not one.[40] As Arius would say: "There was a time when He was not."[41] The Son of God would be the highest of creatures, but a creature nonetheless.[42]

As the controversy raged and spread beyond Alexandria, Emperor Constantine's hand felt forced to act. Since he had promulgated the Edict of Milan, Christianity had become a social force to be reckoned with. Many Romans abandoned their pagan roots, either out of sincere conversion, or because they sensed opportunity in converting to the emperor's preferred religion. The Church's numbers skyrocketed. Therefore, the emergence of different factions within the Church now threatened imperial unity.[43] Furthermore, some clergy had tried to excommunicate Constantine's good friend, the historian Eusebius of Caesarea (whom I quoted earlier,) for his sympathy with Arius.[44] As an emperor, Constantine needed to quell this controversy once and for all, before things would get out of hand.

The problem was: how to quell it? What rule should be applied to distinguish between those who were right and those who were wrong? In the early Church, as we have seen, the concept of "tradition" was still in its embryonic stage. Namely, the best way to access tradition as handed down by the apostles was through what they had written down. But there was a problem: both the Arians and their opponents quoted scripture in favor of their conclusions.[45]

---

39 Mullin. *A Short World History of Christianity*, 64.

40 Bickerton. "The Development of a Theology of Tradition," 10.

41 Mullin. *A Short World History of Christianity*, 64.

42 Bickerton. "The Development of a Theology of Tradition," 10.

43 Bickerton. "The Development of a Theology of Tradition," 10.

44 Mullin. *A Short World History of Christianity*, 65.

45 See Bickerton. "The Development of a Theology of Tradition," 16: "the bishops and teachers of the fourth century realized that they and their opponents could both use Scripture to defend their theological positions." See also Price. *Chalcedon in Context*, 9: "Complex doctrinal debates divided the expanding Church on a new scale, debates in which all involved appealed to Scripture and the issues at stake could not be decided on scriptural terms."

For example, Arius would cite the book of Proverbs in his defense: "Yahweh *created* me, *first-fruits of his fashioning*, before the oldest of his works."[46] He would also quote the epistle to the Hebrews, where it said: "Thou art my Son, *today have I begotten thee*. And again, I will be to him a Father, and he shall be to me a Son."[47] On the other hand, the anti-Arians counter-argued that this "begotten" referred to Jesus's incarnation, not to His alleged creation as the Logos, the Word of God.[48] They could then quote the gospel according to St. John: "I and the Father are one;"[49] and "In that day you shall know, that I am in my Father, and you in me, and I in you."[50]

Merely appealing to scripture would not do. A new way to solve the problem was needed. Therefore, to untangle this mess, Constantine decided to convene the bishops of his empire in a single council, just like the apostles had done in the first century. Legend says that, at the emperor's behest, 318 bishops gathered at the city of Nicaea, in Asia Minor (modern day Turkey)—though the actual number was probably around 220.[51]

The year was 325, and this became the largest Christian council ever held until then. It was also the first council since the apostolic age that could plausibly claim to represent the entire Christian body.[52] For this reason, the First Council of Nicaea (henceforth called simply "Council of Nicaea") is considered the first ecumenical council. From that point onward, Christian tradition would be defined not solely by scripture, but also by the councils.[53]

At the end of the discussion, the bishops decided to define orthodoxy by promulgating a creed. This was, in itself, an innovation. As Robert Mullin once again explains: "Heretofore, creeds were directed at *catechumens*

---

[46] Pr 8:22. NA: I used the New Jerusalem Bible version in this quotation instead of the usual Douay-Rheims, in order to make Arius's point clearer. See Corbellini. "A Participação de Atanásio," 401 (in Portuguese).

[47] Heb 1:4.

[48] Corbellini. "A Participação de Atanásio," 401.

[49] John 10:30.

[50] John 14:20. See also Corbellini. "A Participação de Atanásio," 406.

[51] Price. *Chalcedon in Context*, 10. See also Mullin. *A Short World History of Christianity*, 65.

[52] Price. *Chalcedon in Context*, 9.

[53] Price. *Chalcedon in Context*, 9.

and were meant to *instruct*—now, the Nicene creed was directed at the *clergy* and was meant to *define*."[54]

In this new creed, a single word stood out: *homoousios*. This word was meant to describe the proper relation between the Father and the Son. It means "same substance" in Greek and is roughly translated in Latin / vernacular as "consubstantial." The Father and the Son were of the same substance. Nowadays, "consubstantial" is undeniably and uncontrover-sially a keyword for orthodoxy. However, at the time, *homoousios* raised a lot of problems.

Scholars debate who came up with *homoousios* at the Council of Nicaea. A theory postulates that the *homoousios* was a triumph of Western bishops expressing a Western theology. However, it has been pointed out that the Westerners (including the papal legates) would have trouble following the discussion in Greek.[55] Also their reception of the word after Nicaea was lukewarm at best.[56] Consequently—and if we can take the word of Eusebius of Caesarea for it—the main culprit seems to be Constantine himself. The emperor played an active role in the council. Furthermore, he spoke Greek and probably discussed the *homoousios* with the Eastern bishops beforehand.[57]

This does not mean that the *homoousios* was an imposition from an absolute monarch, bent on forcing his clever ideas upon the council. But, after carefully apprehending where the balance of power lay among the bishops, the emperor probably sought unity through his active—even vehement—participation.[58] If Arianism could not triumph, then it needed be decisively condemned, so as to cease to create division in the Church and in the empire. At the end of the proceedings, all but three bishops signed

---

[54] Mullin. *A Short World History of Christianity*, 65.

[55] Cristescu. "The Expression of True Faith," 110.

[56] This is true especially as regards to Hosius of Cordoba, the president of the council, whom some scholars credited as the main promoter of the word. For a refutation of this claim, see Cristescu. "The Expression of True Faith," 111-112. See also Beatrice. "The word 'homoousios.," 255-256.

[57] Cristescu. "The Expression of True Faith," 111.

[58] Cristescu. "The Expression of True Faith," 110.

the creed with the *homoousios* on it.[59] However, even if a significant majority of bishops signed the creed, the new word left many of them uneasy. Contrary to the rest of the Nicene creed, this term did not figure anywhere in scripture[60]—in other words, it was untradi-tional.[61]

In fact, not only was the *homoousios* an innovation, but its pedigree was also highly questionable. Few, if any, orthodox authors had employed the term before, at least in trinitarian theology.[62] To make matters worse, the first authors to ever use *homoousios* were Gnostic theologians in the second century.[63] Since a Gnostic philosopher named Basilides spoke of a "a threefold sonship consubstantial with the god who is not," and a certain Mark the Magician said that "the original Tetrad Dynamis (Power) is consubstantial with the Monas (Unit),"[64] it is very likely that the *homoousios* probably sounded to our fourth century Fathers very similarly as New Age concepts like "energies" sound to the traditionalists of today.

Furthermore, *homoousios* was also associated with the Sabellians. In the mid-third century, some Christians from Libya asked Pope St. Dionysius to condemn the bishop of Alexandria, himself also named Dionysius, because the bishop had refused to proclaim that the Son was *homoousios* with the Father. Though we do not know who these Christians were, it is highly likely that they were Sabellians. Dionysius of Alexandria seems to have suppressed the *homoousios* precisely to oppose the spread of Sabellianism. Dionysius of Rome did take this opportunity to criticize certain erroneous doctrines that went in the opposite direction of the Sabellians—a correction that Dionysius of Alexandria accepted. Even so, the pope never defended

---

[59] Bickerton. "The Development of a Theology of Tradition," 10.

[60] Mullin. *A Short World History of Christianity*, 66. See also Bickerton. "The Development of a Theology of Tradition," 16, and Beatrice. "The word 'homoousios,'" 244.

[61] Lossky. *In the Image and Likeness of God*, 159.

[62] Origen seems to have used it in this context, but only as a way of analogy. See Beatrice. "The word 'homoousios,'" 251.

[63] See Beatrice. "The word 'homoousios,'" 248: "The word 'homoousios'": "Surprising though it may seem, there is total agreement among scholars on at least one point. . . all without exception agree in claiming that the Gnostics were the first theologians to use the word *homoousios*, or at least that before the Gnostics there is no trace at all of its existence."

[64] Beatrice. "The word 'homoousios,'" 249.

the term *homoousios*, thereby suggesting that Rome viewed this word with suspicion.[65]

But where did Constantine get this word from? The answer to that question is still unclear.[66] There is a theory that *homoousios* was meant to firmly exclude Arianism, while being vague enough to allow for the variety of interpretations within the council, conceding latitude of theological debate in a matter still unresolved.[67] On the other hand, it is highly likely that Constantine was acquainted with Egyptian Hermetic theosophy, where the use of *homoousios* was prevalent.[68] It is plausible that he wished to untie the knots of complex trinitarian considerations by taking recourse to the most sophisticated theological concepts of his day, even if they were of pagan origin.[69] A "thinking outside the box," if you will.

Be that as it may, at the end of the Council of Nicaea, Arianism stood condemned. But to do so, the bishops had "innovated" by drawing up a creed with an ambiguous word with shady provenance that very few were very excited about.[70] To make matters worse, the council did not instantaneously end the Christological debates. In some respects, the controversy was yet to peak.[71]

---

[65] Beatrice. "The word 'homoousios,'" 251. See also Cristescu. "The Expression of True Faith," 114-118.

[66] Cristescu. "The Expression of True Faith," 111.

[67] Bickerton. "The Development of a Theology of Tradition," 19.

[68] Beatrice. "The word 'homoousios,'" 264.

[69] Beatrice. "The word 'homoousios,'" 269.

[70] Cristescu. "The Expression of True Faith," 111: "The Eastern attitude regarding homousios can be fully clarified probably due to the Gnostic resonance of the word and of the materialistic ideas given by this."

[71] Bickerton. "The Development of a Theology of Tradition," 19. See also Mullin. *A Short World History of Christianity*, 66: "Nicaea did not end the controversy over Arianism; it was but the first round." As a sidenote, I cannot but notice how traditionalists rail against the Second Vatican Council for allowing confusion and chaos to spread in its aftermath, at the same time that they advance a romanticized view of past councils, as if they had clarified everything very neatly and immediately.

"Innovators, revolutionaries, coiners of new words"

In the years following the council, the polemic did not die out. Rather, it intensified. For three decades, the creed went mostly ignored. Again, the *homoousios* was not universally accepted, given its Gnostic reverberations. Furthermore, as we have seen, the term was ambiguous enough to allow several interpretations. At that time, there was not yet a deep understanding of what the word actually meant.[72] Just like as in pre-Nicene times, when both orthodox and heretics could quote scripture in their favor, now different bishops could cite the creed in diverse and contradictory ways.[73] Since neither scripture nor creed could answer the controversy directly, the interpretation had to come from within the living, believing community. Thus the concept of "tradition" (and most importantly, of "living tradition") matured.[74]

How then, did *homoousios* came to be identified as a hallmark of orthodoxy, as we know it today? As the Eastern Orthodox theologian Vladimir Lossky beautifully summarizes, this word that had been used by Gnostics and heretics was "transformed" by the Church "into words that are pure silver, refined in a furnace on the ground, purified seven times[75] in the crucible of the Holy Spirit and of the free consciousness of those who judge within the tradition."[76] Namely, we must thank two great saints and Fathers of the Church: St. Athanasius of Alexandria and St. Basil of Caesarea. Let us see how they achieved it.

The greatest resistance to the *homoousios* came from Eusebius. Not solely Eusebius of Caesarea—now rehabilitated by the council, thanks to the emperor's influence—but most especially Eusebius of Nicomedia,[77] the priest who ended up baptizing Constantine in his deathbed. After Eusebius's death, his followers tried to achieve a sort of compromise, a

---

[72] Bickerton. "The Development of a Theology of Tradition," 14.

[73] Price. *Chalcedon in Context*, 9. See also Bickerton. "The Development of a Theology of Tradition," 19, 22, and Mullin. *A Short World History of Christianity*, 67.

[74] Bickerton. "The Development of a Theology of Tradition," 18.

[75] Ps 11:7

[76] Lossky. *In the Image and Likeness of God*, 159.

[77] Mullin. *A Short World History of Christianity*, 65-66.

middle-ground position between orthodoxy and Arianism. This "moderate" position would retrospectively be labeled Semi-Arianism.[78]

Semi-Arians tried to soften the *homoousios* by suggesting a replacement: the *homoiousios*. Though the words seem very similar, note that they differ by an "i." Whereas *homoousios* meant that Father and Son were of the "*same* substance," the *homoiousios* meant that they were of "*similar* substances." In the apt words of Robert Mullin, the battle for orthodoxy "hung over one iota, the smallest of Greek letters."[79]

In the 350s, Athanasius started to push back. First, he had to defend himself against the Arian and Semi-Arian charges that the *homoousios* was unscriptural. As we have seen, the Arians were not the only ones who could use scripture to bolster their claim.[80] Athanasius could do the same, namely by quoting the gospel according to St. John. Afterwards, Athanasius would be in solid ground to interrogate his opponents: "So why then, do they bring forward unscriptural phrases for the sake of impiety, and yet accuse those who use unscriptural phrases piously?"[81] As Athanasius would explain, the Council of Nicaea did not try to illegitimately introduce foreign philosophical expressions into the Christian tradition, but *used* those expressions to accurately understand that tradition. Though *homoousios* could not be found in scripture, it accurately expressed the *meaning* of scripture, whereas Arius's misquotations betrayed that meaning.[82]

After establishing that, Athanasius solidified the authority of the council as the measuring stick of orthodoxy and as the proper hermeneutic through which scripture should be read. In his master works, *De Synodis* and *De Decretis Nicaenae Synodi*, Athanasius cemented the primacy of Nicaea over all regional councils that had happened until then.[83] From that point onward, ecumenical councils would be considered authoritative guides to properly distinguish between orthodoxy and heterodoxy.

---

[78] Darras. *General History of the Catholic Church*, 463.

[79] Mullin. *A Short World History of Christianity*, 66. See also Bickerton. "The Development of a Theology of Tradition," 19.

[80] Corbellini. "A Participação de Atanásio," 402-406.

[81] Bickerton. "The Development of a Theology of Tradition," 16.

[82] Corbellini. "A Participação de Atanásio," 405.

[83] Price. *Chalcedon in Context*, 9-10.

St. Basil, on his end, supported the *homoiousios* compromise in the beginning, and only warmed up to *homoousios* by the 360s.[84] Scholars speculate that this delay was due to a certain "discomfort" with the word because of the "lack of clarity in its interpretation."[85] However, Basil was (along with the other Cappadocian Fathers, St. Gregory of Nyssa and St. Gregory of Nazianzus) instrumental in clarifying the meaning of *homoousios*: in God there would be "one *substance*" (*ousia*), but "three *persons*" (*hypostaseis*). This is the trinitarian formulation considered orthodox today.[86]

What pushed Basil into the correct interpretation was his theological work on the Holy Spirit. Since the debate had focused on the proper relation between Father and Son, the third person of the Trinity was left mostly undefined. Basil tried to set things right in his work: *On the Holy Spirit*.[87] Of course, in the hot theological climate of the day, Basil's work could not be left unchallenged. The saint summarizes the accusations leveled up against him:

> They accuse us of innovation, thus framing the charge against us because we confess three Persons. . . [T]hey allege in their charge that their custom does not have this, and that Scripture does not agree. . . What reproachful name have they not called us—innovators, revolutionaries, and wordsmiths?[88]

Please note that, for Basil, "innovator" was a pejorative term: the venerable Father of the Church "connects innovation with moving away from custom and the rule of faith, putting the innovator outside the communion of the Church."[89] And yet, this is precisely what his adversaries accused him of being! Basil needed to defend himself if the theological concept of the three hypostases was to survive. Basil replies:

---

[84] Bickerton. "The Development of a Theology of Tradition," 8.

[85] Bickerton. "The Development of a Theology of Tradition," 21.

[86] Mullin. *A Short World History of Christianity*, 67. See also Bickerton. "The Development of a Theology of Tradition," 21.

[87] Price. *Chalcedon in Context*, 10.

[88] Bickerton. "The Development of a Theology of Tradition," 27-28.

[89] Bickerton. "The Development of a Theology of Tradition," 28.

> How, then, am I an innovator and a coiner of new words, when I furnish on my behalf whole peoples and cities, a custom older than all human memory, and men, pillars of the Church, who were distinguished in all knowledge and power of the Spirit and were the originators and authors of the word?[90]

In other words, St. Basil maintains that his understanding is indeed "apostolic,"[91] but he does so by appealing, not only to scripture, but also to unwritten sources, like custom, the saints, the writings of the Fathers of the Church, worship, and the Christian community. Through this act of *ressourcement*, Basil develops the concept of unwritten tradition that we have explored in chapter 1 of this book:

> Both [scripture and tradition] hold the same power with respect to true religion. . . No one would deny these points, at least no one who has even a little experience of ecclesiastical institutions. . . Standing fast in non-scriptural traditions is, I think, apostolic[92]

Though, of course, the traditions to which St. Basil appeals to are not innovations, his defense is indeed innovative.[93] It would become precedent throughout the history of the Church to argue from tradition, but at the time it was a creative way to use and interpret traditional sources. By showing that unscriptural evidence was a venerable source for the customary use of phrases like "giving glory with the Holy Spirit,"[94] St. Basil effectively developed doctrine in a way Catholics today may take for granted.

In 379 A.D., the new Roman Emperor Theodosius called for another council, this time to take place in the imperial city of Constantinople. This would become the First Council of Constantinople and be considered the second ecumenical council (see chapter 13). Besides confirming Nicaea, the

---

[90] Bickerton. "The Development of a Theology of Tradition," 26.
[91] Bickerton. "The Development of a Theology of Tradition," 26.
[92] Bickerton. "The Development of a Theology of Tradition," 26, 34.
[93] Bickerton. "The Development of a Theology of Tradition," 2, 26, 48.
[94] Bickerton. "The Development of a Theology of Tradition," 32-33.

bishops at Constantinople added a clause to the creed, wherein the Holy Spirit proceeded from the Father and was to be glorified.[95] St. Basil's writings in *On the Holy Spirit* grounded these new creedal statements. The creed as we know it was now fully complete.

But the controversies were not over yet.

Confusion of natures or a natural conclusion?

Though Nicaea and Constantinople had defined the proper relation between the Father and the Son, this in turn raised new tensions. A new *complexio oppositorum* emerged, now as regards to the proper relation between Christ's human and divine natures. Christians now knew that Jesus, while being human, was also God, coeternal with the Father. But what does this mean? How can we say that Jesus was both fully human and fully divine?

One way in which this new *complexio oppositorum* manifested itself more poignantly was in popular devotion. By the fourth century, a relatively recent word started to pop up in Marian prayers, calling the Virgin by the title *Theotokos* ("God-bearer" in Greek, usually translated as "Mother of God.") For obvious reasons, the term found favor among anti-Arian clergy for its clear implications: if Mary was the God-bearer, then this term stood witness to Jesus's full divinity.[96]

Just like the *homoousios*, the word *Theotokos* could not be found anywhere in scripture. The first appearance of the term is often attributed to Origen in 230 AD, being followed in 250 by Dionysius of Alexandria (the same of the "two Dionysii controversy" mentioned earlier in this chapter).[97] However, this origin is contested. The first undisputed use of the word can be found in an encyclical by St. Alexander in 319 AD, announcing Arius's deposition.[98] Later Fathers of the Church, like Athanasius, Basil or Gregory Nazianzene certainly used *Theotokos* as well.[99] But again, it was in Marian popular devotion that the term gained most traction in the fourth and fifth centuries. Some, however, strongly disliked the word. For them,

---

95 Mullin. *A Short World History of Christianity*, 67.

96 Mullin. *A Short World History of Christianity*, 69.

97 Marinou-Boura. "The term Mother of God."

98 Tawfike. "The Mother of God."

99 Artemi. "Cyril of Alexandria's critique."

Mary could never have been the Mother of God, only the mother of the earthly Jesus. These theologians proposed the term *Anthropotokos* as an alternative[100] (meaning "man-bearer.")

The controversy eventually reached the court of Nestorius, the archbishop of Constantinople, in 428 AD. John McGuckin, an Orthodox archpriest and Professor of Theology at the University of Oxford, describes Nestorius in the following terms:

> In fact, in all his doctrinal statements, Nestorius shows himself to be a consistent, if none too clear, exponent of the longstanding Antiochene dogmatic tradition. He is no creative genius; most of what he says being a re-statement of his teacher Theodore of Mopsuestia's viewpoint, but he is an able enough repetiteur of an old tradition, though tragically not one whose genius could extend to remodeling it creatively in the light of a new and pressing need to redraft its understanding of Christ's personal integrity.[101]

Nestorius received and heard both parties: both the *Theotokos* and the *Anthropotokos* supporters had their audience. In the end, Archbishop Nestorius judged that both terms could be interpreted in an orthodox way and that both were imprecise. To avoid confusion, they should adopt the more accurate formulation *Christotokos* ("Christ-bearer") instead.[102]

This ruling did not end the controversy in the least. Those who were in favor of *Anthropotokos* viewed in this decision a confirmation that *Theotokos* was problematic. On the other hand, the adherents to *Theotokos* were not willing to give up their beloved devotion and started to wreak chaos in Constantinople. This, in turn, led Nestorius to crack down on *Theotokos* with even more gusto. In 429 AD, Nestorius initiated a series of lectures wherein both he and his chaplains would preach against the use of *Theotokos.*[103] Eventually, the whole kerfuffle reached Alexandria, where Bishop

---

[100] Mullin. *A Short World History of Christianity*, 70.

[101] McGuckin. *St. Cyril of Alexandria and the Christological controversy*, 22.

[102] McGuckin. *St. Cyril of Alexandria and the Christological controversy*, 28-29.

[103] McGuckin. *St. Cyril of Alexandria and the Christological controversy*, 29-33.

St. Cyril had been following the controversy with much apprehension. Cyril began his own theological study on this question and started to promote the *Theotokos* through a letter to the monks of Egypt.

Nestorius was furious.[104] An exchange of correspondence began between the two bishops. Cyril began by urging Nestorius to reconsider his position. Nestorius's reply is instructive for the purpose of this book:

> *By reading in a superficial way the tradition of those holy men* (you were guilty of a pardonable ignorance), you concluded that they said that the Word who is coeternal with the Father was passible. Please look more closely at their language and you will find out that that divine choir of fathers never said that the consubstantial godhead was capable of suffering, or that the whole being that was coeternal with the Father was recently born, or that it rose again, seeing that it had itself been the cause of resurrection of the destroyed temple. If you apply my words as fraternal medicine, *I shall set the words of the holy fathers before you and shall free them from the slander against them and through them against the holy scriptures.* "I believe", they say, "also in our Lord Jesus Christ, his only begotten Son". See how they first lay as foundations "Lord" and "Jesus" and "Christ" and "only begotten" and "Son", the names which belong jointly to the divinity and humanity. *Then they build on that foundation the tradition of the incarnation and resurrection and passion.* In this way, by prefixing the names which are common to each nature, they intend to avoid separating expressions applicable to sonship and lordship and at the same time escape the danger of destroying the distinctive character of the natures by absorbing them into the one title of "Son". . . *These are the traditions of the holy fathers. These are the precepts of the holy scriptures.*[105]

Meanwhile, Rome was keeping tabs on the whole discussion as well. Cyril of Alexandria had been informing Pope St. Celestine I about the developments of this debate the whole time. Nestorius, on his part, also sent some letters to the pope. In one of them, Nestorius even admitted that he did

[104] McGuckin. *St. Cyril of Alexandria and the Christological controversy*, 33.
[105] Nestorius. "Reply to Cyril of Alexandria."

not oppose the word *Theotokos* in itself, only that it could spread "*confusion*" about the human and divine natures of Jesus.[106]

The pope, however, had taken Cyril's side. In 430, Celestine invested Cyril with his papal authority and charged him to deliver a final letter to Nestorius: either he would disavow his position in ten days, or he would be excommunicated and deposed. Nestorius, however, did not yield. Rather, he used his influence with Emperor Theodosius II to convince him to convoke a new ecumenical council, the third of its kind.[107] This council would be held at Ephesus, in Asia Minor—the place where, according to tradition, the Virgin Mary lived her last years on earth.

Both Nestorius and Cyril, alongside their own suffragan bishops, arrived at the specified date for the opening of the council, but a contingent of bishops from Antioch—supportive of Nestorius—and the legates of Rome were delayed for several days. Two of the Antiochene bishops were sent ahead and asked for the opening of the council to be postponed for five days. Since after sixteen days they were still not at Ephesus, Cyril and his bishops—who were the majority—interpreted this as stalling and voted to initiate the proceedings. Cyril assumed the presidency and summoned Nestorius to appear before the council, which he refused as a protest of how things were being conducted.

The first session began on June 22, 431. Cyril read the Nicene creed and then his own letters to Nestorius, as well as Nestorius's replies, and the letters of the pope to Cyril. The bishops then declared Nestorius anathema and signed a declaration wherein he was deposed. Nestorius refused to receive it. A few days later, the contingent from Antioch arrived. Knowing of what had happened, they refused to be received by St. Cyril and instead held their own parallel synod, where they deposed Cyril of Alexandria and declared that the other conciliar bishops would be forgiven if they recanted the anathemas.

In the meantime, the papal legates arrived and sided with the party of Cyril, allowing the proceedings of the Council of Ephesus to continue. As time went on, Nestorius understood that his defeat was inevitable and

---

[106] Nestorius. "Third Letter to Celestine."

[107] Chapman. "Council of Ephesus."

asked to retire to a monastery.[108] The Council of Ephesus anathematized those who would not confess that the Virgin Mary was the Mother of God. The *Theotokos*, just like the *homoousios* before it, had definitely entered into the Christian tradition.

St. Vincent—an unexpected development

A few years after the closing of the Council of Ephesus, a certain Peregrinus (Latin for "pilgrim") wrote a book called *Commonitorium.* It is widely accepted that Peregrinus was a pseudonym for a monk from Gaul (today France) called Vincent of Lérins. This is the famous author that I mentioned in the beginning of this chapter, the theologian who articulated the rules a true doctrinal development should follow if it were to be legitimate and not a corruption of the faith. Among these rules is the celebrated motto: "in the same sense, with the same meaning."

But why did St. Vincent write this book? What was its purpose? As Thomas Guarino explains, Vincent was concerned with what had happened at Ephesus a couple of years earlier, and also with the resurgence of Arianism. His objective was to defend the authority of the Councils of Nicaea and Ephesus. To do that, he would explain how to differentiate between Christian orthodoxy and heresy.[109] The criteria to determine where proper doctrine lay were threefold: "universality, antiquity, consent."[110]

These three criteria are disposed in their proper order of appeal. So, for instance, the criterium of universality is defined by St. Vincent as confessing "that one faith to be true, which the whole Church throughout the world confesses."[111] But what if "a small portion of the Church" (or even the whole) "have cut itself off from the communion of the universal faith?"[112] In that case, we must appeal to antiquity. This is the rationale

---

[108] The council proceedings described here were based on Chapman. "Council of Ephesus." As a side note, I cannot avoid noticing how the Second Vatican Council was much more orderly and exempt from external political forces than the Councils of Nicaea and Ephesus. And yet, traditionalists believe these earlier councils were guided by the Holy Spirit. Therefore, I find their lack of faith in the Second Vatican Council disturbing.

[109] Guarino. *The Disputed Teachings*, 11.

[110] Vincent of Lérins, *Commonitorium*, chap. 2.

[111] Vincent of Lérins, *Commonitorium*, chap. 2.

[112] Vincent of Lérins, *Commonitorium*, chap. 3.

used by many traditionalists today, since they believe that a significant part of the Church went astray.

But how do we recognize antiquity? Vincent defines it as not departing "from those interpretations which it is manifest were notoriously held by our holy ancestors and fathers."[113] To this rule of antiquity, he opposes "novelty": every heresy is an evil resulting from a novel doctrine.[114]

However, Vincent recognizes a problem, the same problem we mentioned earlier in the chapter. Though the canon of scripture is "complete," it still requires the authority of the Church for interpretation, since "owing to the depth of Holy Scripture, all do not accept it in one and the same sense, but one understands its words in one way, another in another; so that it seems to be capable of as many interpretations as there are interpreters."[115] So, in chapter 25 of his *Commonitorium*, the saint acknowledges that heretics can appeal to scripture to more easily deceive.[116]

So it happens that, though heretics are always innovators, they often try to appropriate the criterium of antiquity for themselves. This *modus operandi*, however, is not limited to the use of scripture. Heretics can also quote passages from ancient writers in support of their novelties, "so that they get the credit of being neither the first nor the only persons who have held it."[117] So, St. Vincent warns:

> *But the more secretly they [the heretics] conceal themselves under shelter of the Divine Law, so much the more are they to be feared and guarded against.* For they know that the evil stench of their doctrine will hardly find acceptance with any one if it be exhaled pure and simple. *They sprinkle it over, therefore, with the perfume of heavenly language, in order that one who would be ready to despise human error, may hesitate to condemn divine words.* They do, in fact, what nurses do when they would prepare some bitter draught for children; they smear the edge of the cup

---

[113] Vincent of Lérins, *Commonitorium*, chap. 2.

[114] Vincent of Lérins, *Commonitorium*, chap. 4.

[115] Vincent of Lérins, *Commonitorium*, chap. 2.

[116] Also, in chapter 26, he points out the precedent that the Devil also quoted scripture when tempting Jesus (cf. Mt 4:6.)

[117] Vincent of Lérins, *Commonitorium*, chap. 7.

> all round with honey, that the unsuspecting child, having first tasted the sweet, may have no fear of the bitter. So too do these act, who disguise poisonous herbs and noxious juices under the names of medicines, so that no one almost, when he reads the label, suspects the poison.
>
> It was for this reason that the Saviour cried, Beware of false prophets who come to you in sheep's clothing, but inwardly they are ravening wolves (Mt 7:15). What is meant by sheep's clothing? What but the words which prophets and apostles with the guilelessness of sheep wove beforehand as fleeces, for that immaculate Lamb which takes away the sin of the world? What are the ravening wolves? What but the savage and rabid glosses of heretics, who continually infest the Church's folds, and tear in pieces the flock of Christ wherever they are able? *But that they may with more successful guile steal upon the unsuspecting sheep,* retaining the ferocity of the wolf, *they put off his appearance, and wrap themselves, so to say, in the language of the Divine Law*, as in a fleece, so that one, having felt the softness of wool, may have no dread of the wolf's fangs.[118]

In fact, the deception can be so great that even "eminent men" i.e., "certain excellent persons, and of position in the Church, are often permitted by God to preach novel doctrines to Catholics."[119] These people could even have been great champions of orthodoxy against heresy, before falling themselves into a heresy of their own. Among many examples, St. Vincent mentions none other than Nestorius, since at the beginning of his episcopate, Nestorius "was zealously inveighing against the blasphemies of all heresies."[120] Vincent both admonishes and comforts the unfortunate

---

[118] Vincent of Lérins, *Commonitorium*, chap. 25.

[119] Vincent of Lérins, *Commonitorium*, chap. 10.

[120] Vincent of Lérins, *Commonitorium*, chap. 11. Cf. McGuckin. *St. Cyril of Alexandria and the Christological controversy*, 23-24: "On assuming office Nestorius set to work, in much the same way as had Cyril sixteen years earlier, by attempting to bring his episcopal city to a common religious view and practice. . . He also dismayed many members of the aristocracy when he began to apply legal proscriptions against the heretics with little regard for the political ramifications. He possibly composed, as his own initiative, the harsh terms of anti-heretical legislation we find issued from the court of Theodosius at this time (428). One of his first acts in fleshing out the legal policy was to order a demolition squad against the last

Catholic who may feel tempted to follow these former defenders of the faith: "And assuredly it is a great trial when one whom you believe to be a prophet, a disciple of prophets, a doctor and defender of the truth, whom you have folded to your breast with the utmost veneration and love, when such a one of a sudden secretly and furtively brings in noxious errors, which you can neither quickly detect, being held by the prestige of former authority, nor lightly think it right to condemn, being prevented by affection for your old master."[121] Finally, the criterium of antiquity may also not be fully applicable when the heresy is "already widely diffused and of old standing. . . seeing that through lapse of time they have long had opportunity of corrupting the truth."[122]

So, just like when the criterium of universality falters, we must take recourse to antiquity, so also when the principle of antiquity is not sufficient, we must fall back to the rule of "consent," defined as: "to the consentient definitions and determinations of all, or at the least of almost all priests and doctors."[123] This is done by appealing, in doctrinal matters already defined, to the decrees of a general (ecumenical) council.[124]

Thus, we have come full circle to St. Vincent's point: the defense of the authority of councils against the heresies of his time, even if heretics also appealed to antiquity for their claims. Writing three years after the Council of Ephesus, Vincent seeks to theologically solidify the decrees of this council and to curtail the spread of the Nestorian heresy. It is no

---

remaining Arian chapel in Constantinople." Also, we must not forget that Arius was a stark opponent of the Sabellian heresy.

121 Vincent of Lérins, *Commonitorium*, chap. 10.

122 Vincent of Lérins, *Commonitorium*, chap. 27.

123 Vincent of Lérins, *Commonitorium*, chap. 2.

124 Vincent of Lérins, *Commonitorium*, chap. 27: "And if at any time a part opposes itself to the whole, novelty to antiquity, the dissent of one or a few who are in error to the consent of all or at all events of the great majority of Catholics, then they must prefer the soundness of the whole to the corruption of a part; in which same whole they must prefer the religion of antiquity to the profaneness of novelty; *and in antiquity itself in like manner, to the temerity of one or of a very few they must prefer, first of all, the general decrees, if such there be, of a Universal Council*, or if there be no such, then, what is next best, they must follow the consentient belief of many and great masters."

wonder then, that the antepenultimate chapter of the *Commonitorium* praises Ephesus as a hallmark of "constancy," "humility and sanctity," so that the conciliar bishops "innovated nothing, presumed nothing, arrogated to themselves absolutely nothing, but used all possible care to hand down nothing to posterity but what they had themselves received from their Fathers."[125] The next chapter is spent praising Pope St. Celestine and his successor Sixtus III, in their "zeal. . . in opposing novelty" throughout the Nestorian ordeal.[126] The *Commonitorium* is a hymn to the magisterial authority of the Catholic Church.

But how can we say, after all that we learned in this chapter, that the Council Fathers "innovated nothing?" Did they not promulgate new words, like the *homoousios* or *Theotokos*? Certainly, St. Vincent did not ignore that these terms were unscriptural, since that was one of the main criticisms coming from the heretic side. So, how can we say that the councils were interpreting tradition (i.e., antiquity) "in the same sense, with the same meaning?"[127]

To answer this question, we must go back to Athanasius's defense of the *homoousios*. This word cannot be found in scripture, but it accurately *expressed* the *meaning* of scripture, a meaning that was present in the Christian community the whole time, even if *this community could not fully articulate this teaching at the time*. This is how "same sense, same meaning" must be interpreted, not as a way to deny that change ever occurs. In fact, that would contravene the clear sense of the *Commonitorium* since, as we have seen in chapter 3, to deny progress in religion—even supervening great variation in form, shape, and outward appearance—would be motivated by "envy of others" and "hate towards God."[128]

The *Commonitorium* accepts "all possible progress." It uses the Councils of Nicaea and of Ephesus as examples of such progress. If we are to reconcile the Vincentian rules with what history tells us about the pedigree of the words *homoousios* and *Theotokos*, then we must accept the rule "same sense, same meaning" properly. Namely, we must read it in tandem with Pope Francis's favorite Vincentian quote, that doctrine be "*consolidated by*

---

[125] Vincent of Lérins, *Commonitorium*, chap. 31.
[126] Vincent of Lérins, *Commonitorium*, chap. 32.
[127] Guarino. *The Disputed Teachings*, 12.
[128] Vincent of Lérins, *Commonitorium*, chap. 23.

years, enlarged by time, refined by age."[129] This is what happened in the first ecumenical councils, as we have seen.

For St. Vincent, doctrinal development is not only possible, but also the *only* possible outcome. It is impossible to stop doctrinal development, as it is impossible to stop a healthy human body from growing (see chapter 3). By defending the use of *homoousios* by the Council of Nicaea and of *Theotokos* by the Council of Ephesus, Vincent exemplifies the true balance between "same sense, same meaning" and "consolidated by years, enlarged by time, refined by age" that a legitimate doctrinal development must meet. It is not, as we have seen, a simplistic appeal to antiquity, as heretics are also capable of doing. Rather, it must be antiquity as read through *consent*, namely the consent of the magisterial agents with authority to interpret tradition (not forgetting the criterium of universality as well.) For St. Vincent, the worse novelties of his time were the attempts to reverse the decisions of the councils, even if those who sought them also appealed to scripture and antiquity.[130]

---

[129] Vincent of Lérins, *Commonitorium*, chap. 23. Cf. Guarino. *The Disputed Teachings*, 12-13.

[130] Guarino. *The Disputed Teachings*, 13.

Chapter 7

"What earlier generations held as sacred . . ."

I emphasize again that the liturgical life, and the study of it, must lead to greater ecclesial unity, not division. When liturgical life becomes something of a banner of division, there is the odour of the devil, the deceiver, in there. It is not possible to worship God and at the same time turn liturgy into a battlefield for issues that are not essential, or indeed for outdated questions and to take sides, starting from the liturgy, on ideologies that divide the Church. The Gospel and the Tradition of the Church demand that we are steadfastly united on the essential matters, and in sharing legitimate differences in the harmony of the Spirit.

—Francis, Address to the Pontifical Liturgical Institute

Let us turn our calendars back to 2016. In a July 5 address to a conference on the liturgy, Cardinal Robert Sarah, then prefect for the Congregation for Divine Worship, said that he believed "it is very important that we return as soon as possible to *ad orientem* worship."[1]

For some context, *ad orientem* ("towards the east" in Latin) means that, during mass, both priest and congregation face the same direction, towards the liturgical "east," (the direction of the rising sun, symbolizing Jesus's resurrection.) This is contrasted with *versus populum* ("towards the people,") where priest and congregation face each other.

These stances, valid as they are, overflowed beyond the realm of liturgical rubrics and into the domain of liturgy wars. Though there are instances of *versus populum* before the Second Vatican Council, this stance is usually associated with the liturgical reforms proceeding from the council. *Ad orientem*, on the other hand, though fitting with the reformed liturgy, is preferred by traditionalists, given its antiquity.[2]

Cardinal Sarah continued, to thundering applause: "[P]riests and congregation facing same direction, eastwards, or at least towards the apse, towards the Lord who comes, at those points when we address God in the liturgical rite. . . And so, dear fathers, I ask you to implement this practice whenever possible, with prudence and the necessary catechesis and

---

[1] Blackman. "Cardinal Sarah Promotes Advent Launch."

[2] Blackman. "Cardinal Sarah Promotes Advent Launch."

pastoral competence, knowing that this is something good for the Church and the people of God."[3]

In the same conference, Cardinal Sarah also declared that Pope Francis had given him a green light to "study the question of a reform of the reform and how to enrich the two forms of the Roman rite."[4] "Reform of the reform" is a term often employed by those who believe that the implementation of the liturgical reforms post-Vatican II has gone awry and that a new reform must be conducted, bringing the liturgy back to a more traditional practice.

Thomas Lawson was delighted to hear this. Maybe this could be the turning point! The first step towards the normalization of traditional-ism! The beginning of the end of the *Novus Ordo* and all its liturgical abuses! One could only wish…

His expectations would soon be dashed. A few days later, the Vatican spokesman Federico Lombardi told the press that the Holy Father had met with Cardinal Sarah on July 9, indicating that there were no new liturgical directives. According to Fr. Lombardi, "Mass can be celebrated at it facing the people, which is desirable wherever possible." Furthermore, it was better "to avoid the use of the expression 'reform of the reform,' referring to the liturgy, given that it's sometimes the source of misunderstandings." Also, Pope Francis would have expressly "recalled that the 'ordinary' form of the celebration of Mass is that foreseen by the missal promulgated by Paul VI, and that the 'extraordinary' form permitted by Benedict XVI should not take the place of that 'ordinary' form."[5]

A month later, Cardinal Sarah would also clarify that the way his remarks were relayed was not accurate. However, he would also reiterate: "When the modern liturgy is celebrated in the vernacular with the priest 'facing the people,' there is a danger of man, even of the priest himself and his personality, becoming too central."[6]

As for Pope Francis, he was even more forceful one year later when, in an address to Italian liturgists, he placed his whole magisterial authority upon the post-Vatican II liturgical reforms: "We can affirm with certainty

---

[3] Blackman. "Cardinal Sarah Promotes Advent Launch."

[4] Cornwell. "Cardinal Sarah to conduct study."

[5] Catholic News Service. "Vatican rejects Cardinal Sarah's *ad orientem* appeal."

[6] Backler. "Cardinal Sarah reiterates *ad orientem*."

and with *magisterial authority* that the liturgical reform is *irreversible*."[7] He would also explain that "to speak of 'the reform of the reform' is an error."[8] Though Pope Francis acknowledges that we must avoid the liturgical abuses undertaken under the cover of the council's reforms, we must also avoid a resistance to the council's reforms undertaken under the cover of the expression "reform of the reform."[9] As legitimate as the concerns for liturgical abuse are, this expression now carries a heavy ideological baggage that one must avoid.

Of course, Thomas Lawson was furious with this throwback. In an email to his friend Justin, he wrote: "How dare Bergoglio stop us from

---

[7] Francis. "To Participants in the 68th National Liturgical Week." N.A., I wish to avoid future misunderstandings here, like the one advanced by traditionalists, when they claim that the TLM cannot be reformed because St. Pius V, in *Quo Primum*, decreed that this missal should be followed "in perpetuity." Neither Pius, nor Francis, meant to bind future popes and councils. This language is meant to be sweeping and forceful so that the full authority of the magisterial agent is placed on the intended liturgical reforms, to quell the resistance of their day and age. It means that the pope "intended to bind the Church to his liturgical policy until such time as it was changed by competent (i.e., papal) authority, and therefore 'in perpetuity' if it was never changed." (See Mirus, "Pope St. Pius V and *Quo Primum*.") Though there is a strong possibility—given the wide span of human history that the future still holds—that the reforms of the Second Vatican Council may one day themselves be reformed, this cannot serve as an excuse for resistance in the present. If the pope used his magisterial authority to say that the reform is irreversible, traditionalists who resist the liturgical reforms because they are waiting for a sympathetic pope are being disobedient to the manifest mind and will of the pope. This is the error of the progressive dissenters: not to follow the magisterium as it is, but as one hopes it to be some day.

[8] Connell. "Pope Francis: There will be no 'the reform of the reform.'" See also

[9] See Francis, "Letter to the Holy Father Francis to the Bishops of the whole world that accompanies the Apostolic Letter Motu Proprio Data '*Traditionis Custodes*'": "At the same time, *I am saddened by abuses* in the celebration of the liturgy on all sides. In common with Benedict XVI, I deplore the fact that 'in many places the prescriptions of the new Missal are not observed in celebration, but indeed come to be interpreted as an authorization for or even a requirement of creativity, which leads to almost unbearable distortions.' But I am nonetheless saddened that the instrumental use of *Missale Romanum* of 1962 *is often characterized by a rejection not only of the liturgical reform, but of the Vatican Council II* itself, claiming, with unfounded and unsustainable assertions, that it betrayed the Tradition and the 'true Church.'"

celebrating *ad orientem*, when this liturgical tradition goes back to the first centuries of the Church, and was celebrated by so many saints?" Justin tried to explain that no one had stopped anyone from doing anything, merely that the *status quo* had not changed. But Tom doubled down. He sent his friend a quote from Benedict XVI:

> "In the history of the liturgy there is growth and progress, but no rupture. *What earlier generations held as sacred, remains sacred and great for us too, and it cannot be all of a sudden entirely forbidden or even considered harmful.* It behooves all of us to preserve the riches which have developed in the Church's faith and prayer, and to give them their proper place."[10]

This quote would become one of Tom's favorites. He would make a meme out of it, with a black and white picture of Benedict XVI on the background. He would then recirculate this meme whenever he was faced with some kind of liturgical stumbling block. Two occasions would trigger this meme reflex. The first one was in the 2020, at the height of the COVID-19 pandemic, when the Church imposed sensible restrictions on the attendance of mass to contain the spread of the virus.[11] The second one was, obviously, when Pope Francis issued *Traditionis Custodes.*

But where did this quote come from? When Benedict XVI issued *Summorum Pontificum*, turning the pre-Vatican II edition of the Roman missal into an extraordinary form of the Roman Rite, he also published a letter to all the bishops of the world to better explain how he wished his *motu proprio* to be implemented. Of course, if Tom had read this letter in its totality he would have seen the proper context of his quote. The very sentence before the quote said: "There is no contradiction between the two

---

[10] Benedict XVI. "Letter to the Bishops in the occasion of the publication of *Summorum Pontificum*."

[11] Hall. "'Prayers answered'": "When the lockdowns were imposed in March 2020, millions of Catholics in North America had no access to Mass at all. For many, this was a time of spiritual trial and a test of faith, as Catholics are required — under normal circumstances — to attend Mass every Sunday, but could not. As fears about COVID began to fade after it was clear that a new plague had not emerged, many Catholics were frustrated that their bishops did not stand up for their right to receive Christ in the Eucharist."

editions of the Roman Missal."[12]—something that Tom denied, as he considered the *Novus Ordo* illicit. The very sentence after the quote reads: "Needless to say, in order to experience full communion, the priests of the communities adhering to the former usage cannot, as a matter of principle, exclude celebrating according to the new books. The total exclusion of the new rite would not in fact be consistent with the recognition of its value and holiness."[13]—which, again, was not Tom's position.

Also, as Justin took care to point out, *Summorum Pontificum* was not meant to be the final word on the matter. Benedict asked the bishops to send an account of their experiences three years afterwards. He specifically said that: "If truly serious difficulties come to light, ways to remedy them can be sought."[14] Surely the amount of resistance to papal and conciliar authority coming from traditionalist circles constitutes a "serious difficulty."

However, the question remained: was Benedict's quote to be taken as an immutable truth, to be applied indiscriminately always and everywhere? Or was it a revisable statement made in a particular context, not at all parallel to 2021, when a significant part of traditionalist Catholic media was severely attacking the Vicar of Christ?

"Obeying God rather than man"

By the second century AD, the Church was divided. The point of contention: how to observe Easter, the most important celebration of the Christian calendar. There were two different ways to go about it:

On one side, the vast majority of the Church used a solar calendar, developed by a Jewish sect called "the Essenes." In this calendar, feast days would always fall on the same weekday each year. In other words, Easter

---

[12] Benedict XVI. "Letter to the Bishops in the occasion of the publication of *Summorum Pontificum*."

[13] Benedict XVI. "Letter to the Bishops in the occasion of the publication of *Summorum Pontificum*."

[14] Benedict XVI. "Letter to the Bishops in the occasion of the publication of *Summorum Pontificum*."

would always fall on a Sunday,[15] for Jesus had resurrected on the day after the sabbath.[16] In effect, several scholarly articles suggest that the *weekly* Christian Sunday, so familiar to us today, could have evolved from the *annual* Easter Sunday celebration.[17]

The other side of the dispute, comprised mainly by the Church in the Roman province of Asia (current day Turkey,) used a lunar calendar wherein feast days could fall on different days of the week each year.[18] In this practice, Christians would celebrate Easter on the same day as the Jewish *Pascha*, on the fourteenth day of the Hebrew month of *Nisan*.[19] These Christians were called Quartodecimans, from the Latin *quarta decima*, meaning "fourteenth."

By the mid-second century, the bishop St. Polycarp of Smyrna—a disciple of St. John the apostle—came to Rome to meet Pope St. Anicetus and settle the Easter dispute. According to the historian Eusebius of Caesarea (see chapter 6): "Polycarp could not persuade the Pope, nor the Pope, Polycarp. The controversy was not ended but the bonds of charity were not broken." In other words, the pope permitted diversity of practice, allowing Polycarp to keep celebrating Easter as he was accustomed.[20] But soon, this division would grow into a major rift…

By the year 189 AD, a certain Victor was elected pope. He would have a significant impact in the liturgy for millennia to come, for two reasons. The first reason has to do with the Easter controversy. The second has to do with the use of Latin. Let us explore the latter for a bit, since the insights we can gain here are extremely interesting in their own right.

Before Victor's papacy, the Church had historically used two languages in its liturgy: 1) Hebrew and 2) *Koine* Greek. The former had been the language Jesus and the apostles used in their prayers, both at the synagogue and at the temple. But it was soon replaced as a sacred language by Greek,

---

[15] Strand. "John as a Quartodeciman," 251.

[16] Luke 23:53-24:6. Also, there could have been an influence of the Essene practice of observing the first-fruits celebration of the barley harvest on a Sunday, so that a parallel would be established between the concept of firstfruits and the resurrection of Christ. See Strand. "Sunday Easter and Quartodecimanism," 131.

[17] Strand. "Sunday Easter and Quartodecimanism," 127, 131.

[18] Strand. "John as a Quartodeciman," 251.

[19] Strand. "Sunday Easter and Quartodecimanism," 127.

[20] Campbell. "Pope St. Anicetus."

the *lingua franca* across the Roman Empire, particularly its eastern half (where the Christianization of the Gentiles was initially more intense—see chapter 5).[21] Even today, some words in the Christian lexicon have vestiges from the time when these languages were seen as the only ones capable of accurately relaying certain religious elements. So, we have amen, hosanna, and alleluia in Hebrew, and Eucharist, apostle, and bishop (*episcopus*) in Greek.[22] We must not forget that even the words "Christian" and "Catholic" come from the Greek.

This would change under Pope St. Victor. According to St. Jerome, a Father of the Church, Victor was the first Latin writer of the Church, since he wrote several letters and theological treatises in Latin instead of Greek.[23] This in effect made Latin the official language of the Roman Church during Victor's papacy.[24] It has also been argued that Victor may have been the first pope to use Latin in his liturgy.[25]

With these small, subtle steps, Victor set in motion a trend towards a progressive Latinization of the Church. This would deeply shape the face of Catholicism as we know it today. As Christianity spread more and more into the western half of the Roman Empire, the number of colloquial Latin speakers gradually overtook the number of Greek speakers inside the Church. For a couple centuries, Greek remained the liturgical language, since it had been introduced by eastern missionaries who had brought Christianity to the West. After all, liturgical languages tend to be conservative, as people are reluctant to change them out of respect for their predecessors.[26] As Prof. Christine Mohrmann, a twentieth century specialist in ancient Greek and Latin says: "at the moment the Western Christian communities were latinized, there existed already a well-established Greek patrimony: several generations of Christians had spoken Greek and consequently all the ecclesiastical institutions had got Greek names; Christian

---

[21] Groen. "The Interplay of Hebrew, Greek and Latin," 40-41.

[22] Mohrmann. "How Latin Came to Be," 284. See also Groen. "The Interplay of Hebrew, Greek and Latin," 43.

[23] Kirsch. "Pope St. Victor I."

[24] Editors of Encyclopaedia Britannica. "Saint Victor I."

[25] Catholic News Agency. "Pope St. Victor I."

[26] Groen. "The Interplay of Hebrew, Greek and Latin," 49-50.

ideas were formulated in Greek; the Bible circulated for several generations in Greek."[27]

But by the mid-third century, Greek had become almost unintelligible for most Christians. Mixed services, both in Greek and in the vernacular Latin, became more common. This had a positive impact in the evangelization of the empire, as it made Christianity more accessible. For example, in rural, isolated areas, Latin might have been the exclusive language of the liturgy, as these regions did not have substantial contact with Greek. In keeping with the tradition started by Pope Victor, the Roman diocese's official correspondence started to be issued in Latin (at least, when addressing the western part of the empire.)[28]

When the Roman Empire (of the West) fell in the fifth century, Latin had already become a Christian language, modified to address the demands of the Christian religion.[29] Without the empire's framework, Latin gradually transformed into the several Romance languages of today, falling into disuse in everyday life. But the Church kept Latin alive in her liturgy, scripture, and tradition.[30] Nowadays, Latin is no longer the vernacular, but the liturgical language of the Catholic Church. Traditionalists today resist the implementation of vernacular at mass, while indefatigably seeking the restoration of the central role of Latin—not Greek or Hebrew.

But let us now return to the Easter controversy. Pope St. Victor revolutionized the Church also on this point. In fact, some of those theological treatises that Victor wrote in Latin were precisely about the proper dating of Easter.[31] Victor wanted a consensus on the universal Church about this matter. So, he requested synods to be held across the globe to settle this question.[32]

According to Eusebius, synods were held in Rome, Jerusalem, Gaul (present-day France), Pontus (Turkey), Osrhoene (Turkey and Syria), and Corinth (Greece). All these synods voted unanimously in favor of the

---

[27] Mohrmann. "How Latin Came to Be," 282.

[28] Groen. "The Interplay of Hebrew, Greek and Latin," 50-51.

[29] Mohrmann. "How Latin Came to Be," 277.

[30] Mohrmann. "How Latin Came to Be," 279.

[31] Kirsch. "Pope St. Victor I."

[32] Ybarra. "Pope Victor I & the Roman Primacy."

Sunday Easter celebration.[33] One sole Quartodeciman dissent remained: the church of Asia, led by the bishop Polycrates of Ephesus.

Polycrates sent a letter to Victor explaining his reasoning. He drew a very impressive list of irreproachable saints who had celebrated according to the Quartodeciman tradition. Among them was St. Polycarp of Smyrna, as we have seen, but also—and most importantly—the apostles St. Philip and St. John.[34] In response to this letter, Victor excommunicated, not only Polycrates, but all the Quartodeciman Christians in the Roman province of Asia.

Bishops of the day and historians of today both judge Pope Victor's actions very harshly as a disproportionate exercise of sheer authority. However, they tend to overlook one important fact. Polycrates did not merely argue that the Quartodeciman practice was apostolic and legitimate. The Asian bishop also claimed that his was the older practice.[35] In his letter, Polycrates wrote that he had "kept the fourteenth day of the Passover according to the gospel, never departing from it but obeying the *rule of faith*. . . We ought to obey God rather than man." This is very strongly worded. "Rule of faith" was the term used to describe that which separated orthodoxy from heterodoxy. By saying he was following the rule of faith, Polycrates was implicitly accusing, not only Victor, but also all the synods held in the rest of the world, of heterodoxy.[36] Pope Victor's drastic measures were aimed at restoring the Catholic unity broken by Polycrates's letter.

Either way, Pope Victor did indeed receive some rebukes from his fellow bishops. Amongst these was St. Irenaeus of Lyons, the formidable confuter of Gnostics discussed in the beginning of chapter 6. Though a bishop in Gaul, Irenaeus was born in Asia, and so was sympathetic towards the Quartodecimans. In his letter to the pontiff, Irenaeus recalls the cordial

---

[33] Daneshmand. "When Heresy was Orthodox."

[34] Daneshmand. "When Heresy was Orthodox." Prof. Strand from Andrews University raises an interesting question: maybe this divergence really happened in apostolic times, and this might explain the discrepancies in the chronology of the events of the Passion week as they are depicted in the gospel according to St. John and the synoptic gospels (see Strand. "John as a Quartodeciman," 254.)

[35] Daneshmand. "When Heresy was Orthodox."

[36] Ybarra. "Pope Victor I & the Roman Primacy."

relations that Rome had traditionally established with the Quartodecimans. He lists none other than five popes who had allowed diversity in practice, including the aforementioned Pope Anicetus (the one who received Polycarp of Smyrna.)[37] For him, both traditions were apostolic and, therefore, legitimate.

Be that as it may, even if St. Irenaeus, alongside other bishops, disagreed with Pope Victor's actions as being too harsh or imprudent, none contended that Victor was acting outside the bounds of his authority.[38] As bishop of Rome, Victor had the authority to summon synods to settle a liturgical question and to excommunicate whole churches outside of his diocese. Here we can already see a consolidation of the concept of papal primacy, which would develop further as centuries went on.

We do not know if Pope Victor relented of his excommunications or not.[39] But we know the problem needed be addressed once again in the fourth century. As we have seen in chapter 6, Emperor Constantine wanted to quell doctrinal disunity within the Church. It was only fitting that he would take the opportunity to also tackle liturgical disunity. So, he asked the Council of Nicaea to look into this matter once more.

Interestingly, though it seems like the Quartodeciman practice did become more widespread by the fourth century, its demographics had shifted in the meantime. Now, the Roman province of Asia overwhelmingly celebrated Easter on a Sunday. The Quartodeciman tradition, on the other hand, had moved eastward, away from Rome's sphere of influence, into the regions of Syria and Mesopotamia.[40]

Predictably, the Council of Nicaea reaffirmed the more popular tradition of Easter Sunday. A letter was sent asking "all the brethren in the East who have hitherto followed the Jewish practice" to "henceforth observe the custom of the Romans."[41] The Quartodeciman practice survived a couple hundred years more but had already received its final death blow at the

---

[37] Strand. "Sunday Easter and Quartodecimanism," 128-129.

[3838] An impressive collection of quotes from historians—some even hostile to the papacy—agreeing with this proposition can be found in Ybarra. "Pope Victor I & the Roman Primacy."

[39] Ybarra. "Pope Victor I & the Roman Primacy."

[40] Strand. "Sunday Easter and Quartodecimanism," 134-135.

[41] Ybarra. "Pope Victor I & the Roman Primacy."

hands of pope and council. Slowly, but surely, the ancient and apostolic Quartodeciman tradition withered into oblivion…

Imposing on people's rites

Nowadays, the Catholic Church allows the coexistence of no less than seven liturgical traditions—also called "rite families"—in her bosom.[42] Among these, the most predominant (namely in the West) is the Latin rite family. In turn, this family of rites encompasses several rites, like the Roman rite. The latter is the source of the controversy with traditionalists today. Before the liturgical reforms called for the Second Vatican Council, the Roman rite in use was the missal of Pope St. Pius V, last revised by St. John XXIII. Since many traditionalists seemed to refuse Vatican II's liturgical reforms, Pope Benedict XVI sought to achieve unity by making the previous missal an *extraordinary* form of the Roman rite, whereas the reformed missal would be the *ordinary* (common) form. *Traditionis Custodes* tried to restore uniformity within the post-Vatican II liturgy by rolling back on Benedict's concessions.

Just by looking at this recent example we can appreciate how, as regards to liturgy, the Church seems to wobble between periods of tolerance of diversity and imposition of uniformity. But how did the Roman rite come to be? Studying its history will certainly allow us to understand what is happening today.

Though some first century authors like St. Justin Martyr provide a general outline of how mass was celebrated in earlier times, we still do not have many details about the primitive liturgy of the first three centuries. *The Catholic Encyclopedia* states that "there was a certain uniformity of type . . . not a uniformity of detail, but one of general outline." In other words, we cannot speak of a fixed rite, but of a more fluid liturgy, with certain significant and recurring expressions eventually crystallizing into liturgical formulas.[43]

---

[42] CCC 1203.

[43] Fortescue. "Liturgy."

Eventually, this proto-rite condensed into the main "mother" liturgies we know today, namely the Antiochene (from Antioch-Jerusalem), the Coptic (Alexandrian), the Byzantine (Constantinopolitan) and the Roman.[44] This is not surprising, given that these were the five ancient patriarchates, with the highest-ranking bishops. In other words, the spread of a particular rite was not solely associated with its antiquity or beauty, but most especially to the "exalted position of the see that used it." [45] Given these considerations, it is not strange that the rite from Rome, the see of the successor of Peter, would become the most widespread of all.

Our knowledge of the liturgy increases enormously as we delve on the fourth century and onwards. Here, we need not rely on scattered and casual references from non-liturgical works but can consult actual liturgical texts.[46] Regarding the Roman rite, the oldest extant liturgical book is the sacramentary attributed to Pope St. Leo the Great in the fifth century. The second oldest is the Gelasian sacramentary from Pope Gelasius I, though in this source the rite is no longer purely Roman but contains a mix of Roman and Gallican elements (more on that soon.) Finally, we have the sacramentary composed by Pope St. Gregory the Great in the transition from the sixth to the seventh centuries[47]. This was the pope who gave his name to Gregorian chant.[48]

Gregory did not merely transcribe the Roman rite as he received it from his predecessors. John the Deacon, his biographer, wrote that "he brought together the Gelasian Codex about the solemnities of masses, taking out many things, adapting some things, adding several things."[49] Among his many liturgical reforms, Gregory 1) inserted words into the canon of the mass; 2) ordered the Our Father to be recited before the breaking of the host; 3) provided that the Alleluia should be chanted after the Gradual out of paschal time; 4) prohibited the use of the chasuble by subdcacons assisting at the mass; and 5) forbade deacons to perform any

---

44 Fortescue. "Liturgy." See also Griffin. "Rites."

45 Fortescue. "The Roman Rite." See also Ramis. "Liturgical Families in the West," 26.

46 Fortescue. "Liturgy."

47 Ramis. "Liturgical Families in the West," 26.

48 The Editors of Encyclopaedia Britannica. "Gregorian Chant."

49 Mews. "Gregory the Great," 126.

of the musical portions of the mass other than singing the gospel.[50] In many respects, the mass of the Roman rite did not evolve organically, but through papal *fiat.*

By the end of Gregory's pontificate, the Roman liturgy had materialized in a form we can recognize as the "Roman rite,"—sometimes also named "Gregorian rite" in attention to the great pontiff. And though Gregory never imposed his reforms or rite on the broader Church, his fame would gradually evolve into an idealized figure symbolizing liturgical unity.[51]

Be that as it may, for many centuries, the popes did not enforce their own rite. Rather, they allowed liturgical diversity in their patriarchate.[52] This, however, represents an anomaly. The other "mother" liturgies (Antiochene, Alexandrian, and Byzantine) were used uniformly across their respective patriarchates. The natural principle was for rite to follow patriarchate. No other patriarch beside the bishop of Rome would allow a foreign liturgy in his domain.[53]

One of the historical reasons for this may have to do with the atomization of the Roman patriarchate from the fifth century onward, something not experienced by the Eastern patriarchates until very much later. In 476 AD, the Roman Empire of the West fell, leaving no single political entity to enforce unity, whether religious or otherwise. The vacuum of power attracted barbarian peoples from the north, further aggravating the fragmentation. This happened just as the Roman rite was beginning to crystallize. We must not forget that it was Pope St. Leo the Great—the purported author of the first sacramentary—who went outside of Rome's walls to plead with Attila the Hun to spare the city.[54]

Many different barbarian peoples eventually settled upon the shambles of the empire, creating many new kingdoms in their wake. For the purpose of this chapter, it is important just to retain three peoples: 1) the Franks,

---

50 Huddleston, Gilbert. "Pope St. Gregory I ("the Great")."

51 Mews. "Gregory the Great," 125.

52 Griffin. "Rites."

53 Griffin. "Rites."

54 Mullin, *A Short World History of Christianity*, 86.

who conquered modern day France (and eventually Germany and northern Italy); 2) the Suebi, occupying the northwestern part of the Iberian Peninsula; and 3) the Visigoths, who subjugated the Iberian Peninsula and part of Southern France. The Franks converted directly from paganism to Catholicism, but the Suebi and Visigoths were originally converted by Arian missionaries.[55] All of this made it impossible for Rome to have a single rite within the borders of its patriarchate.

In Frankish Gaul, there reigned liturgical anarchy. Again, there was no single political entity to regulate the liturgy. A new rite developed simultaneously in several places,[56] a rite so heterogeneous that it can be best described as a group of many rites, sharing solely the general outlines: the Gallican rite. This Gallican rite eventually cross-pollinated with the emerging Roman rite, thus explaining the mixed nature of the Gelasian sacramentary.

However, as was said before, the Roman rite shared a certain amount of prestige due to its being the rite used by the revered bishop of Rome.[57] Barbarian kings seeking to capitalize on the past glories of Rome sought to imitate the deceased empire's customs: including Catholicism. Eventually, Charlemagne was able to unify the Franks and much of Europe, creating the greatest empire since the fall of the Roman Empire of the West. Though some authors of the time claimed (wrongly) that the Gallican rite had arrived at Gaul through St. Irenaeus of Lyon (see chapter 6), who had received it from St. Polycarp of Smyrna, who had received it from St. John the apostle,[58] Charlemagne sought to replace it with the Roman rite. The new emperor requested the Holy Father's help for this endeavor. Pope Adrian I sent Charlemagne a copy of the Gregorian sacramentary. From its source at the imperial chapel, the Roman rite spread through all the Frankish empire and gradually supplanted the Gallican rite,[59] not allowing it to fully develop before fading away.[60]

---

55 Mullin, *A Short World History of Christianity*, 67.

56 Jenner. "The Gallican Rite."

57 Fortescue. "The Roman Rite."

58 Jenner. "The Gallican Rite."

59 Jenner. "The Gallican Rite." See also Cowdrey. "Pope Gregory VII and the liturgy," 60.

60 Ramis. "Liturgical Families in the West," 28.

The situation was much more complex in the Iberian Peninsula, though. The ruling class—nobles and kings from the barbarian conquering peoples—was Arian, but the populace—descended from the natives of the fallen Roman empire—remained Catholic. In 538 AD, the Suebi bishop of Braga asked the pope for information on the Roman usages of the mass. From this information, a new rite began to emerge, regulated by local councils, and revised by great saints like Leander of Seville and his famous brother Isidore. Eventually, both the Suebi and Visigoth kings converted to Catholicism, and the Visigoths conquered the entirety of the Suebi territory.[61] Finally, a completely new element also left its mark. Islam, founded in the seventh century, expanded militarily from Africa, swallowing the Visigoth kingdom, conquering the entirety of the Iberian Peninsula, save for a small Christian remnant in the north. From this vestige, the Christians mounted the *Reconquista* (Spanish and Portuguese for "reconquest") and founded the Spanish kingdoms of Léon, Castille, Aragon, and Navarre.

Throughout all this process, the Iberian rite kept brewing and consolidating. Even in Moorish Spain, Christians kept celebrating their masses. This rite came to be known as the Mozarabic Rite, since it was practiced by the *Muzarabes* (Spanish word derived from the Arabian *musta'rab*, meaning "someone who was naturalized Arabian.")[62]

Naturally, this raised suspicion in other parts of the West: maybe this Mozarabic rite could be syncretic, a heterodox amalgamation of Christian, Arian, and Muslim elements. Frankish diplomacy, deeply influenced by the papacy, pressured their southern neighbors to adopt the Roman rite.[63] Eventually, Pope John X sent a legate to Spain to examine the Mozarabic rite in 924 AD. After hearing positive reports, Pope John approved the rite with minor modifications.[64]

However, this diversity was not to last. Until then, as we have seen, liturgical uniformity was not imposed by popes—who tolerated variety of practice—but by kings, seeking to strengthen Catholicism within their

[61] Jenner. "Mozarabic Rite."
[62] Jenner. "Mozarabic Rite."
[63] Vones. "The Substitution of the Hispanic Rite," 43.
[64] Jenner. "Mozarabic Rite."

borders by celebrating it the same way as the bishops of Rome did. Popes were usually very careful not to tread on other liturgical practices, since doing so would usually offend conservative sensibilities and upset delicate political balances.[65] Also, popes were wary of introducing liturgical reforms, as the liturgy was viewed as divinely given and unchanging.[66] Yet, the pontiffs would have to balance these considerations with the defense of their authority and prerogatives in their own patriarchate.

The first attempt to suppress the Mozarabic rite and replace it with the Roman rite happened in 1064, with Pope Alexander II. For this purpose, he sent a cardinal named Hugus Candidus to the Spanish kingdoms. The cardinal encountered incredible resistance, not only from the nobles, but also from the local bishops. A delegation of Spanish bishops went to Rome to meet the pope, so that their traditional rite should be respected. They reminded the pontiff that this rite had been approved by his predecessor John X a century earlier.[67] A local synod was held in Mantua in the presence of the pope and the Mozarabic rite was pronounced not only free from heresy, but also worthy of praise.[68]

Nevertheless, the campaign for liturgical centralization was far from over. It reached its peak in the next pontificate, during the reign of another Gregory: Pope St. Gregory VII, whose anticorruption reforms we have already discussed in chapter 2 of this book. Though Gregory was very careful in allowing liturgical diversity in Rome itself, he was not willing to do the same regarding the Mozarabic rite. The Spanish church had been founded by bishops sent by St. Peter and St. Paul. Therefore, the region fell under the Roman patriarchate.[69] For the pontiff, the Arian heresies and the Muslim invasions had undermined the loyalty owed to Rome and replaced the Roman observance with a rite he considered nothing less than superstitious.[70] Thus, Gregory VII mounted his full-on campaign to abolish the Mozarabic rite.

---

[65] Cowdrey. "Pope Gregory VII and the liturgy," 58.

[66] Cowdrey. "Pope Gregory VII and the liturgy," 55-56.

[67] Vones. "The Substitution of the Hispanic Rite," 45-46.

[68] Jenner. "Mozarabic Rite."

[69] Cowdrey. "Pope Gregory VII and the liturgy," 78. See also Vones. "The Substitution of the Hispanic Rite," 46.

[70] Cowdrey. "Pope Gregory VII and the liturgy," 78.

Just eight days after being elected (in fact, even before his papal coronation) Gregory VII sent letters reinstating Hugus Candidus as his legate and claiming his jurisdiction over Spain. He also promoted the order of Cluny, which had been making inroads in Spain and was tightly connected with the papal party. In the next years, Gregory would effectively force the Roman rite in the kingdoms of Aragon and Navarre, through the actions of his legates and through several episcopal nominations in the region, purging those who he deemed unfavorable.[71]

But perhaps the most clear-cut example of Gregory's liturgical zeal was the case of Léon-Castille. The pontiff found an ally in King Alfonso VI, who introduced the Roman rite in his domains in 1077. However, he also found great resistance, namely in the pews. On Palm Sunday of the same year, the faithful organized an act of defiance, demanding God be the direct judge between both liturgies. They organized a joust between two knights, one representing the Roman ordo and the other the Spanish one. They also set up a fight between two bulls, one named "Roma" and the other "Toledo." In both instances, the Mozarabic rite won the "judgment of God."[72]

King Alfonso, however, refused to accept the results of the ordeals. He appealed to Rome and in response the pope sent a new envoy carrying a golden key with a relic of St. Peter's chain as a sign of good faith. Slowly, through the influence of his envoy and the order of Cluny, the Roman rite started to seep into Castilian parishes and monasteries. In 1080, a local council was convened in Burgos to settle the question. The synod declared the Roman rite to be compulsory.[73]

However, Gregory's victory was still not assured. In the same year, a Cluniac monk named Robert was appointed as abbot of Sahagún. This appointment was due to King Alfonso's influence, without any due canonical election. Although his purpose was to establish the Roman rite in the monastery, abbot Robert was influenced by the convent's conservatives and

---

[71] Vones. "The Substitution of the Hispanic Rite," 46-47.

[72] Vones. "The Substitution of the Hispanic Rite," 48-49. See also Jenner. "Mozarabic Rite."

[73] Vones. "The Substitution of the Hispanic Rite," 49. See also Jenner. "Mozarabic Rite."

eventually sided with the Mozarabic rite. The scandal was evident. Pope Gregory was furious. He sent a letter branding abbot Robert as an imitator of Simon Magus[74]—since he had led thousands of people to lapse into the old error, undoing all the pontiff's good work—and relieved him of his duties. Gregory also threatened to excommunicate King Alfonso for his support to Robert and warned that, if the Spaniards kept disobeying his manifest mind and will, he would travel to Spain himself to take care of the situation personally.[75] But soon, Crown and Tiara would reconcile in the pursuit of their common goals.

In 1085, King Alfonso reconquered Toledo, the great center of the Mozarabic rite, from the Muslims. Once again, the faithful there resisted the imposition of the Roman rite and organized a new ordeal. They threw two missals into the fire, a Roman and a Toledan. Again, the Roman book was consumed by the flames, whereas the Toledan was not. This could be ascribed to the thicker vellum of the Toledan book, but the victory still belonged to the Mozarabics. Enraged, King Alfonso threw the Toledan missal back into the fire.[76]

However, the symbolism of the ordeal was too strong, and the resistance too great, to be defied. Furthermore, Pope Gregory had died in the meantime and could no longer support Alfonso in his liturgical reform. The monarch sought a compromise. The Roman rite would be celebrated everywhere except in six churches, where the Mozarabic rite could continue, both for the faithful of the day and their descendants.[77]

Nevertheless, the discouragement initiated by Alfonso and Gregory took a toll on the Mozarabic rite. The Roman rite became so widespread, it gradually was introduced even into Mozarabic churches. There were some punctual attempts to revive the rite in the fifteenth century,[78] but it was too late. Nowadays, the Mozarabic liturgy is celebrated daily only in Toledo and in certain days in certain chapels of Salamanca and Madrid.

Later on, Pope St. Pius V—the pontiff who promulgated the Roman missal that traditionalists revere today—called Popes Gelasius and Gregory

---

[74] In reference to the biblical character opposing the apostles in Acts 8:9-24.

[75] Vones. "The Substitution of the Hispanic Rite," 49-50.

[76] Vones. "The Substitution of the Hispanic Rite," 48-49. See also Jenner. "Mozarabic Rite."

[77] Jenner. "Mozarabic Rite."

[78] Jenner. "Mozarabic Rite."

I "the main creators of the Roman breviary," and Gregory VII its "restorer."[79] Of these three popes, one mixed the purity of the Roman rite with the now defunct Gallican rite; another undertook several changes and additions to the sacramentary; and the last imposed his rite on a resisting population, which was clinging to the liturgy of their ancestors, a mass revised by saints and previously accepted by popes and councils.

Bohemian controversy: is this the real Blood, or is this fantasy?

During the Last Supper, Jesus took bread, blessed it, broke it, and gave it to His disciples, saying: "Take ye. This is my body." Afterwards, He took a chalice, gave thanks, and gave it to them, saying: "This is my blood of the new testament, which shall be shed for many."[80] From that point onward, the Eucharist became "the source and summit of the Christian life."[81] But the way the Eucharist has been distributed has changed throughout the centuries.

In the first twelve centuries of Christian history, communion was usually given and taken *sub utraque specie*. This is a Latin term meaning "under both kinds" i.e., both bread and wine.[82] However, from the thirteenth century onward, communion under both kinds gradually fell into disuse, at least in the West. In place of the old custom, communion was now administered to the laity only in one kind (*sub una specie*): bread. As for the chalice with the wine, it was now reserved for the clergy.[83]

We do not know exactly when the new discipline became widespread. Nor can we attribute it to a single factor. However, it is interesting to note that there is a certain temporal coincidence between the abandonment of the shared chalice[84] and the peak of the bubonic plague in Europe, which

---

[79] Cowdrey. "Pope Gregory VII and the liturgy," 82.

[80] Mark 14:22-24

[81] CCC 1324.

[82] Toner. "Communion under Both Kinds."

[83] Sparks. "*Sub Utraque Specie*," 2.

[84] See Lee. "Coronavirus and Communion": "although sharing the communion cup at church services had been common practice among many Christian communities for a long time, for we Catholics the practice had been outlawed since the

killed around fifty million people (60% of the continent's total population) between 1346 and 1353.[85] *The Catholic Encyclopedia* mentions the "not unreasonable objection on hygienic grounds"[86] as one of the reasons for allowing communion only under one species for the laity.

Other reasons exist, though, preceding the plague. Throughout the Middle Ages, the Eucharist's sacredness made the laity increasingly more hesitant to consume it. This heightened reverence, coupled with an increase of the popularity of Eucharistic adoration, led to a shift of the devotion "away from the chalice and towards the monstrance."[87] *The Catholic Encyclopedia* also mentions the danger of spilling the Eucharistic wine, the inconvenience and delay in administering the chalice to large crowds, and the deterrent of promiscuous drinking from a shared chalice.[88]

In order to substantiate the new practice, medieval theologians formulated the doctrine of *concomitance*. According to this doctrine, Christ is indivisible, so it is not possible to separate His body from His blood. Therefore, Christ is wholly present in *both* Eucharistic species.[89] The bread does not contain only the body, but the whole of Christ, including His blood.[90]

So it happened that, as Mark Wedig, Professor of Liturgical Theology at Barry University, so aptly puts it, the Church of the High Middle Ages had "developed a complete amnesia concerning the chalice."[91] But forgotten memories would soon be rattled.

By 1412, a certain priest from Bohemia (current day Czechia) called Jan Huss was in trouble with the authorities. Formerly, he had been a rector of the University of Prague and the preacher at the Chapel of Bethlehem in the same city. But he had been excommunicated and exiled for supporting extremist views on clergy property and for inciting university and populace against the pope.[92] It was around this year that he began to develop

---

14th century because of a bubonic plague - the Black Death - that peaked in Europe from 1347-51."

[85] Benedictow. "The Black Death"

[86] Toner. "Communion under Both Kinds."

[87] Wedig. "Reception of the Eucharist."

[88] Toner. "Communion under Both Kinds."

[89] Hardon. *Catholic Dictionary*, 102.

[90] Sparks. "*Sub Utraque Specie*," 8.

[91] Wedig. "Reception of the Eucharist."

[92] Wilhelm. "Jan Hus." See also Spinka. "Jan Hus."

his ideas about a return to the ancient and venerable practice of communion *sub utraque.*[93] These ideas would, therefore, eventually become known as Utraquism.

Huss's reasoning was simple. Jesus had said "Except you eat the flesh of the Son of man, *and drink his blood*, you shall not have life in you."[94] Receiving the host would be "eating" the Blood of Christ, not "drinking" it.[95] Therefore, communion under one kind was a violation of a divine precept coming from Jesus Himself, a precept that could not, therefore, be abrogated by subsequent custom.[96] However, Huss still believed in the orthodox doctrines of transubstantiation (see chapter 3) and concomitance. For Huss, it was a matter of both elements being "better" than just one since both would aid more efficaciously with spiritual communion.[97]

But the greatest exponent of Utraquism would be Huss's main supporter (and eventual successor as leader of the Hussite movement) Jacob of Mies. Around a year after Huss started to advocate for communion under both species, Jacob began publicly supporting the lay reception of the chalice, since Jesus's actions at the Last Supper had direct, perduring, and universal application.[98] Jacob taught that "it must be believed that according to the Gospel precept, the faithful community of the people should spiritually and sacramentally receive the body of Christ under the form of bread and His blood under the form of wine."[99] Jacob also denied transubstantiation and, obviously, concomitance. Finally, Jacob broke academic protocol by taking his disputations from the classroom and into the streets. From that point onward, it was not just a matter of doctrinal error any longer—the very unity of society and of the Church was at stake.[100]

In 1414, a new ecumenical council was convoked. Its main focus was not the Bohemian controversy, but to end one of the most confusing

---

[93] Sparks. "*Sub Utraque Specie*," 2.
[94] John 6:54
[95] Hughes. "Utraquism."
[96] Levy. "Interpreting the Intention of Christ," 174.
[97] Sparks. "*Sub Utraque Specie*," 4.
[98] Levy. "Interpreting the Intention of Christ," 174.
[99] Sparks. "*Sub Utraque Specie*," 4.
[100] Levy. "Interpreting the Intention of Christ," 177.

chapters in the history of the Church: the Great Schism of the West. During this period, there were no less than three claimants to the title of successor of Peter. A council was held in the city of Constance (present-day Germany), where all three pontiffs either resigned or were deposed, and a new, single pope was elected.

However, the Council of Constance decided to not only end the schism, but also investigate the Hussite doctrine. Several theological experts were summoned to Constance to confute Huss's and Jacob's Utraquist doctrine. Reading their arguments bears a striking, even if not uncanny, resemblance with what we are witnessing today.

One of those experts was Peter Pulka, a master of the University of Vienna who was asked to review the debate between Jacob and one of his earlier opponents, Andrew of Brod, another master from Prague (as Huss was). Andrew had argued on the basis of doctrinal development: God does not change, but as supreme lawgiver, he gives laws that suit the needs of the times. Therefore, *one immutable faith can be expressed through different sets of laws* (see chapter 1). The Church can change some traditions and ceremonial practices and these decisions—not only Jesus's biblical word—were also divine precepts.[101] *If salvation hinges on obeying God, then we must also obey the prelates God has constituted.*[102] As for Peter Pulka himself, he acknowledged that the Church could not alter the substance of the sacrament of the Eucharist, but that she could indeed change usages that were accidental i.e., not essential to that immutable substance. It all came down to the ecclesiastical authority to depart from old traditions and institute new ones.[103]

Another expert summoned at Constance was Nicholas of Dinkelsbuhl, also from the university of Vienna. Nicholas took issue with Jacob's argument that communion under both species proceeds from gospel and is therefore divine, immutable law. For Nicholas, communion under one kind was a "custom that has been approved for the longest time and by all throughout the kingdom of Bohemia." Therefore, this practice had "obtained the force of law through longstanding public acceptance which

[101] Levy. "Interpreting the Intention of Christ," 178.
[102] Levy. "Interpreting the Intention of Christ," 176.
[103] Levy. "Interpreting the Intention of Christ," 179.

cannot now be overturned by some private person merely on his own whim."[104]

We must bear in mind that communion under one kind, though not as usual, was already possible even before the twelfth century, namely 1) when Eucharistic bread was brought to the faithful's homes for private domestic communion; 2) when administered to the sick; 3) when administered to children (either wine alone or bread alone); and 4) at the Mass of the Presanctified.[105] Never before had it been said that the Church was violating a divine precept by doing so.

So, Nicholas surmised that Huss and Jacob were interpreting the Bible in a rigorist way (*ad rigorem verborum*) and not trying to grasp the authentic meaning of the text by looking at the intention of the writer.[106] Nicholas made a distinction between two kinds of eating and drinking: sacramental and spiritual. The spiritual sense had been explained by medieval theologians and, for Nicholas, was the sense in which we should interpret "eat and drink" in John 6:53.[107] Thus, the exegesis of scripture was to be dynamic. Development of practice and doctrine was a process directed by the Holy Spirit. After all, the Holy Spirit had not only authored scripture, but also guided the Church in reasonable changes in matters that are extrinsic and accidental to the sacrament.[108]

The Council then deliberated. Of course, the Conciliar Fathers could not deny that communion under both species had been practiced by the early Church or even by Jesus Christ Himself. The traditional and orthodox pedigree of *sub utraque* made it impossible for the Council to deem it heretical.[109] Instead, the Council decreed:

> For it should be very firmly believed, and in no way doubted, that the whole body and blood of Christ are truly contained under both the form of bread and the form of wine. Therefore, since this

---

104 Levy. "Interpreting the Intention of Christ," 181.
105 Toner. "Communion under Both Kinds."
106 Levy. "Interpreting the Intention of Christ," 181.
107 Levy. "Interpreting the Intention of Christ," 182.
108 Levy. "Interpreting the Intention of Christ," 181.
109 Levy. "Interpreting the Intention of Christ," 173.

> custom was introduced *for good reasons* by the church and holy fathers, and has been observed for a very long time, *it should be held as a law which nobody may repudiate or alter at will without the church's permission. To say that the observance of this custom or law is sacrilegious or illicit must be regarded as erroneous.* Those who stubbornly assert the opposite of the aforesaid are to be confined as heretics[110]

In other words, though communion *sub utraque* was not deemed heretical, Utraquism—the belief that *only* communion *sub utraque* is legitimate—was indeed judged as such. It was not a matter of condemning the old custom, but of condemning those who would say that only the previous practice was valid. The new custom had been introduced for *good reasons.* What good reasons? Though *The Catholic Encyclopedia* clarifies those reasons (see above), the Council itself does not.[111] What mattered was that one could not say that the withdrawal of the chalice was impious. That would be calling the Council's authority into question.

Was this an overreach? Did Constance exceed its authority? Here, I would like to quote Dr. Ian Levy, Professor of Historical Theology at Marquette University:

> The great question to be resolved, however, was whether the council had actually exceeded its authority by attempting to derogate from divine law. In its attempt to elevate custom to a principle of law was it overturning a direct precept of Jesus Christ? . . . The fundamental issue was development of doctrine; *not whether doctrine develops, however, but the means to determine legitimate development.* The Utraquists were not primarily attempting to prove that the early church had communicated the laity under both species; everyone already knew that. Rather, they contended that lay chalice reception remained an integral part of the sacrament that could not be lawfully altered. It was this claim that forced the Romanists to

---

[110] Constance. "Session 13."

[111] Levy. "Interpreting the Intention of Christ," 173. See also Jong, "On receiving communion in one kind": "Constance does not say what these 'good reasons' are. The assertion seems mostly to have been a reaction against those Bohemian reformers who argued for lay communion under both kinds . . . With all due respect to those at Constance, this is quite hysterical."

> provide warrant for chalice withdrawal based upon the analysis of a set of mutually recognized authoritative texts: Holy Scripture, the church fathers, and canon law. *The stage was set for a battle over access to, and ultimately control over, a shared tradition.*
>
> When the tradition is shared, and the authoritative sources are embraced by both sides, the debate is soon narrowed to questions of methodological competence. *Who possesses the hermeneutical skills requisite* for the discovery, and subsequent application, of the intended meanings that rest within these sacred texts? *Who, moreover, can rightfully claim to be guided by the Spirit which speaks throughout, and by means of, the tradition?. . .*
>
> As we shall see, however, Roman attempts to fit central texts into this tradition, to demonstrate seamless conformity, could result in over-readings as texts were pressed to address a specific set of concerns that had only recently emerged. Indeed, it *was the inherent ambiguity of so many authoritative texts relied upon by both sides that rendered the debate all but intractable.*[112]

Obviously, this meant that the debate was far from over. Though some, like the Parisian theologian Jean Gerson, invoked the precedent of the Council of Jerusalem (see chapter 5) to justify Constance's infallible judgments,[113] the Hussites refused to accept the Council's decision. The Hussites broke from Rome, began to use the Czech liturgy, and administered communion *sub utraque* to the laity.[114]

Several wars broke out in Bohemia between the Hussites and the pope's supporters. Peace negotiations would only start in 1431, when a new ecumenical council at Basel agreed to hear a Hussite delegation. Once again, the Council called orthodox theologians to argue with the Hussite party.

---

[112] Levy. "Interpreting the Intention of Christ," 175-176.
[113] Levy. "Interpreting the Intention of Christ," 185.
[114] The Editors of Encyclopaedia Britannica. "Hussite."

One of them was John of Ragusa, a Dominican, who also quoted scripture to posit that the Holy Spirit would teach the Church all truth[115] in matters necessary for salvation. The Hussites would reply that this promise applied only to the primitive Church, which was the one who followed Christ's precept. But now that the Church had fallen away, it was them, the Hussites, who held up the perfect model of the primitive Church. John replied that there were not two churches, but solely one. Christ's promise did not apply exclusively to the primitive Church, but to the Church forever. If the fifteenth century Church could err, then Christ's promise was false and there would be no assurance that the Church had not erred before, even in primitive times. John's case, therefore, was one of *continuity*.[116]

Another theologian assigned to the negotiation table was Nicholas of Cusa. He dismissed the Hussite claim that they were obeying Christ by disobeying the Church. For Nicholas, it was presumptuous that private individuals would judge their own understanding of divine commands to be more conformed to God than that of the Church, namely the see of Peter. Also, regarding scripture, Nicholas argued that it was both adapted to the times and understood in various ways, and that the Church cannot be bound to the letter of scripture but must instead follow its spirit.[117]

The Council of Basel could not contradict the infallible decrees from Constance, so it sought a compromise, stretching as far as it could go—granting the Hussites the possibility of communion under both kinds, as long as they acknowledged the doctrine of concomitance.[118] Thus, they could practice as they pleased, as long as they submitted to the doctrines promulgated by the Church.

The Hussites were divided on whether to accept Basel's concessions or not. The moderate party—called precisely Utraquists—wanted to accept these concessions, but a more radical party—named Taborites—did not. Catholics and Utraquists allied against the Taborites and defeated them in battle.[119]

---

[115] John 16:12
[116] Levy. "Interpreting the Intention of Christ," 187.
[117] Levy. "Interpreting the Intention of Christ," 189-190.
[118] Toner. "Communion under Both Kinds."
[119] The Editors of Encyclopaedia Britannica. "Hussite."

Later, in 1462, Pope Pius II revoked the concessions of Basel.[120] However, the Protestant Reformation was already at hand. Many Protestants were sympathetic to the Utraquists' plight. A new council was convoked, this time at Trent. Here, the council fathers acknowledged that the early Church practiced communion *sub utraque*, but also that the Church had authoritatively altered this practice. Furthermore, Trent affirmed the dogmas of transubstantiation and concomitance, and condemned the *necessity* of Utraquism i.e., the claim that it was *necessary* for salvation to commune in both kinds. Communion *sub utraque* could, in theory, be practiced, but always at the pope's discretion.[121]

In the next couple of centuries, popes granted and abrogated the practice of communion s*ub utraque* in different places,[122] but in the end, the Counter-Reformation triumphed in Bohemia. By the 1620s, the Utraquists had been absorbed by the Catholic Church.[123] Yet another liturgical controversy had ended in favor of the newer custom.

---

[120] Toner. "Communion under Both Kinds."
[121] Sparks. "*Sub Utraque Specie*," 6, 10.
[122] Toner. "Communion under Both Kinds."
[123] The Editors of Encyclopaedia Britannica. "Hussite."

Chapter 8

"If anyone preach another gospel unto you. . ."

We are being asked to reform, which - in this case - does not consist of words, but rather an approach that has the courage to face this crisis, to accept the reality, wherever that will lead. And every reform begins with oneself. Reform in the Church has been brought about by men and women who were not afraid to expose themselves to crisis and let the Lord reform them. That is the only way; otherwise we would only be "ideologues of reform" without putting our own flesh on the line. The Lord never engaged in "reformation" (if I may permit myself this phrase): neither the project of the Pharisees, nor that of the Sadducees, the Zealots or the Essenes.
—Francis, Letter to Cardinal Reinhard Marx

On February 4, 2019, during his official trip to the United Arab Emirates, Pope Francis signed a joint declaration with the Grand Imam of Al Azhar, Ahmed Al-Tayeb, one of the leading authorities in Muslim Sunni world. In this declaration, the two religious leaders laid the groundwork for a new stage of cooperation between Islam and Catholicism for a more fraternal and peaceful future.[1] This declaration, however, caused quite the stir because of this isolated snippet:

> *The pluralism and the diversity of religions*, colour, sex, race, and language *are willed by God* in His wisdom, through which He created human beings.[2]

Once again, Catholic social media exploded with cries of heterodoxy. Many believed this declaration affirmed that God willed other religions ("false religions") besides the Catholic faith. Thomas Lawson saw many commenters sharing many conspiracy theories about the pope being a freemason bent on creating a syncretic, one-world religion.[3] Others called him an antichrist. A benevacantist was arguing that Jorge Bergoglio had publicly

---

[1] Francis, "Document on Human Fraternity."

[2] Francis, "Document on Human Fraternity."

[3] For example, see the replies to the article on Gloria.tv, "Viganò: Not Even The Most Optimistic Freemason Would Have Dreamed Francis' Papacy."

and manifestly apostatized from the Catholic Faith.[4] A sedevacantist interjected that the apostasy had occurred many decades before, for the problem laid at the feet of the Second Vatican Council's teachings on ecumenism and religious freedom.[5] A discussion ensued as to when exactly the apostasy had taken place, with no agreement being reached between the contending parties.

Thomas Lawson disliked the apocalyptic rhetoric. It reminded him of the Jack Chick tracts he used to read during his Evangelical years. But he could not make heads or tails of the declaration. What was Pope Francis thinking? Had he just overturned 1960 years of solid Catholic precedent, to just go along with a modernist assertion like "all religions are the same?"

He asked his good friend Justin what he thought about all this. The next day, Justin sent him a link to the in-flight press conference after the pope's historical visit. In this conference, Francis clarified that the document "does not pull away one millimeter from Vatican II."[6] While the pontiff acknowledged that there was a development ("[it is a] step forward that comes after 50 years, from the Council, that must be developed") he assured that this development had been made in continuity with previous teachings.

That was the trouble—Tom explained—This indifferentist idea towards the Catholic faith was a fruit of the council. The Second Vatican Council had revolutionized Catholic doctrine on ecumenism and religious freedom, contradicting all previous councils and popes. How could the statements from Gregory XVI (see chapter 9) in *Mirari Vos*[7] be reconciled with Vatican II's declaration *Dignitatis Humanae*?[8] How could the error

---

[4] Cf. Gracida. "What next?"

[5] Cf. Derksen. "Apostasy in Abu Dhabi: Francis says God wills Diversity of Religions."

[6] Catholic News Agency, "Full Text of Pope Francis' in-Flight Press Conference from Abu Dhabi."

[7] Gregory XVI. *Mirari Vos*, 14.

[8] See Vatican II. *Dignitatis Humanae*, 2. For an article that reconciles the preconciliar pronouncements on this topic and the teachings from Vatican II, see Harrison. "Vatican II's Declarations on Religious Freedom." For a contextualization that explains the differences between pre- and post-conciliar views based on how they address different socio-political contexts, see Gurian. "Lamennais," 226-227.

condemned by Pius IX's Syllabus[9] be compatible with Francis's Abu Dhabi declaration? It was impossible!

But while Tom simply dismissed this continuity as self-evidently unfeasible, Justin sent him additional links. Some apologists were already taking up the task of trying to find an accurate interpretative lens through which they could read this declaration in continuity with Catholic doctrine.[10] One of the justifications that eventually gained more traction came from theologian Chad Pecknold, who made a distinction between God's active will and permissive will.[11] God actively willed Catholicism but he only tolerated (on account of man's freedom) the existence of other religions. Since everything that happens comes about through God's will, we call this tolerance of evils "God's permissive will."

This interpretation would be confirmed later on. During an *ad limina* visit to the Vatican, Bishop Athanasius Schneider asked Francis to clarify the meaning of this polemical passage. Schneider then relayed this information to LifeSiteNews, a media outlet very critical of the pope. According to him, the pope explicitly stated he could share the contents of their exchange on this point: "You can say that the phrase in question on the diversity of religions means the permissive will of God."[12] Later, in one of his general audiences, Pope Francis clarified even further: "Why does God allow many religions? God wanted to allow this: scholastic theologians used to refer to God's *voluntas permissiva*" (i.e., permissive will).[13]

Tom thanked Justin for keeping him informed throughout all the controversy, but he was still not pleased. It seemed to him that Justin was just over-contextualizing something that was pretty straightforward. The faithful in the pews should not need a theology diploma to be able to reconcile these obvious contradictions. On the contrary, tradition was simple and

---

[9] See Pius IX. *Syllabus of Errors*, 15.

[10] My own attempt was published on *WPI*: "Pluralism and the will of God . . . is there another way to look at it?"

[11] Farrow, "Pope Francis Signs Peace Declaration on 'Human Fraternity' with Grand Imam."

[12] Montagna, "Exclusive: Bishop Schneider Wins Clarification on 'Diversity of Religions' from Pope Francis."

[13] Francis, "General Audience of April 3, 2019."

clear, unlike the papal and conciliar confusion. The faithful should just study what the Church taught for ages and then decide for themselves whether the "magisterium of the moment" was compatible with them. If not, they could—or should—discard the current teaching, for a fidelity to a higher truth so compelled them.[14]

Justin replied that having everyone interpret tradition by themselves, even contrary to the magisterium, would open the door to subjectivism and relativism. If no interpretation was authoritative, then who was to say which of two contradictory interpretations was true? But Tom dismissed him. There was no need for an authoritative interpretation when tradition was quite clear.[15] What could open the door to subjectivism and relativism would be to allow the pope to contradict the plain meaning of perennial doctrine, as if everything the pope said would be automatically true.[16] The Pope was not an oracle, that all his utterances were to be considered infallible and divinely inspired.

---

[14] See, for example, Kwasniewski. "My Journey from Ultramontanism": "Sometimes traditional Catholics are presented with the objection: 'Should we all have to be theologians and historians to maneuver our way in the Church today? Surely, that's not what Jesus had in mind. He wanted simple faith and trust.' This objection is true in one way and false in another. *It is true in the sense that the Catholic Faith is indeed accessible to all and at all times: what we need to know and to do in order to be saved is mercifully compact.* We find it in the Creeds and Commandments taught by the Church in all of her trustworthy old catechisms. In this sense, *one who knows his catechism knows what the truth is and how to get to Heaven.*"

[15] Kwasniewski. "My Journey from Ultramontanism": "To the objector who says: 'this traditionalist position is subjective!', I reply: No, it is not. The Catholic Tradition includes generally accepted readings of Scripture by the Church Fathers and Doctors as well as copious magisterial determinations, such as the dogmas and anathemas of ecumenical Councils. There are numerous objective and mutually reinforcing indications of Catholic teaching, and these constitute true limits on what the current Magisterium (Pope/bishops) may legitimately teach, or what a Catholic today may accept as rationally consistent"

[16] Kwasniewski. "My Journey from Ultramontanism": "Recognizing that Catholicism is inherently a religion of Tradition, *Where Peter Is* sidesteps the awkwardness of patent contradiction between earlier magisterial teaching and Francis's 'creativity' by arguing that Tradition actually means 'whatever the pope says.' Tradition is not something given in the past or cumulative, but something constituted by the Pope's endorsement of it here and now. Therefore, Catholics must assent to *Amoris Laetitia*, the abolition of the death penalty, human fraternity among a plurality of divinely willed religions, and every other kind of novelty 'proposed' by the pope."

During this back and forth, Tom stumbled upon yet another interview by Bishop Schneider, also published at LifeSiteNews. Even if the Pope's clarification had allowed for an orthodox reading of the Abu Dhabi statement, it was no longer enough. Although Catholic media had previously praised this elucidation as a victory, saying that Schneider had "won" a clarification, now they were asking for more. Bishop Schneider claimed that, with papal explanation or not, the Declaration on Religious Freedom was still "valid" and thus: "there is being proclaimed a new Gospel, a Gospel that is not the one taught by the Incarnate Word of God, that was loyally preached by the Apostles and passed on to the Church. . . There can be no doubt, that Saint Paul would say today, concerning this controversial formulation in the Abu Dhabi statement: '*But though we, or an angel from heaven, preach a gospel to you besides that which we have preached to you, let him be anathema*' (Galatians 1:8–9)."[17]

As he read this Pauline quote, Tom felt a shiver down his spine. He recognized this quote. It had been undug from a past he thought long buried, from his Protestant years. At that time, Tom had used that quote to oppose the papacy and its "traditions of men."[18] Several Catholic apologists had told him that that quote could not be construed in such a way as to attack the pope or the Church.[19] That happened during Benedict XVI's

---

[17] Hickson. "Bp. Schneider: Pope Must Formally Correct Statement."

[18] As an example of such Protestant rhetoric, see Adeyemi. "6 Reasons": "These passages of Scripture prove so clearly that we are saved through faith, and not by works, that no honest or right-thinking man can deny this. . . By placing its anathema on the Biblical Gospel, Rome has placed itself under the anathema of God Almighty (Galatians 1:8, 9). Let all those who affirm this doctrine be blessed, but let Rome's curse fall on her own head."

[19] Kovach. "An Interactive Detective Story": "What does Jesus say? We read in Matthew 16:18 that Jesus 'established a Church': '[U]pon this rock I will build my church, and the gates of hell will not prevail against it.' This tells us Jesus promised us 'an enduring Church'. Galatians 1:8 gives us another clue we should track: 'But even if we or an angel from heaven should preach a gospel other than the one we preached to you, let that one be accursed!' Let's see how these verses help us in our hunt. We turn to biblical scholars, who tell us that Galatians was written around A.D. 48-55. When Paul wrote it, Jesus' true Church already existed. Paul said that any new church or new gospel that came after Jesus was 'accursed'; it would be a 'false gospel.' History, then, can help us find the true Church, since a

pontificate. But now, many Catholic apologists and commentators were using that very same quote to criticize Francis![20] Tom was confused. Could this biblical quote not be used then and yet be used now for the same purpose?

"Traditions of men"

When Martin Luther, an Augustinian friar from the Holy Roman Empire (currently Germany,) nailed his "Ninety-Five Theses" to the door of the cathedral of Wittenberg in 1517,[21] he could not anticipate the impact his actions would have for the future of Christianity. Luther's main goal was to challenge the practice of selling indulgences, a source of ecclesial corruption in his day. What he sought was reform, not a Reformation.

But the movement Luther started soon spun out of control. In a debate at Leipzig in 1519, Luther's followers moved the discussion away from the question of indulgences and into the authority of the Church as a whole. To maintain the coherence of his position, Luther admitted that he believed that ecumenical councils had erred in the past. Pope Leo X would not stand for this. The very next year, he promulgated the bull *Exsurge Domine*, condemning Luther's theology as heresy.[22]

Luther did not stand down. He kept writing and preaching. In 1521, he was summoned before the Imperial Diet[23] at Worms to acknowledge and repudiate his books. Luther refused, saying: "I do not accept the authority of popes and councils, for they have contradicted each other."[24] In

---

church that can't trace its origins or teachings to Jesus' time, by Paul's definition, is 'accursed' as a false gospel."

[20] For example, in an interview to the National Catholic Register, Cardinal Burke (see chapter chapter 5) said: "What's binding is the Tradition. Ecclesial authority exists only in service of the Tradition. I think of that passage of St. Paul in the [Letter to the] Galatians (1:8), that if 'even an angel should preach unto you any Gospel other than that which we preached unto you, let him be anathema.'" (see Pentin, "Cardinal Burke on *Amoris Laetitia Dubia*.")

[21] Mullin, *A Short World History of Christianity*, 122-123.

[22] Mullin, *A Short World History of Christianity*, 123.

[23] A legislative assembly of the representatives of the political units within the Holy Roman Empire.

[24] Mathison. "Solo scriptura" 3. See also the later Westminster Confession of Faith: "All synods or councils, since the apostles' times, whether general or particular, may err; and many have erred. Therefore they are not to be made the rule of

a famous but apocryphal account, he declared: "Here I stand. I can do no other. God help me. Amen." [25] Luther fled, and the Holy Roman Emperor Charles V drew an edict declaring him an outlaw and banning all his books.

Lutheranism, however, kept spreading throughout the empire and even beyond, in Scandinavia. In 1529, some reform-minded imperial princes and nobles sided with Luther in the Diet of Speyer and issued a *Protestatio* (Latin for "protest.") From this occurrence emerged the word "Protestant." One year later, Protestant theology was summarized and consolidated in the Augsburg Confession. [26]

However, Luther's antiestablishment rhetoric could not but backfire. By undermining the concept of authority within the Church, Luther was sawing the branch where he sat on and sowing the fragmentation of his own movement. Soon, the Reformers split into two groups: the moderates (more closely aligned with Luther) and the radicals. [27] The latter would congregate in Switzerland under the leadership of Ulrich Zwingli and, later, John Calvin. This faction would become known as the Calvinists or simply as "the Reformed." But this wing of the Reformation movement would soon branch into more extreme positions, with some going into such lengths as denying even the trinitarian dogmas—Luther would call these fringe elements "Schwarmers" ("crawling things" in German). [28] To add more confusion to the mix, King Henry VIII declared himself head of the Church of England in 1531, therefore establishing the Anglican Church.

To oppose the doctrinal and ecclesial chaos taking hold of Northern and Central Europe, Emperor Charles asked for an ecumenical council to be convoked in neutral ground. Eventually, the pope acquiesced, and the city of Trent was chosen, as at the time it was both Italian and imperial. The Council of Trent dealt both with the doctrinal side of the problem and with reform of the corrupt practices denounced by Luther—something

---

faith, or practice; but to be used as a help in both" (Westminster Divines. *Westminster Confession of Faith*, Chapter XXXI, Article IV).

[25] Hillerbrand. "Martin Luther."

[26] Mullin, *A Short World History of Christianity*, 127.

[27] Mullin, *A Short World History of Christianity*, 123.

[28] Mullin, *A Short World History of Christianity*, 127.

that even the pope admitted being true.[29] After the council, many measures were implemented to counter the Reformation—measures collectively known by the apt name "Counter-Reformation." Among these was the homogenization and unification of the Western Church around the Roman rite, according to the missal later promulgated by Pope St. Pius V (see chapter 7). This is the TLM so revered by the traditionalist community of today.

The Reformation poses two challenges for this book. First, as we have seen, the Protestant movement quickly became fragmented. Therefore, it is not easy to summarize in a single chapter its whole history down to the present day or to take into consideration all the nuances and differences of such a heterogeneous group. So, unlike previous chapters (or the following ones), I will not delve much deeper into the history of the Reformation but focus solely on some limited doctrinal aspects of Protestant theology.

Second, Protestants are the first group in this book to not use the word "tradition" in an honorific way, but in a pejorative way. The Augsburg Confession, for instance, is full of negative references to "human traditions" and "traditions of men."[30] These do not refer solely to ecclesial and culturally contingent traditions, like pious devotions and ceremonial practices, but also to tradition itself as a mode of transmission of the Word of God (see chapter 1, "Tradition and traditions"). Protestants considered scripture *alone* as a valid mode of transmission and were highly suspicious of any unwritten traditions. For them, it was difficult to prove that such traditions had come down from the apostles and not from later, corrupt Church authorities. This led to a reversal of many of the rulings we examined before in this book. For example, the Protestants revived the Utraquist controversy, demanding communion in both kinds to the laity[31] (see chapter 7, "Bohemian controversy"). Sunday would no longer be the day of the

---

[29] O'Malley. *Trent: What happened at the Council*, 13 14. The entirety of this book is fundamental to have a grasp of the Catholic response to Luther's doctrinal and disciplinary challenges.

[30] As a non-exhaustive example, see Luther et al. *Smalcald Articles*, Part III, Article XV - "Of Human Traditions": "The declaration of the Papists that human traditions serve for the remission of sins, or merit salvation, is [altogether] unchristian and condemned, as Christ says Matt. 15:9: In vain they do worship Me, teaching for doctrines the commandments of men. Again, Titus 1:14: That turn from the truth. Again, when they declare that it is a mortal sin if one breaks these ordinances [does not keep these statutes], this, too, is not right."

[31] John, et al. *Augsburg Confessions*, Article XXII.

Lord—instead, the holy day of observance would be the sabbath, per the scriptural practice of the Old Testament (see chapter 7, "Obeying God rather than man").[32] Some, more radical (like Servetus), would even question the doctrine of the Holy Trinity (see chapter 6).[33]

It would appear then, that Protestants would be anti-traditionalists and, therefore, be outside the scope of this book. However, that is not the case. If we pay close attention to what Protestants mean by "traditions of men," we notice that they actually mean "innovations," instituted by the papacy after the Church became corrupted.[34] In order to parse through these corruptions and access the teachings of the primitive Church, Protestants proposed the authority of scripture, as this would be immutable.[35] As we have seen in chapter 1, scripture can be considered tradition, if we apply the broad definition of the word. So, even if Protestants appear, at first glance, to be anti-traditionalists, they are actually invoking tradition (in its broad sense) to resist the alleged innovations approved by the Church's authority throughout the centuries. As the Westminster Confession of Faith would postulate:

---

[32] John, et al. *Augsburg Confessions*, Article XXVIII. Mullin, *A Short World History of Christianity*, 129.

[33] Mullin, *A Short World History of Christianity*, 127.

[34] See, for example, Luther et al. *Smalcald Articles*, Part III, Article XXVII: "There are monstrous disputations concerning the changing of the law, the ceremonies of the new law, the changing of the Sabbath-day, which all have sprung from the false belief. . . that Christ had given commission to the Apostles and bishops to devise *new ceremonies* as necessary to salvation. *These errors crept into the Church when the righteousness of faith was not taught clearly enough*. . . They ask only that they would release unjust burdens *which are new and have been received contrary to the custom* of the Church Catholic."

[35] See Chemnitz. *Examination of the Council of Trent, Part I*: "There is therefore a very great difference between (1) the witness of the primitive church, which was at the time of the apostles and (2) the witness of the church which followed immediately after the time of the apostles and which had received the witness of the first church and (3) the witness of the present church concerning the Scripture." See also Mullin, *A Short World History of Christianity*, 125-126: "Throughout sixteenth-century Europe there were those who, inspired by Scripture, believed it possible not merely to reform the church, but to restore the primitive model of Christianity."

> The whole counsel of God, concerning all things necessary for His own glory, man's salvation, faith, and life, is either expressly set down in Scripture, or by good and necessary consequence may be deduced from Scripture: *unto which nothing at any time is to be added, whether by new revelations of the Spirit, or traditions of men.*[36]

Therefore, for the remainder of this chapter, I am going to explore three major tenets of Protestant theology, at least during the first couple of centuries after the Reformation: 1) the great apostasy theory, 2) *sola scriptura*; and 3) the perspicuity of scripture. For the latter two points, it will be important to remember that scripture and tradition are both modes of transmission of the same deposit of faith. Therefore, if scripture is being incorrectly contrasted against the living magisterium, then the same must, *a fortiori*, hold true for tradition. What is deemed erroneous for scripture must also be deemed erroneous for tradition.

The great apostasy

The thesis of this book is that those who dissent from orthodoxy as defined by the Catholic Church often claim that they are the ones holding to the traditional position. For all their rhetoric against "traditions of men" or "human traditions," the Protestant Reformers were no exception. After all, for a Christian, the ultimate authority is Jesus Christ, who lived 1,500 years before the Reformation. The Catholic Church could establish a connection to Jesus, through Peter and his successors down to the pope of the day. But Protestants had to grapple with the embarrassing question: "where was your church before Luther?" Though the Protestants could theoretically claim that their new interpretation of scripture was still the most faithful to Jesus, they still tried to legitimize themselves through appeals to antiquity. As the eighteenth-century editors of the book "The History of Popery" would reply: "we can shew, and undeniably prove the continued succession of our doctrine in entire visible churches, from the primitive times to the present age."[37]

---

[36] Westminster Divines. *Westminster Confession of Faith*, Chapter I, Article VI.
[37] Barnett. "Where was your Church before Luther?" 34.

A direct historical line to Jesus would grant their theology the authority to challenge the Catholic Church. The Reformers tried to do so through a two-step process. First, they would have to prove that the line claimed by the Church of Rome had been severed along the way. In other words, that the Catholic Church had apostatized and could not be the church that Jesus had founded. Second, they would have to demonstrate that Protestants were the actual spiritual descendants of that church created by Christ. This twofold process started with none other than Martin Luther himself, as he formulated two theories: 1) the great apostasy; and 2) the hidden church.

In 1520, Luther published a book called "The Babylonian Captivity of the Church." Drawing from biblical imagery, Luther recalled the time when the people of Judah were taken captive and exiled to the heathen capitol of the Neo-Babylonian Empire.[38] Luther then applied that biblical episode to the Church of his time, writing that "the papacy is the kingdom of Babylon and the power of Nimrod,[39] the mighty hunter. . . The Papacy is the mighty hunt of the Bishop of Rome."[40] According to Luther, the Catholic Church was trying to hold the faithful captive in three ways: 1) by withholding the cup from the laity (see chapter 7); 2) by teaching the doctrine of transubstantiation (which made sacramental access contingent on priests); and 3) by claiming that mass was a sacrifice and work to gain divine favor.[41]

Later, in the Smalcald Articles, Luther would once again take recourse to biblical imagery, this time to denounce the Pope as the "very Antichrist, who has exalted himself above, and opposed himself against Christ, because he will not permit Christians to be saved without his power".[42] Luther would also compare the papacy with the Beast of the book of Revelation, and the Catholic Church with the harlot.[43] Nowadays, this exegesis of the book of Revelation has been largely abandoned, and many

[38] Jer 39-43

[39] Legendary hunter-king from Gen 10:8-9, associated with the episode of the Tower of Babel and traditionally regarded as the mythical founder of Babylon.

[40] Luther. *The Babylonian Captivity*, 15.

[41] Luther. *The Babylonian Captivity*, 11.

[42] Luther et al. *Smalcald Articles*, Part II, Article IV. Cf. 1 John 4:3 and 2 Tess 2:3-4.

[43] Tanner. "Apostate Jerusalem," 5.

commentators have pointed out that Luther was merely reading the Bible through the lens of his historical situation (namely his struggles with the Catholic Church).[44]

Coupled with this, Luther also wrote about what he considered to be the "true" church. For him, the true church was also a "hidden church." This true/hidden church was pure and could not err. She stood in opposition to a false, man-made church, that spurned the word of scripture and arrogated to itself the role of Christ's body on earth. This false church was the church of the Antichrist. However, even if the true church could be identified with the hidden church, the false church was not necessarily the "visible church." The true church was hidden insofar as it lived in spirit, buried under errors, infirmity, and sin so that it appeared nowhere to the secondary senses.[45]

Later, Martin Chemnitz, a sixteenth-century Protestant polemicist who endeavored to refute the Council of Trent, acknowledged that the divine Word of God could have been handed down through unwritten traditions. Scripture itself attested to that fact, since various patriarchs of the Old Testament had passed on their knowledge to later generations by word of mouth. However, scripture also proved that, as time went by, these unwritten traditions were "repeatedly corrupted, adulterated, and perverted by those whose duty it was to preserve, propagate, and deliver to others the traditions received from the fathers. These examples show what kind of guardianship and preservation of the heavenly doctrine is exercised by later generations."[46] The only way to keep tradition unadulterated was to follow it as it had been written down in immutable scripture.

In 1646, the Westminster Confession of Faith redefined the "catholic and universal church" as the "invisible" church, composed "of the whole number of the elect, that have been, are, or shall be gathered into one, under Christ the head thereof."[47] This "catholic and universal church" was also "visible" in the sense that it was "not confined to one nation" and

---

[44] Tanner. "Apostate Jerusalem," 11.

[45] Noll. "Martin Luther and the Concept of 'True' Church," 80-82.

[46] Chemnitz. *Examination of the Council of Trent, Part I.*

[47] Westminster Divines. *Westminster Confession of Faith*, Chapter XXV, Article I.

consisted "of all those throughout the world that profess the true religion."[48] The Confession would go on to say:

> This catholic church hath been sometimes more, sometimes less, visible. And particular churches, which are members thereof, are more or less pure, according as the doctrine of the gospel is taught and embraced, ordinances administered, and public worship performed more or less purely in them.
>
> The purest churches under heaven are subject both to mixture and error: *and some have so degenerated as to become apparently no churches of Christ.* Nevertheless, there shall be always a church on earth, to worship God according to His will.
>
> There is no other head of the church but the Lord Jesus Christ: nor can the pope of Rome in any sense be head thereof.[49]

From this foundation, subsequent Protestant apologetics sought to better ground these concepts by furbishing them with historical—and many times, pseudo-historical—data. Particularly in England, this endeavor started with Anglican thinkers, since Anglicanism had retained a hierarchical system similar to the Catholic Church. In order to salvage the legitimacy of their episcopate, they tried to set the great apostasy at a later date: the papacy would have become fully corrupted only in the eleventh century, under Pope Gregory VII. The coincidental choice of this pope was not due to his anti-corruption reforms (chapter 2), nor to his attempt to eliminate the Mozarabic rite (chapter 6) but was based purely on apocalyptic chronologies about the binding and unbinding of Satan in the book of Revelation. [50]

Other Anglicans, however, tried to circumvent Rome entirely by claiming that Christianity had been brought to England through a legendary visit

---

[48] Westminster Divines. *Westminster Confession of Faith*, Chapter XXV, Article II.

[49] Westminster Divines. *Westminster Confession of Faith*, Chapter XXV, Articles IV-VI.

[50] Barnett. "Where was your Church before Luther?" 16.

from St. Joseph of Arimathea to the British Isles. John Foxe, an Anglican martyrologist, was one of the first to propose this connection. From there, he tried to establish a succession of true, proto-Protestant piety, from the apostles to the sixteenth century.[51] As the Anglican Bishop John Bale wrote:

> He [Joseph of Arimathea] published there [in Britain] among them the Gospel of salvation which Christ first of all and afterwards his apostles had taught at Jerusalem. Untruly therefore are we reported by the Italian writers and the subtle devisers of holy legends that we should have our first faith from Rome and our Christian doctrine from their unchristian bishops. *From the school of Christ himself have we received the documents of our faith. From Jerusalem and not from Rome* whom both Peter and also Christ called Babylon for that she so aptly thereunto agreed in *ministering confusion to the world.*[52]

Other branches of Protestantism, however, were not so keen in defending an episcopate. For the Puritans, for example, the episcopate was unscriptural, and they rallied against the "popery of Anglican Episcopalianism." They pushed the date of the apostasy backwards, before medieval times that Anglicans were not comfortable in criticizing.[53] If the episcopate-based hierarchy was the source of corruption within the Church, then the historical roots of Protestantism would be found in the early Church, when the hierarchy system was still underdeveloped. They eventually found their scapegoat in Emperor Constantine. By granting his favor and riches on the Church, Constantine had corrupted her and turned her worldly. The first pope to start this journey of corruption would have been Pope Silvester I, the reigning pontiff during the last years of Constantine's rule.[54]

Having thus demonstrated that the Catholic Church had apostatized, the Puritans sought to determine their own pedigree. In order to forge the link between the Reformation and the pure primitive Church, the

---

[51] Barnett. "Where was your Church before Luther?" 15-16.

[52] Barnett. "Where was your Church before Luther?" 16-17 (my translation from Early Modern English).

[53] Barnett. "Where was your Church before Luther?" 17-18.

[54] Barnett. "Where was your Church before Luther?" 21-22.

Protestant apologists took hold of Luther's "hidden church," a collection of true Christians who remained invisible amid the deep anti-Christian corruption of their religious milieu. These Christians would have been persecuted by Rome but would have survived and eventually triumphed in the Reformation.[55] Therefore, many heretical movements persecuted by the Church during the Middle Ages were reexamined under the lens of this historical bias and transformed into proto-Protestants, suffering for their opposition to the corruptions of the faith. The Hussites (see chapter 6) were appropriated for this role, but also the Waldensians, the Cathars, and the Lollards.[56] Theodore Beza, the successor of Calvin at Geneva, taught that the Waldensians had opposed Roman corruptions since "times immemorial," as back as the year 120 AD (though he did not specify why he chose this date in particular.)[57] The connection to apostolic times had thus been completed.

Sola scriptura, sola traditio[58]

In order to better expound their theology, the early Reformers summarized it in the three "solas": *sola fide* (Latin for "faith alone,") *sola gratia* ("grace alone,") and *sola scriptura* ("scripture alone.")[59] *Sola scriptura*, in particular, can be defined as understanding scripture "as the *sole* source of divine revelation" and as "the *only* inspired, infallible, final, and authoritative norm of faith and practice."[60]

The proper relation between scripture and tradition had been under discussion since the Middle Ages. According to Prof. Heiko Oberman, a Dutch historian and theologian specialized in the study of the Reformation, there were two major currents regarding this medieval debate. Confusingly

---

[55] Barnett. "Where was your Church before Luther?" 17-18.

[56] Barnett. "Where was your Church before Luther?" 16-18.

[57] Barnett. "Where was your Church before Luther?" 20.

[58] This section was inspired by my article at *Where Peter Is*: Gabriel. "Sola Traditio."

[59] Hindson. *The Popular Encyclopedia*, 310. Some may add two more "solas": *solo Christo* ("through Christ alone") and *soli Deo gloria* ("glory to God alone.")

[60] Mathison. "Solo scriptura" 3.

enough, he calls these two currents "traditions." According to the first current ("Tradition 1,") scripture was the sole source of divine revelation, and the Church was to be its interpreter in the hermeneutical context of the "rule of faith." As for the second current ("Tradition 2,") it postulated a double source, in which unwritten tradition was to supplement biblical revelation.[61] Both of these currents could claim the support of at least some early Fathers of the Church. During the scholastic period, theologians and canonists stressed the primacy of scripture, but also presupposed the magisterial authority of the Church. By the sixteenth century, there was a spectrum of opinion between Tradition 1 and Tradition 2, so a doctrinal consensus was yet to emerge.[62]

The Reformers saw themselves as merely continuing this debate, resisting what they saw as the abuses of Tradition 2 by returning to the most ancient and venerable Tradition 1.[63] However, this introduced a novel instability. During the medieval debates, theologians and canonists acknowledged the "tension" (*complexio oppositorum*) between scripture and tradition, but usually did not see both as in contradiction with one another.[64] Rather, scripture, tradition, and magisterium enjoyed a *complementary* relationship: scripture was the authority in the Church but could not be properly understood without the interpretation of the Church Fathers and the guidance of the magisterium.[65]

Catholics reacted against the Reformers' appropriation of Tradition 1. To better understand this reaction, it is instructive to examine the case of Jacob van Hoogstraten, an inquisitor of several German ecclesiastical provinces at the time, and a notorious controversialist.[66] At first, van Hoogstraten tried to answer Luther by writing a fictional dialogue with St. Augustine, one of the earliest Church Fathers who could be ascribed to Tradition 2. But here, van Hoogstraten's objective was not to enroll the aid of Augustine as a Church Father, but as an exegete. He sought to show the compatibility between scripture and certain Catholic tenets on baptism and

[61] Mathison. "Solo scriptura" 2.
[62] Ickert. "Catholic Controversialist," 16.
[63] Mathison. "Solo scriptura" 2.
[64] Ickert. "Catholic Controversialist," 16.
[65] Ickert. "Catholic Controversialist," 17.
[66] Ickert. "Catholic Controversialist," 13-14.

justification that the Protestants deemed unscriptural.[67] Later on, the inquisitor got embroiled in polemics involving the theological faculties of Cologne and Louvain, as he tried to defend scholastic theology by basing it on scripture. In other words, van Hoogstraten was trying to find scriptural evidence for contested doctrines and practices. He was starting from Tradition 1,[68] as this was common ground with Protestants.

However, this soon would cease to be enough. As Scott Ickert, a doctor in Church History, writes in an article about van Hoogstraten:

> "As it became more and more evident to Catholic defenders that the Reformers eschewed patristic authority to stress its discontinuity with Scripture, it was clear that the traditional symbiotic relationship that had existed between Scripture and its authoritative interpreters no longer could be taken for granted or simply assumed uncritically."[69]

Therefore, van Hoogstraten would have to move his defense up to Tradition 2, asserting the dual mode of transmission of divine revelation. For the inquisitor, the traditions that the Protestants denied for being unscriptural—like the veneration of saints or the existence of purgatory—had been passed on orally by Christ to the apostles, who passed them on to the Church, who later amplified and expounded them through the Fathers of the Church[70] (see chapter 1). For van Hoogstraten, the Church Fathers represent tradition in general and the magisterium in particular.[71] Patristic authority stemmed from the same foundation upon which scripture had been built, so the bond between scripture and extra-scriptural tradition had to be maintained.[72]

---

[67] Ickert. "Catholic Controversialist," 19-22.
[68] Ickert. "Catholic Controversialist," 22.
[69] Ickert. "Catholic Controversialist," 22.
[70] Ickert. "Catholic Controversialist," 25.
[71] Ickert. "Catholic Controversialist," 22.
[72] Ickert. "Catholic Controversialist," 26.

Extra-scriptural tradition was not to be regarded as *un*scriptural.[73] To prove this, van Hoogstraten had gone to great lengths to find scriptural basis for the allegedly unscriptural traditions of the Church. Luther and his followers did not see those foundations because their view of scripture was, at the same time, "too restrictive" and "fragmented."[74] Sometimes, scripture was to be read figuratively, not literally.[75] Also, scripture should be read as a whole, not in a patchy way. For this reason, van Hoogstraten would say that "Lutherans listen to scripture with only half an ear."[76]

Not only were extra-scriptural traditions to be found in a figurative and holistic reading of scripture, but they could also even help to better illustrate the deeper meaning of scripture. As we have seen in chapter 6, this was the rationale St. Athanasius used to defend the unscriptural *homoousios* as an accurate expression of the teachings on the Trinity that are only implicit in scripture. If Luther was to reject the traditions of the church merely because they were extra-scriptural, —van Hoogstraten asserted—then he would also have to deny that the Son was unbegotten or that Mary was a perpetual virgin,[77] since *homoousios* and *Theotokos* were also not present in scripture (chapter 6).

When van Hoogstraten moved from Tradition 1 to Tradition 2, he underwent a "structural," not an "essential metamorphosis," as regards to his reliance in scripture.[78] In both apologetical strategies, he was defending the true meaning of scripture against what he saw as Luther's innovations.

It bears emphasizing, however, Luther and other early Reformers did not outright reject all the tradition that preceded them.[79] As van Hoogstraten so well highlighted, they upheld the *homoousios*, for instance. As I said above, Tradition 1 postulates that, though scripture is the sole source of divine revelation, *it has to be interpreted in and by the Church.*[80] The disagreement was on what constituted the "church," as we have seen above. Tradition 1 never meant that "all of theology ought to be

[73] Ickert. "Catholic Controversialist," 23.
[74] Ickert. "Catholic Controversialist," 27.
[75] Ickert. "Catholic Controversialist," 23.
[76] Ickert. "Catholic Controversialist," 27-28.
[77] Ickert. "Catholic Controversialist," 23.
[78] Ickert. "Catholic Controversialist," 33.
[79] For a collection of quotes proving this, see Mathison. "Solo scriptura" 3-4.
[80] Mathison. "Solo scriptura," 2.

constructed anew, without reference to the church's tradition of interpretation, by the lonely exegete confronting the naked text."[81]

However, Catholic controversialists of the time were sensitive enough to understand the logical implications of Luther's theology. By challenging the authority of the Catholic Church to interpret scripture, Luther's *sola scriptura* eventually evolved into what is called "Tradition 0" (what Reformed theologian Keith Mathison derogatively calls "*solo scriptura*," in opposition to *sola scriptura*.) In practice, it is an absence of tradition. Tradition has no authority since each individual believer needs nothing more than the Bible and the guidance of the Holy Spirit.[82] The final standard is each individual's personal judgment, opening the doors to subjectivism and relativism.[83]

In the meantime, Catholic doctrine evolved, through the Council of Trent and the Counter-Reformation, to what Oberman termed "Tradition 3," placing the emphasis on the "magisterium of the moment."[84] This is also a hermeneutic that many traditionalists—at least of the "recognize and resist" variant—reject as a caricature of Catholicism.[85] However, in my opinion, this shows precisely a proper doctrinal development, perfectly harmonizing Tradition 1 and Tradition 2. If there are two modes of transmission of divine revelation, one written and the other oral (Tradition 2) and if the Church is to be the authoritative interpreter in the hermeneutical

---

81 Mathison. "Solo scriptura" 3.

82 Mathison. "Solo scriptura" 3.

83 Mathison. "Solo scriptura" 5-6.

84 Mathison. "Solo scriptura" 3.

85 Ferrara, "*Amoris Laetitia*: Anatomy of a Pontifical Debacle": "Nor can it be argued that the faithful have no capacity to recognize these contradictions but rather must blindly presume that somehow they do not exist. This is the Catholic Church, whose deposit of Faith is objectively knowable, not a gnostic sect headed by the Oracle of Rome, who announces what 'Jesus wants' today." See also Kwasniewski, "My Journey from Ultramontanism": "The conservative, by indiscriminately taking 'the Magisterium of the Moment' as his guide in all things, unmoors himself from the established content of cumulative teaching and risks being guided by the whims of a capricious monarch or the synthetic dogmas of an ideologue. The conservative would have no basis for questioning or disagreeing with a pope on any matter, no matter how much it departed from the teaching of his predecessors or even that of Scripture."

context of the "rule of faith" (Tradition 1), then Tradition 3 is the logical conclusion. This is what eventually became defined in *Dei Verbum* and beautifully summarized in the Catechism:

> *Sacred Tradition and Sacred Scripture*, then, are bound closely together, and communicate one with the other. *For both of them, flowing out from the same divine well-spring*, come together in some fashion to form one thing, and move towards the same goal. . . *The task of giving an authentic interpretation of the Word of God, whether in its written form or in the form of Tradition, has been entrusted to the living teaching office of the Church alone.* Its authority in this matter is exercised in the name of Jesus Christ. This means that the task of interpretation has been entrusted to the *bishops in communion with the successor of Peter, the Bishop of Rome.*[86]

Early Reformers would appeal to their own concept of tradition—defined in the broad sense—to turn this definition on its head. It would not be the magisterium to authoritatively interpret scripture, but scripture that would be used to judge the fidelity of the magisterial agents, as the Westminster Confession of Faith defends:

> The Supreme Judge, by which all controversies of religion are to be determined, and all decrees of councils, opinions of ancient writers, doctrines of men, and private spirits, are to be examined, and in whose sentence we are to rest, can be no other but the Holy Spirit speaking in the Scripture.[87]

Martin Chemnitz, whom as I said before, tried to refute the Council of Trent, had this to say:

> But when that body of men which has the title of the church departs from the true doctrine of the Word of God, it does not follow on that account, either that the sound doctrine is false, or that the errors, which that body of men holds, are the truth; but this

---

[86] CCC 80, 85.

[87] Westminster Divines. *Westminster Confession of Faith*, Chapter I, Article X.

> follows that that body of men, when it no longer has the true doctrine, is not the true church . . . For the church is not an autocratic or independent body of men, but it ought to show and prove by sure and firm testimonies that the doctrine which it holds and confesses is divinely revealed, true, and sound. These testimonies she takes from the canonical books of the Scripture, *as we have proved from expressions of the ancients.* [88]

It is impressive how much this rhetoric mimics today's traditionalists, if we simply replace "canonical books of Scripture" with "tradition." Yet, what many traditionalists seem to defend is a kind of *sola traditio*, in every way similar to *sola scriptura* except on the mode of transmission of divine revelation that it overemphasizes. [89] Many of the Catholic arguments presented by van Hoogstraten could be equally applied to tradition—not as a way to downplay tradition (just like he never sought to downplay scripture,) but to place it in its proper hermeneutical context.

Does this mean that the Catholic Church, by adopting Tradition 3, also falls into its own extreme? A kind of *solo magisterio*, if you will? [90] Not at all. Even if the Church has three pillars (scripture, tradition, and magisterium,) they are not all on the same plane. Scripture and tradition are two different modes of transmission of the same deposit of faith, but the magisterium is not a third mode. Rather, the magisterium is the authoritative interpreter of the other two. It is through the magisterium that we know the true meaning of both scripture and tradition. Therefore, Catholics do not believe in any "sola." Instead, they hold that the three must be in harmony, as a tightly held threefold cord. Even if the cord may be in tension sometimes, it must remain unbroken. Any interpretation that sets scripture or tradition against the magisterium is driving a wedge between what is indivisible and should, therefore, be abandoned.

---

88 Chemnitz. *Examination of the Council of Trent, Part I.*

89 Gabriel. "Sola Traditio."

90 Kwasniewski. "How Protestants, Orthodox, Magisterialists and Traditionalists differ."

The perspicuity of the Word of God[91]

Sola scriptura rests on another major Protestant tenet: the perspicuity of scripture. We have already seen that the Reformers believed that scripture alone was the source of divine revelation. The Catholic Church responded to this, affirming that, though scripture was the written Word of God, it required the authoritative interpretation of the magisterium. To eschew the need of an interpreter, the Reformers answered that scripture was "clear enough for the simplest person to live by"[92] i.e., perspicuous. The Westminster Confession of Faith illustrates the concept of perspicuity:

> All things in Scripture are not alike plain in themselves, nor alike clear unto all; *yet those things which are necessary to be known, believed, and observed, for salvation, are so clearly propounded and opened in some place of Scripture or other*, that not only the learned, but the unlearned, in a due use of *the ordinary means*, may attain unto a sufficient understanding of them.[93]

We must remember, however, that the early Reformers did not believe in Tradition 0, but in Tradition 1. For them, scripture was to be interpreted by and in the Church. Therefore, it was often necessary to take recourse to a teacher for an accurate interpretation.[94] After all, sometimes the meaning of scripture was indeed obscure—though they attributed this phenomenon to humankind's sinfulness.[95] However, this authoritative interpretation was made not by bishops, but by learned men versed in scripture, through the ministry of Bible teacher. This teacher was not to use magisterial authority to interpret scripture, but *ordinary means* i.e., normal rules of grammar and syntax.[96]

Of course, this notion flies in the face of historical reality. As we have seen, namely in chapter 6, both Arius and his opponents could use scripture

---

[91] This section was inspired by my article at *Where Peter Is*: Gabriel. "The Perspicuity of Tradition."

[92] Pettegrew. "The Perspicuity of Scripture," 214.

[93] Westminster Divines. *Westminster Confession of Faith*, Chapter I, Article VII.

[94] Pettegrew. "The Perspicuity of Scripture," 213.

[95] Pettegrew. "The Perspicuity of Scripture," 214.

[96] Pettegrew. "The Perspicuity of Scripture," 215.

to support their mutually exclusive positions. The Council of Nicaea had to use its magisterial authority to break the impasse, by promulgating a creed. Yet not even this was enough, for in the aftermath of the council, there were several divergent interpretations of the same creed. Consequently, neither scripture nor tradition are perspicuous. "Dead" documents cannot interpret themselves or signal when someone interpreted them accurately. To interpret a "dead" document, one needs a living agent, someone with a voice and with authority. In sum, an interpreter, a reliable guide amid a turmoil of conflicting analyses.[97] This is the *living* magisterium (see chapter 1).

Catholic apologists at the time of the Reformation already understood this. Jacob van Hoogstraten, for instance, appropriating an old dictum, would have said: *scriptura non est autentica sine authoritate ecclesiae* ("scripture is not authentic without the authority of the Church.")[98] For him, *sola scriptura* was "a smokescreen for selectivity,"[99] leading to dangerous scriptural interpretations. It would not be implausible to think that, at the end of his apologetical journey, the inquisitor might say, in the same vein: *traditio non est autentica sine authoritate ecclesiae* ("tradition is not authentic without the authority of the Church.)[100]

Diogo Paiva de Andrade, a Portuguese theologian and participant in Trent who contended with Chemnitz (see above), would concede that scripture was true and unchangeable, but he also brought attention to the fact that heretics could obscure parts of scripture and twist them to their ends—which, as we have seen before, has indeed happened before. As Andrade would have said, as quoted by Chemnitz himself:

> "Produce some passage which requires no interpreter and by which one cannot be convinced that it is spoken of something else, but you are attempting to twist it to your own sense. . . What is put ambiguously and may be interpreted in our favor and in yours will

---

[97] Gabriel. "Sola Traditio."
[98] Ickert. "Catholic Controversialist," 32.
[99] Ickert. "Catholic Controversialist," 30.
[100] Ickert. "Catholic Controversialist," 32.

> not help your cause at all; but it is evident that such things only sustain a bad cause by delaying settlement. . . These passages are mysterious, they are veiled, they are figurative; we urgently ask for something clear which does not need an interpreter."[101]

Martin Chemnitz, in his reply to Andrade and Trent, would defend perspicuity against these charges. For him, scripture was sufficient. If there were obscure passages in scripture, these could be clarified in light of plain passages also found in these same scriptures.[102] According to the doctrine of perspicuity, every Christian has the right to read and interpret scripture for himself, so that his faith may rest on the testimony of scriptures and not on that of the Church.[103]

For Chemnitz, therefore, the decrees of the Council of Trent were to be examined according to the norm of scripture. No one could forbid or condemn this "right of examination." For him, to "simply agree without examination, without investigation and judgment to the bare decrees of the Council of Trent, in which one and the same person is the accuser" was an exercise of "papalist tyranny." It would, in effect, "grant to councils infinite license to invent and decree what they pleased outside of, beside, and against the Word of God." Consequently, it would be dangerous to "take away the liberty of judging and diligence. . . lest we under the authority of a synod be led astray from the true, life-giving faith."[104]

In this sense, the authority of councils was indeed "most salutary in the church," but only insofar as "they judge according to the rule and norm of the sacred scripture. And when they prove their decisions by means of sure and clear testimonies of scripture, the church owes them obedience with the greatest reverence as to a heavenly voice. . . But when the mere name 'council' is heard, it ought not at once turn us into rocks, treetrunks, and stocks, as though it were the head of Gorgo,[105] so that we thoughtlessly

---

[101] Chemnitz. *Examination of the Council of Trent, Part I.*

[102] Chemnitz. *Examination of the Council of Trent, Part I.* See also Pettegrew. "The Perspicuity of Scripture," 213-214.

[103] Pettegrew. "The Perspicuity of Scripture," 216.

[104] Chemnitz. *Examination of the Council of Trent, Part I.*

[105] The gorgons were three mythological sisters, with hairs as serpents, that would turn to stone anyone who dared look at them. The most famous of these sisters was Medusa.

embrace any and all decrees without examination, without inquiry and careful judgment. For scripture tells us that there are also councils of the wicked."[106]

The Reformed polemicist vigorously asserted that the Council of Trent clamorously violated this principle. Whereas—according to Chemnitz—"the ancient councils did not thrust bare decrees, dictatorial and accountable to no one, upon the churches," but had explained their reasoning so that the faithful may more easily judge them, "the Tridentine judges promulgate *only the bare decrees, without reasons*, with praetorian authority in the Christian word, and immediately they seem ready to threaten with fire and sword those who contradict, or rather, who *only ask questions*. This is the shortcut which the canonists follow, that the Roman *pope may substitute his will for his reason in things he wants*."[107]

Chemnitz also complained that, when Protestants asked that this formula from the Council of Basel (see chapter 6) be inserted "And expressly, that in controversies of the divine law, the practice of Christ, of the apostles, and *of the primitive church*, together with the councils and teachers which genuinely take their stand on these, *are to be admitted as the truest judge in this council*," the Council of Trent replaced it with this alternative statement: "And expressly, that matters of controversy be dealt with. . . according to the Holy Scripture, *the traditions of the apostles, the approved councils, the consensus of the Catholic Church, and the authority of the holy fathers*."[108]

In all this exchange, we can see the slow gestation of both Tradition 0 and Tradition 3, mentioned in the last section. We cannot forget that what came about from the Protestant doctrine of perspicuity of scripture was, as we have seen, a subjectivist and relativist reading of scripture, that even Protestant scholars lament today.

As regards to the Catholic understanding, we can consult the current Catechism to appreciate the fruits of the development sowed in Trent. As we have seen before, the Catechism states that "the task of giving an authentic interpretation of the Word of God, whether in its written form or

---

[106] Chemnitz. *Examination of the Council of Trent, Part I.*
[107] Chemnitz. *Examination of the Council of Trent, Part I.*
[108] Chemnitz. *Examination of the Council of Trent, Part I.*

in form of Tradition, has been entrusted. . . to the bishops in communion with the successor of Peter."[109] But the Catechism goes even further. The proper interpretation of scripture requires more than grammar and syntax. To "interpret Scripture correctly, the reader must be attentive to what the human authors truly wanted to affirm, and to what God wanted to reveal to us by their words."[110] Furthermore, "the reader must take into account the conditions of their time and culture, the literary genres in use at that time, and the modes of feeling, speaking and narrating then current."[111]

In other words, Protestants may say that it is self-evident that, for example, the Catholic usage of statues of saints contradicts the plain meaning of scripture. Fine distinctions, like *latria* (worship) and *dulia* (veneration)[112] may seem like apologists "twisting themselves into pretzels" to justify practices that "obviously" go against scripture. But Catholics know that these fine distinctions provide a broader and more informed perspective on the Old Testament prohibition of carving images. Through this perspective, one can grasp the real reason why idolatry is wrong, and that idolatry can exist in relation to other things besides statues.

Doing so is not about finding farfetched explanations for the Catholic view, but about deepening our understanding of an issue or question. Rather than contradicting reason, theological insights that consider historical and literary contexts and cultural conditions are much richer and more intellectually edifying than simplistic and literal interpretations of scripture.

The same is true regarding the interpretation of tradition and historical magisterial pronouncements. They must account for "the conditions of their time and culture, the literary genres used, and the modes of feeling, speaking, and narrating." One must consider nuance, such as the distinction between tradition and traditions (see chapter 1), or between doctrine and discipline, or between different degrees of magisterial authority.

The Catechism goes on to explain that there is another principle for the correct interpretation of scripture that is equally important:

---

[109] CCC 85.
[110] CCC 109.
[111] CCC 110.
[112] Schiffer. "Dulia and Hyperdulia."

> Read the Scripture within "the *living* Tradition of the whole Church." According to a saying of the Fathers, Sacred Scripture is written principally in the Church's heart rather than in documents and records, for *the Church carries in her Tradition the living memorial of God's Word, and it is the Holy Spirit who gives her the spiritual interpretation of the Scripture* (". . . according to the spiritual meaning which the Spirit grants to the Church")[113]

This does not mean that scripture does not "exist in itself," simply that it does not exist in isolation. This point was superbly conveyed in an article by contemporary Catholic apologist Dave Armstrong:

> It's not that Scripture is so unclear and esoteric that it is an utter mystery and an undecipherable "code" that only Holy Mother Church can break, and that no individual can possibly understand. Rather, the Church is required to speak authoritatively as to what Holy Scripture teaches, just as it spoke authoritatively with regard to what books were to be included in Scripture. Holy Scripture remains inherently what it is: God's inspired, infallible written revelation.
>
> *Tradition* in the Bible (particularly for St. Paul) *is not an individualistic thing*, kept by each person as an esoteric "secret," as the gnostic heretics would have it. No, it is obviously a *corporately held entity*. It is held in common by the Church, as the collectivity of Christians.[114]

If this is true for scripture, it is also true for tradition. Tradition flows from the same source as scripture. Tradition is a mode of transmission of the Word of God, just like scripture is. And both have the same authoritative interpreter: the magisterium.

If traditionalists, following Trent and traditional Catholic teaching, reject the concept of perspicuity of scripture, then it logically follows that

---

[113] CCC 113.

[114] Armstrong. "The Clearness, or 'Perspicuity'"

they must reject perspicuity of tradition. If they do not, then they will have to explain why tradition is clear, sufficient, and perspicuous, yet scripture (which, as we have often seen, derives its authority from the same source, being transmitted only through a different medium) is not. Likewise, they will have to explain why they accept the magisterial contextualization of the many alleged contradictions between scripture and Catholic doctrine or practice, and yet eschew the same magisterial contextualization when it comes to alleged contradictions with tradition.

No one is privy to an authentic understanding of Catholic scripture or tradition apart from the rest of the Church. The traditional understanding is that scripture—which does indeed exist in itself—does not, and cannot, exist in isolation. *A fortiori*, the same holds true regarding unwritten tradition.

Chapter 9

"They have made a new church"

After the First Vatican Council, for example, the last vote, the one on infallibility, a well-sized group left and founded the Old Catholic Church so as to remain "true" to the tradition of the Church. Then they developed differently and now they ordain women. But in that moment they were rigid, they rallied behind orthodoxy and thought that the council had erred.

—Francis, In-flight press conference from Antananarivo to Rome

On October 4, 2019, the Vatican was bustling with activity. In a couple of days, a new synod of bishops would begin. Francis had decided that this 2019 synod would be dedicated to the Pan-Amazon region, so neglected by a western-centric Church and so attacked by economic and political interests.

On that day, to celebrate the start of the synod, there was a ceremony at the Vatican gardens. The service was thoroughly Catholic through and through, with prayer, preaching, and a symbolic planting of a holm tree from Assisi using soil coming from the Amazon. But what caught most people's eyes was a five-minute segment at the beginning of the ceremony where some indigenous people bowed before a mandala with many figurines symbolizing the Amazonian daily life and, most especially, two wooden statuettes of pregnant native women.[1]

Though the identity of these pregnant women left some people scratching their heads for a while, Catholic news outlets filled the informational void by saying that the dance resembled "the '*pago a la tierra*,' a traditional offering to Mother Earth common among indigenous peoples in some parts of South America."[2] From that point onward, the idea that there had been a pagan ceremony in honor of the goddess Pachamama

---

[1] A video of the whole event can be seen on YouTube at Vatican News. "Pope Francis-Feast of Saint Francis 2019-10-04." The relevant bits happen from the 07:00 to the 12:40 marks.

[2] Mares. "Amazon Synod: Ecological ritual."

(Quechua for "Mother Earth") became an undeniable truth for some Catholics.

Almost as soon as he became aware of it, Thomas Lawson sent Justin a screenshot of the indigenous Amazonians prostrating before the naked statues in the presence of the pope. He sent it alongside a challenge, which was more rhetorical than anything else: "I'm curious to see how you're going to spin *this*." The implication being that the "Pachamama" interpretation of events was obviously correct, and any other possible explanation would be mere apologetical exercises to cover up the evident and ugly truth. Tom was so scandalized; he had shielded his mind from considering any possibility that he may be wrong in his assessment of the situation.

Justin, as usual, did not reply immediately. He knew he should not be baited into stampeding by the heat of the controversy. Usually, clarity would appear when the dust settled. And, as predicted, that is exactly what happened. Some apologists, who had seen the whole ceremony from beginning to end, noticed that when the natives presented one of the statuettes to the pope for him to bless, they called it "Nuestra Señora de la Amazonia," which is Spanish for "Our Lady of the Amazon."[3] Even later, official Vatican spokespeople clarified that the statues were a mere representation of life and of the Amazonian peoples, and had been placed there "without idolatrous intentions."[4]

Tom, unfortunately, had closed himself to these explanations. He would push the Pachamama explanation even onto the denials. If the official spokespersons would say that the statues had no Marian connotation, he would see this as confirmation that it was not Our Lady of the Amazon, but rather a pagan goddess, even if the spokespeople denied the pagan connotation in the same breath as they denied the Marian one. Tom would not accept that the statues might hold different (and non-pagan) meanings to the indigenous people participating in the ceremony and to the officials who had organized it.[5] Only the pagan explanation, that neither natives nor

---

[3] See Vatican News. "Pope Francis-Feast of Saint Francis 2019-10-04," from the 13:20 to the 13:35 marks. See also Gabriel, "Paganism in the Vatican?"

[4] For a collection of these official statements, see Gabriel, "Our Lady of the Amazon, Pray for us"

[5] See Gabriel. "Our Lady of the Amazon: solving the contradictions."

organizers held, was truthful, because that was what Catholic websites were promoting—they knew better.

When Justin pointed this out to him, Tom reacted with indignation. "You're just defending the pope because you're an Ultramontanist! You think that everything the pope says or does is infallible! But that is not true Catholicism!"[6] His virtual voice calmed down, as he said: "I understand that temptation. I was an Ultramontanist myself once. But now, I have taken the red pill[7] and can see clearly. This pope is a liberal and is taking the side of liberals against the conservatives who are the true standard bearers of Catholicism!"

Thomas was, however, thrown off his guard when Justin replied that, yes, he was an Ultramontanist, and there was nothing wrong with that. In fact, that was what true Catholicism was. Tom did not know what to say! In every Catholic media he consumed, "Ultramontanist" was used as an insult.

To avoid scandalizing Tom even further, Justin clarified that he did not think that everything the pope said or did was infallible. He simply gave his submission of mind and will to the pope's magisterium, even his non-infallible teachings. As for the pope's actions, it is not that Justin believed the pope to be impeccable, but that he had examined the evidence and found it wanting. On the contrary, Justin knew that many Catholic pundits and websites had tried, since the beginning, to scrutinize every of Francis's actions and spin them in the worst possible light, to paint him as the worse pope of history. This Pachamama kerfuffle was just the latest instance of this.

Tom cackled. "So, all these theologians and faithful clergymen who have a problem with the pope are just wrong? How arrogant and imprudent can you be to dismiss the concerns of people with this intellectual statute! They are just trying to defend the perennial tradition of the Church! Yet,

---

[6] See, for example, Kwasniewski. "My Journey from Ultramontanism."

[7] This is a pop culture reference, often used in social media, that eventually took on a life of its own. In the movie *The Matrix*, taking the "red pill" means waking up from an illusory and comfortable world and facing reality as it really is. See Marshall. "Red Pilled on Pope Francis."

they have been sidelined, as usual, for this synod of the Amazon! Only the liberals are invited to talk! Do you really think that this is not just Pope Francis once again promoting his liberal agenda? The Pachamama ceremony is just setting the tone for the synod. It is a rigged synod,[8] a charade to make it seem like Francis consulted the bishops before doing what he wants. The synod's outcome is already preordained."

Tom once again copy-pasted the screenshot of the indigenous Amazonians bowing before the wooden statue: "Just look at this picture! What am I supposed to believe? The Ultramontanists' gaslighting or my own lying eyes? Knock it off! Do you think I'm stupid?" Afterwards, Thomas sent another picture, this time of a TLM priest consecrating the Eucharist according to the pre-conciliar rite: "Now tell me to my face that these two pictures are of the same Church. Francis and his followers have made a new Church!"

Traditionalism versus Ultramontanism

A distracted reader could be surprised if, while browsing *The Catholic Encyclopedia*, he would stumble upon the entry for "Traditionalism." After all, this encyclopedia was published at the height of the anti-modernist campaign (see chapter 10). But this bastion of orthodox knowledge defines traditionalism in *a negative way*,[9] not as a position that a Catholic should hold. On the contrary, the same encyclopedia's entry on "Ultramontanism" says: "A term used to denote integral and active Catholicism . . . being applicable to all Roman Catholics worthy of the name . . . For Catholics it would be superfluous to ask whether Ultramontanism and Catholicism are the same thing: assuredly, those who combat Ultramontanism are in fact combating Catholicism, even when they disclaim the desire to oppose it."[10]

---

[8] Eli. "Cardinals decry the misuse of the synod": "After the rigged synods in 2014 and 2015 and the sham sex abuse summit in February, savvy Catholics will be little surprised if revolution comes in October." See also Eli. "Vatican 2022 Synod on Synodality": "The synods under Pope Francis have been plagued by scandal, however, leaving many Catholics feeling they are 'rigged' in order to produce a preconceived outcome."

[9] Sauvage, "Traditionalism."

[10] Benigni, "Ultramontanism." See also O'Neill, "A Defense of Ultramontanism": "But how does the historical usage of the term 'ultramontane' hold any

However, what *The Catholic Encyclopedia* means by traditionalism is not the same as what we mean when we use that word today. Rather, it is referring to a very specific theological movement, circumscribed to the nineteenth century.

One of the major proponents of this nineteenth century traditionalism was the French priest and philosopher Felicité de la Mennais (penname Lamennais).[11] In 1817, he published the first volume of his *Essai sur l'indifférence en matière de religion* (French for "Essay on the indifference in religious matters.") His house became "the spiritual and intellectual capital of French Catholicism,"[12] and several Catholic personalities of the time came to him for advice and inspiration. In a century still recovering from the radical ideals of the French Revolution, or from the exaggerated rationalism and scientific positivism of the Enlightenment, or from a profound religious indifferentism, Lamennais emerged as a new, vibrant voice, revitalizing Catholicism, and turning it once more into a social force to be reckoned with. For Lamennais, the only way to oppose all the evils of his time was by advocating a papal theocracy,[13] wherein the Roman pontiff would rule over everyone, including kings and emperors. In other words, Lamennais was an Ultramontanist.

Ultramontane is a term that originated in the Middle Ages to describe a pope hailing from outside Italy. A *papa ultramontano* was a pope from the "other side of the mountains" i.e., the Alps. Later, the French and the Germans, while defending the power of their local churches against papal overreach, inverted the perspective: now it was the pope who dwelled in a distant world from the other side of the mountains. Ultramontane thus became a pejorative term to insult those who supported papal authority.[14]

---

significance for us today? Given that the term arose as an insult against those who challenged the claims of Gallicanism, and given that those who championed papal primacy over local kings and bishops were legitimized at Vatican I, the term ought not to be associated with heterodoxy but rather orthodoxy."

[11] Gurian. "Lamennais," 205.

[12] Gurian. "Lamennais," 207-208.

[13] O'Malley. *Vatican I*, 66-67.

[14] O'Malley. *Vatican I*, 60. See also Benigni, "Ultramontanism."

The Ultramontanes were, however, a very diverse group. Though they all agreed that papal authority was to be exalted above both episcopal and secular authorities,[15] the particulars of how that papal authority was to be exerted was not so consensual among them. Lamennais is proof of such diversity. His particular brand of Ultramontanism would eventually evolve into Traditionalism and liberalism.

It is important to understand the historical-social context that motivated Lamennais's ideas. After the waning of the French Revolution and the final defeat of Napoleon Bonaparte, Louis XVIII of the House of Bourbon reinstituted the French monarchy in 1814. The Catholic Church, having suffered severe persecution at revolutionary and Napoleonic hands, aligned itself with this restoration.

But Lamennais was not pleased with this arrangement. For him, the Bourbon regime was a vessel for Gallican beliefs, like the need for the Church to submit to secular rulers (more on that later). This restorationist regime was slowly dying[16] and the Pope should jump ship before he was caught up on the whirlpool. Whereas other Ultramontanes applauded the marriage between throne and cathedra, Lamennais supported its divorce. For him, the papacy should not ally with princes, but with the people. The philosopher conceived of a strange chimera where papal maximalism was combined with laicism and freedom of speech, press, and religion. A theocratic democracy if you will.[17] In 1826, he published the essay *De la religion considérée dans ses rapport avec l'ordre politique et civile* ("On religion considered on its relationship with the political and civil order"). In 1830, he founded the journal *L'Avenir* ("the tomorrow").

To bind all the pieces of his chimera together, Lamennais formulated a metaphysical philosophical-theological system which would later be called "Traditionalism." According to this system, all the instruments by which humans apprehend the world—senses, reason, feelings—are fallible and, therefore, unreliable. To achieve the rule of certitude, therefore, one cannot rely on oneself, but on something external. This can be done by comparing one's own senses, feelings, and reason with the senses, feelings, and reason of other people. The rule of certitude is the common consent

---

[15] O'Malley. *Vatican I*, 61.

[16] Gurian. "Lamennais," 208.

[17] O'Malley. *Vatican I*, 66-67.

or agreement of all. Before trusting on reason, a person must take a leap of faith, blindly believing in what is the *sens commun* ("common sense") or *raison générale* ("general reason").[18] This way, Lamennais sought to oppose the rationalism of his age by falling on the extreme opposite, a kind of fideism.[19]

According to Lamennais, faith was identified with the original beliefs of the human race, revealed by God to our first ancestors. These original beliefs were later restored by Jesus Christ and preserved by the Catholic Church.[20] Before trusting in reason, one must trust in tradition, here identified with the *raison générale*—hence the name "Traditionalism."

Lamennais was not only skeptical of each individual's senses, feelings, and reason. He also had a profoundly negative opinion about the present, imperfect world. To escape this world, Lamennais would project his dreams onto a better world, that could exist either in the Catholic afterlife or in an earthly future where the Church would shepherd a utopian society built upon freedom.[21] The monarchs of Bourbon France and of all of Europe were adversaries of this project. They should, therefore, be rejected. Thus, Lamennais was one of the founders, not only of Traditionalism, but also of Catholic liberalism.

Of course, Lamennais's theology and philosophy contains many logical holes. For example: if each individual's senses, feelings, and reason are unreliable, why would the agreement of all individuals' fallible senses, feelings, and reason somehow become a rule of certitude? Furthermore, Lamennais's Traditionalism was a kind of fideism: divine revelation replaced reason instead of being ascertained by it.[22] Yet, the Catholic Church had condemned fideism as erroneous, for human reason is indeed capable of knowing with certitude some fundamental truths of the natural, moral, and religious order.[23] Regarding Lamennais's liberalism, it was based on a romantic, lyric notion that justice would inevitably be realized once the

[18] Sauvage, "Traditionalism."
[19] Gurian. "Lamennais," 215.
[20] Gurian. "Lamennais," 215.
[21] Gurian. "Lamennais," 212.
[22] Sauvage, "Traditionalism."
[23] Sauvage, "Traditionalism."

people were free from the tyrannies of princes. He never seemed to consider that injustices could be committed in the name of oppressed peoples.[24]

Obviously, his ideas gathered him many enemies among the Gallicans who, as we will see later, emphasized submission to the rulers Lamennais so much despised.[25] But it was the Holy Father's opposition that surprised Lamennais the most. After all, Gregory XVI had, prior to his election as pope, published a book called *Il Trionfo della Santa Sede e della Chiesa contro gli assalti dei novatori* (Italian for "The Triumph of the Holy See and of the Church over the attacks of innovators,") effectively kickstarting the Ultramontane movement.[26] Yet, in his eagerness to defend freedom for all, Lamennais significantly misread his historical context.

In 1830, many rebellions popped up through Europe, inflamed by revolutionary ideals. One such rebellions toppled the Bourbon king of France, replacing him with his cousin. The Papal States were not spared from this wave of revolutionary fervor. The papal army was manifestly insufficient to quell the uprising. Order could be restored only with the aid of troops sent by Austria and France.[27] Though Lamennais had accurately predicted the decadence of the Bourbon regime, Gregory XVI had been attacked by his own subjects and saved by the power of the monarchs. The pope had every reason to mistrust the peoples Lamennais supported, and to trust the kings Lamennais despised.

In a bout of naïve enthusiasm, Lamennais set out to Rome in 1831 to ask for the pope's approval.[28] The timing could not, obviously, have been more unfortunate. The ashes of the 1830 rebellion were still looming over the Papal States. Gregory XVI would respond in 1832 through his first encyclical *Mirari Vos*. In this encyclical, the pope condemned the separation of Church and State and the freedoms of speech and press, so dear to Lamennais.[29] Though the pontiff did not name the French philosopher by name, *Mirari Vos* made Lamennais's political philosophy untenable from a Catholic perspective. Two years later, Gregory would issue another

---

[24] Gurian. "Lamennais," 223.
[25] Gurian. "Lamennais," 217.
[26] O'Malley. *Vatican I*, 51.
[27] O'Malley. *Vatican I*, 52.
[28] Gurian. "Lamennais," 219.
[29] O'Malley. *Vatican I*, 53.

encyclical, basically reasserting the principles of *Mirari Vos*. Its title was *Singulari Nos* and its subtitle was literally *On the Errors of Lamennais.*

Lamennais's utopian fantasies laid now utterly crushed. The foundations of his faith had been shaken to their core. Though at first, the philosopher replied "We must submit to papal judgment,"[30] soon he started to drift away from said judgment. The pope had acted not like a father, but as a diplomat, swayed by the political intrigues of the European princes.[31] Lamennais tried to make a distinction between the pope as head of the Church and the pope as a private person expressing political opinions.[32] This was, evidently, just wishful thinking on his part, a conclusion in search of an argument, a clumsy way to solve the cognitive dissonance between being a papal defender and disagreeing with the pope. It could not last long.

Lamennais's inner clash between his Ultramontanism and his liberalism continued, but his political ideals were the ones that won the battle for his soul. Previously, he had advocated for a kind of theocratic democracy. Since theocracy and democracy were now deemed incompatible, he would drop the former and keep the latter. Soon, he would consign the pope to the same contempt as the monarchs he so hated. The Roman pontiff was just another prince, another tyrant, another obstacle to the fulfilment of freedom. Lamennais took the infallible character once ascribed to the pope and gave it to the people instead.[33] Since the Church disappointed him, Lamennais replaced her with humanity itself.[34] At the end of his life, the philosopher had abandoned the priesthood, renounced his Catholicism, and professed instead a vaguely spiritualistic progressive humanitarianism.[35]

The spiritual decline of such a luminary as Lamennais is one of the greatest tragedies of nineteenth century Catholicism. However, though we may agree that the philosopher was treated quite harshly, the pope's

---

30 Gurian. "Lamennais," 220-221.
31 Gurian. "Lamennais," 219.
32 Gurian. "Lamennais," 221.
33 Gurian. "Lamennais," 224.
34 Gurian. "Lamennais," 211.
35 Gurian. "Lamennais," 213.

position is also understandable. As Waldemar Gurian, a twentieth century political scientist explains on his work on Lamennais:

> The system of Lamennais was an expression of his belief in his particular mission which brought him in conflict with the Papacy. He was the standard-bearer of an ultramontanism fighting against a Gallicanism which was trying to limit the Papal authority in the interest of egoistic and particular power. But in reality, he sought to determine the action of that authority in whose name and for whose rights he was acting . . . He did not realize that his policy tried to bind the Church to a political-social system, and thus subordinated her supra-temporal and supra-political mission to a temporal social and political movement in the same way that his opponents, the defenders of the unity between Church and the regimes of the Restoration, had done. That was the crucial issue behind the condemnation. . .
>
> Lamennais tried to impose his leadership on the Church, and to replace the authority of the Papacy. And he tried to identify this leadership with certain political and social demands. Surely, Pope Gregory XVI overestimated the practical possibilities of cooperation with the princes—he himself later regretted the confidence which he put in Czar Nicholas I. It may be that the Pope did not always judge the actual political situation correctly, overestimating the Christian character of the conservative regimes and not trying to discover, as the *Avenir* did, the true longing of the masses behind antireligious speakers. But Lamennais created a situation unacceptable to the Papacy; a group of men without authority, Lamennais and his friends, tried to impose its views on the whole Church by mobilizing public opinion. Lamennais himself had always stressed the Papal authority—he had done it also in the *Avenir* with unquestionable sincerity; how could he hope that Papal authority would subordinate itself to his interpretation of history and of the duties of the Church in contemporary society?[36]

[36] Gurian. "Lamennais," 225-226.

In the end, not only Lamennais's liberalism, but also his Traditionalism would stand condemned. A few decades later, the First Vatican Council dedicated chapter 4 of *Dei Filius* to the relationship between faith and reason. Here, the Council Fathers defined a twofold order of knowledge: on the one hand we know by natural reason, on the other hand we know by divine faith.[37] Reason does indeed attain some understanding of the divine mysteries when it persistently, piously, and soberly seeks such understanding.[38] The Fathers would go on to say:

> Not only can faith and reason never be at odds with one another but they mutually support each other, for on the one hand right reason established the foundations of the faith and, illuminated by its light, develops the science of divine things; on the other hand, faith delivers reason from errors and protects it and furnishes it with knowledge of many kinds.[39]

However, the First Vatican Council did much more than condemn Traditionalism. Its main target was not so much Traditionalism, as Gallicanism. And though Lamennais had split the Ultramontane movement in two,[40] the faction that remained Ultramontane had in Gallicanism a much greater, much more ancient foe.

"Ultramontane innovations"

To understand what Gallicanism is, we must turn our calendars back to the seventeenth century. At that time, political tensions were at a peak. Pope Innocent XI's papal primacy clashed with the monarchical absolutism of King Louis XIV of France. The French clergy's fidelity was split between two competing duties, the religious and the secular. The Assembly of the Clergy of France gathered in 1682 and discussed the matter.

---

[37] Vatican I. *Dei Filius*, Chapter 4, 2.
[38] Vatican I. *Dei Filius*, Chapter 4, 4.
[39] Vatican I. *Dei Filius*, Chapter 4, 10.
[40] O'Malley. *Vatican I*, 68.

Historians nowadays do not believe that this meeting was commandeered by the king, but rather that it expressed the French clergy's authentic and traditional beliefs.[41] At the end, the assembly produced a declaration with four articles:

1. Jesus Christ gave Peter and his successors authority over spiritual, not temporal matters.
2. Papal authority on spiritual matters did not hinder the authority of ecumenical councils, as defined by the decrees of the fourth and fifth sessions of the Council of Constance.
3. The authority of the Holy See must also be regulated according to the liberties of the French church, namely long-standing rules, customs, and constitutions sanctioned by time and by the whole church at some time.
4. The pope's judgment is not irreformable unless it receives the consent of the whole church.[42]

This was the birth of Gallicanism as we know it. But even though these principles were codified by the 1682 declaration, they were not created by it.[43] For Gallicans, these principles went back to the first centuries of Church history.[44] During the first millennium, it was customary for the governance of the Church to be done by bishops, either individually or collectively through councils both local and ecumenical.[45] The Gallicans would point out that the Roman church had been saved several times by

---

[41] O'Malley. *Vatican I*, 27.

[42] O'Malley. *Vatican I*, 26-27. See also Dégert, "Gallicanism."

[43] Dégert, "Gallicanism."

[44] O'Malley. *Vatican I*, 29. See also Dégert, "Gallicanism": "If we are to credit these authors, what the Gallicans maintained in 1682 was not a collection of novelties, but a body of beliefs as old as the Church, the discipline of the first centuries. The Church of France had upheld and practiced them at all times; the Church Universal had believed and practiced them of old, until about the tenth century; St. Louis had supported, but not created them, by the Pragmatic Sanction; the Council of Constance had taught them with the pope's approbation. Gallican ideas, then, must have had no other origin than that of Christian dogma and ecclesiastical discipline."

[45] O'Malley. *Vatican I*, 28.

the action of the whole church, namely when the papacy had to be liberated from the Roman nobility in the eleventh century.[46]

As for France in particular, the popes had made several concessions throughout the centuries, divesting some of their authority in favor of French bishops and kings. After all, the French church had always distinguished itself by its exactitude in the preservation of the faith and the maintenance of ecclesiastical discipline (see chapter 7: "Imposing on people's rites").[47] As a Gallican author would remark: "Of all Christian countries, France has been the most careful to conserve the liberty of her Church and *oppose the novelties introduced by Ultramontane* canonists."[48]

For the Gallicans, therefore, the Ultramontane claims of papal primacy and infallibility[49] were later additions, not sustained by tradition. Throughout history, the papacy had gradually usurped the prerogatives belonging to the local bishops.[50] Also, the Gallicans believed that the papacy's independence from secular powers had been a novelty introduced by our old friend St. Gregory VII, who, unlike his predecessors, had excommunicated kings and nobles for the grievances they had inflicted upon the Church.[51] Consequently, Gallicanism was viewed as a revival of the most ancient traditions of Christianity.[52]

This did not mean that Gallicans did not believe in the pope's primacy. They were simply against what they perceived as novel excesses of papal authority. As historian John O'Malley explains: "For them, the Holy See was the center where everything came together, not the source from which everything flowed."[53] Papal primacy was limited by the temporal power of

---

[46] O'Malley. *Vatican I*, 28.

[47] Dégert, "Gallicanism."

[48] Dégert, "Gallicanism."

[49] Papal primacy refers to the supreme episcopal jurisdiction of the pope as pastor and governor of the Universal Church. Papal infallibility refers to the pope's immunity from teaching error when defining dogma.

[50] O'Malley. *Vatican I*, 29.

[51] Dégert, "Gallicanism." See also O'Malley. *Vatican I*, 61. For an account of the excommunication of the Holy Roman Emperor Henry IV by Pope Gregory VI, see Mullin, *A Short World History of Christianity*, 99-100.

[52] Dégert, "Gallicanism."

[53] O'Malley. *Vatican I*, 56.

princes, by the authority of ecumenical councils, by the consent of bishops, and by the canons and customs of the local churches.[54] In doing so, they were, in their view, accepting a notion of papal authority that was more in conformity with scripture and tradition.[55]

In 1691, Innocent XI's successor, Alexander VIII, issued the bull *Inter Multiplices*, proclaiming the 1682 French declaration null and void of every authority. Alexander, however, did not fully condemn Gallicanism out of fear of political retaliation. This allowed the Gallicans to interpret the bull in a more generous way than what the pontiff intended. The pope had shown disfavor, but had not proscribed Gallicanism, so it was still an allowed opinion.[56]

Gallicanism would not remain confined inside French borders. As the eighteenth century advanced, more statist politicians felt that the Gallican principles could be useful in establishing national churches with a greater fidelity to king than to pope. These politicians were more the sons of the Enlightenment than of the Church, but they saw the Church as a convenient division of the state, serving the state for its purposes.[57] In 1763, von Hontheim, the auxiliary bishop of Trier, published a book "On the constitution of the Church and the legitimate power of the Pope," under the pseudonym Justinius Febronius.[58] For Febronius, Germany had as much right to concessions as France, since the German emperors were also heirs to Charlemagne.[59] Emperor Joseph II of Austria would use Febronius's writings to justify his modernizing and enlightened reforms.[60] Thus, Febronianism and Josephism became the names of the German and Austrian versions of Gallicanism, respectively.

When the French Revolution erupted, the National Assembly applied Gallican principles in their anticlerical Civil Constitutions of the Clergy, stripping the Church of her property, unilaterally reducing the number of dioceses in France, decreeing that bishops should be locally elected without the need of papal approval, and forcing every member of the clergy to

---

[54] Dégert, "Gallicanism."
[55] Dégert, "Gallicanism."
[56] O'Malley. *Vatican I*, 28.
[57] O'Malley. *Vatican I*, 34.
[58] O'Malley. *Vatican I*, 29. See also Dégert, "Gallicanism."
[59] Dégert, "Gallicanism."
[60] O'Malley. *Vatican I*, 30.

swear allegiance to the state.[61] When Napoleon took power, he signed a concordat with the Holy See reasserting all these measures.[62]

When the Bourbon reinstated the monarchy (see above), Gallicanism was severely weakened from years of serving discredited political powers. In the meantime, Ultramontanism emerged as a reaction against this political instability. The best antidote to all the evils the Church had experienced in the past century or two was to strengthen papal authority against the encroachment of the statists.

Though considered as an innovation by the Gallicans, Ultramontanism also boasted of a venerable pedigree. The previous chapters of this book witness to many instances of papal primacy. The fact that Peter had a special preeminence among the other disciples was widely recognized in the Church of the first centuries. It was solidly grounded in scripture[63] and acknowledged by the early bishops both of east and west.[64] By the fifth century, there was already a tradition that the Roman church could not err in matters of contested doctrines, since 1) it had been the place where Peter had been martyred, 2) it had double apostolicity (being founded also by Paul), and 3) had an impeccable record of supporting the position that ended up being considered orthodox in hotly contested doctrinal debates.[65] We will see more of that in chapter 12.

But it was during the Middle Ages that the issue of papal authority matured the most. The pope became the ruler of the Papal States, a monarch as any other in Europe. Papal power became more centralized and claimed authority even over secular rulers. Theologians and canonists started deliberating and debating on papal infallibility and what this entailed.[66] The Council of Florence, in particular, seemed to affirm papal supremacy.[67]

---

[61] O'Malley. *Vatican I*, 42.
[62] O'Malley. *Vatican I*, 57.
[63] Mt 16:17-20; John 21:15-17; Luke 22:31-34
[64] O'Malley. *Vatican I*, 6-7.
[65] O'Malley. *Vatican I*, 8.
[66] O'Malley. *Vatican I*, 6, 9, 61.
[67] O'Malley. *Vatican I*, 204-205.

Ultramontanism received an additional boost during the Reformation. As Protestants rejected papal teachings, Catholics reacted by emphasizing papal infallibility and the reliability of the magisterium (see chapter 8). Particularly important to outline the later Ultramontane claims, was Cardinal St. Robert Bellarmine, the famous Jesuit Counter-Reformer theologian, whose writings on the papacy soon became considered the gold standard on the issue. Bellarmine also wrote against some Parisian theologians (namely Jean Gerson, whom I have mentioned in chapter 7) that had promoted concepts which would later form the basis for the 1682 Gallican declaration.[68] The emerging Ultramontanism was on an inevitable collision course with Gallicanism.

Ultramontanism suffered a mutation during the eighteenth and nineteenth centuries. The greatest adversaries for Catholics were no longer the Protestants, but the princes and revolutionaries that demanded Catholics to set fidelity to the state above their religious commitments. As time went on, allegiance to the papacy ceased to be "an opposition to the Reformation" and became more an "opposition to the times."[69]

We have come full circle to Gregory XVI's papacy and his publication of the *Triumph of the Church.* The Ultramontane movement was now in full force, taking advantage of Gallicanism's weakened state. The two factions were now warring for the heart of the Church. As O'Malley once again explains, these two parties were separated by a "*methodological variance regarding the church's tradition.* The difference was the result of two divergent approaches to the deeply disturbing problem of how the church was to deal with at least *seemingly discrepancies between past teaching and their present counterparts.*"[70]

Nevertheless, it would be Gregory's successor who would take the most important steps for—as O'Malley says in the subtitle of his seminal book on Vatican I— "the making of the Ultramontane Church."

---

[68] O'Malley. *Vatican I*, 6, 61-62.

[69] O'Malley. *Vatican I*, 49.

[70] O'Malley. *Vatican I*, 5.

A "rigged" council

When Pius IX succeeded Gregory XVI in 1846, he was considered more sympathetic to liberal ideas than his conservative predecessor. He was young, friendly, and eager to undertake necessary reforms in the Papal States. However, these would never go far enough to please the revolutionaries. In 1848, a revolt exploded in Rome. Pius had to be smuggled outside of his palace and escape to the countryside. A popular assembly was established in Rome stripping the pope of his temporal power. Only the following year was the pope's rule reestablished with the aid of French troops. Pius IX's sovereignty, however, was still precarious, and would remain so throughout all his pontificate.[71] This traumatic experience severely hardened Pius IX against liberalism. The most Ultramontane pope in all of history had just been born.

His most formidable foe was also slowly coming to light. In 1826, a German priest named Ignaz von Döllinger became a professor at the University of Munich. Soon, his scholarship and intellectual acumen became widely known across Germany and the world. His contemporaries referred to him as "Germany's most internationally celebrated theologian" and "*primus doctor Germaniae*"[72] ("greatest professor of Germany.") He counted Cardinal Newman as one of his admirers and became provost of the Royal Church of St. Cajetan, as well as privy councilor to the crown.[73] His future seemed bright, his career unassailable, his work impeccable.

Unfortunately, as Pius IX shifted from a more liberal to a more conservative stance, Döllinger's position also moved away from his original Ultramontanism. The professor became increasingly worried with what he saw as the "Romanizing tendencies of the Pope and his Jesuit backers."[74] In 1861, Prof. Döllinger delivered a series of lectures that generated a wave of controversy all around Europe. He advocated for the dissolution of the Papal States, praised Bishop Bossuet (one of the leading Gallican

[71] O'Malley. *Vatican I*, 96-98.
[72] Howard. *The Pope and the Professor*, 3.
[73] Howard. *The Pope and the Professor*, 3-4.
[74] Howard. *The Pope and the Professor*, 5.

theologians of the seventeenth century) as a "Church Father," and defended the prerogatives of Catholic theologians in the face of Rome's obscurantism.[75]

The pope's reaction was predictable. In 1863, Pius IX published an apostolic letter to the Archbishop of Munich, titled *Tuas Libenter*, in which he reminded the archbishop of the duty of German theologians to submit to papal authority.[76] Later, Pius IX promulgated the encyclical *Quanta Cura* with an appendix: the famous Syllabus of Errors. Here, the pope condemned a series of modern propositions, including many that could be attributed to Döllinger. In the meantime, a series of Ultramontane articles started to pop up in Catholic periodicals favorable to the pope, namely in the semiofficial *La Civiltà Cattolica.*

Döllinger did not sit idly. If the pope and the ultramontanes were going to use the press, then the professor would fight fire with fire. He published five articles in the German newspaper *Augsburger Allgemeine Zeitung*, responding to the *Civiltà*'s position.[77] Though Döllinger certainly accepted papal primacy, he believed the kind of primacy envisioned by Pius IX had no support from tradition. It was a later (and questionable) development from the Middle Ages.[78] Some Gallican thinkers joined the fray, publishing books and articles of their own, using historical precedent in support of their position. Among them was Bishop Dupanloup of Orleans, who accused the Ultramontanes of "fomenting discord among bishops, deliberately polarizing opinions, agitating for infallibility with amateur and ill-informed arguments, labeling legitimate opinions heresy, speaking of the papacy in ways that equated it with the divinity."[79]

This animosity did not exist in a vacuum. The Italian nationalist movement had rallied around the figure of King Victor Emmanuel of Savoy, seeking to unify the whole Italian peninsula under one single nation. This, of course, included the Papal States. By 1860, most of these lands had been successfully conquered, and only the city of Rome itself and its vicinity

---

[75] O'Malley. *Vatican I*, 121-122.
[76] O'Malley. *Vatican I*, 122.
[77] O'Malley. *Vatican I*, 124.
[78] Howard. *The Pope and the Professor*, 5. See also O'Malley. *Vatican I*, 124.
[79] O'Malley. *Vatican I*, 129.

remained under papal control. The dispute between Gallicans and Ultramontanes had clear political implications.

Five years later, Pius IX convoked a council to be gathered at the Vatican. This would be the First Vatican Council. The Gallicans panicked. They feared that this new council would set the Ultramontane doctrines on infallible stone. Döllinger in particular had fought long and hard to explain why defining papal infallibility in the explosive context they were living in was an incredibly bad idea. It would be turning a shaky movement of the medieval papacy into the irreversible teaching of the Catholic Church.[80] The Gallicans felt the pontiff pulling the strings behind the *Civiltà*'s articles and concluded that the council was rigged against them.[81]

However, all the controversy involving Döllinger and the Gallicans backfired against them. The reasons why Pius IX asked for a council are unclear,[82] but the suggested order of business at the beginning focused on rationalism, materialism, and indifferentism. Gallicanism and papal infallibility seemed not to be a central point of the planned proceedings of the council.[83] But now, thanks to the downpour of Gallican articles, papal

---

[80] Howard. *The Pope and the Professor*, 5.

[81] O'Malley. *Vatican I*, 123.

[82] O'Malley. *Vatican I*, 107.

[83] O'Malley. Vatican I, 109. See also De Mattei. *Pius IX,* 130—131: "Pius IX confided in a group of cardinals his project of calling a new ecumenical council as a remedy against the grave evils of the time. . . The bull of convocation [Aeterni Patris] explained that the purpose of the Council was to 'offer a remedy to the ills of the present century in the Church and society'. . . In the bull *Aeterni Patris*, no mention was made of the problem of Papal infallibility." See also Sheridan. "A Note on Mr. Blanshard," 692: "Mr. Blanshard implies that the Council was convened solely for the purpose of defining infallibility, a view which is thoroughly unhistorical. Infallibility did become the most violently agitated question in the Council, but the latter accomplished a great deal of other important work and projected more which was interrupted by the outbreak of war. . . The Council convened in December 1868, and the matter of infallibility was not opened in the Council until May the following year. Since the Council closed in mid-July, only about one-third of its time was spent on infallibility. It was on December 6, 1864, that Pius IX instructed the curial cardinals to consider the advisability of an ecumenical council. Within a few months he was in receipt of some twenty-one reports, of which only two saw no need for a council and only two mentioned papal

primacy and infallibility had turned into the controversy of the day. It would be very hard for the council to ignore those topics.[84] The outcome Döllinger and his likeminded fellows so much feared became a self-fulfilling prophecy because of their preemptive and aggressive defensiveness. An ecumenical council, led by the most Ultramontane pope yet, was about to discuss the merits of Ultramontanism and of its rival theology, Gallicanism.

On December 8, 1869, the First Vatican Council was opened, assembling seven hundred bishops from around the world, becoming the greatest Catholic (or even European) gathering up to that time.[85] Soon, the bishops coalesced into two factions. On one side were the Gallicans, joined by the liberals (the latter influenced by Lamennais). As historian O'Malley describes:

> At the council, the gallicans wanted above all to preserve the *traditional role of bishops and councils* in the governance of the church. They opposed the definition of papal infallibility in principle, because they saw it as unnecessary or inopportune. . . . Their fundamental theological objection to the doctrine as formulated by many of its advocates was that *it destroyed the traditional organic structure of the church* by separating the head from the body.[86]

The Gallicans brought up, as was usual in their argumentation, many historical examples for their position, namely the traditional role of bishops in defining doctrine, especially when gathered in ecumenical councils[87]—an ironical stance to take in an ecumenical council poised to define a doctrine they disagreed with. They also argued by wielding the precedent of

---

infallibility. The supposedly subservient Roman party seems to have mistaken the mind of its master."

[84] O'Malley. *Vatican I*, 130. Here, O'Malley quotes Schatz. Vaticanum I, 1:272-273, which in turn cites an axiom said at the time by Bishop Charles Couseau of Angouleme: *Quod inopportunum dixerunt, necessarium fecerunt* ("by talking inappropriately, they made it necessary").

[85] O'Malley. *Vatican I*, 133.

[86] O'Malley. *Vatican I*, 131.

[87] O'Malley. *Vatican I*, 207.

the so-called heretical popes, like Pope Honorius. We are going to discuss this with more detail in chapter 13.

However, the other party constituted the majority of the episcopacy. Even more, it enjoined the full weight of Pius IX's support. And the pope did indeed intervene many times behind the scenes of the council. For example, when it was already obvious that infallibility was going to be defined in one way or another, Cardinal Filippo Guidi proposed a sort of compromise: infallibility did not belong to the pope as a person, but to the act the pope undertook when defining dogma. It was the act, not the person, who was infallible. Also, the pope should not exert this power before consulting the bishops to understand what the sense of the Church was. Any conciliar definition of papal infallibility should include the caveat: "after due inquiry, as is the custom."[88]

In that very same day, Pius IX summoned Cardinal Guidi to his presence in a bout of rage. Guidi defended his thesis: the pope should consider the tradition of the Church. In reply to this, the pontiff famously cried: "I, I am the tradition! I, I am the Church!"[89] It was obvious that papal infallibility was now an inevitability and there would be no compromise at all with the Gallican faction.

On the sidelines, Döllinger kept his journalistic resistance, casting a shadow over the legitimacy of the council. He questioned whether the bishops were really free to vote as they discerned, or if they were under papal duress.[90] Still, there was nothing he or the Gallican bishops could do.

On July 11, the final texts to be voted were presented to the assembly. The idea that secular powers could somehow obstruct the communication between the pope and the faithful was condemned as erroneous. Papal authority did not require local or secular ratification. This was, in effect, banning the Gallican position.[91] Also, Bishop Gasser of Brixen read his famous *relatio* dealing with the thorny issue of papal infallibility. This infallibility was personal, but the pope had to make it clear that he was intending

---

88 O'Malley. *Vatican I*, 211.
89 O'Malley. *Vatican I*, 212.
90 O'Malley. *Vatican I*, 230.
91 O'Neill. "A Defense of Ultramontanism."

to infallibly define a teaching. He should do so through *ex cathedra* pronouncements. As for ecumenical councils, they were infallible as well, but only if their decrees were approved by the pope.[92]

In order to avoid voting against their consciences, the Gallican bishops excused themselves from the council and departed early to their respective dioceses.[93] Unsurprisingly given this context, the text of *Pastor Aeternus* as we know it today was approved by an overwhelming majority. The dogmas of papal primacy and infallibility were now a part of Catholic teaching.

This happened just on the brink of time. A couple months later, King Victor Emmanuel conquered Rome, the final stronghold standing in the way of his project of a unified Italy. Rome became the Italian capital and Pius IX declared himself "prisoner in the Vatican." Since there were no conditions for the council to proceed unencumbered, the Holy Father adjourned it indefinitely.[94] The First Vatican Council, however, would never again be reopened.

The Old Catholic Church

The council's outcome was received with much perplexity among Europe's enlightened elites. In an age of progress and freedom, the Church had—so they thought—decided to remain mired in an obsolete obscurantism, which should have been confined to the Middle Ages. Of course, dazzled as they were by their modern ideals, they did not understand that the Church was merely pushing back against the secular overreach that had taken place in the previous couple of centuries. Embracing Ultramontanism was the only way to defend the independence of the Church to preach truth as it was, without any undue pressure from the state. This was especially important now that the pope had lost his age-old territorial sovereignty. After all, Rome was now under the rule of a king, whose interests did not always align with the Church's.

Of course, Ultramontanes did not get everything they wanted either. The conditions for papal infallibility were much more restrictive than what they intended in the beginning. If the pope wanted to be infallible, he

---

[92] O'Malley. *Vatican I*, 216-217.
[93] O'Malley. *Vatican I*, 220-221.
[94] O'Malley. *Vatican I*, 223.

needed to define the dogmas with an *ex cathedra* formulation. This would cause problems later on, as theologians tried to use the non-infallible nature of certain teachings as an excuse to wiggle out of the obedience owed to them. Already during Pius IX's pontificate, the Church sought to protect those non-infallible teachings by enunciating the concept of "ordinary magisterium," as we shall see in chapter 12.

Be that as it may, it was undeniable that the Ultramontane faction had won. The First Vatican Council had moved the Church in an Ultramontane direction—indisputably and irreversibly.[95] In Germany, this was seen as intolerable. An academic named Friedrich Michelis published an article calling the pope a "heretic" and a "destroyer of the Church."[96] But Döllinger was the major concern for those who wanted to implement the council. As soon as he returned home, Gregor von Scherr, Archbishop of Munich, asked for a meeting with the professor. This is how the historian O'Malley recounts their conversation:

---

[95] It is true that the CDF issued a document about papal primacy in which Ultramontanism is listed among Febronianism and Gallicanism as a "biased and one-sided position already rejected by the Church in the past" (see CDF, "The Primacy of the Successor of Peter") However, Ultramontanism is not defined—or even mentioned again—in that document. Given the historical records mentioned here and given that there is no formal condemnation of any Ultramontane claim, it is obvious that the CDF is talking about the extreme Ultramontane views that did not get everything they wanted in the council. See O'Neill, "A Defense of Ultramontanism": "Of course, there is an extreme theory of papal authority which ought to be rejected. Neither Vatican I nor any other ecumenical council teach that each jot and title of every papal appearance or interview is infallible, nor even that it demands the complete assent of the faithful. However, this phenomenon would be better termed something like 'super-ultramontanism' or 'ultra-ultramontanism.' Both of these terms are admittedly clumsy but at least they are doctrinally and historically proper." Papal critics usually ascribe those extreme views to those who defend pope and council nowadays (see Giunta, "Where Peter Isn't"), but that is a strawman. Continuists today do not believe that everything the pope says is infallible (see Lewis, "A Myth that won't die"). Rather, they: 1) simply accept what the Church herself teaches on submission of mind and will to non-infallible teachings, 2) oppose a concerted effort in certain Catholic media to spin the pope and council in the worst possible light, and 3) resist a Orwellian reinterpretation of the narrow boundaries for legitimate dissent as delineated in *Donum Veritatis*.

[96] O'Malley. *Vatican I*, 232.

Scherr: Let us now begin to work again for our Holy Church.
Döllinger: Indeed, for the Church of old.
Scherr: There is only one Church, that is neither old nor new.
Döllinger: They have made a new church.[97]

Only a month later, Döllinger gathered fourteen German university teachers to protest *Pastor Aeternus*, arguing that it was "a new doctrine that the church had never before recognized."[98] The German bishops defended themselves by penning a letter saying that the doctrine was not new.[99] Archbishop Scherr kept insisting with Döllinger that he accept the decision of the council.

On March 1871, Döllinger answered that "as a Christian, as a theologian, as a historian, as a citizen, I cannot accept this doctrine."[100] On April 2, Scherr replied with impatience: the matter "has now assumed the form of a direct revolt against the Catholic Church."[101] With the Vatican's backing, Scherr offered an ultimatum: Either the professor would recant his position, or he would face excommunication. According to Döllinger, this was his only sleepless night of his life, as he tried to reconcile his conscience with the dogma of infallibility, "thinking it over and over and coming to the conclusion" that he "could not."[102] On April 17, Scherr formally excommunicated Döllinger.

Döllinger's career might have finished then and there, were it not for the intervention of the Bavarian king and the German elites, who saw in Döllinger the only bastion of light that could bring the Church to conform with the times.[103] He was unanimously elected as rector of the University of Munich.[104] Oxford and many other universities granted Döllinger an honorary degree for his defiance of Rome's obscurantism.[105]

---

[97] O'Malley. *Vatican I*, 233.
[98] O'Malley. *Vatican I*, 233.
[99] O'Malley. *Vatican I*, 234.
[100] Howard. *The Pope and the Professor*, 5.
[101] Howard. *The Pope and the Professor*, 5.
[102] Howard. *The Pope and the Professor*, 5.
[103] Howard. *The Pope and the Professor*, 6.
[104] O'Malley. *Vatican I*, 234.
[105] Howard. *The Pope and the Professor*, 6.

Since Döllinger did not step down from the limelight, he became an appealing symbol for the resistance to Vatican I. It is not strange, therefore, that disgruntled Catholics, especially in the German-speaking world, would try to enlist Döllinger into their movement—or even more, crown him as their leader. These disgruntled Catholics would go on to call themselves "Old Catholics," in opposition to the "new" Catholics adhering to the council's innovations. This designation had been started a few years before, by a German judge named August Beck. Protesting against the Syllabus, Beck referred to the "original and traditional Catholics . . . fostering as an ideal the notion of the '*ecclesia primitiva*'"[106] i.e., the primitive church.

After the council, Döllinger and other prominent theologians chaired a series of lectures. In these lectures the idea of an "Old Catholic Church" gained traction among the audience—a church with the traditional parish and hierarchical system, but also with greater local autonomy,[107] as the Gallicans affirmed was practiced in the primitive church.

Of course, Döllinger's name appeared as a prospective bishop to lead the emerging Old Catholic Church.[108] But this was a step too far than what Döllinger was willing to take. Even if the Old Catholics claimed Döllinger was one of their spiritual founders, the professor always maintained an ambivalent position regarding the newly formed church.[109] For all his faults, the professor was too traditional to become a new Luther.[110]

The Old Catholics, however, kept treading ahead. They gathered at Cologne in 1873 and elected Joseph Reinkens, a priest and theology professor, as their new bishop. Since the Vatican would obviously not accept their nomination, the Old Catholics took recourse to the bishop of the schismatic Church of Utrecht—whose episcopacy did not have Roman approval since 1702[111]—to consecrate Reinkens. However, for all its vibrant

---

106 Visser. "The Old Catholic churches," 68-69.

107 Visser. "The Old Catholic churches," 71.

108 Howard. *The Pope and the Professor*, 185-186.

109 Howard. *The Pope and the Professor*, 6.

110 Howard. *The Pope and the Professor*, 8.

111 Visser. "The Old Catholic churches," 70.

beginnings, the Old Catholic Church peaked at fifty-four thousand members in 1877.[112] The dreaded schism fizzled away.

Today, the Old Catholic Church still exists and is in active talks with the Vatican for a possible rapprochement. They still maintain, though, that they are following the Church as it was in the first ten centuries, under the guiding principles laid out by St. Vincent of Lérins[113] (see chapter 6).

As for Döllinger, Pope Leo XIII (Pius IX's successor) made several attempts to reconcile him with the Catholic Church, but to no avail.[114] The German professor would die in 1890, still excommunicated. With him died most of the resistance against the First Vatican Council. The Ultramontane church, as defined by the council, would continue to the present day.

---

112 O'Malley. *Vatican I*, 235.

113 Visser. "The Old Catholic churches," 82.

114 Howard. *The Pope and the Professor*, 8.

Chapter 10

"What would Jesus do?"

[We must] be attentive to that old and always new temptation from the promoters of gnosticism. They wanted to make a name for themselves and expand their doctrine and fame, so they sought something always new and distinct from what the Word of God gave them. That's what St. John describes with the word proagon, *i.e. the one who is too ahead, the one at the forefront, the one that always wants to go beyond of the ecclesial 'Us' which protects the community from excesses.*

—Francis, Letter to the People of Germany

As the Synod on the Amazon progressed, it became clear that one of the main challenges was how few priests there were to minister to such a vast region. Within the synod—and most especially outside it—this issue became a battleground between liberals and conservatives. The liberals, on their end, took this opportunity to push for an exception that would allow the ordination of married men ("*viri probati*") in the Amazon, like what already happens in the Eastern rites or in the Anglican ordinariate. They also advocated for the reopening of a commission to study the possibility of ordaining female deacons.[1]

Conservatives perceived these proposals, not so much as trying to solve the vocational shortage in the Amazon, but as a kind of Trojan horse[2] that would eventually abolish priestly celibacy as a whole and allow the ordination of women as priests, a very common position among progressive Catholics.[3] Unfortunately, conservatives presented few other alternatives

[1] Winfield, "Pope's Amazon synod proposes married priests."

[2] Tossati, "The Amazon Synod: a Trojan Horse to destroy Priestly Celibacy?"

[3] Dougherty, "Roma Locuta Est, deal with it": "But of course, there was nothing — nothing at all — novel or surprising discussed at the Synod, and very little that was particularly Amazonian. It was all the half-century-old preoccupations of liberal European and American clerics: married priests, women in ordained offices, and non-traditional liturgy. . . The Amazonian Synod itself was a brainchild of an old European, Bishop Kräutler, an advocate of women's ordination to the priesthood. Though the step toward ordaining married men as priests in the Amazon is justified to the world as meeting the specific needs of one region, in fact Kräutler says it 'can be the cause of an epochal step in the Universal Church.' This is of

besides simply restating the value of priestly celibacy and of an all-male priesthood, as if by consolidating the Church at the doctrinal and disciplinary levels, the vocations would automatically grow.[4] In one thing liberals and conservatives alike agreed: the solution for the problems in the Amazon consisted in implementing what they already passionately defended for the whole Church before the synod. A remarkable and convenient coincidence.[5]

In online Catholic forums—the same ones Thomas Lawson usually attended—one commenter was particularly giddy about the synod. Her name was Lilly Eveson and she was the one usually spearheading the liberal position in these discussions. Tom remembered the first time he had seen one of her comments in favor of homosexual marriage. He twisted his nose, while thinking to himself: "why is this person in a Catholic forum anyway?" He browsed her profile, and everything became clear. Her bio contained pronouns and rainbow/trans symbols alongside the Vatican flag. Her pinned tweet had a link to Catholics for Choice. "Of course, typical liberal."—he sneered. From that moment onward, he made a point of not letting any of Lilly's claims go unanswered. Lilly, on her end, tried to return the favor.

As I said before, Lilly was absolutely pumped up about the synod, especially after the final document seemed to validate her stance.[6] Surely, Pope Francis would approve it, in the interest of synodality. Tom thought so too, and that is why he did not argue based on what he thought the Holy Father would do, but on "perennial tradition and Church doctrine." As for Justin Peterson, he just kept quiet, serenely waiting for the pope's final decision.

In the end, Francis surprised both Tom and Lilly. On February 2, 2020, the pontiff published his post-synodal apostolic exhortation *Querida Amazônia*. In this document, he would write:

---

course how revolutions work: Allow an exception in one theoretical case, and then watch as the implementation of this exception obliterates the principle in fact."

[4] Cronin, "Abandoning Apostolic Celibacy would be a mistake."

[5] I deal with this at Gabriel, "Married priests and Querida Amazônia."

[6] Winfield, "Pope's Amazon synod proposes married priests."

> Consequently, it is not simply a question of facilitating a greater presence of ordained ministers who can celebrate the Eucharist. That would be a very narrow aim. . . Such a reductionism would lead us to believe that women would be granted a greater status and participation in the Church only if they were admitted to Holy Orders. But that approach would in fact narrow our vision; it would lead us to clericalize women, diminish the great value of what they have already accomplished, and subtly make their indispensable contribution less effective. . . In a synodal Church, those women who in fact have a central part to play in Amazonian communities should have access to positions, including ecclesial services, that do not entail Holy Orders and that can better signify the role that is theirs.[7]

Lilly was crushed. Suddenly, all her support and fervor for the Holy Father vanished. The successor of Peter had, after all, shown himself to be a stumbling block for progress once more, an instrument of the oppressive patriarchy. As for Tom, —who had until then opposed Pope Francis every step of the way—he started to pontificate "*Roma locuta est, causa finita est.*"[8]

Of course, this did not sit well with Justin. In a private message to Tom, Justin denounced his inconsistency. So, he would adhere to the pope when he taught something Tom approved of, but not when the Holy Father magisterially taught something Tom disagreed with? Did Tom submit to the Holy Father or only when their positions matched? Tom, however, did not think he was being inconsistent. The pope's teachings were to be adhered to, as long as they were in harmony with Tom's idea of tradition. Of course, that meant that when the pope taught something contrary to what Tom believed was tradition, he was to be dismissed.

"You are again being an Ultramontanist that treats the pope as if he's God."—Tom replied— "But our religion is Catholicism, not

---

[7] Francis, *Querida Amazônia*, 93, 100, 103.

[8] "Rome has spoken, the discussion is over": paraphrase from St. Augustine's Sermon 131, 10. This sentence has been used for centuries by Catholic apologists in support of the papacy.

hyperpapalism. If the pope teaches something that goes against the teachings of Christ, then we must not heed him. We follow Jesus, not the pope."[9]

As soon as Tom finished typing this reply, a ping sounded on the background. In another tab, in a parallel conversation he was holding, someone had replied to *him*. It was Lilly Eveson. She had posted a new comment on their thread about clerical celibacy and women's ordination. She said:

"I don't think Jesus would agree with the pope on this. Jesus was all about love, he never discriminated, he never judged. What would Jesus do? I'd rather follow Jesus than the pope on this one."[10]

Tom's smile suddenly vanished. Both tabs were simultaneously opened on his computer. He could see both his and Lilly's comments, uncannily echoing each other: "I follow Jesus, not the pope."[11] Within Thomas Lawson's soul, something clicked…

The quest for the historical Jesus

For all his hostility or indifference towards Christianity, modern man cannot avoid a certain fascination with Jesus Christ and His teachings. Jesus appears to modern man as someone of undeniable moral stature, a reference, an inevitable influence that one cannot simply ignore or evade. But

---

[9] See Mallett, "On Vatican Funkiness": "Even if a pope were to deny Jesus Christ, we ought to hold fast to Sacred Tradition and remain faithful to Jesus unto death. Indeed St. John did not 'blindly follow' the first pope into his denial. . . . This is what I intend to do, by God's grace, even should a pope deny Christ himself. My faith is not in Peter, but Jesus. I follow Christ, not a man." Also see Steve Skojec's tweet from December 17, 2016: "We worship Christ, not the pope. @Pontifex is fomenting doctrinal error and souls are at stake" (this tweet was posted before Skojec's crisis of faith).

[10] See, for example, Hanna, "On holiest of days": "While during these holy days *we would presume to hear Pope Benedict XVI echoing Jesus' call for love and inclusion,* instead the Pope put forth a message of fear, intimidation, and oppression. In his homily earlier today, he denounced 'disobedience' within the church and strongly reprimanded priests who support women's ordination. The Women's Ordination Conference (WOC) is discouraged that the Pope would use this sacred time in our religious tradition to attack his fellow priests, who in good conscience, support women's full inclusion in the Roman Catholic Church. *It is not these priests who are disobedient, it is the hierarchy who has lost touch with the people of God.*"

[11] I tackle this argument in Gabriel, "Following Christ, but Not His Vicar."

this poses a problem. The Jesus presented by the Church conflicts with many values and ideas that modern man deems non-negotiable.

Resorting to a typical *modus operandi*, modern man resolves this tension by trying to separate that which cannot be separated (chapter 4). Therefore, we see an attempt to separate Jesus Christ from His Church. This is often done by trying to split the human and divine natures of Jesus Christ (see chapter 6)—or as it is usually said, by excising the "historical *Jesus*" from the "*Christ* of faith."[12] In order to oppose *Christianity*, modern man replaces it with a "*Jesusanity*," a pious veneration of the human (and only human) example given by Jesus.[13]

For modern man, Jesus cannot have risen, for He remains buried. Not so much in a sepulcher, but buried underneath layers and layers of tradition, accumulating through millennia. Beneath these strata of tradition, lie the real object of the faith: Jesus of Nazareth. As centuries went by, this core of the faith became increasingly obscured and blurred,[14] as an old picture from a bygone generation.

This belief grounds modern man's anti-traditional bias, a bias that traditionalists so often (and rightly) decry. Traditions seem to be hiding the real Jesus, whom modern man admires so much. But this too, is a superficial way to look at what is happening. What we see here is an unconscious—yet misguided—urge to retrieve a purer, more primitive tradition from the clutches of Church innovations. Jesus, as we have seen, is the source of true tradition (chapter 1). This is acknowledged, even by modern man—hence his search for the historical Jesus. The "layers of tradition" beneath which Jesus is buried were novelties added by the Church later on. That these alleged "innovations" have become so ancient by now that they are considered traditions, does not negate the fact that they are indeed viewed as innovations.

For three times already, modern man undertook the expedition to retrieve this "historical Jesus." The first quest happened during the nineteenth century, the second one around the 1950s, and the third one

---

[12] Ratzinger. *Jesus of Nazareth: from the Baptism*, xi.

[13] Deines. "Can the 'Real' Jesus be identified with the Historical Jesus?" 26.

[14] Ratzinger. *Jesus of Nazareth: from the Baptism*, xii.

between the 1970s and 1980s. This last quest set out to the ancient Jewish world, where the explorers claimed to have finally taken a glimpse at the "Jesus of flesh and blood." The historical Jesus was a Jewish man: it stood to reason that He could only be found within the original Semitic, Aramaic-Hebrew, cultural and religious traditions of the time.[15] The third quest's historical Jesus should be viewed as a "Galilean itinerant healer, exorcist, and preacher—and nothing more."[16] The Jesus of the gospels would be a later distortion of this historical Jesus according to foreign pagan and Greek traditions.[17]

Of course, no adventurer sets out on an expedition or quest with bare hands. These kinds of endeavors need appropriate tools. And the search for the historical Jesus has indeed a very fundamental tool: the historical-critical method. In 1678, an Oratorian monk named Richard Simon published a book titled *Critical History of the Old Testament.* A decade later, he followed it up with *Critical History of the Text of the New Testament.* Thus, he became "the founder of modern biblical criti-cism."[18] This historical-critical method was perfected and refined during the nineteenth century. It was further developed in the twentieth century by the great German academics Rudolf Bultmann and Martin Dibelius,[19] who were skeptical that Jesus could even be described with any historical certainty.

To put it succinctly, the historical-critical method consists in answering a set of questions like:

1) "Why did the writer present this passage of the gospel to the community? What was its function?"—Form criticism.
2) "Why did the author write about these particular events and not others? Why did he synthesize these events in this particular way?"—Redaction criticism.[20]

---

[15] Deines. "Can the 'Real' Jesus be identified with the Historical Jesus?" 13.

[16] Deines. "Can the 'Real' Jesus be identified with the Historical Jesus?" 14.

[17] Deines. "Can the 'Real' Jesus be identified with the Historical Jesus?" 13. See also p. 37: "one might see Jesus as an itinerant sage in a cynic-like garb as promoted by adherents of the Jesus-Seminar, who was only retrospectively transformed into a messianic-like figure and eventually become God."

[18] Moss. "Hubristic Specialists," 35.

[19] Waldstein. "Historical-Critical Scriptures."

[20] Waldstein. "Historical-Critical Scriptures."

Form criticism means, among other things, analyzing the literary form of a particular passage and its possible relations with questions that preoccupied a community. As for redaction criticism, it compares the different places in which parallel passages are found, their function in the overall outline of the text, etc.[21]

I must be very clear, lest the purpose of this chapter be misunderstood, that I do not believe there is anything inherently heterodox with this method. It has brought to light many interesting and important insights that allow us to better understand scripture today. In his groundbreaking encyclical *Divino Afflante Spiritu*, Pius XII spoke favorably of this method, namely when he said:

> In the present day indeed this art, which is called *textual criticism* and which is used with great and praiseworthy results in the editions of profane writings, is also quite rightly employed in the case of the Sacred Books, because of that very reverence which is due to the Divine Oracles. For its very purpose is to insure that the sacred text be restored, as perfectly as possible, be purified from the corruptions due to the carelessness of the copyists and be freed, as far as may be done, from glosses and omissions, from the interchange and repetition of words and from all other kinds of mistakes, which are wont to make their way gradually into writings handed down through many centuries.[22]

Our current Catechism also implicitly acknowledges the value of this method when it says:

> In order to discover the sacred authors' intention, the reader must take into account the conditions of their time and culture, the literary genres in use at that time, and the modes of feeling, speaking and narrating then current. For the fact is that truth is

---

[21] Waldstein. "Historical-Critical Scriptures."

[22] Pius XII. *Divino Afflante Spiritu*, 10, 17.

> differently presented and expressed in the various types of historical writing, in prophetical and poetical texts, and in other forms of literary expression.[23]

However, the historical-critical method has also been viewed with suspicion right from the start. Fr. Richard Simon himself, the founder of biblical criticism back in the sixteen hundreds, had his fair share of dealings with the religious authorities.[24] Later, during the twentieth century, the famous *ressourcement* theologian Henry de Lubac (see chapter 2), criticized the biblical critics in these terms: "They are primarily specialists, and their function has become very necessary and very important during the last few centuries. They must realize (and this realization is something they have occasionally lacked) that their very specialization imposes *limitations* on them; that their 'science' thus *cannot be the whole of scriptural science*; but they are not required, in their role as scientific exegetes, to give us the whole of scriptural science; and they should not even aspire to do so."[25]

But the most impactful criticism in recent history came from Benedict XVI when, in his capacity as a personal theologian, he wrote his Christological treatise *Jesus of Nazareth.*[26] It is important to note that Joseph Ratzinger does not dismiss the historical-critical method at all. He calls it an "indispensable dimension of exegetical work."[27] After all, if the Christian faith is grounded on real *historical* events, faith itself demands that it must be assessed through a *historical* method.[28] Catholicism accepts that there is a *tension* (see chapter 4) between the truth of the historical event and the veracity of its narrative transmission, and in typical fashion endures this tension to avoid a fundamentalist perspective.[29] Rather, the Catholic Church will resolve the tension on a higher plane, by arguing that she does

---

[23] CCC 110.

[24] See Lambe. "Biblical Criticism and Censorship."

[25] As quoted by Moss. "Hubristic Specialists," 33-34.

[26] Benedict XVI, *Jesus of Nazareth: from the Baptism*, xxiii. Here, the pope clarifies that "this book is in no way an exercise of the magisterium."

[27] Benedict XVI, *Jesus of Nazareth: from the Baptism*, xv, xvi.

[28] Benedict XVI, *Jesus of Nazareth: from the Baptism*, xvi. See also Deines. "Can the 'Real' Jesus be identified with the Historical Jesus?" 38.

[29] Deines. "Can the 'Real' Jesus be identified with the Historical Jesus?" 25-26.

not adhere (and never has) to a merely literalistic view of the Bible[30] (see chapter 8).

Ratzinger's main point of contention is not that the historical-critical method is wrong, but that it is *insufficient.* As he says in his book, the historical-critical method "does not exhaust the interpretative task for someone who sees the biblical writings as a single corpus of Holy Scripture inspired by God."[31] Echoing his master de Lubac, Ratzinger contends that the historical-critical method, while valuable and true, must be able to recognize its *limits*, if it is to remain a tool in service of the truth.

For one thing, the historical-critical method is, as its name suggests, a *historical* method. Therefore, not only must it "investigate the biblical world as a thing of the past, but it has to let it remain in the past."[32] This is, at the same time, a strength, but also a limit. Also, since everything divine goes beyond the empirical, this method must treat the Bible as mere human words. Finally, though it can consider each book of scripture in its individual context, it cannot recognize the unity of all those books as one single "Bible." Ultimately, the historical-critical method, as a scientific method, can never go beyond the domain of hypothesis.[33]

Other academics before Ratzinger also noted other limitations. In the nineteenth century, as the first quest for the historical Jesus was unfolding, Catholic scholars and theologians decried the philosophical foundations of this new method, namely: 1) a rejection of the possibility of divine intervention and miracles; 2) an objection to any notion of historical uniqueness when dealing with the Jesus event; and 3) a characterization of the gospel as mythology.[34]

From these limitations, we can grasp why Catholics were so suspicious of this historical-critical method. As a tool, it is perfectly acceptable. A tool is intrinsically neutral—its value depends on how it is used. The problem lies when the limits of the method are not acknowledged. Or worse, when

---

[30] Moss. "Hubristic Specialists," 36, 37.

[31] Benedict XVI, *Jesus of Nazareth: from the Baptism*, xvi.

[32] Benedict XVI, *Jesus of Nazareth: from the Baptism*, xvi.

[33] Benedict XVI, *Jesus of Nazareth: from the Baptism*, xvi-xvii.

[34] Moss. "Hubristic Specialists," 36.

the void left out by those limitations is filled with certain philosophical or ideological presuppositions that then co-opt the method to gain credibility.[35]

Let us take one of the limitations that I mentioned above: that the historical-critical method does not accept the possibility of divine intervention or miracles. From a scientific standpoint, this methodology makes sense. The historical-critical method is an historical method: therefore, it cannot ascertain realities that go beyond the empirical, like miracles.[36] But when we go beyond a mere methodological constraint like this to extrapolate from this a philosophical claim—that miracles are impossible—then we have already crossed the limit of legitimate scientific inquiry.[37]

It goes even deeper than that, though. As is usually the case, by proceeding like this, we are betraying our goal of finding a purer tradition under the pretext of defending it. The third quest for the historical Jesus claimed to have found the "Jesus of flesh and blood" within the historical context of first century messianic Judaism. For methodological (and

---

[35] See Waldstein. "Historical-Critical Scriptures": "If one understands the historical-critical method in this way as a set of questions of a certain type and a set of tools used to answer these questions, one can hardly find fault with it in principle. . . it is clearly, as such, legitimate. The difficulty experienced by concerned Catholics when they come in contact with historical-critical Scripture scholarship lies on a different level: it lies in particular examples of historical- critical exegesis, which are unavoidably the products, not simply of the historical-critical method, but of certain philosophical and theological premises as well."

[36] Deines. "Can the 'Real' Jesus be identified with the Historical Jesus?" 37.

[37] See Deines. "Can the 'Real' Jesus be identified with the Historical Jesus?" 39: "But Hoppe is convinced that this is not the case because God is not a subject for the historical method and consequently, confessional theological statements cannot be excluded by it. He further admits: 'one might consent to the thought, that God entered history with Jesus', but then he adds, that this 'of course cannot be a historical statement but only a confession.' That is precisely the point: From where does the certainty of the 'of course' come? Why is it 'natural' ('natürlich') to take such a statement about God acting in history as confession only and not as a starting point for a historical enquiry when it can be taken as a true proposition? This implies that a secular understanding of history is more natural, more appropriate, and has a higher truth claim, than a theological one. The point is not that this is evident for scholars working right from the beginning within such a positivist paradigm. But why, and this leads back to the Pope's methodological concerns, why should this claim be accepted without qualification by Christians? And why by Christian scholars as well?"

unfortunately, often philosophical and ideological) reasons, the possibility that God ever acted in the history of Israel is excluded from consideration. But Jewish heritage, the same one where we can find this historical Jesus, "rejects the deistic assumption of a distant God removed from the world, and speaks instead of the God of Abraham, Isaac, and Jacob, the God of the living and not the dead, the One who continually engages with his creation in giving and receiving."[38] To find the historical Jesus in the midst of ancient Jewish world is to find Him immersed in a culture filled with stories of miracles and divine intervention.

Ratzinger's critique goes in the same vein. For the pope, the Jesus of the gospels is the true Jesus, because it is the historical Jesus.[39] We cannot separate that which should not be separated. Both the historical and theological components of the gospel story cannot be excised from one another, because they were woven into a single, inextricable whole by the very authors themselves. As Prof. Roland Deines from the University of Nottingham says: "Less emphasis, however, is given to the discussion that the truth claim of the Gospel message is nonetheless closely related to the historical veracity of the narrated events from which God's participation cannot be dissolved in a clear-cut way, having 'pure' historical facts on one side and 'dogmatic' interpretations on the other."[40]

To supplement the deficiencies of the historical-critical method, Joseph Ratzinger proposed the so-called "canonical exegesis,"[41] developed by the Protestant scholar Brevard Childs.[42] Canonical exegesis means

---

[38] Deines. "Can the 'Real' Jesus be identified with the Historical Jesus?" 14-15.

[39] Benedict XVI, *Jesus of Nazareth: from the Baptism*, xxii. See also Deines. "Can the 'Real' Jesus be identified with the Historical Jesus?" 18: "What Ratzinger does is to take as his starting point an inherited tradition about Jesus' relation to God, because he is convinced not least for historical reasons advanced by many scholars from very different scholarly milieus that the traditional faith correctly formulates an 'ontological truth-claim'"

[40] Deines. "Can the 'Real' Jesus be identified with the Historical Jesus?" 27

[41] Benedict XVI, *Jesus of Nazareth: from the Baptism*, xviii.

[42] Moss. "Hubristic Specialists," 39.

"reading the individual texts of the Bible in the context of the whole."[43] As we have seen above, one of the limitations of the historical-critical method is that it can only take into account each individual text of the Bible, but not the whole, since the unity of scripture is a theological assertion,[44] not a historical one. Therefore, canonical exegesis does not contradict, nor replace the historical-critical method, but complements it and expands upon it.[45] It takes one of biblical criticism's limitations and starts working from there, accepting what the historical-critical method offers up to that boundary which it cannot cross. Through canonical exegesis, scripture is "read anew, evolving in continuity with its original sense, tacitly corrected and given added depth and breadth of meaning."[46] This is true doctrinal development[47] (see chapter 3).

Besides canonical exegesis, Catholic scholars have also become increasingly fascinated by another method, called "reception history," which consists of taking a theme, text, or figure in the Bible and tracing the interpretation of that theme, text, or figure over the course of history.[48] Intentionally or not, this method also brings up another interesting contradiction in the historical-critical method: that this method in itself is also a chapter in the ongoing history of biblical interpretation. Not only scripture, but the *historical-critical method itself* is "a product of its day," "bound by the philosophical and cultural conventions of its time."[49] The fact that some modern thinkers (not necessarily biblical criticism scholars) have not understood this important limitation, led to some of the distortions that we are going to see further along this chapter.

---

[43] Benedict XVI, *Jesus of Nazareth: from the Baptism*, xix. See also Moss. "Hubristic Specialists," 39.

[44] Benedict XVI, *Jesus of Nazareth: from the Baptism*, xviii.

[45] Benedict XVI, *Jesus of Nazareth: from the Baptism*, xix.

[46] Benedict XVI, *Jesus of Nazareth: from the Baptism*, xviii-xix.

[47] See Benedict XVI, *Jesus of Nazareth: from the Baptism*, xix: "This is a process in which the word gradually unfolds its inner potentialities, already somehow present like seeds, but needing the challenge of new situations, new experiences and new sufferings, in order to open up. This process is certainly not linear, and it is often dramatic, but when you watch it unfold in light of Jesus Christ, you can see it moving in a single overall direction."

[48] Moss. "Hubristic Specialists," 39.

[49] Moss. "Hubristic Specialists," 40.

"The synthesis of all heresies"

By the end of the nineteenth century and the beginning of the twentieth, a German Protestant scholar named Adolf von Harnack was making inroads in academic circles. His goal was to use a historical method to retrieve Christianity's original essence, separating it from subsequent accretions of dogma.[50] For Prof. Harnack, Christian dogma as we know it had only originated in the fourth century, when Greek philosophy shaped the Christological ecumenical councils we have explored in chapter 6.[51] If Christianity was to survive in the modern world, it should be freed from the shackles of dogma, a liberating process that had started during the Reformation.[52]

As for Jesus, Prof. Harnack believed that to understand the gospel, one must understand the concept of the *kingdom of God.* For Jesus, this was a purely spiritual kingdom, "the rule of God in the individual heart."[53] However, soon after Jesus's death, the apostles would have distorted this kingdom. It ceased to be something lived in the present, and was instead projected into the future, to an eschatological utopia.[54]

It was true—not even Harnack disputed this—Jesus saw Himself as a messiah.[55] However, Jesus's messiahship was so incredibly different and

---

[50] Pauck. "Adolf von Harnack."

[51] Pauck. "Adolf von Harnack." See also Keating. "Christianity": "Abandoning the Apostolic Age, Harnack, in his 'History of Dogma', ascribes the hellenization of Christianity to the apologists of the second century . . . It was the transference of Christianity from a Semitic to a Greek soil that explains, according to Dr. Hatch (Hibbert Lectures, 1888), 'why an ethical sermon stood in the forefront of the teaching of Jesus, and a metaphysical creed in the forefront of the Christianity of the fourth century'. Professor Harnack states the problem and solves it in similar fashion. He ascribes the change, as he conceives it, from a simple code of conduct to the Nicene Creed."

[52] Pauck. "Adolf von Harnack."

[53] Gilbert. "Harnack, Loisy, and the Gospel," 92-93.

[54] Gilbert. "Harnack, Loisy, and the Gospel," 92-93.

[55] See Keating. "Christianity": "Most modern rationalists (Harnack, Wellhausen, and others) acknowledge that Christ from the beginning of His preaching knew Himself as the Messias, and accepted the various titles which belong in the

rich, the very idea of "messiah" had gone haywire. But this had been a side effect, not intended by Jesus. For Harnack, Jesus's gospel "did not include the Son, only the Father," because Jesus was not "part of the gospel," but its "realization."[56] Jesus shared the views of His age, but Harnack's modern view was, for him, the truth of the message of Jesus. In this way, Jesus was made both ancient and modern at the same time.[57] Harnack conceived of Christianity as a fruit that one must peel away,[58] so as not to confuse the husk for the kernel.[59]

Some wondered, though, if there would be anything left after that fruit had been peeled away. Fr. George Tyrrell, an Anglo-Irish priest of the time, famously remarked: "The Christ that Harnack sees, looking back through nineteen centuries of Catholic darkness, is only the reflection of a liberal Protestant face seen at the bottom of a deep well."[60] We will return to this metaphor later in this chapter.

One of Harnack's most influential critics in Catholic circles was a French priest and theologian called Alfred Loisy. For Loisy, the gospel had everything to do with the announcement of the kingdom of God indeed, but this gospel *also included Jesus.* The gospel was not something abstract, but a *living faith.* The gospels were inseparable from the things this living faith had produced throughout the centuries.[61] As someone raised in the bosom of Catholic popular piety,[62] Loisy could not accept Harnack's dismissal of the Church. The Church was needed, because no religion can exist without a cultus.[63] Furthermore, the Church had also been a product of this living faith that had emerged from the gospel: the papacy, the veneration of Mary and of the saints, the sacramental system, all of this had

---

Scripture to that personage — Son of David, Son of Man (Daniel 7:13), the Christ (see John 14:24; Matthew 16:16; Mark 14:61-62)."

[56] Gilbert. "Harnack, Loisy, and the Gospel," 94.

[57] McCown. "Alfred Loisy: Unfaltering Critic," 33.

[58] Gilbert. "Harnack, Loisy, and the Gospel," 93.

[59] McCown. "Alfred Loisy: Unfaltering Critic," 33.

[60] McCown. "Alfred Loisy: Unfaltering Critic," 33. See also Moss. "Hubristic Specialists," 43.

[61] Gilbert. "Harnack, Loisy, and the Gospel," 95.

[62] McCown. "Alfred Loisy: Unfaltering Critic," 20.

[63] McCown. "Alfred Loisy: Unfaltering Critic," 30.

sprouted from this living faith.[64] In this sense, Loisy did not see Christianity as a fruit to be peeled, but as a seed to be grown.[65]

Unfortunately, for all their astute critiques of Harnackian historiography, both Tyrrell and Loisy would be marred by an inescapable fault: they were both Modernists. Loisy was even considered the "father of Modernism."[66] In spite of his pietist upbringing, Loisy lost faith in every dogma of the Church by the ripe age of 29 years[67]—not because he thought those dogmas were wrong, but because he rejected the very notion of dogma.

As an intellectual son of the nineteenth century, Loisy had been deeply influenced by the concept of evolution. Evolution had overflown beyond the boundaries of Biology and had left a profound mark on the mindsets of the elites and academics, who started to apply evolutionary principles to all areas of knowledge. Through the use of the new historical-critical method, Loisy would apply these evolutionary principles to religion. If the Church had the authority to interpret scripture, then it could "reinterpret it according to modern critical principles in order to suit them to modern times."[68] This idea that the Church can (and must) evolve with the times was at the heart of the Modernist movement.[69]

It stands to reason then, that Loisy would abhor the idea that we should return to an earlier version of Christianity.[70] Such would amount to a regression, the complete antithesis of his evolutionary mindset. Regression, like stagnation (i.e., unaltered dogma), were not the way forward.

---

64 Gilbert. "Harnack, Loisy, and the Gospel," 95.

65 Gilbert. "Harnack, Loisy, and the Gospel," 93.

66 Burke. "Loisy's Faith," 138.

67 Burke. "Loisy's Faith," 138.

68 McCown. "Alfred Loisy: Unfaltering Critic," 31.

69 Vermeersch, "Modernism": "A remodeling, a renewal according to the ideas of the twentieth century—such is the longing that possesses the modernists. 'The avowed modernists', says M. Loisy, 'form a fairly definite group of thinking men united in the common desire to adapt Catholicism to the intellectual, moral, and social needs of today' (*Simples réflexions sur le décret 'Lamentabili' et sur l'encyclique 'Pascendi' du 8 September, 1907*, p. 13). 'Our religious attitude,' as *Il programma dei modernisti* states (p. 5, note l), 'is ruled by the single wish to be one with Christians and Catholics who live in harmony with the spirit of the age.'"

70 McCown. "Alfred Loisy: Unfaltering Critic," 30.

Here, it would seem like Loisy's Modernism was utterly anti-traditional and, therefore, unfit for this book.

However, even with these tenets in mind, Loisy could not but turn his head back to the past. After all, his most fascinating study subjects—Jesus and the early Church—lied there, in a bygone era. Unwittingly, Loisy's Modernism aimed at creating a new tradition, and this new tradition was grounded on his ideas, and these ideas had been formed through his studies and publications on primitive Christianity.

For someone so keen to see the old Church in light of the modern Church, it is not strange that Loisy would formulate hypotheses based on his personal experience. Loisy's revolutionary ideas led to his dismissal from his teaching position at the Catholic Institute of Paris in 1893.[71] During a six-year period, he was confined to teaching the catechism to groups of young girls. These catecheses, far from dissuading him, sharpened Loisy's vision: for him, the New Testament was largely about catechetical instruction.[72] And one of the most important catecheses of the New Testament was precisely the thing that Harnack so detested: the eschatological catechesis.[73]

The eschatological catechesis, concerned with the return of the glorious Jesus, was the most central feature of early Church instruction. It had started with the writings of St. Paul and his *maranatha* (Aramaic for "the Lord is coming") in 1 Cor 16:22. The Christian, instructed by this catechesis, was supposed to repent of his sins and prepare the coming of the Lord. Repentance of sins also entailed a moral catechesis, which was then tied to the eschatological one.[74]

The relentless march of evolution kept driving Christianity forward, transforming it. Completely inverting Harnack's theory that Jesus had focused on the present and had been distorted by his disciples' eschatology, Loisy affirmed that the eschatological catechesis had come first, and an evangelical catechesis had arisen later. This evangelical catechesis was focused on the idea of salvation in the present, effective already in this earthly life, though still finding its completion after the apocalypse. The gospel

[71] Borto. "From an Apologism," 501.
[72] McCown. "Alfred Loisy: Unfaltering Critic," 32.
[73] McCown. "Alfred Loisy: Unfaltering Critic," 33.
[74] McCown. "Alfred Loisy: Unfaltering Critic," 34.

according to St. John had actually been a way to reinterpret both the eschatological and evangelical catecheses according to Gnostic principles (see chapter 6).[75]

No wonder then, that Loisy rejected the gospel according to St. John as a reliable source of information on Jesus. Here, for once, Loisy agreed with his rival Harnack. But Loisy went even beyond what Harnack was willing to accept. Not only the gospel according to St. John, but also the three other gospels, the synoptic gospels, had been subjected to thorough revisions.[76] Mark had emphasized Jesus's Baptism and Last Supper. Matthew added to Mark the eschatological and moral catechesis of St. Paul. Luke took Matthew's work and turned it into an apologetics for Christianity. Either way, all the gospels had been written too late to be historically trustworthy.[77]

Through his work, Loisy revolutionized the very historical-critical method, by introducing *form criticism* (see above). The gospels were not records of what Jesus had done or said, but interpretations.[78] In the end, though, this meant that the gospels were so much a product of the creative imagination of the Church, nothing certain could be known about the life and teaching of Jesus.[79] If Harnack's fruit could be peeled so much that nothing would be left, Loisy's seed had been so filled with his own ideas, that nothing religious was left as well to grow from it.[80]

But then, if nothing certain could be known from this Jesus, how could the Christian faith be sustained? Here ended Loisy as a biblical critic and Loisy as a philosopher began. As Rev. George Gilbert, a twentieth century theologian explains:

> Again, the whole sacramental system, though not all given in the gospel narrative, is a Christian institution and so comes from the gospel "seed." *The immortal Christ acts through it.*

[75] McCown. "Alfred Loisy: Unfaltering Critic," 34.
[76] Gilbert. "Harnack, Loisy, and the Gospel," 92-93.
[77] McCown. "Alfred Loisy: Unfaltering Critic," 35-36.
[78] Burke. "Loisy's Faith," 145.
[79] McCown. "Alfred Loisy: Unfaltering Critic," 35-36.
[80] Gilbert. "Harnack, Loisy, and the Gospel," 93.

> True, Loisy as a critic admits that the worship of the saints does not belong to the gospel, and yet he holds that it truly proceeds from the "*primitive revelation.*" Here, as it appears to me, the critic is lost in the philosopher. For this "primitive revelation," out of which proceeds the worship of saints, is the truth that God reveals himself *to* man *in* man. To this we naturally assent, and say with Loisy that the most divine thing in the world is not the crash of the thunder, nor the light of the sun, nor the unfolding of life, but is beauty of soul, purity of heart, perfection of love in sacrifice. *But this primitive revelation is far more "primitive" than the gospel. For centuries prior to the gospel God had been revealing himself to man in man.* This fact, then, is not distinctively Christian, and therefore nothing based upon it can be distinctively Christian. *But is it not also the philosopher rather than the critic* who speaks in the assertion that, because God reveals himself to man in man, therefore the worship of the saints and of Jesus is justified?[81]

This idea that God reveals Himself *to* man and *in* man is the principle of *theological immanence* (i.e., God is immanent in man.) It is connected to another principle, the principle of *divine permanence*, the notion that Jesus did not institute the Church and the sacraments, at least not directly, but in a *mediate* way. Rather, the Church and the sacraments had been instituted by Christians. Christian consciences, on their end, were virtually included in the conscience of Christ, as all Christians are said to live the life of Christ. So, the Church and the sacraments were created by Christ only insofar as they were created by Christians who are a part of Christ.

Loisy's efforts were not only academic, but also apologetical. He did not merely want to renew the Catholic Church and her theology—he wanted to defend them.[82] To mount this defense, Loisy used the historical-critical method, the approach in which he was so proficient. However, Loisy did not take into account the limits of this method (see above). Specifically, he had turned the historical-critical method from a neutral tool into a carrier of certain philosophical premises, namely that we cannot

---

[81] Gilbert. "Harnack, Loisy, and the Gospel," 96.

[82] Borto. "From an Apologism," 505.

adduce God's actions in history and so are constrained to study only human and natural causes through critical methods.[83]

Loisy and his fellow Modernists had mounted an apologetics that tried to reconcile the Church with the modern scientific discoveries in the realms of history and biblical-criticism, if not with modern thought in general,[84] so as to reverse the tide of rejection of Catholicism by modern society. However, when they did so, they crossed the boundary between apologist and Modernist. Pius IX, in his famous Syllabus of Errors (see chapter 9), had condemned the proposition that the "Roman Pontiff can, and ought to, reconcile himself, and come to terms with progress, liberalism and modern civilization."[85]

It would be another Pius who would enforce the correction of this error. Pope St. Pius X is a name that evokes admiration—even nostalgia—among current-day traditionalists. Mons. Lefebvre resisted the Second Vatican Council's reforms precisely by founding a priestly society bearing Pius X's name. This is because Pius X was the pope that most notably fought against the Modernist heresy, a heresy that traditionalists believe has infected the modern Church, up to the higher echelons.[86]

In 1907, Pius X promulgated his most important document: the encyclical *Pascendi Dominici Gregis* (PDG), paving the way for Loisy's excommunication the very next year.[87] If one sentence jumps out of *Pascendi* is the common aphorism: "Modernism is the synthesis of all heresies."[88] We see this sentence often in social media, wielded by traditionalists to accuse the modern Church and even modernity itself. However, there is a difference between modernity and Modernism. Modernism has been very

---

[83] Borto. "From an Apologism," 507-508.

[84] Burke. "Loisy's Faith," 142.

[85] Pius IX. *Syllabus of Errors*, 80.

[86] See, for example, Kwasniewski. "Pius X Condemns Modernism": "all the errors that Pius X analyzes in *Pascendi* are still being taught today – indeed, in the most scandalous dereliction of duty yet seen in Church history, by the pope himself, not just once or twice, but frequently, across a wide range of subjects."

[87] Borto. "From an Apologism," 502.

[88] PGD, 39.

carefully defined, by none other than Pius X. In fact, this pope takes almost two thirds of his key encyclical explaining what Modernism is.

In order to properly define Modernism, Pius X tried to characterize the Modernist in all its facets. Firstly, he described the Modernist as a philosopher. The philosopher would ground his ideology in two roots, one negative and another positive. The negative root would be *agnosticism*. "According to this teaching human reason is confined entirely. . . to things that are perceptible to the senses, and. . . it has no right and no power to transgress these limits."[89] Since this negative root blocks the road to divine revelation, the void left behind must be filled with something else. Here is where the "positive" root comes in: the principle of *vital immanence* i.e., the idea that "every vital phenomenon, and religion. . . is due to a certain necessity or impulsion; but it has its origin, speaking more particularly of life, in a *movement of the heart, which movement is called a sentiment*."[90] Hence, both "science and history are confined within these two limits, the one external, namely, the visible world, the other internal, which is consciousness. When one or other of these boundaries has been reached, there can be no further progress, for beyond is the unknowable."[91]

Since religion rests merely on sentiment, it befalls the intellect to provide it structure, namely through formulas. If these formulas are approved by the Church, they constitute dogmas. But since religious sentiment proceeds from the believer, then dogmas must be adapted to the believer, and therefore dogmas can "evolve" i.e., "change."[92]

From here, then, we proceed from the Modernist as a philosopher to the Modernist as a believer. Whereas the philosopher does not concern himself with whether divine reality exists outside the heart of the believer, the believer on the other hand does indeed believe in such divine reality, a reality independent of the person who believes in it. But this believer will state that the foundation of his faith rests on the "experience of the individual."[93]

---

[89] PGD, 6.
[90] PGD, 7.
[91] PGD, 7.
[92] PGD, 11-12.
[93] PGD, 14.

And here, in this section of the encyclical dealing with the Modernist believer, is where Pius X discovers the old trick that we have been exploring throughout this book. Even here, even in Modernist thought, we witness an attempt to hijack tradition to serve heresy. The section "Religious Experience and Tradition" from *Pascendi Dominici Gregis* deserves to be quoted in full:

> But this *doctrine of experience* is also under another aspect entirely contrary to Catholic truth. *It is extended and applied to tradition*, as hitherto understood by the Church, and *destroys it.* By the Modernists, *tradition is understood as a communication to others, through preaching by means of the intellectual formula, of an original experience.* To this formula, in addition to its representative value, they attribute a species of suggestive efficacy which acts both in the person who believes, to stimulate the religious sentiment should it happen to have grown sluggish and to renew the experience once acquired, and in those who do not yet believe, to awake for the first time the religious sentiment in them and to produce the experience. *In this way is religious experience propagated among the peoples; and not merely among contemporaries by preaching, but among future generations both by books and by oral transmission from one to another.* Sometimes this communication of religious experience takes root and thrives, at other times it withers at once and dies. For the Modernists, to live is a proof of truth, since for them life and truth are one and the same thing. *Hence again it is given to us to infer that all existing religions are equally true, for otherwise they would not live.*[94]

Pius X would go on to condemn the Modernist as a theologian, namely by censoring the principles of theological immanence[95] and divine permanence[96] that we have seen above. Afterwards, he would deal with the Modernist as an historian and critic, showing how the historical-critical method

---

[94] PGD, 15.
[95] PGD, 19.
[96] PGD, 20.

at the time was fraught with philosophical and ideological premises that were incompatible with the faith, as we have also seen.[97] Finally, he would reprimand the Modernist as an apologist,[98] and the Modernist as a reformer.[99] Loisy was in check in all fronts.

But can we infer from all that we have seen that Pius fostered an immobilist conception of the Church, utterly unmoved by any evolutionary principle? It depends. When Pius and Loisy were facing each other about evolution, they were speaking of *dogma*, of infallibly defined doctrines. These are indeed unchangeable, as the First Vatican Council—once again, infallibly—defined in his constitution *Dei Filius*: "the meaning of the sacred dogmas is ever to be maintained which has once been declared by holy mother church, and there must never be any abandonment of this sense under the pretext *or in the name of a more profound understanding*."[100] But the council quickly goes on to clarify that it accepted doctrinal development according to the principles of St. Vincent of Lérins (see chapter 6): "*May understanding, knowledge and wisdom increase as ages and centuries roll along*, and greatly and vigorously flourish, in each and all, in the individual and the whole church: but this only in its own proper kind, that is to say, in the same doctrine, the same sense, and the same understanding"[101]

As a meticulous follower of the First Vatican Council and of Catholic tradition, Pius X would also admit the possibility of such doctrinal development. One of the criticisms that Pius X levied against Modernists, was that they did not allow for the refinement of a dogmatic formula "in itself and *according to logical development*, but as required by circumstances."[102] He condemns evolution, but on the terms laid out by the Modernists, as a conflict between two forces: a conservative force, embodied by the clergy, and a progressive force, personified in the laity. Of course, such a notion was unacceptable to the pope, for it saw the magisterium as something that would eventually and inevitably be superseded.[103] Pius turned to the

---

[97] PGD, 29-33.

[98] PGD, 35.

[99] PGD, 38.

[100] Vatican I. *Dei Filius*, Chapter 4, 14.

[101] Vatican I. *Dei Filius*, Chapter 4, 14.

[102] PGD, 21.

[103] PGD, 21. But is it not here present a certain parallel with a certain traditionalism of today that, disillusioned by Church hierarchy, places its hope instead

magisterium instead, to the Syllabus and to the part of *Dei Filius* that I have quoted earlier, and said: "Nor is the development of our knowledge, even concerning the faith, impeded by this pronouncement - on the contrary it is aided and promoted."[104] In another encyclical, titled *Il Fermo Proposito*, Pius X would write:

> In passing it is well to remark that it is impossible today to re-establish under the same form all the institutions which have been useful and even the only effective ones in past centuries, so numerous the new needs which changing circumstances keep producing. But the Church in its long history and on every occasion has wisely shown that she possesses the marvelous power of adapting herself to the changing conditions of civil society. Thus, while preserving the integrity and immutability of faith and morals and upholding her sacred rights, she easily bends and accommodates herself to all the unessential and accidental circumstances belonging to various stages of civilization and to the new requirements of civil society.[105]

So how can one know where true development lies? As has been shown time and again throughout the course of this book, that can be done by turning to the magisterium. In a 1912 speech Pius X would say: "we do not set above the authority of the Pope that of other persons, however learned, who dissent from the Pope, who, even though learned, are not holy, because whoever is holy cannot dissent from the Pope."[106] In an earlier address from 1909, Pius X taught:

> For the first and greatest criterion of the faith, the ultimate and unassailable test of orthodoxy is obedience to the teaching

---

on a traditionally-minded laity, securing the fort until the post-conciliar magisterium is reversed by a future pope?

[104] PGD, 28.

[105] Pius X. *Il Fermo Proposito*, 9.

[106] Pius X, "Discorso."

> authority of the Church, which is *ever living* and infallible, since she was established by Christ to be the *columna et firmamentum veritatis*, "the pillar and support of truth" (1 Tim 3:15).
>
> And so, with a system of sophisms and errors they falsify the concept of obedience inculcated by the Church; they arrogate to themselves the right of judging the actions of authority even to the extent of ridiculing them; they attribute to themselves a mission to impose a reform — a mission which they have received neither from God nor from any authority. They limit obedience to purely exterior actions. . .
>
> Do not let yourselves be deceived by the subtle declarations of others who do not cease to pretend that they wish to be with the Church, to love the Church, to fight for her so that she will not lose the masses, to work for the Church so that she will come to understand the times and so to win back the people and attach them to herself. Judge these men according to their works. If they maltreat and despise the ministers of the Church and even the Pope; if they try by every means to minimize their authority, to evade their direction, and to disregard their counsels; if they do not fear to raise the standard of rebellion, what Church are these men speaking about?[107]

Again, the answer rests on the ecclesiastical magisterium. *Pascendi* was, in itself, a muscular exercise of magisterial authority. The pontiff posited many practical remedies to combat the spread of Modernism, from the promotion of scholastic thought (see chapter 2),[108] to the censorship of publications,[109] to the implementation of diocesan watch committees,[110] and even the creation of an anti-modernist oath that all clergy should take.[111] When Pius X's pontificate ended, the Modernist movement had been successfully stopped on its tracks. As for Loisy, he kept writing and publishing even after his excommunication, and much ink has been spilled

---

[107] Benedictine Monks. *Papal Teachings: The Church*, 380-382.

[108] PGD, 45-47.

[109] PGD, 50-53.

[110] PGD, 55.

[111] Pius X, *The Oath Against Modernism.*

on whether he kept believing in any sort of personal God until the end of his life.[112]

"Whom do you say I am?"[113]

Even if moderns and Modernists alike have tried their best to answer the question of who Jesus is, this question is not new. In fact, one can say that this question is as old as Jesus's ministry itself. One bright day, two millennia ago, Jesus was passing with His disciples by the vicinity of a town, named Caesarea Philippi. There were some caverns nearby where, according to legend, the gates of Hades stood. Suddenly, Jesus halted His steps. Turning to the disciples, He asked:

"Whom do men say that the Son of man is?"[114]

This disconcerting question took the disciples by surprise. The replies to this question were multiple, then as now. "Some say you are John, the Baptist."—they replied— "Others that you are Elijah, or Jeremiah, or any other prophet…"[115]

However, Jesus was also interested in knowing, not only the thoughts of the world, but the thoughts of His disciples: "But whom do *you* say that I am?"[116]

The door was opened for a new multiplication of answers. After all, the disciples' guess could be as good as any other. That would not be the case, though. The gospels say that one of the disciples took the lead and dared answer the question that multitudes have been answering since then. This disciple was Peter, the same one whose adventures we followed in chapter 5—though at the time, he was known by a different name: Simon, son of Jonah.

"Thou art Christ, the Son of the living God."[117]

---

[112] Burke. "Loisy's Faith."
[113] Mt 16:15.
[114] Mt 16:13
[115] Mt 16:14
[116] Mt 16:15
[117] Mt 16:16

If we keep reading the gospels, we will find that this answer was the one that pleased Jesus the most. He proclaimed that this response had been revealed to Simon by none other than God, the Father Himself.[118] As recognition for Simon's answer, Jesus changed his name to Peter, and gave him authority over the newborn Church, and even over the same gates of hell legend said opened nearby.

We will return to this episode later in chapter 12. For now, let us try to keep focusing on the answer to the age-old question: "Whom do men say the Son of man is?" The replies are manifold, and even more so now since the Christ of faith has been amputated from the Jesus of history. Some have claimed that Jesus was a revolutionary that went against the oppression of the established order,[119] or even a proto-Marxist.[120] Coincidentally, the authors who think this belong to the left-wing half of the political spectrum. Also coincidentally, it is possible to find people on the other side of the spectrum claiming that Jesus was actually a capitalist.[121] On their hand, feminists will say that Jesus was a feminist,[122] and pro-choice activists that Jesus would be pro-choice.[123] Those who advocate for the end of priestly celibacy posit that Jesus was married with Mary Magdalene,[124] and those who advocate for LGBTQ, that He had a romance with the apostle John.[125]

---

118 Mt 16:17

119 See for example, Gasper, "Jesus the Revolutionary?": "The Gospels offer two different pictures of Jesus. On the one hand, there is the divine being who preaches salvation in another world. On the other hand, there is a Jesus in the tradition of Jewish popular revolution—a figure of this world who opposes kings and oppressors, and who promises his followers real material benefits in this life. There is plenty of evidence that the first of these pictures was a later elaboration. . . In any case, the first three gospels never claim that Jesus is divine. It is only in the Gospel of John, written last and rejected by some Christians as late as the 3rd century, that Jesus is represented as a deity. Meanwhile, the second picture of Jesus fits with the social and political circumstances in which he lived. . . All the evidence points to Jesus as one of the self-proclaimed messiahs fighting to end Roman occupation, and for an egalitarian society in which the division between rich and poor has been erased. According to Celsus, Jesus was a 'ringleader of sedition.'"

120 For an example, see Arel, "Sorry Republicans, but Jesus was a Marxist."

121 See "Jesus was a capitalist," *Reclaiming America for Jesus Christ.*

122 Swidler, *Jesus was a feminist.*

123 See for example, Currie, "Here's why I'm a pro-choice pastor."

124 As an example, see Phips, "Did Jesus marry?"

125 One example can be found in Oestreicher, "Was Jesus gay? Probably."

Faced with this cacophony of contradictory interpretations, I cannot but recall what the great twentieth century writer G.K. Chesterton wrote, when faced with this same babel:

> I maintain therefore that a man reading the New Testament frankly and freshly would not get the impression of what is now often meant by a human Christ. The merely human Christ is a made-up figure, a piece of artificial selection, like the merely evolutionary man. Moreover there have been too many of these human Christs found in the same story, just as there have been too many keys to mythology found in the same stories. . . [O]thers said he was indeed an original teacher because he cared about nothing but Socialism; or (as others said) about nothing but Pacifism. Then a more grimly scientific character appeared who said that Jesus would never have been heard of at all except for his prophecies of the end of the world. He was important merely as a Millenarian like Dr. Cumming; and created a provincial scare by announcing the exact date of the crack of doom. Among other variants on the same theme was the theory that he was a spiritual healer and nothing else; a view implied by Christian Science, which has really to expound a Christianity without the Crucifixion in order to explain the curing of Peter's wife's mother or the daughter of a centurion. There is another theory that concentrates entirely on the business of diabolism and what it would call the contemporary superstition about demoniacs, as if Christ, like a young deacon taking his first orders, had got as far as exorcism and never got any further. Now, each of these explanations in itself seems to me singularly inadequate; but taken together they do suggest something of the very mystery which they miss. *There must surely have been something not only mysterious but many-sided about Christ if so many smaller Christs can be carved out of him.* If the Christian Scientist is satisfied with him as a spiritual healer and the Christian Socialist is satisfied with him as a social reformer, so satisfied that they do not even expect him to

> be anything else, it looks as if he really covered rather more ground than they could be expected to expect.[126]

Or, paraphrasing Fr. Tyrrel's insight, it might seem that what all these interpreters may be seeing is not the historical Jesus, but their own reflection at the bottom of a deep well.

However, as tempting as it might be to think so, this is not an exclusively modern phenomenon, created by the chronological distance that separates us from those days when Jesus walked the earth. Even in the early Church we find a great interpretative diversity, with great disagreements about the proper interpretation of scripture or other historical events related to Jesus.[127] Some scholars, then, will postulate that acknowledging this "tradition" of diversity and disagreement undercuts "the notion of an unbroken tradition,"[128] which would amount to an unhistorical "whitewashing of biblical and early church history into a narrative of continuous and harmonious agreement."[129] According to this worldview, the fact that the early Church contained both Gnostic factions and a faction that would eventually be called orthodox means that the latter does not have any more inherent value than the former—it is simply the position that became consensual at a later time and, eventually, rewrote history in its own image and likeness. But this is, once again, a philosophical and ideological presupposition.

Then as in now, the principle of non-contradiction applies. We know that it is impossible that Jesus would be a proto-Marxist and a proto-capitalist at the same time. We know that it is untenable that Jesus would be married to Mary Magdalene and have a gay affair with John the apostle at the same time. Likewise, it is also impossible that both Gnostics and

---

126 Chesterton, *The Everlasting Man*, 190-191. See also Deines, "Can the 'Real' Jesus be identified with the Historical Jesus?" 33-34, 37: "In between is space for all other kinds of Jesuses: the revolutionary, the liberator from all kind of real or imagined oppressions, the feminist and first 'real man', the magician, the social reformer, the Galilean *chasid*, the Jewish prophet, or more precisely the apocalyptic or milleniaristic prophet, the helper of the poor, or just a lazy swindler who was lucky enough to find people who were willing to support him with their money."

127 Moss. "Hubristic Specialists," 40.

128 Moss. "Hubristic Specialists," 40.

129 Moss. "Hubristic Specialists," 43.

orthodox would be right about Jesus, for both interpretations contain mutually exclusive elements. One interpretation, therefore, must be truer than the other—in other words, more authoritative. And, if we go back to that sunny day at Caesarea Philippi two thousand years ago, when Jesus asked, "Whom do you say I am?" one answer was more pleasing than all others.

To know where this authoritative answer lies, we must question the widespread modern idea that faith invented events to express itself. Maybe this is a non-proved premise that is held as true only because of philosophical and ideological prejudices. Maybe it was the opposite: faith came into being and expressed itself as a *reaction* to an event. Maybe something real, something historical, happened to those who would then interpret their experience and formulate it in terms of faith.[130] In this sense, faith is viewed retrospectively instead of prospectively. The Christians of yore were looking to the past and making sense of their historical experiences.

This faith reaction to a historical experience crystallized, as we have seen in chapter 1, first as oral tradition and then as scripture. Scripture became so through a process of incessant re-readings, corrections, deepenings, and dilatations. Ancient texts are read in a new situation and understood in a new way, progressively revealing their inner possibilities.[131] In this sense—and contrary to what Harnack and Loisy thought—the chronological distance between the actual experience and its later expression is not a sign that the biblical writings are not reliable. On the contrary, this chronological distance adds "meaningfulness and correlation with other historical or spiritual realities that were absent to them or imperceptible when the event itself took place."[132]

Scripture grew *in* and *from* a living subject.[133] This living subject is not merely the authors of the books of the Bible, since these writers are not autonomous in the modern sense of the word: rather, they belong to a collective subject, which is called "the people of God." This people of God is the *Church*, the living subject of scripture. In the Church, the words of

---

[130] Deines, "Can the 'Real' Jesus be identified with the Historical Jesus?", 28.
[131] Benedict XVI, *Jesus of Nazareth: from the Baptism*, xviii-xix.
[132] Deines, "Can the 'Real' Jesus be identified with the Historical Jesus?", 28.
[133] Benedict XVI, *Jesus of Nazareth: from the Baptism*, xx.

the Bible are a permanent presence.[134] This dynamic process is, as we saw in chapter 1, what constitutes the *process of tradition.* As Joseph Ratzinger says in another book:

> *Tradition, we said, always presumes a bearer of tradition, that is, a community* that preserves and communicates it, that is the vessel of comprehensive common tradition and that becomes, by the oneness of the historical context in which it exists, the bearer of concrete memory. *This bearer of tradition in the case of Jesus is the Church.* That is not a theological judgment in the true sense of the word but rather a simple statement of fact. The Church's role as bearer of tradition rests on the oneness of the historical context and the communal character of the basic experiences that constitute the tradition. This bearer is, consequently, the *sine qua non* of the possibility of a genuine participation in the *traditio* of Jesus which, without it, would be, not a historical and history-making reality, but only a private memory.[135]

As we have seen in chapter 1, tradition only exists within the community, for it is within the community that the contents of tradition are passed on, from person to person, from generation to generation. In our case, the community is the Church. Any effort to try to "save the Church" by taking recourse to any kind of "archaeologism" is not true tradition, but a false tradition. For Ratzinger, this archaeologism can be either conservative or liberal. Progressive archaeologism goes beyond the Protestant archaelogism of *sola scriptura* (see chapter 8) and regards with suspicion everything that comes after St. Paul, defining "tradition according to the need of the moment" and depending "extensively on reconstructions that are but the reflections of their own *a priori* conceptions." But, as Ratzinger says, "the difference between such progressivisms and a false traditionalism is not a fundamental one; it is merely a question of when tradition ends."[136]

---

[134] Benedict XVI, *Jesus of Nazareth: from the Baptism*, xx-xxi.

[135] Ratzinger, *Principles of Catholic Theology*, 100. I am also reminded of the words from St. Joan of Arc, quoted in the CCC 795: "About Jesus Christ and the Church, I simply know they're just one thing, and we shouldn't complicate the matter."

[136] Ratzinger, *Principles of Catholic Theology*, 101.

Of course, one can say that this diversity of opinions about who Jesus is also exists within the confines of this ecclesial community that is the bearer of tradition. Even within the Church, there are progressive and traditionalist factions, with contradictory interpretations. This is the reason why the Church, where tradition dwells, recognizes an authoritative interpreter. This authoritative interpreter is the magisterium, whose agents are the pope and the bishops in communion with him.[137]

And this brings us back to that hot day in Caesarea Philippi, when Jesus told a certain Simon son of Jonah that his interpretation of His identity was the right one amidst all other versions. This episode initiated a tradition, solid as any other, that has shaped the Church ever since. We will explore it with more detail in chapter 12. For now, I would like to end this chapter by quoting Pope Pius XII:

> *They, therefore, walk in the path of dangerous error who believe that they can accept Christ as the Head of the Church, while not adhering loyally to His Vicar on earth.* They have taken away the visible head, broken the visible bonds of unity and left the Mystical Body of the Redeemer so obscured and so maimed, that those who are seeking the haven of eternal salvation can neither see it nor find it.[138]

It is folly to try to separate that which cannot be separated. We cannot separate Christ from His Vicar, the pope. The pope is the head of the visi-

---

137 CCC 85, 100.

138 Pius XII, *Mystici Corporis Christi*, 41.

ble Church,[139] the guarantor of unity.[140] Therefore, those who follow a different Jesus from the pope are, in effect, separating themselves from the Church, the community that is the bearer of tradition. And, as we have seen throughout this chapter, tradition can only exist within the community. Those who want to return to a Jesus separated from the living Church are, once again, unwittingly attacking tradition under the pretext of defending it.

In summary:

We have now completed a tour through time, from the first to the twenty first century. Throughout this travel, we have seen a tradition at play, a tradition running deeper than mere restatements of ancient texts and pronouncements. This is the tradition of doctrinal development, always expanding, even in surprising directions, sometimes even with the appearance of contradiction with what came before.

However, alongside this venerable tradition, we have also seen another counter-parallel tradition—or rather, an anti-tradition. It is the anti-traditional tradition of traditionalism. Whenever a development is at hand, forces of resistance will inevitably emerge to stifle the growth of living tradition, while non-authoritatively claiming guardianship over tradition.

---

[139] Pius XII, *Mystici Corporis Christi*, 40: "On the contrary, our Redeemer also governs His Mystical Body *in a visible and normal way through His Vicar on earth.* You know, Venerable Brethren, that after He had ruled the 'little flock' Himself during His mortal pilgrimage, Christ our Lord, when about to leave this world and return to the Father, entrusted to the Chief of the Apostles the visible government of the entire community He had founded. Since He was all wise He could not leave the body of the Church He had founded as a human society without a visible head. Nor against this may one argue that the primacy of jurisdiction established in the Church gives such a Mystical Body two heads. For Peter in view of his primacy is only Christ's Vicar; so that there is only one chief Head of this Body, namely Christ, who never ceases Himself to guide the Church invisibly, though at the same time He rules it visibly, through him who is His representative on earth. After His glorious Ascension into Heaven this Church rested not on Him alone, but on Peter, too, its visible foundation stone. *That Christ and His Vicar constitute one only Head is the solemn teaching of Our predecessor of immortal memory Boniface VIII in the Apostolic Letter* Unam Sanctam*; and his successors have never ceased to repeat the same.*"

[140] See John Paul II, *Ut Unum Sint*, 88.

But if we cannot trust mere appearances, how can we distinguish between a true doctrinal development (*profectus fidei*) and a corruption of the faith (*permutatio fidei*)? I think that, until now, I have already hinted at the answer. Nevertheless, let us try to address the topic from a different perspective.

We have seen that Jesus Christ is the source of all tradition (see chapter 1). It would stand to reason, then, that Jesus would also have been affected by the phenomena we have explored so far. Namely, if Jesus would have taught something that could be understood as a development, then the anti-traditional forces of traditionalism would have resisted Him as well. This is what we are going to investigate in the next chapter. In the process, we will be able to better grasp where to find the safety of the barque of tradition amidst a tempestuous sea of competing interpretations.

Section III

Tradition Recognized

Chapter 11

"Not one iota"

In this passage, Jesus wants to help his listeners to reread the Mosaic law. What had been said in the ancient covenant was true, but that was not all: Jesus came to bring to fulfillment and to promulgate in a definitive way the Law of God, up to the last iota. He manifests its original aims and fulfils its authentic aspects, and he does all this through his preaching and, even more, with the offering of himself on the Cross. In this way, Jesus teaches how to fully carry out God's will, and he uses these words: with a 'righteousness' that 'exceeds' that of the scribes and the Pharisees. A righteousness enlivened by love, charity, mercy, and hence capable of fulfilling the substance of the commandments, avoiding the risk of formalism. Formalism: this I can, this I cannot; up to this point I can, up to this point I cannot.

—Francis, Angelus

2020 had been a very sad year. Most people were imprisoned inside their homes. Only "essential workers" were allowed outside of their domiciliary prisons, but only to carry the whole society on their shoulders. Churches were closed, malls were empty, the roads were deserted. In the words of Pope Francis, for weeks it had been evening. Thick darkness had gathered over the squares, the streets, the cities. It had taken over everyone's lives, filling everything with a deafening silence and a distressing void. It could be felt in the air, in people's gestures, in their glances: the specter of COVID-19 hovering over the globe, as an invisible Damocles sword. The world found itself afraid and lost.[1]

Sure, the authorities kept assuring everyone, it was just a matter of "riding this wave." If everyone waited out, strictly upholding the lockdowns and distancing measures, the spread would diminish. Scientists were working tirelessly to find vaccines or treatments for the virus—it was just a matter of time. But even apart from the constant naysayers spreading misinformation, even among those who were following all the recommendations from national and international health specialists, the exhaustion of this complete societal overhaul was taking its toll. People kept feverishly accompanying the numbers of new cases and deaths, incessantly being updated by the news broadcasts, hoping for any favorable evolution in the

[1] Francis, "Extraordinary Moment of Prayer."

statistics, praying for any budging of the graphs, waiting that today would be better than yesterday. But days kept pilling up, with no end in sight. As usual, Pope Francis had enough discernment to understand that something needed to be done. It was paramount to restore hope to the people.

On March 22, the Holy Father delivered his usual Angelus address. The "usual" Angelus address. . . How could it be usual if it had not been preached to the habitual crowds at St. Peter's Square, but livestreamed from the papal palace's almost empty library? Yet, Pope Francis would make this address even more unusual. He announced: on March 27, he would give an extraordinary "*Urbi et Orbi*" blessing. These blessings "to the city and the world" were usually done only on Easter and Christmas, the peaks of liturgical importance in the Church. But Francis would give an additional one on that Feast of the Annunciation, because the world needed it. He also granted a plenary indulgence to all those who would follow the blessing's broadcast, and also asked all Catholics (in fact, every Christian, regardless of denomination) to join him in prayer at that time.[2]

Thomas Lawson twisted his nose. "Here is the diva pope, always showing off"—he thought to himself. This had been the pope that had condoned the lockdown of churches, depriving the faithful of the sacraments and of mass. As if these were not "essential services"! And how much did Tom miss his beautiful Latin mass, the smell of incense, the echo of the chants! His soul was wilting as a flower without water. All of that was Francis's fault, who had given himself up to fear, the same fear stoked by godless authorities for whom physical wellbeing was more important than spiritual goods.[3]

Still, the pope had convoked all Catholics to pray for the world. How could Tom refuse? God knew that the world was in dire need of prayers.

---

[2] Wells, "Pope announces extraordinary *Urbi et Orbi* blessing."

[3] As an example of this criticism, see Reno, "Questioning the Shutdown": "Cancelling services and closing churches underlines the irrelevance of institutional Christianity in our technocratic age. We are bombarded by the gospel of perpetual youth won through diet and exercise (supplemented by the ersatz immortality of social media fame). If churches are darkened in the face of sickness and death, only TV talking heads, media pundits, and public health officials will speak to our anxieties and fears. This reinforces the secular proposition: Life in this world is the only thing that matters. The docility of religious leaders to the cessation of public worship is stunning. It suggests that they more than half believe that secular proposition."

If, in order to storm the heaven with prayers in unison with all Church, he would have to do it at Francis's beckoning, so it would be done!

On March 27, at the prespecified time, Tom turned on his laptop. Forevermore, he would always remember the exact place where he watched that extraordinary *Urbi et Orbi*. When the live broadcast started, he could see the immense St. Peter's Plaza, completely empty. It was raining. It was dark. The lights in the distance reflected on the water in the ground, imparting a phantasmagorical appearance to the bluish hue of the background. The ambience could not be more attuned to Tom's general spirits.

Suddenly, against the backdrop of this disheartening void, a lonely figure emerged, his whiteness contrasting with the darkness around. By his side there were icons that, in the past, had been associated with warding off epidemics. Amongst these was the cross of San Marcello al Corso which, in the sixteenth century, had been processed through all the districts of Rome to end a great plague.[4] Now, during this twenty first century plague, the cross was once again retrieved, this time to be virtually processed through the four corners of the earth. The rain did not stop, pouring over the image of the crucified Christ, just like the moment when He expired 2,000 years ago.

The downpour, however, did not deter the Holy Father. He preached his homily, reflecting on the gospel story of Jesus calming the storm, reassuring troubled hearts that the Savior was present even during the deadliest tempest, for He had the God-given authority to command even the forces of nature. The pope then delivered a litany of supplication before the cross of San Marcello. The empty plaza notwithstanding, everyone could sense it: at that moment, the pope was not praying there alone—the whole world was praying with him. Yet, nothing was more poignant than the adoration of the Blessed Sacrament, followed by the pope blessing both the city and the world with the monstrance, to the sound of the bells.[5]

At that moment, hardened hearts could not but melt away; their criticism faded. It was undeniable for anyone with faith that the Spirit was present in St. Peter's at that moment. The entire Church had united with the pope that night, regardless of their personal opinions on Francis, as it

---

[4] Daud, "Miraculous crucifix from 1522 plague."

[5] Gabriel, "*Urbi et Orbi*: Meeting the real Pope Francis."

should have been since the beginning of his pontificate. And Tom was no exception. That night, he slept in peace, filled with hope in the Lord.

Online, a common refrain began to emerge among the voices who, until then, had been most critical of Francis: that this blessing (and not any of Francis's magisterial teachings or acts) was the high point of his pontificate. Tom agreed. But the pope's apologists were quick to note "Here's one of the best kept secrets about Francis: he talks like that all the time."[6]

"Why is this a well-kept secret?"—Justin rhetorically asked Tom— "Is it Francis's fault? Not at all: most of his speeches, homilies, and documents are publicly available on the Vatican website, as well as credible media sources. Anyone with a computer or cellphone and an internet connection can access them at any time. But it's a well-kept secret because the media outlets on which many Catholics rely for information about the Church have been distorting Francis's image. They've been trying to sell him as a worldly pope, one who sacrifices the mystical and spiritual dimensions of the faith in order to accommodate the values of the secular and political world. The difference is that this *Urbi et Orbi* was so widely disseminated *in its entirety*, that it was impossible to bury the pope's spirituality under layers of misinterpretation and misinformation, as is usually the case. That evening, Francis was allowed to shine to all the faithful, as he really is, without the usual dark filters."

Tom was still reluctant to accept this, but soon another event gave him pause for reflection. Not another blissful event, but its opposite. The breaking of bliss. The breaking of this beautiful state of grace. Soon, the nagging resumed on social media. Reports started to circulate that the cross of San Marcello had been damaged by the exposure to the rain, to the point of being "on the verge of exploding."[7] This would later prove to have been grossly exaggerated.[8] Also, soon after the *Urbi et Orbi* blessing, the numbers of COVID-19 cases began to subside in Italy.[9] But all this was not enough to quell the barrage of criticisms against the Holy Father.[10]

---

[6] See @mfjlewis tweet from March 28, 2020.

[7] Giansoldati, "Danneggiato il crocifisso 'miracoloso.'"

[8] Allen, "Damage to 'miraculous crucifix' not as serious as reported." See also Gabriel, "The disfigured crucifix."

[9] Henley, "Italy records lowest coronavirus death toll."

[10] Gloria.tv. "Cross Crumbles - Coronavirus Continues."

And frankly, at that point, Tom was starting to grow weary of all the negativity. . . The cross of San Marcello might not have really cracked, but the walls around Tom's soul were indeed showing signs of fracture.

A gospel tension with the gospel's flavor

One day, Jesus and His disciples gathered with some Pharisees and scribes from Jerusalem. The table was ready and filled with good food and merry drink. The Pharisees certainly expected this to be a pleasant meal, with an enriching exchange on the side. But soon, their delight gave way to pure disgust. Jesus's disciples had started eating without washing their hands. The problem here was not merely lack of hygiene. It had much deeper religious connotations. The ritual hand washing had to do with a well-established purity system. As the gospels remark, it was a venerable "tradition of the ancients." Not only the hands, but cups and pots also, should be washed in a particular way, lest the food and participants be defiled.[11]

The Pharisees turned to Jesus. As the master, He was the one responsible for the misbehavior of His disciples. The Pharisees asked: "Why do not thy disciples walk according to the tradition of the ancients, but they eat bread with unwashed hands?"[12] They were expecting Jesus to harshly rebuke His disciples. Instead, Jesus harshly rebuked the Pharisees:

> Well did Isaias prophesy of you hypocrites, as it is written: This people honoureth me with their lips, but their heart is far from me. And in vain do they worship me, teaching doctrines and precepts of men. For leaving the commandment of God, you hold the *tradition of men*, the washing of pots and of cups: and many other things you do like to these. And he said to them: *Well do you make void the commandment of God, that you may keep your own tradition.*[13]

This was not the first time that Jesus had done something similar. On another occasion, Jesus had brought His disciples to a field, so that they

---

[11] Mark 7:1-4.

[12] Mark 7:5.

[13] Mark 7:6-9.

would glean some food. The problem: that day was a sabbath, a day of obligatory rest for Jews. Once again, the Pharisees confronted Jesus, asking Him: "Why do they do on the sabbath day that which is not lawful?"[14] And, once more, Jesus replied: "The sabbath was made for man, and not man for the sabbath. Therefore, the Son of man is Lord of the sabbath also."[15]

Many other examples abound. Jesus was constantly breaking the purity codes that the Jews had inherited from their forebears. Jesus touched people whom these codes deemed unclean: a leper,[16] a hemorrhaging woman,[17] a corpse.[18] Furthermore, He often shared meals with sinners.[19] In this sense, Jesus perfectly anticipated the purity controversies that we have seen in chapter 5 of this book.

It seemed like Jesus's actions were obviously—even self-evidently—discontinuous with the tradition the Jewish people had received. So, why should anyone listen to this Jesus? This was the Pharisees' reasoning, and at a first glance, it was reasonable. But not so fast. At a later time, Jesus would say something that would throw the Pharisees completely off guard. As He delivered His most famous "sermon on the mount", Jesus said:

> Do not think that I am come to destroy the law, or the prophets. *I am not come to destroy, but to fulfill.* For amen I say unto you, till heaven and earth pass, *one jot, or one tittle shall not pass of the law*, till all be fulfilled. He therefore that shall break one of these least commandments, and shall so teach men, shall be called the least in the kingdom of heaven. But he that shall do and teach, he shall be called great in the kingdom of heaven.[20]

What a confusing thing to say! After all, a jot (or iota) and the tittle (dot) are the smallest strokes of the Hebrew alphabet![21] This meant that the law

---

[14] Mark 2:23-24.

[15] Mark 2:27-28.

[16] Mark 1:41.

[17] Mark 5:27.

[18] Mark 5:41.

[19] Mark 2:15-16. See also Loader, *Jesus' Attitude Towards the Law*, 11.

[20] Mt 5:17-19.

[21] Crowe, "What did Jesus mean when He said, 'Not an Iota'?"

would not be changed even to the most infinitesimal detail. This coming from a person that had patently broken the law every step of the way! Did Jesus mean that He would be the least in the kingdom of heaven?

The Pharisees were still scratching their heads at this puzzling statement when Jesus proceeded with His sermon. And as He did, He put an uncomfortable spotlight on them: "For I tell you, that unless your justice abound more than that of the scribes and Pharisees, you shall not enter into the kingdom of heaven."[22] He then explained to the multitude how their justice could exceed that of the Pharisees. He did so through a series of antitheses, contrasting "You have heard that it was said to them of old" (i.e., tradition) with "But I say to you."[23] So, if the law the Pharisees obeyed said "Thou shalt not kill," Jesus's followers should surpass them by not even being angry at their brothers.[24] If tradition commanded "Thou shalt not commit adultery," Jesus invited the multitudes to not even "look on a woman to lust after her."[25] Jesus's teaching was much more radical than the Torah.[26] We will see why this is important later in this chapter.

Jesus ended His sermon and descended from the mount. But He was not through yet. At another time, He would complete what He had said, once again focusing on the Pharisees:

> "*The scribes and the Pharisees have sitten on the chair of Moses. All things therefore whatsoever they shall say to you, observe and do*: but according to their works do ye not; for they say, and do not. For they bind heavy and insupportable burdens and lay them on men's shoulders; but with a finger of their own they will not move them. And all their works they do for to be seen of men."[27]

The Pharisees must have been very angry at these words. After all, they boasted of being perfect in the observance of the law. Now this Jesus had come along, telling ordinary people that they could exceed the Pharisees,

---

22 Mt 5:20.

23 Benedict XVI. *Jesus of Nazareth: from the Baptism*, 102.

24 Mt 5:21-22.

25 Mt 5:27-28.

26 Benedict XVI. *Jesus of Nazareth: from the Baptism*, 122-123.

27 Mt 23:2-5.

all the while calling their inner faults out in public! But let us forget this for a moment. Let us rather focus on the confusion that these apparently self-contradictory assertions must have caused. Jesus said He did not come to destroy the law, but He also urged His disciples to break the law. He said that not one iota of the law would be changed, but He constantly flipped the law on its head. Was Jesus being deliberately ambiguous, trying to undermine the foundations of the law while preemptively defending Himself from the accusations of doing so by issuing some fig-leaf disclaimers here and there? Was Jesus being a sophist, like Siger of Brabant (see chapter 4), holding two conflicting statements at the same time?

Not at all. Rather, what we have here is a tension between continuity and discontinuity.[28] A true tension with the flavor of the gospel, for this tension exists in the very gospels themselves. If this is a tension with the flavor of the gospel, in the way Pope Francis envisions those (see chapter 4), then one must resolve it in a higher plane. Would this even be possible?

Hardened hearts: a *ressourcement*

The discontinuity here seems obvious and there is no need to rehash it again. Jesus constantly broke the law by eating with sinners, touching unclean people, feasting with unwashed hands, and working on a sabbath, among other things. But the continuity is also there, and not just on the "not one iota" disclaimer. For example, when justifying His disciples' gleaning on sabbath, Jesus brought up a historical precedent, connecting His actions to the line of King David (from where the Messiah was foretold to come):

> Have you never read what David did when he had need, and was hungry himself, and they that were with him? How he went into the house of God, under Abiathar the high priest, and did eat the loaves of proposition, which was not lawful to eat but for the priests, and gave to them who were with him? And he said to them: The sabbath was made for man, and not man for the sabbath.[29]

---

[28] Loader, *Jesus' Attitude Towards the Law*, 55.
[29] Mark 2:25-27.

In other words, Jesus did not make His maxim up out of thin air. The utterance "the sabbath was made for man, not man for the sabbath" had been grounded on King David eating the holy loaves of the temple.[30] These loaves had a connection with the sabbath, for they should be changed every Saturday and could only be eaten by a priest within the sanctuary.[31] But David and his companions ate them anyway. Jesus had retrieved a forgotten and ancient tradition to substantiate His behavior. The reason why this tradition had been forgotten was because it had been practiced only by King David, who had divine permission to act this way. By appealing to Davidic precedent, Jesus was also asserting His authority and messiahship.[32]

This would not be the only time Jesus would practice a kind of *ressourcement.* There was another occasion when the Pharisees tried to embarrass Jesus, by asking Him whether it was lawful for a man to put away his wife. Jesus replied to them:

> Have ye not read, that *he who made man from the beginning*, made them male and female? And he said: For this cause shall a man leave father and mother, and shall cleave to his wife, and they two shall be in one flesh. Therefore, now they are not two, but one flesh. What therefore God hath joined together, let no man put asunder.
>
> They say to him: Why then did Moses command to give a bill of divorce, and to put away?
>
> He saith to them: Because Moses by reason of the *hardness of your heart* permitted you to put away your wives: *but from the beginning it was not so.*[33]

Once again, Jesus appeals to an ancient and forgotten tradition, a tradition older than Moses's concessions, a tradition hearkening back to Adam and Eve. Nothing could be more primordial than that.

But Jesus's greatest exercise of *ressourcement*—and the one most important for better understanding His perspective on the law—is the

[30] 1 Sam 21:3-6.

[31] Lev 24:5-9.

[32] See Benedict XVI, *Jesus of Nazareth: From the Baptism*, 107.

[33] Mt 19:4-8.

reawakening of the concept of "hardness of heart." In fact, Jesus mentions this "hardness of heart" as the reason for Moses's allowances for divorce in the passage above.

"Hardness of heart" is a common accusation from Old Testament prophets whenever the people went astray. Psalm 94 evokes an episode in Exodus—where the Hebrews quarreled with Moses about lack of water[34]—as an example of hardness of heart and urges the reader not to harden his heart in the same way.[35] Prophet Zechariah said that the people had "made their heart as the adamant stone."[36] The book of Chronicles explains that King Sedecias "hardened his neck and his heart from returning to the Lord."[37]

Against this hardness of heart, the prophet Ezekiel foretells that God will cause Israel to walk in His commandments by "taking away its stony heart and giving it a heart of flesh."[38] Prophet Jeremiah talks of a "new covenant" with Israel where God is going to write the law "in their hearts."[39] In other words, the perfection of the commandments rests not on legalistic religious observance, but in following them interiorly, in one's own heart.[40]

Jesus picks up on this tradition and expands upon it. During the incident of the unwashed hands, Jesus explains that a person is not defiled by anything coming from without (like food tainted by unclean hands,) but by what comes from within (the heart.)[41] Jesus then proceeds to turn the accusations against the accusers. He mentions the practice of *Corban* (i.e., offerings dedicated to the temple that could not be used for any other purpose) and how it was being abused by temple authorities to enrich themselves, while defrauding people of the money they should spend supporting their parents in their old age—which was also a commandment of the law.[42] This practice was lawful if one stuck to the letter of the law. But, in

---

[34] Exod 17:1-7.
[35] Ps 94:8-9.
[36] Zech 7:12.
[37] 2 Chron 36:13.
[38] Ezek 36:26.
[39] Jer 31:31-33.
[40] Vilijoen, "Jesus' Teaching on the 'Torah,'" 149-150.
[41] Mark 7:15.
[42] Grondin. "Why Did Jesus Condemn the Practice of Corban?"

practice, it divided the people between religion of the heart and their actual behavior.[43] It was a loophole in the law, encouraging abuse. Jesus did not have an argument with the law, but with a particular interpretation of the law that deliberately sought to circumvent it.[44]

A similar dynamic plays out during the gleaning episode. After proclaiming that "the sabbath was made for man, not man for the sabbath," Jesus goes into a synagogue and asks: "Is it lawful to do good on the sabbath days, or to do evil? To save life, or to destroy?" Jesus then proceeds to heal a crippled man. When they saw this, the Pharisees went out and immediately started to conspire on how to dispose of Him.[45] Jesus "worked" on sabbath to do good and to save a life, whereas the scandalized Pharisees tried to stop Him from "working" on sabbath. In doing so they worked evil on a sabbath, trying to destroy His life. Jesus had made their hypocrisy manifest once again.[46]

This brings us back to the sermon of the mount when Jesus affirmed that not one iota or dot would be removed from the law. He said He had come not to destroy the law, but to fulfill it. As I mentioned previously, during His speech, Jesus taught the multitudes how to surpass the Pharisees in the observance of the law. Jesus establishes a series of antitheses, wherein He contrasts external behaviors with internal attitudes. So, not only must one not kill, but one must also not be angry with one's brother. Not only must one not commit adultery, but one must also not look lustfully at a woman. To do otherwise makes one a murderer or an adulterer in one's own heart.[47]

It is interesting that, in His antitheses, Jesus does not disagree with what "is written," but with "you have heard."[48] So, we can see that Jesus did not abrogate the commandments, but reinterpreted them, so that the inward obedience to the law would take precedence over the outward and material obedience. The law remains authoritative. Not one iota or dot was removed from it. But just because the law is still authoritative, it does not

---

[43] Loader, *Jesus' Attitude Towards the Law*, 72.

[44] Loader, *Jesus' Attitude Towards the Law*, 73.

[45] Mark 3:4-6.

[46] Loader, *Jesus' Attitude Towards the Law*, 37.

[47] Mt 5:21-28.

[48] Crowe, "What did Jesus mean when He said, 'Not an Iota'?"

mean it will always continue to function in the same way.[49] This is how the law could be fulfilled. Jesus combats legalistic behavior[50] because, as we have seen with the errors of the Pharisees, this formalism breaks the law under the pretext of upholding it.

The same holds true as regards the gleaning controversy. When Jesus says that the sabbath was made for man, not man for sabbath, what He is saying is that the sabbath should be interpreted as a gift to be inwardly enjoyed, not as a demand outwardly imposed. Jesus challenges the Pharisees to think differently about the same reality. There is no need for so much strictness,[51] for that will lessen the enjoyment of this God-given gift and, therefore, thwart its purpose.

What God wanted was mercy, not sacrifice.[52] The Pharisees had failed to understand this simple truth. It was not about setting limits to the application of the law but about showing its correct application.[53] It was not about eschewing sacrifice, but prioritizing mercy over sacrifice.[54]

This reinterpretation of the law did not happen in a vacuum either. It was closely related to the developing Jewish tradition of the prior two centuries.[55] There is a famous episode where the Pharisees tried to ensnare Jesus by asking Him what the greatest commandment in the law was. Jesus replied to them:

> Thou shalt love the Lord thy God with thy whole heart, and with thy whole soul, and with thy whole mind. This is the greatest and the first commandment. And the second is like to this: Thou shalt love thy neighbour as thyself. On these two commandments dependeth the whole law and the prophets.[56]

We are used to thinking that this controversy has to do with Jesus explaining the ethical core of the law. This is correct and adjusted to Jesus's

---

49 Vilijoen, "Jesus' Teaching on the 'Torah,'" 150.
50 Vilijoen, "Jesus' Teaching on the 'Torah,'" 150.
51 Loader, *Jesus' Attitude Towards the Law*, 45, 52.
52 Mt 9:13.
53 Vilijoen, "Jesus' Teaching on the 'Torah,'" 151.
54 Loader, *Jesus' Attitude Towards the Law*, 76, 101.
55 Stern. "Jesus' Citation of Dt 6,5," 312.
56 Mt 22:36-40.

ministry, as we have seen above. But there is more at play here. The Pharisees knew that the question of the "greatest and first commandment" had been a hot topic for two hundred years already. The reason why they sought to "ensnare" Jesus, was because they thought He would give an incorrect answer. His ignorance of the law would therefore be made manifest, and they could more easily refute Him.[57] On the other hand, it would be very hard for Jesus to give an accurate answer to this question, for it would be like asking a "specialist in any field to condense the whole of his lifetime of study into a few sentences."[58]

The Pharisees' second intentions are made even more manifest if we take into account that this episode mirrors very closely what had happened with Hillel the Elder, a rabbi from the first/second centuries BC. According to Jewish sources, a heathen mocked Hillel by making an unreasoned demand: "I'll convert if you teach me the whole Torah while I stand on one foot." Hillel replied: "What you dislike, do not do to others. This is the whole Torah. The rest is commentary. Go and learn the commentary."[59] The Pharisees were certainly aware of this incident when they asked the same to Jesus.

Jesus frustrates their plans by answering in the same vein as Hillel, thereby showing His familiarity with the best Jewish normativity of His time.[60] By doing this, Jesus showed Himself to be in continuity with the developing Jewish tradition, but at the same time proved His point about the interiority of the commandments. On the one hand, Jesus showed a great handle of the law, since He subsumes the law into two commandments, one for sins affecting a person's relationship with God, and another for sins affecting a person's relationship with their brethren.[61] On the other hand, by summarizing the law into "love God and thy neighbor," Jesus formulates the two greatest commandments as internal attitudes from which the external actions should flow.[62]

---

[57] Stern. "Jesus' Citation of Dt 6,5," 312.
[58] Stern. "Jesus' Citation of Dt 6,5," 313-314.
[59] Stern. "Jesus' Citation of Dt 6,5," 313-314.
[60] Stern. "Jesus' Citation of Dt 6,5," 314.
[61] Stern. "Jesus' Citation of Dt 6,5," 316.
[62] Loader, *Jesus' Attitude Towards the Law*, 101.

Fulfilling the law: a continuity

As we have seen, when Jesus summarizes the law into the two greatest commandments, He is trying to show continuity with Jewish tradition. Throughout the gospels, the evangelists put a great deal of effort to illustrate this continuity. For example, they try to illustrate many Old Testament episodes by using typology i.e., when someone or something in the Old Testament is viewed as foreshadowing someone or something in the New Testament.[63] The transfiguration shows Jesus in continuity with Moses (the law) and Elijah (the prophets.) And scattered through the gospels we see Jesus fulfilling many ancient prophecies.[64] The evangelists seek to establish this continuity with Jewish tradition so thoroughly, they connect Jesus with the last link of this tradition: John the Baptist[65] (though the latter also clashed with the Jewish tradition of his time; but the evangelists only reveal it implicitly,[66] so as not to highlight the discontinuity).

Why was this continuity important? It was not just Jesus that was being ensnared by the Pharisees. The evangelists recounting the life of Jesus were trying to avoid their own traps as well. As we have seen in chapter 5, the Hellenization of Jewish culture led to the persecution of orthodox Jews by the Greek King Antiochus Epiphanes in the second century BC. This led to the development of another Jewish tradition: the notion that the Greek persecution had been divine punishment for the people's infidelity, since by their actions they had "abolished the law."[67] In the first century AD, this tradition was in full steam. The temple, the most sacred thing in Jewish religion, had been destroyed by the invaders. Just like in the time of the Maccabees, someone's actions needed to be at fault. The scapegoat befell the zealot rebels who, in order to fight against Roman rule, had ceased to observe the sabbath, thereby "abolishing the law." Furthermore, during their revolt, the zealots occupied the temple, showing less respect for its hallowed grounds than the Romans had had.[68] Certainly, the ensuing

[63] Nash. "A Primer on Biblical Typology."
[64] Loader, *Jesus' Attitude Towards the Law*, 125.
[65] Loader, *Jesus' Attitude Towards the Law*, 14, 55.
[66] Loader, *Jesus' Attitude Towards the Law*, 14.
[67] Thiessen. "Abolishers of the Law in Early Judaism," 545-548.
[68] Thiessen. "Abolishers of the Law in Early Judaism," 549-550.

temple destruction had been a divine punishment for the zealots' disregard for the law.

So, when St. Matthew stressed that Jesus came not to abolish the law,[69] he was preemptively defending Christianity from a loaded term. The Pharisees had certainly thought the Jesus had abolished the law, and Israel was blaming the destruction of the temple on those who had abolished the law through their actions. Both Jesus and the evangelists answer this charge by turning the tables: it was the Pharisees who, by upholding the letter of the law while betraying its heart, had not fulfilled the law. Jesus, on His end, had come not to abolish the law, but to fulfill it. How? By holding the law to a higher standard than the Pharisees, internalizing it into the heart.[70]

It is interesting, therefore, that when Jesus rejects the charge that He is abolishing the law, He does not contrast "abolishment" with "confirmation" or "enforcement" or even "obedience," but with "fulfillment" of the law—meaning bringing the law to its full intent and expression.[71]

How does Jesus fulfill the law? When He subsumed all the law into the two greatest commandments, He also subsumed the whole law into love: love for God and love for one's neighbor. And mercy—which God desires more than sacrifice, as we have seen—is carried out through love.[72] Jesus fulfilled the law in His own life, by loving God and humanity till death on the cross. Love is the fulfilment of the law, mercy is the fulfilment of love, and Jesus is the fulfilment of mercy.[73]

St. John Chrysostom, the great Eastern Father of the Church, said that Jesus fulfilled the law in a threefold fashion. The first one we have already seen, in His own life, by transgressing none of the precepts of the law. Secondly, not only did He fulfill it Himself, He granted us to do likewise. Therefore, we are to be merciful because of the mercy Jesus has shown us.[74] Thirdly, and most importantly for this book, Jesus fulfilled the law by

---

69 Mt 5:17.

70 Thiessen. "Abolishers of the Law in Early Judaism," 551-555.

71 Vilijoen, "Jesus' Teaching on the 'Torah,'" 147.

72 Vilijoen, "Jesus' Teaching on the 'Torah,'" 152.

73 See Crowe, "What did Jesus mean when He said, 'Not an Iota'?": "This does not mean Christians should have no concern to follow God's law. Christ frees us to obey it. Jesus' disciples are called to a genuine love of God and neighbor. This is a lofty calling, but Jesus Himself embodied it throughout His life."

74 Crowe, "What did Jesus mean when He said, 'Not an Iota'?"

drawing up a new code of laws, that brought the law to its most perfect expression. However, this code of laws did not repeal the former, just like saying "be not angry" does not annul "do not kill," or saying "do not look at a woman with lust" does not rescind "do not commit adultery."[75]

Therefore, we can see that, when Jesus claimed to have come "not to abolish the law but to fulfill it," He did so to allay the fears in His listeners that He had come to abrogate the ancient institutions. To prevent the notion that His antitheses placed both sets of commandments against each other, Jesus first clarified the apparent contradiction by explaining that there is no contradiction at all. However, as St. John Chrysostom points out, at the same time Jesus was also changing the whole world, by introducing another discipline.[76] Thus, we see the tension between continuity and discontinuity being resolved in a higher plane.

Nevertheless, these caveats did not prevent the Pharisees from accusing Jesus of the same things He disclaimed. Despite Jesus's clarifications, they saw Him as an innovator, just like they had done with John the Baptist before Him.[77] During the beginning of Jesus's ministry, we can hear the Pharisees asking each other in bewilderment: "What thing is this? What is this new doctrine?"[78] And even St. John Chrysostom affirms that, though Jesus did not repeal the ancient code of law, He came to draw up a new one. So how could this be? As Jesus and the evangelists tried to show—and as the Pharisees also understood—it all boiled down to the issue of authority.

"By what authority?"

In his Christological treatise, Benedict XVI notes a curious detail during the episode of the cleansing of the temple. Jesus fashioned a whip from small cords, drove out the sacrificial animals that were there for sale, and overthrew the moneychangers' tables.[79] However, even after all this

---

[75] Chrysostom. *Homily 16 on Matthew.*

[76] Chrysostom. *Homily 16 on Matthew.*

[77] Loader, *Jesus' Attitude Towards the Law*, 17.

[78] Mark 1:27.

[79] John 2:13-15.

ruckus, neither the temple police nor the Roman soldiers intervened.[80] The priests interrogated Jesus but did not accuse Him at that moment (that would happen later.) This is because Jesus was not violating the law. Jesus was attacking a relatively novel practice, that had been set up by the temple aristocracy (and, by doing so, attacking the corruption that came along with this practice.) Furthermore, when He cried "Is it not written, My house shall be called the house of prayer to all nations? But you have made it a den of thieves,"[81] Jesus was actually invoking an older tradition, dating back to prophets Isaiah[82] and Jeremiah.[83] Certainly, these references would not have gone unnoticed among the scripturally literate temple elites. Once again, Jesus was not violating the law, but fulfilling it.[84]

No, the temple authorities did not accuse Jesus of violating the law. Rather, they proceeded to ask Him: "By what authority dost thou these things?"[85] As we have seen above, it was a matter of authority. It is only when Jesus says, "Destroy this temple, and in three days I will raise it up,"[86] that the temple authorities start plotting to accuse Jesus. This utterance would become one of the charges during Jesus's trial at the Sanhedrin.[87]

So let us return to the question of authority. Benedict XVI tells us of a book called *A Rabbi talks with Jesus*, written by Rabbi Jacob Neusner. In this book, Rabbi Neusner imagines himself at the mount where Jesus preached His most famous sermon, listening to Him and then entering into a dialogue with Him.[88] Neusner then returns to the company of his fellow Jews and begins relaying what he heard and saw. The rabbi shows the

---

[80] Benedict XVI, *Jesus of Nazareth: Holy Week*, 11. See also Loader, *Jesus' Attitude Towards the Law*, 111: "One would certainly expect the temple authorities to have objected to Jesus's action. It would have been seen as an unnecessary interference in their domain; they had their own temple police! . . . Jesus' actions must have been confined enough in space and time, not to expose him to immediate arrest. This already suggests an action of a symbolic nature, rather than a general clean up."

[81] Mark 11:17.

[82] Is 56:7.

[83] Jer 7:11.

[84] Benedict XVI, *Jesus of Nazareth: Holy Week*, 11-12.

[85] Mark 11:28. See also Benedict XVI, *Jesus of Nazareth: Holy Week*, 12.

[86] John 2:19.

[87] Mt 26:61.

[88] Benedict XVI, *Jesus of Nazareth: From the Baptism*, 69.

continuity between Jesus's summary of the two greatest commandments and an ongoing tradition of law simplification: "Rabbi Simelai explains that Moses received six hundred and thirteen precepts; David reduced them to eleven; Isaiah reduced them to six and later to two; Then Habacuc summarized them in one single precept: 'the just shall live in his faith.'"[89]

Then, someone asks Neusner: "So is this what Jesus came to say?" The rabbi replies: "Almost, but not exactly." New question: "What did Jesus omit?" Neusner responds: "Nothing." New query: "Then, what did Jesus add?" And finally, Neusner gives the answer at the crux of the whole matter: "Himself."[90]

Rabbi Neusner was not alone in his conclusions. All those who had listened to Jesus' sermon on the mount are said to have been "in admiration at his doctrine. For he was teaching them as one having authority, and not as the scribes and Pharisees."[91] In other words, Jesus is not like the others that came before Him. He is not a mere speaker with impressive rhetorical quality.[92] He is not a prophet in the traditional sense, acting as an ambassador or trustee from another, but rather makes Himself the point of reference for a righteous life.[93] He is not to be reduced to a rebel[94] or liberal reforming rabbi, for He is not stating His own personal opinion, or else His authority would be merely human or scholarly.[95] On the contrary, Jesus claims a normativity that no other teacher has ever claimed.[96] The authority of Jesus's new interpretation cannot be lesser than the one from the original text. It must be a *divine* authority.[97]

Jesus had encouraged the people to follow the Pharisees and scribes, even if their lives contradicted their doctrines, for they "sat in the chair of Moses."[98] But now, as Jesus sat on the mount to teach,[99] Jesus also sat in the cathedra of Moses. He did not sit as the Pharisees and scribes, though.

---

[89] Benedict XVI, *Jesus of Nazareth: From the Baptism*, 104-105.
[90] Benedict XVI, *Jesus of Nazareth: From the Baptism*, 105.
[91] Mt 7:28-29. See also, related to another episode, Mark 1:22.
[92] Benedict XVI, *Jesus of Nazareth: From the Baptism*, 102.
[93] Benedict XVI, *Jesus of Nazareth: From the Baptism*, 90.
[94] Benedict XVI, *Jesus of Nazareth: From the Baptism*, 126.
[95] Benedict XVI, *Jesus of Nazareth: From the Baptism*, 119-120.
[96] Benedict XVI, *Jesus of Nazareth: From the Baptism*, 90.
[97] Benedict XVI, *Jesus of Nazareth: From the Baptism*, 120.
[98] Mt 23:2.
[99] Mt 5:1.

He did not sit as a master taught in the school of Moses, or as Moses's disciple, receiving authority from His master. Rather, Jesus sat as the *new Moses*. The mount is also charged with symbolism. This unnamed Galilean hill is the *new Sinai*, where *the law is given anew*.[100]

Was this within His power to do? Since we Christians know that Jesus is God incarnate, we know that the answer is yes. But would the people of Israel by the time of Jesus be able to know it? Or would they be justified in thinking that Jesus had come to abolish their divinely instituted traditions and should, therefore, be rejected if one wanted to remain faithful to God? Here, the answer is complex. Clearly, Jesus's message should have the ability to be well received in the religious milieu of first century Israel, otherwise Jesus should not even have tried to preach it—and He would not have had any followers either. But its continuity might not have been *obvious*, or at least it might have seemed less cogent than the simpler alternative: that Jesus was a law abolisher.

It was not a strange concept for first century Judaism to have the Mosaic character shift to later teachers and legislators. Most importantly, Jesus presents Himself as the Messiah. There was an expectation at the time that the Messiah would bring the Torah, but there was disagreement about how this would come to be. Some thought the Torah would stay unchanged forever, others that certain rituals and purity laws would cease or be revised, and finally there were some that thought that a new Torah would be installed—the "messianic Torah."[101] Paradoxically, Jesus fulfills all these currents of thought, but this might not be obvious for everyone, especially those who believed the Torah would always remain immutable.

This is the reason why the evangelists emphasize so much all the events in Jesus's life that fulfill Old Testament prophecies regarding what the Messiah would do. From the protoevangelium, when it is said that the "seed of woman shall crush the Serpent's head,"[102] to Micah's prediction that He would be born in Bethlehem[103] or Zecharia's prophecy that He would enter

[100] Benedict XVI, *Jesus of Nazareth: From the Baptism*, 66. See also Vilijoen, "Jesus' Teaching on the 'Torah,'" 149.

[101] Vilijoen, "Jesus' Teaching on the 'Torah,'" 149. See also Benedict XVI, *Jesus of Nazareth: From the Baptism*, 99.

[102] Gen 3:15.

[103] Mic 5:2.

Jerusalem to great acclamation while riding a donkey,[104] Jesus seems to check all the boxes.[105] But some may disagree. After all, this Jesus messiah did not bring with Him universal peace, nor did He vanquish poverty and misery once and for all.[106] The Jewish people, thirsty for liberation from Roman oppression, was expecting the Messiah to bring about this messianic kingdom. They saw this kingdom in a political light, so they were expecting a political messiah. The failure to see Jesus's primarily spiritual mission explains many of the misunderstandings around Jesus, even coming from His disciples.[107]

One can say that these more "secular" prophecies were not fulfilled in the first coming but will be fulfilled in Jesus's second coming.[108] We can also say that this world peace was achieved in a more abstract way, by bringing God's peace to the world,[109] a peace we must strive to maintain. But, though the Jewish people of the time (understandably) were more focused on the messianic prophecies involving political freedom, there were other prophecies, more obscure, that were still there from the beginning. These were prophecies involving uncomfortable realities that were closed to the disciples' understanding until much later.[110] There were prophecies that the Messiah would be betrayed by a friend during supper, that this betrayal would be for thirty pieces of silver, that the Messiah would remain silent before His accusers, that He would be spat upon and beaten, that He would be pierced, that He would be killed alongside transgressors, and that He would rise from the dead on the third day.[111] So, one could reasonably believe that Jesus, through His death and resurrection, was the Messiah, but this might not be immediately obvious.

Another possible stumbling block was Jesus's claim of divine authority, as we have seen above. Rabbi Neusner, of whom we have read before, is not scandalized by Jesus when He teaches that it is lawful for the disciples

---

[104] Zech 9:9.

[105] See Marshall. *The Crucified Rabbi*, 38-41.

[106] Benedict XVI, *Jesus of Nazareth: From the Baptism*, 116.

[107] See, as an example, Mt 20:20-28.

[108] Marshall. *The Crucified Rabbi*, 57.

[109] Benedict XVI, *Jesus of Nazareth: From the Baptism*, 44.

[110] Compare what the disciples of Emmaus said in Luke 24:21 and what Jesus says to them in Luke 24:25-27.

[111] Marshall. *The Crucified Rabbi*, 42-48.

to glean on the sabbath. This could have been the interpretation of any liberal or reform-minded rabbi.[112] What concerns Neusner is the justification given by Jesus. Jesus brings up the Davidic precedent, when David ate the consecrated bread of the temple. Neusner remarks that, by doing so, Jesus and the disciples have taken the place of the priests in the temple.[113] But even more shocking is the sentence: "the Son of Man is the lord of the sabbath."[114] The good rabbi is quick to understand that this utterance goes beyond the reforming program of a liberal teacher—Jesus is proclaiming Himself God.[115]

Throughout the gospels, we see Jesus ascribing to Himself tasks and prerogatives that belong only to God. For example, Jesus forgives the sins of a sick man with palsy. The Pharisees become outraged. How can this Jesus, a mere man, forgive sins? Sins are an offense against God. Therefore, only God should be able to forgive sins![116] Truly, Jesus's actions are only legitimate when we acknowledge that He is God incarnate.

This raises the question: would it be licit to ask the people of Israel to believe in such strange and novel concepts as incarnation or trinity? Would this not rightfully conflict with their profoundly monotheistic faith? Not quite. After all, we Christians, believers in the mysteries of incarnation and trinity, are also monotheistic. However, though it would be possible for a first century Jew to believe in these concepts, these might not have been obvious at first glance.

In his book *The Bodies of God*, Jewish biblical scholar Benjamim Sommer explains that, in ancient Mesopotamian and Canaanite culture, gods exhibited a "baffling mixture of distinctiveness and interchangeability. . . They usually appear as individuals. . . Yet on occasion, the boundaries separating gods in these texts are porous."[117] One way this could happen was through a phenomenon called "fragmentation." Two divinities might share the same name (e.g., Ishtar of Arbela and Ishtar of Nineveh) and being and not being the same entity at the same time.[118] On the other hand, there is

---

[112] Benedict XVI, *Jesus of Nazareth: From the Baptism*, 106-107.
[113] Benedict XVI, *Jesus of Nazareth: From the Baptism*, 108.
[114] Mark 2:28.
[115] Benedict XVI, *Jesus of Nazareth: From the Baptism*, 110.
[116] Mark 2:5-7.
[117] Sommer. *The Bodies of God*, 18.
[118] Sommer. *The Bodies of God*, 13.

also the concept of "fluidity," in which the gods not only had bodies, but could hold several bodies at the same time.[119] This is the reason why ancient Mesopotamians could believe that the god was manifestly present in an idol (in that the idol could see, speak, hear, and smell,) while the same god still remained in heaven.[120] By undergoing a specific ritual, the idol would become an incarnation of the god, whose substance was identical with that of the god, while not being the *only* body of the god.[121]

Is this important for ancient Israelite religion? After all, the Israelites rightfully condemned these Mesopotamian and Canaanite mythologies as sinful idolatry. Be that as it may, it stands to reason that ancient Hebrews were also somehow influenced by their cultural environment, so that certain concepts would not be so strange for them.[122] In this regard, we can see several biblical instances of fluidity and even "incarnation" of divine realities, namely the One True God. The most paradigmatic example is Abraham meeting the three men by the oak of Mambre. The book of Genesis is clear that "the Lord appeared to him in the vale of Mambre."[123] So it is heavily implied that God appeared in the form of three men, or at least one of the three men. They also possess physical bodies, for they all eat with Abraham.[124] Then, one of the men speaks in the name of God, prophesying what is about to happen to Sodom and Gomorrah: "*I* will go down."[125] In this sense, we can see that God is, at the same time, speaking through that man, but also mysteriously remains in heaven, from whence He will come down to judge Sodom.[126] Many Church Fathers saw in this event a manifestation of God's trinity.[127]

---

119 Sommer. *The Bodies of God*, 19.

120 Sommer. *The Bodies of God*, 19, 21.

121 Sommer. *The Bodies of God*, 22.

122 Sommer. *The Bodies of God*, 38.

123 Gen 18:1-2.

124 Gen 18:9.

125 Gen 18:21.

126 Sommer. *The Bodies of God*, 40-41.

127 See, for example: Hilary. *On the Trinity*, Book V: "But perhaps it will be argued that, when the Angel of God is called God, He receives the name as a favour, through adoption, and has in consequence a nominal, not a true, Godhead. If He gave us an inadequate revelation of His Divine nature at the time when He was styled the Angel of God, judge whether He has not fully manifested His true Godhead under the name of a nature lower than the angelic. For a Man spoke to

Another cryptic episode relates to how Jacob fought a mysterious man in a mountain that he later called Peniel (i.e., "face of God"). After calling that place Peniel, Jacob says: "I have seen God face to face, and my soul has been saved." [128] We can see that the patriarch has an inkling of an idea of the identity of this mysterious man, and it seems to be divine. Later, prophet Hosea muddies the waters even more, by calling the mysterious man "an angel," and then proclaiming that Jacob made supplication there to "the Lord of hosts." [129]

Abraham, and Abraham worshipped Him as God. Pestilent heretic! Abraham confessed Him, you deny Him, to be God." See also Augustine. *On the Trinity*, Book II: "And certainly, as to those who are moved by the visions of waking men to believe that not the Father, but only the Son, or the Holy Spirit, appeared to the corporeal sight of men,—to omit the great extent of the sacred pages, and their manifold interpretation, such that no one of sound reason ought to affirm that the person of the Father was nowhere shown to the eyes of waking men by any corporeal appearance;—but, as I said, to omit this, what do they say of our father Abraham, who was certainly awake and ministering, when, after Scripture had premised, 'The Lord appeared unto Abraham,' not one, or two, but three men appeared to him; no one of whom is said to have stood prominently above the others, no one more than the others to have shone with greater glory, or to have acted more authoritatively? Wherefore, since in that our threefold division we determined to inquire, first, whether the Father, or the Son, or the Holy Spirit; or whether sometimes the Father, sometimes the Son, sometimes the Holy Spirit; or whether, without any distinction of persons, as it is said, the one and only God, that is, the Trinity itself, appeared to the fathers through those forms of the creature: now that we have examined, so far as appeared to be sufficient what places of the Holy Scriptures we could, a modest and cautious consideration of divine mysteries leads, as far as I can judge, to no other conclusion, unless that we may not rashly affirm which person of the Trinity appeared to this or that of the fathers or the prophets in some body or likeness of body, unless when the context attaches to the narrative some probable intimations on the subject. For the nature itself, or substance, or essence, or by whatever other name that very thing, which is God, whatever it be, is to be called, cannot be seen corporeally: but we must believe that by means of the creature made subject to Him, not only the Son, or the Holy Spirit, but also the Father, may have given intimations of Himself to mortal senses by a corporeal form or likeness."

[128] Gen 32: 24,30.

[129] Hos 12:3-5. See commentary on this biblical episode in Sommer. *The Bodies of God*, 41. See also Augustine. *On the New Testament*, Sermon LXXII: "And when the man had prevailed against the Angel, he kept hold of Him; yes, the man kept hold of Him whom he had conquered. And said to Him, 'I will not let Thee go, except Thou bless me.' When the conqueror was blessed by the Conquered, Christ was figured. So then that Angel, who is understood to be the Lord Jesus, saith to

However, though ancient Judaism might have had an idea of the physicality of God (as when Adam hears the steps of God in the garden of Eden,[130] or when God protects Moses with His hand as He passes by,)[131] the truth is that other biblical texts start to push back against this perception.[132] This is the reason why later scholarship has attributed these puzzling biblical excerpts to an attempt to anthropomorphize God, in order to illustrate complex, abstract, divine realities through simple, day-to-day, down-to-earth language.[133] Be that as it may, the truth is that ancient Jews would have had the tools to at least accept the possibility of an incarnational and trinitarian concept of the monotheistic God, and not reject it outright.

In summary, Jesus's claims for His reinterpretation of the Torah rest on authority, or rather, His messianic and divine authority. This authority was based on traditions that first century Judaism would be able to recognize—though those traditions might have remained obscure until Jesus's manifestation. Those who accept Jesus's authority will be more amenable to receive His interpretation of the law and read it through a hermeneutic of continuity. Those who do not accept it will be more prone to reject it as a self-evident contradiction with ancient, immutable tradition, and to eschew any continuity as mental gymnastics.

That is precisely what happened with the Pharisees, who outright ruled out any possibility of legitimacy for Jesus's actions, for they did not recognize His authority. When Jesus forgave the sins of the man with palsy, the Pharisees believed He was usurping, not the priests' role, but God's rights. But the evangelist defends Jesus against these charges, by saying that, as the Son of Man, Jesus indeed had this authority to forgive sins.[134]

Jacob, 'Thou shall not be any more called Jacob, but Israel shall thy name be,' which is by interpretation, 'Seeing God.' After this He touched the sinew of his thigh, the broad part, that is, of the thigh, and it dried up; and Jacob became lame. Such was He who was conquered. So great power had this Conquered One, as to touch the thigh, and make lame. It was then with His Own will that He was conquered. For He 'had power to lay down' His strength, 'and He had power to take It up.' He is not angry at being conquered, for He is not angry at being crucified."

[130] Gen 3:8.

[131] Exod 33:22-23.

[132] Sommer. *The Bodies of God*, 38-57

[133] Sommer. *The Bodies of God*, 4-10.

[134] Loader, *Jesus' Attitude Towards the Law*, 30.

If Jesus has that authority, He certainly can bequeath some of this authority to someone else, that this person may act as His representative. What would this authority look like and what are its limits? This is what we are going to explore in the next chapter.

Chapter 12

"Upon this rock"

And this is freedom, it is actually the freedom that is found in the Church. Everything happened "cum Petro and sub Petro"*, that is to say, in the presence of the Pope, who is the guarantor for everyone of freedom and trust, and who guarantees orthodoxy.*

—Francis, General Audience

While the pandemic was still raging on, Pope Francis promulgated a new encyclical. This was a very timely encyclical, as it was focused on human fraternity, something that was very much needed at the time. All humankind should work together if all were to emerge victorious from the profound societal upheaval of the previous year.

However, as was usual, *Fratelli tutti* was barely out, and papal critics were already attacking it. The pope had finally codified his teaching on the inadmissibility of the death penalty in his own papal encyclical (see chapter 6).[1] But more than that, he had tackled a wide range of social issues through the lens of Catholic Social Doctrine, namely immigration[2] and private property.[3] The critics claimed that when Francis taught that the right to private property was not absolute, he was directly contradicting Leo XIII.[4] Here and there sprouted the all-too familiar notion that Francis was only teaching on prudential matters and could be disregarded on those

---

[1] Francis, *Fratelli tutti*, 263.

[2] Francis, *Fratelli tutti*, 59-61.

[3] Francis, *Fratelli tutti*, 120.

[4] Lawler. "Pope's new encyclical ignores previous social teaching": "Here is a flat contradiction: Pope Leo says the right to private property is inviolable; Pope Francis says it is not inviolable—and tosses in the obviously false claim that the magisterium has never suggested otherwise."

grounds.[5] It was just a leftist pope spouting out his usual Marxist drivel—they would say.[6]

This time, though, Tom had actually read *Fratelli tutti* from start to finish, and found it to be Pope Francis's most traditional document.[7] In all of those contentious teachings, the pontiff had tried to find scriptural, Patristic, and other authoritative sources to back them up.[8] And even the supposed contradiction with Leo XIII was based on a mistranslation[9]: the original wording was a direct quote from the Compendium of Social Doctrine.[10] Nor could one say that *Fratelli tutti* was a leftist encyclical, since it spoke favorably of the principle of subsidiarity and condemned "assistentialism."[11]

Tom was beginning to develop a distaste for this kneejerk negativity towards the Holy Father. This was certainly not what Catholicism was meant to be! His traditionalist friends kept assuring him that Francis was not being magisterial, but only expressing his prudential judgment on these matters, that could be safely ignored. But Tom was starting to question, why was Francis always not being magisterial when it came to the teachings his friends found difficult to accept? Was that not too convenient? We were

[5] Gregg. "Fratelli Tutti is a familiar mixture of dubious claims": "[T]he encyclical reflects the broader pattern of the commentary which has long characterized Francis's pontificate. Genuine insights which spring directly from the Gospels and often profound meditations on the Hebrew and Christian Scriptures go hand-in-hand with. . . generalized assertions about highly prudential matters which are unsupported by evidence, and a fair amount of what I can only describe as utopianism."

[6] See, for example, Solimeo. "*Fratelli Tutti*: A Socialist-Utopian, Ecumenical-Interreligious Encyclical."

[7] Gabriel. "*Fratelli tutti* – Francis's most traditional document?"

[8] Gabriel. "*Fratelli tutti* – Francis's most traditional document?"

[9] Gabriel. "*Fratelli tutti* – Francis's most traditional document?"

[10] See the Spanish version of the Compendium of Social Doctrine: "La tradición cristiana nunca ha aceptado el derecho a la propiedad privada como absoluto e intocable" (Pontifical Council for Justice and Pease. Compendio de la Doctrina Social de la Iglesia, 177). Compare this wording with the Spanish version of *Fratelli tutti*, 120. "la tradición cristiana nunca reconoció como absoluto o intocable el derecho a la propiedad privada"

[11] Francis, *Fratelli tutti*, 162, 186. See also Gabriel. "Is *Fratelli Tutti* a 'leftist' encyclical?"

talking about a papal encyclical! —Tom reasoned. Surely it must have some kind of magisterial authority! Otherwise, what are encyclicals for?

Preserved ever immaculate

At this point of the book, we should already be able to answer our central question in a conclusive way: since true tradition may not be obvious or perspicuous, where can we find where true Catholic tradition is? Theologians have several signposts that can guide them in this endeavor: the canons of St. Vincent of Lérins[12] (see chapter 6), the theological *loci* of Melchor Cano,[13] or the seven notes of doctrinal development from Cardinal Newman.[14] But could there be a surest, more reliable way to find tradition amidst a vortex of competing interpretations?

We may still have not answered the question of where true Catholic tradition is. But we have seen where it most likely is not. From all the precedents in this book, we can conclude that a mere private interpretation of tradition is not a reliable indicator of orthodoxy. In the last chapter, we have seen from Jesus Himself—the source of all tradition (chapter 1)—that one needs an authoritative interpreter.

Who is this authoritative interpreter? Jesus, of course. But since Jesus does not dwell on earth in a visible way anymore, where can one find this authoritative interpretation? Let us go back to an episode we have already examined in chapter 10. Let us go back to that hot day 2,000 years ago when, in Caesarea Philippi, Jesus asked His disciples "Whom do men say I am?" The true interpretation was given by a certain Simon, son of Jonah: "Thou art Christ, the Son of the living God." Jesus was so pleased with this answer, He renamed Simon right there on the spot, uttering words that would change the face of the Church forever:

> Blessed art thou, Simon Bar-Jona: because flesh and blood hath not revealed it to thee, but my Father who is in heaven. And I say to thee: That thou art Peter; and upon this rock I will build my church, and the gates of hell shall not prevail against it. And I will

---

[12] Martins, *Introdução à Teologia*, 114-116.

[13] Martins, *Introdução à Teologia*, 116-121.

[14] Newman, *Development of Christian Doctrine.*

> give to thee the keys of the kingdom of heaven. And whatsoever thou shalt bind upon earth, it shall be bound also in heaven: and whatsoever thou shalt loose upon earth, it shall be loosed also in heaven.[15]

This has even more importance than meets the eye. The quote already seems impressive in itself, but there is a traditional context at play here that evades our modern minds. Jesus proclaimed Himself "Messiah" i.e., descendant and heir to King David's royal line. From Israelite history, we know that the highest office in the land below the king was the royal steward. This office had been instituted by King Solomon, David's successor. Though the royal steward was not the king, he bore the authority of the king.[16] The prophet Isaiah explains that this steward would be called a *father* to the inhabitants of Jerusalem. I recall the etymology of the word "pope," meaning "daddy." The prophet goes on to say that the steward would bear the "keys of the house of David" so that what "he shall open, none shall shut; and what he shall shut, none shall open."[17] The parallels are quite striking and would certainly not have been lost among the disciples, eager as they were for the fulfilment of the messianic kingdom.

As would be expected, the gospels show us that from that point onward, Peter took on the role of the disciples' leader. During the Last Supper, even as Jesus foretold that Peter would deny Him thrice, He also said: "Simon, Simon, behold Satan hath desired to have you, that he may sift you as wheat: But I have prayed for thee, *that thy faith fail not*: and thou, being once converted, confirm thy brethren."[18] After the resurrection, Jesus told Peter thrice: "Feed my lambs."[19] All of these three biblical instances were later used by the First Vatican Council (see chapter 9) to support the teaching on papal primacy and infallibility.[20]

As we have seen in chapter 5, St. Peter performed this Jesus-given commission admirably. At the Council of Jerusalem, Peter defended

---

15 Mt 16:17-19.

16 Marshall. *The Crucified Rabbi*, 54-55. It is also from this office of royal steward that the historical title "vicar of Christ" emerged.

17 Is 22:21-22. See also Marshall. *The Crucified Rabbi*, 55-56.

18 Luke 22:31-32.

19 John 21:15-17.

20 Vatican I. *Pastor Aeternus*, chapters I and IV.

tradition, not according to the "obvious meaning" proposed by the Judaizer faction, but according to the tradition of the messianic Torah given by his master: "Not that which goeth into the mouth defileth a man: but what cometh out of the mouth, this defileth a man" (see chapter 11). Peter was not only the custodian of tradition, but also the sure guide for adequate doctrinal development. In fact, St. Cardinal Newman showcases Peter's position at the Council of Jerusalem as a paradigm of the first note of a true doctrinal development—preservation of type:

> And, in like manner, ideas may remain, when the expression of them is indefinitely varied; and we cannot determine whether a professed development is truly such or not, without some further knowledge than an experience of the mere fact of this variation. Nor will our instinctive feelings serve as a criterion. *It must have been an extreme shock to St. Peter to be told he must slay and eat beasts, unclean as well as clean, though such a command was implied already in that faith which he held and taught*; a shock, which a single effort, or a short period, or the force of reason would not suffice to overcome. *Nay, it may happen that a representation which varies from its original may be felt as more true and faithful than one which has more pretensions to be exact.* So it is with many a portrait which is not striking: at first look, of course, it disappoints us; but when we are familiar with it, we see in it what we could not see at first, and prefer it, not to a perfect likeness, but to many a sketch which is so precise as to be a caricature. On the other hand, real perversions and corruptions are often not so unlike externally to the doctrine from which they come, as are changes which are consistent with it and true developments. . . Nay, one cause of corruption in religion is the refusal to follow the course of doctrine as it moves on, and an obstinacy in the notions of the past.[21]

Such is the nature of doctrinal development. Oddly enough, one of the teachings that underwent proper development was precisely the doctrine of papal primacy. That St. Peter was a historical figure of particular

[21] Newman, *Development of Christian Doctrine*, 176-177.

relevance in the early Church, and that he was seen throughout his life as a reliable guarantor of Jesus's tradition is pretty much undisputed. The question is whether there was, at the time, a concept of a Petrine office that would survive Peter's death.[22] The latter would need to undergo development and maturation, though the seeds of this Petrine tradition were already there.

Alongside the wheat of early Christianity grew the chaff of Gnosticism (see chapter 6). According to Gnostic theology, the faith of ordinary Christians was just the first step on the path of faith, meant for beginners. To grow in the faith, one would need to gain greater knowledge about it, a knowledge that was only accessible to an elite of enlightened individuals.[23] Against this exclusivist Gnostic assertion, the Church would contend that tradition must be open to all, accessible, and understandable even for ordinary Christians. There should not be any secret traditions.[24] But since, as we have already seen, tradition may not always be obvious, how do we resolve this tension? We need just revisit chapter 6 and find the answer in the writings of St. Ignatius of Antioch: "You must all follow the lead of the bishop, as Jesus Christ followed that of the Father. . . Where the bishop appears, there let the people be, just as where Jesus Christ is, there is the Catholic Church."[25] There are no secret traditions, because the bishop is there to guide everyone into the true tradition, which thus becomes accessible to all.

---

[22] Schatz. *Papal Primacy*, 1-2.

[23] Ironically, Pope Francis is being extremely traditional when he denounces—namely in certain Church movements that are critical of him in the name of tradition—a certain "contemporary Gnosticism", defined thus: "a purely subjective faith whose only interest is a certain experience or a set of ideas and bits of information which are meant to console and enlighten, but which ultimately keep one imprisoned in his or her own thoughts and feelings. . . Gnostics think that their explanations can make the entirety of the faith and the Gospel perfectly comprehensible. They absolutize their own theories and force others to submit to their way of thinking" (Francis. *Gaudete et Exsultate*, 36, 39). An astute reader can draw the parallels between this ideology and the Modernism we have explored in chapter 10. It is quite peculiar that Pope Francis and his followers are the ones being accused of Modernism.

[24] Schatz. *Papal Primacy*, 5.

[25] Ignatius. "Epistle to the Smyrnaeans", 8.

Not every local bishop or church had the same authoritative weight, however. Of particular significance were the sees founded by apostles or located where the apostles lived or were buried. And among these, Rome became a "privileged locus of tradition," for the Roman church had been founded both by St. Peter and St. Paul. Besides, both had been martyred and buried there.[26] In his letter to the Romans, St. Ignatius calls the Church of Rome "the Church which is beloved and enlightened by the will of Him that wills all things which are according to the love of Jesus Christ our God, *which also presides* in the place of the region of the Romans, worthy of God, worthy of honour, worthy of the highest happiness, worthy of praise, worthy of obtaining her every desire, worthy of being deemed holy, and *which presides over love* [charity]."[27]

One can argue from this Ignatian quote that it is not the pope, but rather the "Church of Rome" that is deserving of all these epithets. However, the Church of Rome's preeminence is not merely on charity, or material assistance, but also spiritual, in matters of teaching.[28] It would, therefore, be just a matter of time until this authority of the Roman Church would crystallize around its bishop. Already in the second century, we see the bishop of Rome taking the reins of ecclesial disputes, as happened with St. Victor during the Quartodecimanian controversy (see chapter 7). At that time, as we have seen, this power move was criticized as too harsh by some of Victor's fellow bishops, like St. Irenaeus of Lyons. However, they did not dispute his authority to do so. In fact, this same Irenaeus would go on to argue against heretics by "indicating that tradition derived from the apostles, of the very great, the very ancient, and universally known Church founded and organized at Rome by the two most glorious apostles, Peter and Paul. . . For it is a matter of necessity that every Church should agree with this Church, on account of its *preeminent authority*."[29]

It is quite true that, during the doctrinal controversies of the first centuries, the disagreements would be settled by regional synods and ecumenical councils (this is, of course, also a point against those traditionalists who

---

[26] Schatz. *Papal Primacy*, 7-8.

[27] Ignatius. "Letter to the Romans," greeting.

[28] Schatz. *Papal Primacy*, 5-6.

[29] Ireaneus. *Against Heresies*, Book III, Chapter 3, 2. For a commentary on this quote, see Schatz. *Papal Primacy*, 10.

criticize the Second Vatican Council.) But it soon became clear that the position taken by the Roman church, in the person of her bishop, inevitably ended up on the right side of the conflict. In the end, the Roman position always seemed to prevail.[30]

This was especially interesting because Rome was not suited with the best theologians. To find the best theological minds of the time one would have to look to the Greek-speaking East, where the centers of the most vibrant intellectuality flourished. Rome, on the other hand, was a mere backwater of the empire at the time (see chapter 7). Paradoxically, this could have been a protective factor. Unlike the East, where questioning, probing, and debating were commonplace, Rome lacked intellectual sophistication and sensitivity. Rather, Rome's strength lied in common sense in practical questions.[31] Therefore, while most early heresies emerged from the overthinking East, Rome remained untainted by heresy, in spite of its lacks (or maybe precisely because of them.)

As controversies kept being overcome always on the side of Rome, the authority of the Roman bishop became increasingly strengthened. By the fourth century, we would already see St. Ambrose of Milan saying: "Where Peter is, there is the church."[32] A bit later, Pope St. Leo the Great would consolidate the papacy even further, by building upon this preexisting and emerging tradition, and developing it through scriptural and legal arguments. Leo took the "upon this rock" quote from Mt 16:18 to substantiate Peter's foundational role and preeminence among the other apostles. He then proceeded to claim that he was the "heir of Peter," and therefore also the heir to the keys. More than an heir to Peter, Leo was also in a sense "a Peter," or rather, "vicar of Peter."[33] From this point onward, the title "pope" would be applied solely to the bishop of Rome.[34]

It is true, many of the great champions of orthodoxy were not popes. We remember from chapter 6 that St. Athanasius had a paramount role in the combat against the Arian heresy. However, in his seminal essay on

---

[30] Schatz. *Papal Primacy*, 14-16.

[31] Schatz. *Papal Primacy*, 14-16.

[32] Ambrose. *Commentary on Twelve Psalms of David*, 40:30.

[33] Kaiser. "Leo the Great on the Supremacy of the Bishop of Rome," 75-77. See also Schatz. *Papal Primacy*, 29.

[34] Schatz. *Papal Primacy*, 28-29.

doctrinal development, St. Cardinal Newman ascribed an even greater role to Pope Leo in the fight against heterodox teaching:

> There has been a time in the history of Christianity, when it had been Athanasius against the world, and the world against Athanasius. The need and straitness of the Church had been great, and one man was raised up for her deliverance. In this second necessity, who was the destined champion of her who cannot fail? Whence did he come, and what was his name? *He came with an augury of victory upon him, which even Athanasius could not show; it was Leo, Bishop of Rome.*
>
> *Leo's augury of success, which even Athanasius had not, was this, that he was seated in the chair of St. Peter and the heir of his prerogatives.* In the very beginning of the controversy, St. Peter Chrysologus had urged this grave consideration upon Eutyches himself, in words which have already been cited: "I exhort you, my venerable brother," he had said, "to submit yourself in everything to what has been written by the blessed Pope of Rome; for St. Peter, who lives and presides in his own See, *gives the true faith to those who seek it.*" This voice had come from Ravenna, and now after the Latrocinium it was echoed back from the depths of Syria by the learned Theodoret. "That all-holy See," he says in a letter to one of the Pope's Legates, "has the office of heading (hegemonian) the whole world's Churches for many reasons; and above all others, *because it has remained free of the communion of heretical taint, and no one of heterodox sentiments hath sat in it, but it hath preserved the Apostolic grace unsullied.*" And a third testimony in encouragement of the faithful at the same dark moment issued from the Imperial court of the West. "We are bound," says Valentinian to the Emperor of the East, "to preserve inviolate in our times the prerogative of particular reverence to the blessed Apostle Peter; that the most blessed Bishop of Rome, to whom Antiquity assigned the priesthood over all (kata panton) may have place and opportunity of judging concerning the faith and the priests." Nor had Leo himself been wanting at the same time in "the confidence" he had "obtained from the most blessed Peter and head of the Apostles, that he had authority to defend

> the truth for the peace of the Church." Thus, Leo introduces us to the Council of Chalcedon, by which he rescued the East from a grave heresy.[35]

This perception that the see of Rome always remains unblemished from any taint of heresy was so proven by the sixth century, that Pope St. Hormisdas was comfortable enough to require his fellow bishops to sign a formula in order to heal a schism. The formula thus said:

> The first means of safety is to guard the rule of strict faith and to deviate in no way from those things that have been laid down by the Fathers. And indeed the words of Our Lord Jesus Christ: "Thou art Peter; and upon this rock I will build my church" (Mt 16:18), cannot be disregarded; these things which were spoken are demonstrated by the results, for *the Catholic religion has been preserved ever immaculate in the Apostolic See.*[36]

As we have seen in previous chapters, this Petrine precedent of unwavering orthodoxy was all but confirmed in later controversies. If we began this chapter by asking "where can we find the true Catholic tradition," we can go back to all the historical episodes we examined thus far and note that tradition was always whatever the pope and ecumenical councils affirmed. I feel even tempted to paraphrase St. Ambrose: "Where Peter is, there is tradition." Throughout this book, we saw the development of papal primacy, growing ever stronger, from its earliest stages until the First Vatican Council (see chapter 9) and even beyond (see chapter 10). In fact, the First Vatican Council would irrevocably stamp the formula of Hormisdas into Catholic doctrine when it defined the dogma of papal infallibility.[37] In his Syllabus of Errors, Bld. Pope Pius IX would condemn as erroneous the proposition that: "Roman pontiffs and ecumenical councils have. . . erred in defining matters of faith and morals."[38]

---

[35] Newman, *Development of Christian Doctrine*, 306-308.

[36] Kirsch. "Pope St. Hormisdas."

[37] Vatican I. *Pastor Aeternus*, chapters IV.

[38] Pius IX. *Syllabus of Errors*, 23.

This is our tradition and was pretty much undisputed in Catholic circles before Pope Francis (or the Second Vatican Council) came along. It is too convenient, I must say, that after remaining unblemished by heresy throughout millennia, pope and council would start erring precisely at the chronological point traditionalists started disagreeing with them.

Magisterium, the authoritative interpreter

In the last chapter, we have noted that Jesus Christ, by reason of His divine authority, is the source of all tradition and also the ultimate interpreter of the law. In this chapter, we have seen that Jesus can and did bequeath some of His authority to the Church, namely Peter. How does this interpretative task manifest itself? The Catechism sheds some light on the matter:

> *The task of giving an authentic interpretation* of the Word of God, whether in its written form or *in the form of Tradition*, has been entrusted to the living teaching office of the Church alone. *Its authority in this matter is exercised in the name of Jesus Christ.* This means that *the task of interpretation has been entrusted to the bishops in communion with the successor of Peter, the Bishop of Rome*. . . The task of interpreting the Word of God authentically has been entrusted *solely to the Magisterium* of the Church, that is, *to the Pope* and to the bishops in communion with him.[39]

Of course, unlike Jesus, the pope is not God. He cannot do whatever he wants, nor overturn divinely instituted traditions and truths. For this reason, traditionalists are quick to note that the same Catechism immediately adds the following caveat: "Yet this Magisterium is not superior to the Word of God, but is its servant. It teaches only what has been handed on to it."[40] They sometimes also quote Benedict XVI for the same effect:

> The power that Christ conferred upon Peter and his Successors is, in an absolute sense, a mandate to serve. The power of teaching

[39] CCC 85, 100.
[40] CCC 86.

> in the Church involves a commitment to the service of obedience to the faith. The Pope is not an absolute monarch whose thoughts and desires are law. On the contrary: the Pope's ministry is a guarantee of obedience to Christ and to his Word. He must not proclaim his own ideas, but rather constantly bind himself and the Church to obedience to God's Word, in the face of every attempt to adapt it or water it down, and every form of opportunism.[41]

The problem is that, when traditionalists quote these caveats, they are presupposing the thing they are trying to prove. They assume beforehand that the pope did not act as a true servant to the faith. They assume the pope acted as an absolute monarch. They assume he is proclaiming his own ideas or that he tried to water down doctrine. They then use these quotes as a confirmation of their conclusions.[42] But in order to deploy these quotes, they have to prove that the pope has indeed failed his mandate, —or even that he is not fulfilling his mandate when he teaches something they disagree with—otherwise they do not apply.[43] And to prove this, they will have to show that their interpretation is correct whereas the magisterial interpretation (i.e., the authoritative interpretation) is not. In doing so, they are entering into dangerous territory. Not everything is permitted here.

First, one has to ascertain the degree of magisterial authority that a certain statement contains. There are several levels of magisterial teachings:

---

[41] Benedict XVI. *Homily.*

[42] After quoting Benedict XVI's homily, Prof. Edward Feser says: "So, suppose some papal statement or other magisterial document did appear to try to introduce 'some new doctrine,' or appeared to 'water down' the Church's consistent past teaching, or failed to guard that teaching 'scrupulously' or to explain it 'faithfully.' This would be the clearest possible case in which a theologian might raise legitimate criticisms of the kind recognized by *Donum Veritatis.*" See Feser, "The Church permits criticism of popes."

[43] The same holds true for sedevacantists using certain ancient theologians' (most notably St. Bellarmine) writings as proof that a pope automatically loses his office if he professes heresy. The quotes used to justify the papal "error" are different, but the rationale is the same. They assume the error exists. But they have to prove that the pope is, indeed, in error, to assert that he lost his office.

- Extraordinary magisterium: teachings by a pope (when speaking *ex cathedra*) or by an ecumenical council. These teachings enjoy an infallible degree of certitude.
- Ordinary and universal magisterium: teachings of the bishops (including the pope), dispersed throughout the world, but in moral unanimity. These teachings are also infallible.
- Ordinary magisterium (not to be confused with the ordinary *and universal* magisterium): teachings by individual bishops or popes. These teachings are *not* infallible but are nevertheless authoritative.[44]

To better understand the different levels of the magisterium (and how the faithful should respond to each one of them,) we should turn to the Second Vatican Council's dogmatic constitution *Lumen Gentium*, and to two official documents published by then-Cardinal Joseph Ratzinger as Prefect for the CDF: 1) the instruction *Donum Veritatis* on the ecclesial vocation of the theologian; 2) the Doctrinal Commentary on the Concluding Formula of the *Professio fidei*.

Infallible teachings are irreformable[45] (see chapter 10), irreversible, definitive, and irrevocable.[46] These teachings contain truths to be believed as divinely revealed or to be held definitively.[47] In the case of the extraordinary magisterium, these doctrines are taught through a *defining act*.[48] One of the ways this defining act can take form is when the pope proclaims a dogma *ex cathedra*,[49] using the solemn formula "I declare, pronounce, and define." The other way is when an ecumenical council makes a solemn

---

[44] Adapted from a table in Sheehan, *Apologetics and Catholic Doctrine*, 206.

[45] CDF. "Doctrinal Commentary on the *Professio fidei*," 5. See also Vatican II. *Lumen Gentium*, 25: "And therefore his definitions, of themselves, and not from the consent of the Church, are justly styled irreformable, since they are pronounced with the assistance of the Holy Spirit, promised to him in blessed Peter"

[46] Sheehan, *Apologetics and Catholic Doctrine*, 207.

[47] CDF. "Doctrinal Commentary on the *Professio fidei*," 9.

[48] CDF. "Doctrinal Commentary on the *Professio fidei*," 9.

[49] Vatican II. *Lumen Gentium*, 25: "this is the infallibility which the Roman Pontiff, the head of the college of bishops, enjoys in virtue of his office, when, as the supreme shepherd and teacher of all the faithful, who confirms his brethren in their faith, by a definitive act he proclaims a doctrine of faith or morals."

proclamation, namely promulgating a creed, or decrees or canons with notes attached (usually anathemas).[50]

However, it may also happen that an infallible doctrine may be taught through a *non-defining act*, which happens with truths belonging to the ordinary and universal magisterium.[51] Although individual bishops besides the pope do not enjoy the prerogative of infallibility, they can still proclaim a doctrine infallible whenever they are in agreement on one position as definitively to be held, even when they are dispersed throughout the world, while maintaining the bond of communion among themselves and with the pope.[52] In this case, the magisterium is said to be "ordinary" because the bishops are exercising their teaching authority in their respective dioceses through pastoral letters, sermons, catechisms, or other methods. It is also said to be "universal," because their unanimity extends the teaching to the whole Catholic Church. Since it would be almost impossible to determine whether all the bishops of the world were unanimous at any given time, one needs not a total (mathematical) unanimity, but a practical unanimity or majority.[53]

How to know if a certain teaching belongs to the ordinary and universal magisterium? As the Commentary on the *Professio fidei* makes clear, "such a doctrine can be confirmed or reaffirmed *by the Roman Pontiff*, even *without recourse to a solemn definition*, by declaring explicitly that it belongs to the teaching of the ordinary and universal Magisterium as a truth that is divinely revealed or as a truth of Catholic doctrine. The declaration of confirmation or reaffirmation by the Roman Pontiff in this case is not a new dogmatic definition, but a formal attestation of a truth already possessed and infallibly transmitted by the Church."[54]

Infallible doctrines require assent of theological faith by all members of the faithful.[55] The First Vatican Council states that "by divine and

---

[50] Vatican II. *Lumen Gentium*, 25: "This is even more clearly verified when, gathered together in an ecumenical council, they [the bishops] are teachers and judges of faith and morals for the universal Church, whose definitions must be adhered to with the submission of faith."

[51] CDF. "Doctrinal Commentary on the *Professio fidei*," 9.

[52] Vatican II. *Lumen Gentium*, 25.

[53] Berry. *The Church of Christ*, 66-67.

[54] CDF. "Doctrinal Commentary on the *Professio fidei*," 9.

[55] CDF. "Doctrinal Commentary on the *Professio fidei*," 5.

catholic faith *all those things are to be believed*, which are contained in the word of God as found in scripture and *tradition*, and which are proposed by the church as matters to be believed as divinely revealed, whether *by her solemn judgment or in her ordinary and universal magisterium*."[56] The Second Vatican Council completes: "*To these definitions the assent of the Church can never be wanting*, on account of the activity of that same Holy Spirit, by which the whole flock of Christ is preserved and progresses in unity of faith."[57] Thus, whoever obstinately places these infallible teachings in doubt or denies them falls under the censure of *heresy*.[58]

What I have said above is relatively undisputed among traditionalists. The problems start to emerge—at least with traditionalists of the "recognize and resist" variant—when we turn to the ordinary magisterium of the pope. Since the ordinary magisterium is not infallible, these traditionalists will take the logical leap that it is "fallible," and therefore, subject to error. Ergo, from their point of view, these magisterial teachings can be ignored or even vehemently opposed if one perceives them to contradict one's personal interpretation of tradition.[59]

Whether the ordinary magisterium can err is a matter that is still under discussion, though the pious position that it cannot err (a position I personally hold) is legitimate.[60] Sedevacantists, for example, often rely on St. Robert Bellarmine's arguments that a pope would automatically lose his office if he was a heretic[61]—something that Bellarmine only mentioned in the context of theoretical theological speculation. But even St. Bellarmine

[56] Vatican I. *Dei Filius*, Chapter 3, 8.

[57] Vatican II. *Lumen Gentium*, 25.

[58] CDF. "Doctrinal Commentary on the *Professio fidei*," 5.

[59] See, for example Joy. "Disputed Questions": "But if there are non-infallible expressions of the authentic magisterium, then it is possible for the authentic magisterium to teach error. For what is not infallible is fallible; and what is fallible is able to fail. . . This assent may legitimately be withheld in certain cases, although to do so merely on the basis of one's own private judgment would be rash and dangerous. However, assent must be withheld when the teaching in question clearly conflicts with any irreformable doctrine of the Church, i.e. a doctrine that has been taught infallibly."

[60] For example, Scott Smith, who argues that this position is erroneous, concedes that it "does remain a pious opinion which to date has neither been imposed nor condemned by the magisterium." See Smith, "Friends don't let Friends."

[61] Derksen. "Can a Heretical Pope be Deposed?"

holds that it is "pious and probable" (though not "certain") that a Pope, as an individual person or a private teacher, was never able to fall into heresy or teach heresy.[62]

Whatever opinion one may hold in this debate, it is undeniable that the belief on the supposed fallibility of non-infallible teachings has done enormous damage to the Church's unity, especially during Francis's pontificate. Even if one thinks that the ordinary magisterium can err, one can see that the likelihood of such an error is much lesser than an error in one's private interpretation of tradition. Showing these odds has been the sole purpose of this book.

It is significant that no official Church document has ever said that the ordinary magisterium can contain error. *Donum Veritatis* admits that, in matters of the prudential order, it can happen that some magisterial documents might not "be free from all deficiencies."[63] But deficiencies do not necessarily equate with error. "Deficiency" can also mean something that can be developed further (something that, we have seen in chapter 10, is not possible for dogmas, as the First Vatican Council infallibly defines.) This seems to be the meaning behind *Donum Veritatis*, for it goes on to say:

> "Bishops and their advisors have not always taken into immediate consideration every aspect or the entire complexity of a question. . . The theologian knows that some judgments of the Magisterium could be justified at the time in which they were made, because while the pronouncements contained true assertions and others which were not sure, both types were inextricably connected. Only time has permitted discernment and, after deeper study, the attainment of true doctrinal progress."[64]

It is noteworthy how *Donum Veritatis* studiously avoids the word "error." It contrasts true assertions with "others which were not sure." It also says that those judgments could be justified at the time they were made—an odd thing to say if they contained grave error. The document is also quick to clarify: "But it would be contrary to the truth, if, proceeding from some

---

[62] Bellarmine. *On the Roman Pontiff*, 312, 489.
[63] CDF, *Donum Veritatis*, 24.
[64] CDF, *Donum Veritatis*, 24.

particular cases, one were to conclude that the Church's Magisterium can be habitually mistaken in its prudential judgments, or that it does not enjoy divine assistance in the integral exercise of its mission."[65]

It is also clear from the context that *Donum Veritatis* is referring here to doctrinal development, so what it says about "deficiencies" should be read in this light. In fact, that is one of the properties of non-infallible statements. They can be developed, fulfilled, perfected, even reformed. Provisional teachings may be revised, but usually that is not what people have in mind when they speak of the Church admitting that her teaching was wrong.[66] The fact that non-definitive teaching is not necessarily irreformable is not contrary to its reliability, for the reformable nature of such teaching does not come from any unreliability in the teaching but from the non-definitiveness of the magisterial intention.[67] In other words, it is not reformable because it is erroneous, it is reformable because it was never meant to be definitive in the first place.

In this sense, the term "non-infallible" is unhelpful and prone to misinterpretations (like equating it with "fallible".) It is much better to refer to it with the terminology employed by *Lumen Gentium*: "*authentic* magisterium," meaning "authoritative."[68] A proposition contrary to these doctrines can be qualified as erroneous.[69]

As *Donum Veritatis* says, even the ordinary magisterium "enjoys divine assistance," something that traditionalists do not necessarily always possess. This must surely bear some weight in all the precedents we have observed in this book and should give one pause whenever one assumes he is right when the Church is wrong in matters magisterial. Especially, since the ordinary magisterium also requires an answer from the faithful, just like the infallible magisterium does.

This answer is not an "assent of faith," but a "religious submission of mind and will." Contrary to what some "recognize and resisters" claim,[70]

---

[65] CDF, *Donum Veritatis*, 24.

[66] Sheehan, *Apologetics and Catholic Doctrine,* 208

[67] Hausam. "Was Pope Vigilius a heretic?"

[68] Joseph, "The Catholic Magisterium"

[69] CDF. "Doctrinal Commentary on the *Professio fidei*," 10.

[70] As an example, see Holmes. "On non-infallible teachings": "But what does it mean? Sometimes '*obsequium religiosum*' is translated 'religious assent,' at other times 'religious submission,' and at other times 'religious respect'. . . The *obsequium*

this submission is not a mere "respect" that one pays to these teachings, while being free to contradict them. This "submission" means a "thorough following."[71] It cannot be "simply exterior or disciplinary but must be understood within the logic of faith and under the impulse of obedience to the faith."[72] It must be shown in such a way that the pope's "supreme magisterium is acknowledged with reverence, the judgments made by him are sincerely adhered to, according to his manifest mind and will."[73] How can we know the pope's manifest mind and will? "Either from the character of the documents, from his frequent repetition of the same doctrine, or from his manner of speaking."[74]

The necessity for religious submission of mind and will also holds a venerable place in Catholic tradition. Of course, as is usual, from this tradition developed a parallel anti-tradition: the idea that one need not submit to non-infallible teachings. An anti-tradition, ironically, adopted by many a traditionalist today.

In the nineteenth century, as it became clear that the definition of papal infallibility was gaining steam, the debate about what to do with non-infallible teachings also became more opportune. It is no coincidence then, that the first pope to use the term "ordinary magisterium" was also the pope that eventually was responsible for the dogma of papal infallibility. Five years before the First Vatican Council, Pope Pius IX issued a letter to the Archbishop of Munich, explaining that obedience "must not be limited to the truth expressly defined by decrees of the ecumenical councils or by the Pope and this Apostolic See, but must extend also to the truth that the *ordinary magisterium* of the Church, dispersed throughout the world, relays

we give to the Magisterium is specified as "religious": it does not arise from fear for our lives, nor from amorous love, but from reverence. . . While I compared reverence for the Magisterium to reverence for a church or a tabernacle, there is a key difference between reverence for inanimate sacred things and reverence for a sacred person. The sacred thing is simply there, more or less sacred as the Church has made it so. But a person holding a sacred office can choose to bring the sacredness of his office more or less to bear on a situation. . . Disagreeing with a non-infallible teaching does not mean withdrawing the essence of the *obsequium religiosum*."

[71] Fastiggi. "*Amoris Laetitia* and the Magisterium."

[72] CDF, *Donum Veritatis*, 23.

[73] Vatican II. *Lumen Gentium*, 25.

[74] Vatican II. *Lumen Gentium*, 25.

as divinely revealed, in common with the *universal consent* of the Catholic theologians as regards to the faith."[75]

The attentive reader will note that in this letter, Pius IX is not referring to the ordinary magisterium *per se*, but to the ordinary *and universal* magisterium. As we have seen "ordinary and universal" magisterium is what ended up being defined as an infallible agent during the First Vatican Council. But the fact that the term "ordinary magisterium" entered into Catholic lexicon at this time is significant. The term had been coined during the mid-nineteenth century by the Jesuit Joseph Kleutgen, who was concerned with a tendency from contemporary theologians to assume that if a doctrine had not been defined by a judgment of the Church, then it was a matter of free opinion. Kleutgen solved this by describing the living tradition itself as a mode of exercise of the magisterium.[76] It is interesting that there was some resistance to using this term during Vatican I. Not only was Kleutgen a clergyman of suspicious moral character, but some Council Fathers also saw the term as "obscure and ambiguous."[77]

Be that as it may, Pope Pius IX was concerned with dissent, not only from the ordinary and universal magisterium, but with the ordinary magisterium as well. In his Syllabus, Pius IX condemned as erroneous the following proposition: "the obligation by which Catholic teachers and authors are strictly bound *is confined to those things only* which are proposed to universal belief *as dogmas of faith by the infallible* judgment of the Church."[78] His successor, Leo XIII, would write:

> In defining the limits of the obedience owed to the pastors of souls, but most of all to the authority of the Roman Pontiff, it *must not be supposed that it is only to be yielded in relation to dogmas* of which the obstinate denial cannot be disjoined from the crime of heresy. Nay, further, *it is not enough* sincerely and firmly to assent to doctrines which, though not defined by any solemn pronouncement of the Church, are by her proposed to belief, as divinely revealed, in her common and universal teaching, and which the Vatican

[75] Pius IX, *Tuas Libenter* (my translation from the official Italian version).
[76] Joy. "Capital Punishment and the Infallibility of the Church"
[77] Joy. "Capital Punishment and the Infallibility of the Church"
[78] Pius IX. *Syllabus of Errors*, 22.

> Council declared are to be believed "with Catholic and divine faith." *But this likewise must be reckoned amongst the duties of Christians, that they allow themselves to be ruled and directed by the authority and leadership of bishops, and, above all, of the apostolic see.*[79]

Later, already in the twentieth century, Pope Pius XI would teach:

> "*For it is quite foreign to everyone bearing the name of a Christian to trust his own mental powers with such pride* as to agree only with those things which he can examine from their inner nature, and to imagine that the Church, sent by God to teach and guide all nations, is not conversant with present affairs and circumstances; or even that *they must obey only in those matters which she has decreed by solemn definition as though her other decisions might be presumed to be false or putting forward insufficient motive for truth and honesty.* Quite to the contrary, a characteristic of all true followers of Christ, lettered or unlettered, is to suffer themselves to be guided and led in *all things that touch upon faith or morals* by the Holy Church of God through its Supreme Pastor the Roman Pontiff, who is himself guided by Jesus Christ Our Lord."[80]

Finally, Pius XII would also extend this authority to papal encyclicals, explaining that it would be erroneous to believe that they do not demand consent just because they are not exercised through the "supreme power of their teaching authority"[81] (i.e., infallibly.) Rather, papal encyclicals belong to the "ordinary teaching authority, of which it is true to say: 'He who heareth you, heareth Me.'"[82] These are all pre-conciliar sources, so traditionalists are bound to accept them.

One of the ways traditionalists may try to evade this is by arguing that the teachings they disagree with are not magisterial. For example, they can claim that the Second Vatican Council, unlike the other ecumenical

---

[79] Leo XIII, *Sapientiae Christianae*, 24.
[80] Pius XI, *Casti Connubii*, 104.
[81] Pius XII, *Humani Generis*, 20.
[82] Pius XII, *Humani Generis*, 20.

councils, did not define any dogma, but was merely a "pastoral council."[83] This contravenes the manifest mind and will of Pope St. Paul VI. It is true that, in a much-misinterpreted sentence, Paul VI admitted that "given the pastoral character of the Council, it has avoided pronouncing dogmas endowed with the notes of infallibility in an extraordinary way." But Paul VI immediately adds; "But those teachings were still *endowed with the authority* of the supreme *ordinary magisterium*, and this ordinary magisterium is so obviously *authentic*, it must be truly and humbly received by all the faithful, according to the mind of the council about the nature and scope of each document."[84]

Other examples of this strategy are frequent in Francis's pontificate. For example, it has been argued that the controversial apostolic exhortation *Amoris Laetitia* is not magisterial.[85] But apostolic exhortations are some of the most important instruments the pope can use to exercise his ordinary authentic magisterium.[86] Elsewhere, I have written at length why *Amoris Laetitia* belongs to the ordinary magisterium of Pope Francis.[87] Other theologians agree with this conclusion.[88]

Likewise, traditionalists have contested some teachings in *Fratelli tutti* and *Laudato Si'*. But these are encyclicals and, therefore, belong to the ordinary magisterium, per the instructions of Pius XII. Finally, Pope Francis's revision of the Catechism on the death penalty—besides already having

---

[83] See, for example, Fellay. "Interview with Bishop Bernard Fellay": "The Second Vatican Council was intended to be pastoral; it did not define any dogma. It did not add to the articles of faith. . . When people renounce their errors and join the Catholic Church, are they now required to profess their faith in religious liberty, ecumenism or collegiality?"

[84] Paul VI. "General Audience" January 12, 1966.

[85] Burke. "'*Amoris Laetitia*' and the Constant Teaching and Practice of the Church": "Pope Francis makes clear, from the beginning, that the post-synodal apostolic exhortation is not an act of the magisterium"

[86] Travers, "*Amoris Laetitia* and Canon 915," 394. See also Morrisey, "Apostolic Exhortation," 586: "Although not juridically binding, [apostolic exhortations] are a *significant expression of the magisterium* of the Church." Contrast this with Christopher Altieri's objection ("From What, Precisely, Are *Amoris Laetitia* 'Dissenters' Dissenting?"): "A post-Synodal Exhortation is neither *a formal teaching document* nor a governing instrument of any kind."

[87] Gabriel. *The Orthodoxy of Amoris Laetitia*, 3-13.

[88] See Pié-Ninot, "L'Ultima Parola."

been reaffirmed in *Fratelli tutti*[89] —was accompanied by a letter from the CDF, expressly approved by the pope, and ordered by him for publication.[90] As *Donum Veritatis* explains, the documents issued by the CDF and "expressly approved by the Pope participate in the ordinary magisterium of the successor of Peter."[91]

Another way to circumvent the religious submission of mind and will is to appeal to *Donum Veritatis*'s concessions. This document gives instructions on what to do when tensions arise between the theologian and the magisterium. The process is quite long. First, the theologian must assess the authoritativeness of the magisterial teaching in question.[92] The theologian can only proceed with questioning if he is dealing with a teaching of the prudential order. But then, the theologian does not go directly to questioning: he is invited to try to understand the teaching and revise his conclusions.[93] If difficulties persist, he must make the problem known, not to anyone, but to the magisterial authorities.[94] If the magisterium maintains its position, the theologian is invited, once again, to remain open to investigate the question more deeply to give his assent of faith.[95] At last, the theologian is called to suffer, in *silence* and prayer, in the certainty that truth will ultimately prevail.[96] Throughout all this process, the theologian should not present his own opinions or divergent hypotheses as though they were non-arguable conclusions.[97] He must refrain from giving untimely public expression to them,[98] and avoid turning to the mass media, so as not to exert the pressure of public opinion to force the magisterium.[99]

It is hard to argue that this process has been meticulously followed since Francis's election. In the end, as we have seen, *Donum Veritatis* explains that the submission of mind and will is not merely exterior but must be understood within the logic of faith and under the impulse of obedience

---

[89] Francis, *Fratelli tutti*, 263.
[90] CDF, "Letter to the Bishops."
[91] CDF, *Donum Veritatis*, 18.
[92] CDF, *Donum Veritatis*, 24.
[93] CDF, *Donum Veritatis*, 29.
[94] CDF, *Donum Veritatis*, 30.
[95] CDF, *Donum Veritatis*, 31.
[96] CDF, *Donum Veritatis*, 31.
[97] CDF, *Donum Veritatis*, 27.
[98] CDF, *Donum Veritatis*, 27.
[99] CDF, *Donum Veritatis*, 30.

to the faith.[100] The difference between dissent and reverent questioning has to do with the interior attitude towards the magisterium. Is one really seeking to resolve a difficulty?[101] Or is one seeking to force the magisterium to accept one's conclusions?

I would just like to finish by addressing the question of prudential judgments and disciplinary matters. Some traditionalists have argued that the faithful are not bound to adhere to the pope's prudential judgments,[102] or to disciplinary or pastoral matters,[103] since these would not fall under the scope of magisterial teaching. But this an equivocated reasoning. *Donum Veritatis* is clear that there is such a thing as "magisterial decisions in matters of discipline," which, though not enjoying the charism of infallibility, "are not without divine assistance and call for the adherence of the faithful."[104] Also, regarding prudential teachings, *Donum Veritatis* affirms that they enjoy divine assistance as well, and that one cannot conclude that the Church can be habitually mistaken in her prudential judgments.[105]

I remind the reader; the traditionalist does not necessarily enjoy divine assistance, unlike the Church's hierarchy. Once again, the traditionalist is gambling on his intellect when the Church has a more solid standing ground. The Commentary on the *Professio fidei* states that propositions

---

[100] CDF, *Donum Veritatis*, 23.

[101] Fastiggi. "*Amoris Laetitia* and the Magisterium."

[102] See, for example, Horn, "'Prudential Judgment,' and Voting Q+A."

[103] For example, "Brother André Marie" writes in "*Amoris Laetitia* and the 'Authentic Magisterium'": "The defenders of *Amoris Laetitia*, including the Holy Father's official and unofficial spokesmen in the episcopacy, have stated that the document represents no change to doctrine, but merely a different pastoral or disciplinary approach. . . I say this because, by its very nature, something that belongs to the 'authentic Magisterium' is and must be a matter of faith or morals, not merely a matter of sacramental discipline or pastoral practice. Which means that in Chapter eight of *Amoris*, in the Buenos Aires guidelines, and in the Pope's letter to the Bishops of Buenos Aires, we are confronted with a body of propositions that have long been defended as merely pastoral and representing no change in doctrine being elevated to a magisterial category that is strictly doctrinal in nature. . . . This leads the confused student of all this to ask some troubling questions. Do we have here a pastoral discipline that contradicts law and a doctrine that is not doctrine?"

[104] CDF, *Donum Veritatis*, 17.

[105] CDF, *Donum Veritatis*, 24.

contrary to teachings of the prudential order, are "rash or dangerous and therefore '*tuto doceri non potest.*'"[106]

However, the level of adherence here is still lower than with more authoritative magisterial statements. Such adherence requires obedience, but not necessarily agreement with the point of discipline.[107] In this sense, someone may disagree with a certain discipline and even ask the pope to change it. But though one is not bound to agree with the discipline, one must always observe it and respect it, and speak of it respectfully, even if one hopes for a change in some point.[108] Nevertheless, if the pontiff declares that the Church has no intention of changing something, a good Catholic will not foment division and discontent by prolonging the debate.[109] Overstepping these bounds goes against what the First Vatican Council infallibly defined regarding papal primacy:

> *Hence We teach and declare* that by the appointment of our Lord the Roman Church possesses a sovereignty of ordinary power over all other Churches, and that this power of jurisdiction of the Roman Pontiff, which is truly episcopal, is immediate; to which all, of whatsoever rite and dignity, both pastors and faithful, both individually and collectively, are bound, by their duty of hierarchical subordination and true obedience, *to submit, not only in matters which belong to faith and morals, but also in those that appertain to the discipline and government of the Church throughout the world*; so that the Church of Christ may be one flock under one supreme Pastor, through the preservation of unity, both of communion and of profession of the same faith, with the Roman Pontiff. *This is the teaching of Catholic truth, from which no one can deviate without loss of faith and of salvation. . .*
>
> If then any shall say that the Roman Pontiff has the office merely of inspection or direction, and not full and supreme power of jurisdiction over the universal Church, *not only in things which belong to faith and morals, but also in those things which relate to the discipline and*

---

[106] CDF. "Doctrinal Commentary on the *Professio fidei*," 10.
[107] Joseph, "The Catholic Magisterium"
[108] Sheehan, *Apologetics and Catholic Doctrine*, 209
[109] Sheehan, *Apologetics and Catholic Doctrine*, 209

> *government of the Church spread throughout the world . . . let him be anathema.*[110]

In the end, it is an inextricable (and traditional) part of the Catholic faith that the bishops in general, and the pope in particular, are authentic teachers, endowed with the authority of Christ. They bring forth from the treasury of Revelation *new* things and old,[111] making it bear fruit and vigilantly warding off any errors that threaten their flock.[112]

But have popes always succeeded in this most holy task? In the final chapter of this book, I will try to address an important counterargument to everything I have said thus far: what about the bad popes we have had in the past?

---

[110] Vatican I, *Pastor Aeternus*, Chapter 3, 2.
[111] Mt. 13:52.
[112] Vatican II. *Lumen Gentium*, 25.

Chapter 13

"The gates of Hell shall not prevail"

> *Peter, conscious of being "the greatest sinner among the Apostles" — going so far as to have "denied the Lord" — but also aware of being chosen "to feed the people with love", asked to be crucified "upside-down"... The great sinner was chosen to tend the People of God, to "feed" the People of God: it makes us think... Peter denies Jesus and then their eyes meet: when Jesus goes out, He looks at him, and Peter, courageous, even courageous in his denial, is capable of weeping bitterly. And then after all of his life in service to the Lord, he ends up exactly like the Lord: on the cross. But he doesn't boast, saying: "I shall meet the same end as my Lord!". No, he asks: "please, hang me on the cross upside-down, because at least in this way all can see that I am not the Lord; I am his servant".*
>
> —Francis, "We are servants"

Thomas Lawson experienced a severe relapse when Pope Francis promulgated *Traditionis Custodes*. It got even worse when his parish, in accordance with the bishop's directives, stopped offering the usual TLM that Tom had attended for years. He was furious. How dare Francis restrain the TLM? How dare he deprive him of such a source of holiness and reverence? How dare he continue persecuting faithful Catholics, when liberal dissenters were left unaddressed? Where was the dialogue, the listening, the accompaniment for traditionalists?[1]

Justin tried to calm his friend down, but for a while, Tom would not answer his messages. His traditionalist friends were right, after all! Pope Francis was an enemy of tradition! For quite some time, Tom avoided Justin and went back to his traditionalist group.

This would not last, however. In 2022, Pope Francis promulgated an apostolic letter on the liturgy, called *Desiderio desideravi*. When he read it, Tom felt unimpressed, but did not find anything blatantly erroneous either. But soon after, four bishops, alongside several clerics and theologians, would sign their own letter, condemning this papal document as heretical.[2]

[1] Lawler. "*Traditionis Custodes*: a needless extension of papal power."

[2] Strickland et al. *The teaching of the Catholic faith on the reception of the Holy Eucharist.*

Tom was baffled. What was heretical about it? And furthermore, there had been a "filial correction" before, on similar grounds, as regards to *Amoris Laetitia*! Could such a proliferation of accusations of papal heresy be compatible with the belief in an indefectible Church? Did Christ not promise that He would guide the Church? Had He not foreseen a pope like Francis? Had He lied?

His friends reassured him, this was nothing special. There had been heretical popes in the past, like Honorius or Liberius. But Tom did not feel any comfort in these words at all. In fact, they made him feel uneasy. Something clicked on him. He went back to one of those previous corrections, accusing Francis of heresy because of *Amoris Laetitia.* And there it was: the signatories had used Honorius's precedent to justify their actions.[3]

Thomas knew all those instances of heretical popes. He had used them during his Protestant days to argue against the Catholic doctrine of papal infallibility! At the time, he had studied the topic in depth. He had confirmed the arguments presented in Catholic forums. And he had arrived at the conclusion that those popes had not been heretical at all. But now, he was supposed to overturn everything he had learned, in order to concede the possibility of a heretical pope, only to pin Pope Francis on charges of heresy. . .

"But there have been bad popes"

The purpose of this book is to illustrate how one is in more solid grounds if one stands on the Church's magisterial teaching than if one stands on one's own personal interpretation of tradition.[4] This will allow the reader to make the appropriate calculus when tensions arise in his or her mind, and to proceed accordingly. I believe, therefore, that the only

---

[3] See Buscemi *et al.*, "Open Letter to the Bishops of the Catholic Church," formally accusing Pope Francis of heresy because of *Amoris Laetitia*, among other things: "The situation of a pope falling into heresy has long been a subject of discussion by Catholic theologians. This situation was brought into prominence after the ecumenical Third Council of Constantinople anathematized the Monothelite heresy in 681, and posthumously anathematized Pope Honorius for his support of this heresy; this condemnation of Honorius as a heretic was repeated by Pope St. Leo II when he ratified the acts of that Council."

[4] Mt 7:24-27.

counterargument that can hinder this book's purpose is to show that the pope's magisterium is also not reliable. So, I will have to quickly tackle the "bad popes" line of reasoning.

First, we need to make an important distinction when we talk about "bad popes." Sometimes, traditionalists mix different kinds of "bad popes" to make an argument. They will point out the immorality of medieval and Renaissance popes and then place these in the same degree as popes who allegedly taught error.[5] Those are not the same thing. One of my points in chapter 5 was that Paul corrected Peter, not on his magisterial teachings or decisions, but on his behaviors as an individual. Popes may be infallible in certain circumstances, and they may be reliable interpreters of the faith, but that does not mean they are impeccable i.e., without personal sin.[6] This does not hinder the pope's magisterial authority. As corrupt as the Borgia popes were, they upheld the orthodoxy of the faith. Heresy does not figure among the many accusations levelled against them.

So, we are left with the question of the supposedly heretical popes. Interestingly, this charge has historically been associated with Protestant[7] and other anti-Catholic propaganda.[8] Before Francis's papacy, Catholic apologists were concerned with debunking the myth of heretical popes, not on promoting it.[9] It was only after Francis's election—and when certain Catholic influencers began disagreeing with him—that the "heretical popes" claim began to take hold in Catholic circles.[10]

---

[5] Dreher. "The Catholics Left Out In The Cold": "'There have been bad popes in the history of the church,' Mr. Skojec said. 'Popes that murdered, popes that had mistresses. I'm not saying Pope Francis is terrible, but there's no divine protection that keeps him from being the type of guy who with subtlety undermines the teachings of the church to bring about a different vision.'"

[6] Blackburn. "Does papal infallibility mean the pope is perfect or inerrant?"

[7] Harris, *Fundamental Protestant Doctrines*, vol. 2, pg. 13: "Honorius was a heretic according to Roman Catholic standards and was condemned by church councils and popes for 800 years. Such facts are not known to most Protestants as they arise from the technical study of history. They naturally are not publicized by Roman Catholics. But facts they are. And they entirely disprove the papal claims." This claim is quoted in Loraine Boettner's later influential work, *Roman Catholicism*.

[8] Some of these polemicists are listed in Spencer, "The Truth about Pope Honorius."

[9] Spencer, "The Truth about Pope Honorius."

[10] See, for example, Feser. "The Church permits criticism of Popes."

Examining the cases of alleged heretical popes with all the nuance and context that this topic deserves would require a book unto itself. These are very complex cases, and it is not possible to do them justice in a few pages. So, I will very summarily outline the historical details of these episodes and briefly explain why they do not hold up to scrutiny. If the reader wants to know more, I invite him or her to check the references in the footnotes, where this subject is dealt with in more depth.

But I must also bring attention to another crucial detail, so often overlooked by those who bring up these exceptional cases to justify their attitude towards the pope. Even if we do concede that these popes were heretics (something I do not admit,) these instances revolve around a *single* doctrinal issue. These popes would be orthodox in every other subject except for that one. This is fitting, given the divine assistance the magisterium enjoys in the whole scope of its exercise.

However, when traditionalists criticize Pope Francis, they usually bring up a litany of heterodox teachings, ranging from *Amoris Laetitia* to the death penalty Catechism revision, including *Desiderio desideravi*, the pope's homily on the communion of saints—only to amalgamate these instances of magisterial teaching with supposed errors in practice like the Vatican-China deal, the alleged Pachamama idolatry, the signing of the Abu Dhabi declaration, and so forth. Francis would be indeed the worst pope in history, as everything he says, teaches, and does seems to be infallibly *wrong.*[11] Is this likely for someone enjoying the divine assistance of the Holy Spirit in the integral exercise of his mission? Or is it more likely that we are before a hermeneutic of suspicion, combing his every action and word, spinning it through the worst possible lens, and producing a distorted and negative perception of this pontificate?

The same holds true for traditionalists that believe that magisterial errors predate Francis's papacy. They assert that the Second Vatican Council, an ecumenical council, promulgated doctrinal errors—something unprecedented in itself—and that every single pope ever since has perpetuated those errors in a myriad of topics, from religious freedom to the relations with other religions and with the secular states. These traditionalists will

[11] Gabriel. "The infallibly erring Pope."

argue that we live in unparalleled times.[12] But is it probable that the Church was so immaculately protected from the blemish of heresy for nearly 2,000 years, only to be utterly transformed into a den of heresy in current days? Is it not more likely that we are once again experiencing what has been a predictable routine in Church history since the beginning: that some Catholics have preferred to rely in simplistic personal interpretations of tradition instead of relying in the less obvious, but more authoritative magisterial interpretation?[13]

As Rocco Buttiglione, a member of the Pontifical Academy of Social Sciences writes: "There are very few popes in the history of the Church who can be suspected of being heretics. Nevertheless, it is certain that all heretics have claimed that the popes of their time were heretics."[14]

However, as we shall now see, the allegedly "heretical" popes were not heretical at all. Therefore, the current situation would not only be quantitatively, but also qualitatively different from anything that has ever happened before as far as heresy is concerned. So, without further ado, let us examine these cases:

Pope Liberius

Let us return briefly to the Arian controversy and to the heroic part played by St. Athanasius during this dispute. As we have seen in chapter 6, in the aftermath of the Council of Nicaea, the Semi-Arians proposed a compromise: they would deny the consubstantiality between Father and

---

[12] Dobbs. "Taking the Tradpill": "[W]hile the Church has gone through crises in its past, the current crisis is nearly unprecedented in its desolation and heterodoxy."

[13] The same holds true for sedevacantists, who personally judged the conciliar popes as heretics and, therefore, destitute of their office. As of the time of the writing of this book, fifty-six years have elapsed since the closing of the Second Vatican Council. According to sedevacantists, the see has been vacant for this interval of time. The most extended period of *sede vacante* before this has been a little less than three years. At this moment, all living cardinal-electors have been elevated by supposedly illegitimate popes. Apart from the rationalizations put forth in sedevacantist apologetics sites, is it really likely that something like this would occur? Yet, to their credit, sedevacantists do not accept the "heretical popes" rationale, so this section of this book is not particularly aimed at them.

[14] Buttiglione, *Risposte amichevoli*, 113.

Son (and, therefore, reject the term *homoousios*), even though they would agree that the Son would have a *resemblance*, in all things, to the Father (adopting the term *homoiousios.*)[15]

At one point, a vast majority of Eastern bishops subscribed to this opinion.[16] The Emperor Constantius II—Constantine's son—sought to end division, unifying the Church under the banner of the so-called "moderate" position. And he did so aggressively. Someone, however, stood in his way: Athanasius and his unyielding defense of the Nicene creed.

It was not difficult to find bishops who would condemn Athanasius in the largely Semi-Arian East. The Western bishops posed a problem, though. Constantius attempted to pressure them to censure Athanasius, namely by convoking synods at Sardica (343 AD) and later at Arles (353). All these attempts failed. But the emperor kept pushing forward. Finally, in 355, Constantius was able to secure a condemnation of Athanasius at the Synod of Milan, by stacking the council with Arian bishops and beating or exiling the papal legates who resisted his orders.[17]

This, however, was not enough. For the sentence to be valid, it should be "confirmed by the higher authority of the bishop of the Eternal City."[18] At the time, this was Pope Liberius, a staunch defender of Athanasius until then. At first, Constantius tried to bribe Liberius with lavish gifts. But Liberius replied that he could not condemn someone who had been acquitted in two previous synods, or someone who was absent and could not defend himself. "This is no Ecclesiastical Canon;"—Liberius said— "*nor have we had transmitted to us any such tradition* from the Fathers, *who in their turn received from the great and blessed Apostle Peter.*"[19] In short, Liberius could not find in tradition anything that would validate the course of action sought by the emperor.

---

[15] Darras. *General History of the Catholic Church*, 463.

[16] Darras. *General History of the Catholic Church*, 463.

[17] Chapman. "Pope Liberius."

[18] Chapman. "Pope Liberius."

[19] Schaff. *Athanasius: Select Works and Letters*, 761. See also Chapman. "Pope Liberius": "He could not decide against Athanasius, who had been acquitted by two general synods, and had been dismissed in peace by the Roman Church, nor could he condemn the absent; such was not the tradition he had received from his predecessors and from St. Peter."

Enraged, Constantius unleashed a terrible religious persecution upon Rome, and dragged the pope to Milan. There, the emperor interrogated the pontiff: "Who are you to stand up for Athanasius *against the world*?"[20] From this episode emerged the famous Latin expression *Athanasius contra mundum* ("Athanasius against the world"). It is ironic how this expression is often used in traditionalist circles to foment division with the Holy Father,[21] when the phrase originated from the fact that Athanasius was not actually alone against the world—he had the pope on his side.

As Liberius remained unmoved, Constantius banished him from Rome and installed an antipope in his stead: Felix II. Here is where the story becomes muddled. It is said that, as his exile dragged out, Liberius succumbed to pressure and signed a condemnation of Athanasius and/or a Semi-Arian statement. From thence arises Liberius's fame as a heretical pope.

This claim is based mostly on letters attributed to Liberius,[22] one of which implies that he subscribed to the manifestly heretical "second Sirmian formula." Some scholars postulate that these letters are most likely forgeries created by the opposing party.[23] Other academics do not dispute the letters' authenticity,[24] but they counter that it is chronologically impossible for Liberius to have signed the "second Sirmian formula."[25] Instead,

---

[20] Chapman. "Pope Liberius."

[21] See, for example, Douthat. *To Change the Church*, 157-158: "But nonetheless, if Liberius did not fully succumb to Arianism, the papacy was certainly not orthodoxy's greatest champion either. That honor belongs to Athanasius of Alexandria, bishop of that city for forty-five years, and memorialized with the phrase *Athanasius contra mundum*—Athanasius against the world. . . Finally, with Pope Francis's intervention on behalf of the liberal side, the division of the bishops and the simple silence of so many, you have a case not unlike the situation facing figures like Athanasius—where for orthodoxy to win out, it must do so against long odds, in defiance of seemingly authoritative proclamations, without (at certain moments) the clear support of the pope himself."

[22] Chapman. "Pope Liberius": "The same story of the pope's fall is supported by three letters attributed to him in the so-called 'Historical Fragments' ("Fragmenta ex Opere Historico" in P.L., X, 678 sqq.) of St. Hilary. . . so he wrote 'Pro deifico timore' to the Easterns, assuring them not only that he had condemned Athanasius in 'Studens paci', but that Demophilus, the Bishop of Beroea. . . had explained to him the Sirmian formula of 357, and he had willingly accepted it. This formula disapproved of the words *homoousios* and *homoiousios* alike"

[23] Chapman, "The Contested Letters of Pope Liberius."

[24] Barnes, "The Capitulation of Liberius," 264.

[25] Barnes, "The Capitulation of Liberius," 260-261, 265.

Liberius would have signed a more ambiguous statement, that could be read both in a Semi-Arian and in a Nicene way.[26] The fact of the matter is, no one really knows what happened at that time. There are historians who have defended all different possibilities, based on conflicting information from ancient times.[27]

Be that as it may, it does not matter. As we have seen in the previous chapter, a magisterial document must be interpreted according to the pope's manifest mind and will, something that cannot happen if the pope is acting under duress, as was the case here.[28] Even Bishop Bossuet, a staunch Gallican apologist (see chapter 9), who tried to erode Liberius's orthodoxy to undermine papal infallibility,[29] had to admit to that fact: "[C]all to mind, that every act extorted by open violence is null by every title and protests against itself. . . Though one or two sovereign pontiffs, contrary to the custom of their predecessors, should, either from violence or surprise, have failed in maintaining the faith with sufficient constancy, or in explaining its doctrines with perfect clearness, still, personal errors could make no impression on the chair of Peter. Not more traceless are the waters which a ship has cleaved in its passage."[30]

---

[26] Hausam. "Historical Challenges to the Infallibility of the Church, Part Two" See also Chapman. "Pope Liberius": "if Liberius signed a Sirmian formula, it was the harmless one of 351. . . The newest view, brilliantly exposed by Duchesne in 1908, is that Liberius early in 357. . . wrote the letter 'Studens paci,' and, finding it did not satisfy the emperor, signed the indefinite and insufficient formula of 351." See also Sheehan. *Apologetics and Catholic Doctrine*, 214: "Let us suppose he [Liberius] did sign the formulary: it cannot be shown that it contained anything erroneous. Many of the Arian formularies were unobjectionable."

[27] Hausam. "Historical Challenges to the Infallibility of the Church, Part Two"

[28] Chapman. "Pope Liberius": "It should be carefully noted that the question of the fall of Liberius is one that has been and can be freely debated among Catholics. No one pretends that, if Liberius signed the most Arian formulae in exile, he did it freely; so that no question of his infallibility is involved." See also Sheehan. *Apologetics and Catholic Doctrine*, 214: "He [Liberius] did not sign as a teacher of the Universal Church; he signed as a prisoner and under compulsion. Manifestly it cannot be held that, in such circumstances, he intended to bind the consciences of all the faithful."

[29] Apparently unsuccessfully, even by his own standards. See Darras. *General History of the Catholic Church*, 459-460.

[30] As quoted by Darras. *General History of the Catholic Church*, 457, 462.

Most important still is St. Athanasius's opinion on the pontiff. There is no recrimination against Liberius in his voice, nor any attempt to prove that a pope can err in his official capacity:

> Thus they endeavoured at the first to corrupt the Church of the Romans, wishing to introduce impiety into it as well as others. But Liberius after he had been in banishment two years gave way, and from fear of threatened death subscribed. Yet even this only shews their violent conduct, and *the hatred of Liberius against the heresy, and his support of Athanasius,* so long as he was suffered to exercise a free choice. *For that which men are forced by torture to do contrary to their first judgment, ought not to be considered the willing deed* of those who are in fear, but rather of their tormentors.[31]

How did this story end? Though Antipope Felix was not a heretic himself, the people of Rome refused to acknowledge him, since he had communion with those promoting heresy. The other bishops ignored him, and when Felix celebrated mass, no one attended. Liberius's prolonged exile did not merely take a toll on the pope, but on the emperor as well, who saw himself responsible for a protracted and intolerable situation. Some influential Roman women pleaded with the emperor to allow Liberius to return. Eventually, Constantius acquiesced, as long as Liberius would govern the Roman church alongside Felix. When this was announced, the people of Rome are reported to have replied in unison: "One God, one Christ, one bishop!" Riots broke out, until the emperor reluctantly allowed the legitimate pontiff to return.[32]

Some Arian commentators claim that Liberius's return to Rome was not due to the Roman people's heroic resistance, but because he had signed the Semi-Arian statement, thereby satisfying the emperor. But it is also said that, when Liberius reentered the Eternal City, he was received in triumph,

---

[31] Schaff. *Athanasius: Select Works and Letters,* 764-765. Some authors, however, dispute the veracity of this passage (see Darras. *General History of the Catholic Church,* 461-462.)

[32] Chapman. "Pope Liberius." See also Darras. *General History of the Catholic Church,* 459.

as a conqueror.[33] The jubilant people of Rome did not seem to think that Constantius had defeated him.[34] Nor any mention of his lapse was made at a later time, when Liberius decreed that bishops fallen to Arian pressure could not be restored unless they publicly repudiated their previous stance. Yet, there is no mention of any recantation or public atonement on Liberius's part, which would be odd if he had really fallen himself.[35]

A few decades later, we have St. Ambrose of Milan praising him, addressing him as "Pope Liberius of holy memory."[36] The Greek Menology—the Eastern equivalent of a martyrology—calls him "blessed," "defender of the faith," "burning with zeal for the orthodox faith," protector of Athanasius, and "persecuted by the heretics for his bold defense of the truth."[37] In the nineteenth century, Bld. Pius IX would write, in his encyclical *Quartus Supra*: "the Arians falsely accused Liberius, also Our predecessor, to the Emperor Constantine, because Liberius refused to condemn St. Athanasius, Bishop of Alexandria, and refused to support their heresy."[38]

In summary, Pope Liberius was a staunch defender of orthodoxy and of St. Athanasius. For this he was exiled and pressured to subscribe to Semi-Arian heresy. We are not sure if he did this or not. If he did, we are not certain of the exact content of the statement he signed, and whether it could be interpreted in an orthodox way. Be that as it may, if he did sign a heretical statement, he did so under duress, so this act has no magisterial weight and, therefore, has no relevance as to whether the pope can err in his magisterial teaching. After Liberius was reinstated, his memory does not seem to have been tarnished by the lapse, until this was brought up by those opposing papal authority and infallibility.

---

[33] Darras. *General History of the Catholic Church*, 459. See also Chapman. "Pope Liberius."

[34] Darras. *General History of the Catholic Church*, 462.

[35] Chapman. "Pope Liberius": "Further, the pope's decree after Rimini, that the fallen bishops could not be restored unless they showed their sincerity by vigour against the Arians, would have been laughable, if he himself had fallen yet earlier, and had not publicly atoned for his sin. Yet, we can be quite certain that he made no public confession of having fallen, no recantation, no atonement."

[36] Darras. *General History of the Catholic Church*, 457.

[37] Darras. *General History of the Catholic Church*, 462.

[38] Pius IX. *Quartus Supra*, 16.

Pope Vigilius

After Nestorianism was condemned at the Council of Ephesus (see chapter 6), a new theological movement emerged to counter Nestorius's errors. Unfortunately, as is often the case, these Catholics overcorrected in the opposite direction and fell into a heresy of their own. Nestorianism argued that Jesus Christ was one person, but with two hypostases and two natures. These overzealous Catholics, on their hand, believed that Jesus was one person with only one hypostasis and one nature. Since "nature" in Greek is *physis*, these Catholics were called Monophysites ("one nature-ers"). This is not the correct interpretation, however. For an orthodox Catholic, Jesus is one person, one hypostasis and two natures (human and divine).[39] Just like Nestorianism was condemned on the third ecumenical council of Ephesus, Monophysitism would be condemned by the subsequent ecumenical Council of Chalcedon.

The Monophysites were obviously not pleased with this result. Almost a century after Chalcedon, they were still accusing the Church of having fallen prey to a soft kind of Nestorianism. When they were reassured that Nestorius was still regarded as a heretic, the Monophysites would point out that Nestorius's teacher, Theodore of Mopsuestia, had never been condemned. To their litany of accusations, they added Theodoret of Cyrus, who had at a time been a friend and defender of Nestorius yet had been exonerated at Chalcedon. Furthermore, there was a questionable letter from Ibas of Edessa, that had been read approvingly by the council. These writings came to be known by the simple name of "The Three Chapters." [40]

It must be said that there was some truth to these complaints. The Three Chapters could indeed be read in a Nestorianizing way. Theodore of Mopsuestia could be said to be a "Nestorian before Nestorius."[41] Regarding the other two characters, the situation was more complex. It could be argued that Theodoret and Ibas's initial support for Nestorius had to do

[39] Chapman. "Monophysites and Monophysitism."

[40] Bacchus. "Three Chapters."

[41] Bacchus. "Three Chapters." Still, some scholars maintain that Theodore of Mopsuestia was not really a Nestorian. See, for example, Soro. *The Church of the East.*

mostly with misunderstandings with St. Cyril's language (see chapter 6).[42] Furthermore, Theodoret had repented of his earlier attacks against Cyril and had accepted the resolutions of the Council of Ephesus.[43] Be that as it may, these writings from Theodoret and Ibas could be read both in a Nestorian sense and in an orthodox sense.[44] The Monophysites emphasized the Nestorian sense. They could never stand with a Church that did not condemn the Nestorian tendencies observed in these works.

Emperor Justinian was very keen on healing the religious divisions plaguing his domains. But though his intentions were good and just, he went about them the wrong way. In 543-544 AD, the emperor issued an edict anathematizing the Three Chapters. He then coerced the Eastern bishops to subscribe to this edict. But the bishops did not want to do this, since they believed that doing so would be to contradict Chalcedon, an ecumenical council.[45]

Eventually the Eastern episcopate capitulated to imperial pressure. The Western episcopate, though, stood firmly in support of Chalcedon. Vigilius, who was the pope at the time, refused to sign the emperor's edict. Not only that, but he also condemned the fallen patriarchs of the East. For his resistance, the pontiff was kidnapped and forcibly shipped to Constantinople in 545—between this case and Liberius's, we are starting to see a pattern here.

One thing that stood in the way of a satisfactory resolution for this controversy was the Western bishops' ignorance of the Greek language, so that they were unable to judge for themselves the Three Chapter's orthodoxy. Vigilius too, suffered of this shortcoming.[46] So when he arrived at Constantinople, the pope organized three conferences with several bishops to study the matter, with the condition that the bishops were there only to counsel him, and that the final decision was his alone.[47]

From this consultation resulted a papal document in 548, called *Judicatum* (unfortunately now mostly lost to history.)[48] In this judgment, Vigilius

---

[42] Bacchus. "Three Chapters."

[43] Chapman. *Studies on the Early Papacy*, 229.

[44] Hausam. "Was Pope Vigilius a heretic?"

[45] Bacchus. "Three Chapters."

[46] Bacchus. "Three Chapters."

[47] Hefele. *A History of the Councils of the Church*, Vol. IV, 251-252.

[48] Hefele. *A History of the Councils of the Church*, Vol. IV, 253.

condemned the Three Chapters in "moderate terms,"[49] though with a clause stating that "the importance of the Council of Chalcedon should not be called in question."[50] Vigilius would later comment that "in order to remove present offense, he had *condescended*, in order to quiet men's minds, he had *relaxed the severity of right*, and in accordance with the need of the time had ordered things *medicinally*."[51]

Though the emperor was pleased, many Western churches rebelled against what they saw as an affront against Chalcedon. In some cases, like Aquileia or Milan, there would even be a century-long schism.[52] The Illyrian church rejected communion with Vigilius on the all too familiar grounds that "they obeyed St. Leo and the former Popes, and 'must ever hold with the Apostolic Church of the Romans.'"[53] How they purported to hold to the apostolic Roman church while rejecting her current bishop was a kind of cognitive dissonance that remains unresolved to this day.

Given the *Judicatum*'s bad reception, both pope and emperor agreed to withdraw the document in 550, thus appeasing Western hostilities.[54] The change in the pope's position is to be explained by the fact that the condemnation of the writings was justifiable in essence yet appeared inopportune taking into consideration the controversy raging in Western Europe.[55] Instead, the dispute should be settled through an ecumenical council. This would come to be known as the Second Council of Constantinople, the fifth ecumenical council.

The pope, who was still detained at Constantinople, asked the emperor that the following conditions be met: that five or six bishops from each province (including the West) should attend the council, and that should prevail only what was peacefully determined in common. Also, nothing further should be decided for or against the Three Chapters until the council's decision had been made.[56]

---

49 Chapman. *Studies on the Early Papacy*, 229.

50 Hefele. *A History of the Councils of the Church*, Vol. IV, 254.

51 Hefele. *A History of the Councils of the Church*, Vol. IV, 257-258 (emphasis as in the original).

52 Bacchus. "Three Chapters."

53 Hausam. "Was Pope Vigilius a heretic?"

54 Hefele. *A History of the Councils of the Church*, Vol. IV, 265.

55 Kirsch, "Pope Vigilius."

56 Hefele. *A History of the Councils of the Church*, Vol. IV, 265.

But Justinian broke this agreement and issued a new document anathematizing the Three Chapters.[57] Vigilius protested and the relations between the two soured. The pontiff took refuge in the Basilica of St. Peter in Hormisda and the emperor sent soldiers after him, to draw him out of there by force, if needed be. Vigilius clung to the pillars of the altar, while the soldiers tried to drag him by the feet and beard with such violence that the altar table almost fell over the pope and would have crushed him if some clerics had not swiftly held it up. This angered the populace and even some soldiers, so that the emperor was forced to swear not to harm Vigilius.[58]

In the meantime, the council was summoned. Justinian broke his agreement with the pope once again, by stacking the synod with Eastern bishops. The council was, therefore, opened in 553, by imperial command but without papal assent. And though he was summoned to come, Vigilius refused to attend the council.[59] Instead, he submitted his position in writing. He sent a document, called the *Constitutum*, wherein he refused to condemn the persons of Theodore, Theodoret and Ibas, though he did condemn sixty propositions taken from the writings of the former.[60] He also ordained and decreed that no one should "write or bring forward, or undertake, or teach anything contradictory to the contents of this *Constitutum* in regard to the three chapters, or, after this declaration, begin a new controversy about them."[61]

The pope sent the *Constitutum* to Justinian, but the emperor refused to read it, saying: "If it condemns the Three Chapters, it is useless, as the Pope has already condemned them. If it defends them, then he is contradicting himself."[62] After knowing the contents of the document, Justinian sent to the council some of Vigilius's previous letters, in which he had defended the *Judicatum*. The emperor also alleged that, by contradicting himself and refusing to condemn the Three Chapters, the pope had excommunicated

[57] Hefele. *A History of the Councils of the Church*, Vol. IV, 269. See also Chapman. *Studies on the Early Papacy*, 230.

[58] Hefele. *A History of the Councils of the Church*, Vol. IV, 280. See also Chapman. *Studies on the Early Papacy*, 230.

[59] Hefele. *A History of the Councils of the Church*, Vol. IV, 288-289.

[60] Chapman. *Studies on the Early Papacy*, 234.

[61] Hefele. *A History of the Councils of the Church*, Vol. IV, 322-323.

[62] Chapman. *Studies on the Early Papacy*, 234.

himself and should no longer be named among the bishops in communion with the Church (i.e., the *diptychs*).[63] Using a doublespeak that has become all too prevalent with traditionalists today, Justinian said to the council: "We have decided that it is not proper for Christians to recite his [Vigilius's] name in the diptychs, lest we should be found thus to be in communion with Nestorius and Theodore. . . . *But we preserve unity with the Apostolic See*, and we are sure that you [the council] will preserve it."[64] Again, the emperor tried to separate that which could not be separated, by pledging obedience to the see of Rome all the while rebelling against the reigning pontiff. Justinian wanted to have his cake and eat it too.[65]

The council, however, did a more thorough job than the circumstances would foresee. The conciliar bishops did not accept Vigilius's excommunication but rather strove to study the matter of the Three Chapters with great detail. In the end, they did anathematize the Three Chapters but in the following way: they condemned Theodore of Mopsuestia, as well as Ibas's letter and Theodoret's writings in defense of Nestorius against Cyril.[66] In other words, though they reviled Theodore, they did not condemn the *persons* of Theodoret and Ibas—they only censured their writings that could be construed in a Nestorian way.

In the meantime, Vigilius had been exiled and sentenced to labor in the mines. His release was contingent on him ratifying the decision of the council.[67] After studying the matter, Vigilius decided to ratify the council's decision and once again condemn the Three Chapters. The pope wrote:

> The enemy of the human race, who sows discord everywhere, had separated him from his colleagues, the bishops assembled in Constantinople. But Christ had removed the darkness again from his spirit, and had again united the Church of the whole world. . . . There is no shame *in confessing and recalling a previous error*; this had been done by Augustine in his Retractations. He, too, following this and other examples, *had never ceased to institute further inquiries* on

[63] Chapman. *Studies on the Early Papacy*, 234-235.
[64] Chapman. *Studies on the Early Papacy*, 235 (emphasis as in the original).
[65] Hausam. "Was Pope Vigilius a heretic?"
[66] Hefele. *A History of the Councils of the Church*, Vol. IV, 328.
[67] Hefele. *A History of the Councils of the Church*, Vol. IV, 345.

> the matter of the three chapters in the writings of the Fathers. . . . Finally, we subject to the same anathema all who believe that the three chapters referred to could at any time be approved or defended, or who venture to oppose the present anathema. Those, on the contrary, who have condemned, or do condemn, the three chapters, we hold for brethren and fellow-priests. Whatever we ourselves or others have done in defense of the three chapters we declare invalid.[68]

So, does this mean that the pope erred? He explicitly mentions the word "error" in the quote above. However, we have to place this episode in its proper context. Theodore of Mopsuestia was indeed Nestorian, and even in the *Constitutum*, Vigilius condemns several propositions from this author. As for Theodoret and Ibas, things got trickier. They could be read both in an orthodox and in a Nestorian sense. This was never disputed. So, whether the Three Chapters were condemned or not is not so much a matter of doctrinal error, but more of a procedural matter.

On the one hand, there was no precedent for anathematizing deceased people who had died in communion with the Church.[69] On the other hand, since Theodoret and Ibas had been validated by the Council of Chalcedon, it was unclear how one could condemn them without forcing discontinuity with an ecumenical council.[70] Furthermore, whether one decided to sanction the Three Chapters or not, one would create a schism either in the East or in the West. The need to consider all these factors, and not any substantive doctrinal change, explains Vigilius's waffling on this issue. It was never about whether Nestorianism was heretical or not—that much was undisputed. It was about whether the Three Chapters had enough Nestorianizing proclivities to warrant a condemnation, and whether the consequences thereof were worth it.

The Second Council of Constantinople solved these conundrums with a most elegant solution. Though Theodore was indeed condemned, Theodoret and Ibas were not. Only their dubious writings, not their persons,

---

[68] Hefele. *A History of the Councils of the Church*, Vol. IV, 347-348.

[69] Chapman. *Studies on the Early Papacy*, 229. See also Bacchus. "Three Chapters."

[70] Bacchus. "Three Chapters."

were anathematized. This distinction is important. After all, Chalcedon had demanded Theodoret and Ibas to recant of their Nestorian support, something that they had indeed done. So, they could not be condemned, as they had repented of their errors. But this did not mean that their earlier writings had been rehabilitated as well. In fact, if their earlier writings were not problematic, there would not have been a need for recantation. Constantinople pronounced sentence only on the Nestorian past of Theodoret and Ibas, without contesting their recantation and, consequently, their rehabilitation by Chalcedon. Constantinople did what Chalcedon did not, without contradicting it.[71] Since the main difficulties had been resolved, Vigilius saw no need to prolong the controversy further and ratified the council with a clear conscience.

To finalize, it is important also to recall what *Donum Veritatis* 24 mentions about deficiencies in magisterial pronouncements: "some judgments of the Magisterium could be justified at the time in which they were made, because while the pronouncements contained true assertions and others which were not sure, both types were inextricably connected. Only time has permitted discernment and, after *deeper study*, the attainment of true doctrinal progress."[72]

This is exactly what Vigilius says in the quote above. The pope explains that he "never ceased to institute further inquiries," to fill in the gaps of his ignorance in the Greek language. We have seen that, as soon as he arrived at Constantinople, he organized conferences to study the matter in depth. Only when all legitimate objections were addressed in a satisfactory manner, could the pontiff make a final judgment on the whole dispute.

Pope Honorius I

Among all the allegedly heretical popes, no case is more emblematic (and more often brought up) than the one of Pope Honorius.[73] This is not

---

[71] Hefele. *A History of the Councils of the Church*, Vol. IV, 346.

[72] CDF, *Donum Veritatis*, 24.

[73] Harris, *Fundamental Protestant Doctrines*, vol. 2, pg. 13. See also Schneider, "On the question of a heretical pope": "Pope Honorius I was fallible, he was wrong, he was a heretic, precisely because he did not, as he should have done, declare authoritatively the Petrine tradition of the Roman Church. To that tradition he had made no appeal but had merely approved and enlarged an erroneous

strange, since this is the only pope to have been condemned for heresy by three ecumenical councils. But is this really everything that is to know about his story? Let us dive in.

It all started, again, with the Monophysites, who were still wreaking havoc by the seventh century. In 622, Emperor Heraclius got involved in a dispute with the Monophysites. To refute them, he made use of the expression "one operation" (or "one energy") to describe Jesus. A bishop found this expression dodgy and asked Sergius, the patriarch of Constantinople, what he thought about its orthodoxy. Sergius was afraid to settle this matter but noted that the expression seemed to soothe the Monophysites' resistance, allowing their reunion with the Catholic Church. So, he let it slide. Both emperor and patriarch were well pleased with this result,[74] though the ease with which this reunion had been established disquieted Sergius a bit. He had good reason to be troubled, indeed. . .

The proposition "one operation" would eventually be condemned under the name of "Monothelitism" (Greek for "one will.") At the time, it was not clear that this constituted a new heresy. However, for the Monophysites, it was indeed clear that there was no great distinction between Monophysitism and Monothelitism, which explains their willing acquiescence. Both heresies were essentially the same, and Heraclius's "correction" attacked an imaginary error that the Monophysites did not really hold.[75]

Why is "one operation" erroneous? As we have seen earlier in this chapter, Jesus Christ possesses two natures: one human and one divine. So, Jesus is not a demigod or a half-human, but fully God and fully human at the same time. Denying this was, grossly speaking, the error of the Monophysites. From this logic follows that Jesus must have what is essential to both natures. It is essential for a human nature to have a will, and for God's nature to have a will. Therefore, Jesus must have both a human will

---

doctrine. But once disowned by his successors, the words of Pope Honorius I were harmless against the fact of the inerrancy in Faith of the Apostolic See. They were reduced to their true value, as the expression of his own personal view." The only other case mentioned by Bishop Schneider is John XXII, which we will explore later. Another example is Cardinal Burke, who even erroneously affirms that Honorius was "deposed" (see Burke, "Interview With Cardinal Burke.")

[74] Chapman. *The Condemnation of Pope Honorius*, 11-12.

[75] Chapman. "Pope Honorius I."

and a divine will.[76] One person, two natures, two wills. The term "one operation" denied this, implying that Jesus would have only one will, and that Jesus's actions were "theandric" (i.e., "divine-human" meshed together.)[77]

This may seem a bit baffling, and that is probably at the root of Sergius's confusion. This kind of language made it sound like Christ's person is divided, as if there are two Christs, a human one and a divine one, engaging in different activities.[78] How can a single person have two wills? Is this not schizophrenic? Not in Jesus's case. Mark Hausam shows that this is easier to understand if we apply this logic to other aspects of the two natures, such as *mind*. He writes:

> Jesus has both a human mind and a divine mind. That is, he can think and perceive as God and he can think and perceive as a human. We must talk of two minds, for otherwise we will end up erasing either some aspect of Jesus's humanity or some aspect of his divinity. But this doesn't mean that we have two persons. There is one person, but that one person can think and perceive in a human mind or in a divine mind. Similarly, Jesus is one person, but when he wills, he can exercise his human willing capacity as well as his divine willing capacity. Two wills, one person.[79]

Returning to our story, Sergius's beloved reunion with the Monophysites was interrupted by a monk named Sophronius, famed by his holiness. Sophronius correctly noted that the "one operation" language endangered the Council of Chalcedon's decisions. Interestingly, the monk could not bring forward from the Fathers any quotes (i.e., "tradition") that quite clearly and literally would require recognition of the two wills of Christ. Still, Sophronius made a persuasive case. Sergius was in a conundrum: though the patriarch now distrusted the formula, he could not formally withdraw it without endangering the gains achieved so far with the

---

[76] Hausam. "Historical Challenges to the Infallibility of the Church, Part Three"

[77] Chapman. "Pope Honorius I."

[78] Hausam. "Historical Challenges to the Infallibility of the Church, Part Three"

[79] Hausam. "Historical Challenges to the Infallibility of the Church, Part Three"

Monophysites. So, Sergius tried to compromise: there would be no more talk of either "one operation" or "two operations." For the sake of peace, Sophronius agreed, as the "one operation" expression had also been dropped.[80]

But Sergius was still with a hot matter on his hands. He could not hush it forever. So, Sergius appealed to the pope. This, at the time, was Honorius I. In his letter, Sergius explains why he is troubled, but also why he cannot accept Sophronius's "two operations" expression:

> In like manner, to speak of two energies gives offence with many, because this expression occurs in none of the holy Fathers, and because there would follow from thence the doctrine of two contradictory wills in Christ (a false inference!), as though the Logos had been willing to endure the suffering which brings us salvation, but the manhood had opposed it. This is impious, for it is impossible that one and the same subject should have two and, in one point, contradictory wills.[81]

Though Honorius was described as "clever in mind, vigorous in counsel, and clear in doctrine,"[82] he could not see beyond Sergius's leading question. It is obvious that Sergius's tendentious description of the whole affair primed him to reply against the "two natures." Since Honorius was also "gentle and humble in character,"[83] he replied to Sergius in a concurring manner.

> Of this letter of yours to Sophronius we have received from you a copy, and, after having read it, we commend you that your brotherliness has removed the new expression [one energy], which might give offence to the simple. For we must walk in that which

---

[80] Chapman. *The Condemnation of Pope Honorius*, 13. See also Hefele, *A History of the Councils of the Church*, Vol. V, 23.

[81] Hefele, *A History of the Councils of the Church*, Vol. V, 25-26.

[82] Hefele, *A History of the Councils of the Church*, Vol. V, 27.

[83] Hefele, *A History of the Councils of the Church*, Vol. V, 27.

> we have learned. . . *Whence, also, we confess one will of our Lord Jesus Christ.*[84]

This is the whole crux of the matter. In this infamous letter, Pope Honorius simply confessed "one will," a proposition that would later be condemned as heretical. But is this all that this letter conveys? Can we reconcile this mess with orthodoxy in some way? Let us continue reading what Honorius wrote after confessing one will:

> *Whence, also, we confess one will of our Lord Jesus Christ* since our (human) nature was plainly assumed by the Godhead, and this being faultless, as it was before the Fall. . . As He was conceived by the Holy Ghost, so was He also born without sin of the holy and immaculate Virgin, the God-bearer, without experiencing any contamination of the *vitiata natura* [corrupted nature]. . .
>
> It is this, as we said, not the *vitiata natura* [corrupted nature] which was assumed by the Redeemer, which would war against the law of His mind; but He came to seek and to save that which was lost, *i.e.* the *vitiata natura* [corrupted nature] of the human race. In His members there was not another law (Rom. vii. 23), or a *diversa vel contraria Salvatori voluntas* [diverse or contrary will to the Savior's], because He was born *supra legem* [above the law] of human condition;[85]

In other words, when Honorius confesses that Jesus had "one will," he is not denying that Jesus had two wills, but denying He had two *opposing* wills.[86] This is even clearer if we read it in light of Sergius's letter, to which Honorius was giving a response, since Sergius was objecting precisely to the "false inference" of "two contradictory wills." If Jesus's human will opposed God's will, then Jesus would have been sinful—a heretical

---

[84] Hefele, *A History of the Councils of the Church*, Vol. V, 28-29.

[85] Hefele, *A History of the Councils of the Church*, Vol. V, 29-30. The English translations of the Latin expressions (in brackets) are the ones provided by Hausam. "Historical Challenges to the Infallibility of the Church, Part Three."

[86] Hausam. "Historical Challenges to the Infallibility of the Church, Part Three."

proposition. Jesus does not have a fallen, sinful will that would stand in opposition to divine will. But Honorius does not take into account that Jesus has an *incorrupt* human will, perfectly attuned to God's will, so it is obvious he did not grasp the problem from the outset.[87]

Is this reading accurate? Did Honorius merely disagree with "two opposing wills" and not "two wills" altogether? If we read a second letter that Honorius sent to Sergius, we can clearly understand that the pope was not a Monothelitist. While Honorius rejects both the "one operation" and "two operations" formulations, he also says: "both natures are naturally united in the one Christ, that each in communion with the other worked and acted ('*operated*'); the divine works the divine, and the human performs that which is of the flesh."[88] Later, he writes that Christ's two natures "work what is proper to them ('*proper operations*') in the one Person of the only-begotten Son of God, unmingled and unseparated and unchanged."[89]

So, Honorius rejects the wording "one operation" and "two operations," but clearly acknowledges that Jesus had two operations, each working what was proper to them. This is not Monothelitism, it is actually the opposite. It seems that Honorius was objecting more to the introduction of new expressions, involving "wills" and "operations," preferring to rely instead on the well-tried and orthodox Chalcedonian concept of "two natures." This is obvious from another quote from his first letter:

> [B]ut whether on account of the works of the Godhead and manhood (*opera divinitatis et humanitatis*) it is suitable to think and to speak of one or two energies (*operationes*) as present, we cannot tell, we leave that to the grammarians. . .
>
> We, however, wish to think and to breathe according to the utterances of Holy Scripture, rejecting everything which, as a novelty in words, might cause uneasiness in the Church of God, so that those who are under age may not, taking offence at the expression two energies, hold us for Nestorians, and that (on the

---

[87] Hefele, *A History of the Councils of the Church*, Vol. V, 32-33.
[88] Hefele, *A History of the Councils of the Church*, Vol. V, 50.
[89] Hefele, *A History of the Councils of the Church*, Vol. V, 50.

> other side) we may not seem to simple ears to teach Eutychianism, when we clearly confess only one energy.[90]

To recapitulate, Honorius does not make an official pronouncement on whether "one operation" or "two operations" is correct, since he believes that this is more of a semantical war than anything else. He clearly affirms the Chalcedonian understanding that Jesus is one person with two natures, each operating what is proper to them. He affirms the idea but does not use the language. He does not deny Jesus's human will, only His *corrupt* human will.[91] Therefore, he is orthodox.[92] However, while orthodox, Honorius did not see through Sergius's Monothelite tendencies, and expressed himself in a way that could be easily misunderstood.[93] He was on the right track but did not fully draw the inferences of both positions.[94]

His greatest fear was that, if he would affirm either "one operation" or "two operations," he would give scandal to the less theologically savvy, because the former sounds Eutychian (i.e., Monophysite,) and the latter may be judged to be Nestorian[95] (see chapter 6). It is quite ironic that, by proceeding like this, Honorius would produce more scandal in the coming centuries than anything he could have dreamed of! Still, the fact remains that Honorius did not decide the question, did not authoritatively declare

---

[90] Hefele, *A History of the Councils of the Church*, Vol. V, 31.

[91] Hausam. "Historical Challenges to the Infallibility of the Church, Part Three."

[92] Chapman. *The Condemnation of Pope Honorius*, 16: "Honorius is thus logically and theologically as much astray as Sergius, though both are orthodox in intention. It would no doubt be uncharitable to regard either the Pope or the Patriarch as 'private heretics.'" Sheehan. *Apologetics and Catholic Doctrine*, 214: "His words bear an orthodox sense; they were written to contradict the false doctrine, ascribed by Sergius to his opponents, 'that there are two *conflicting* Wills in Christ.'"

[93] Hausam. "Historical Challenges to the Infallibility of the Church, Part Three." See also Sheehan. *Apologetics and Catholic Doctrine*, 214: "He had been misinformed by Sergius as to the point at issue, and thought the controversy was, as he observed, 'a war of words' to be settled by 'grammarians.'"

[94] Hefele, *A History of the Councils of the Church*, Vol. V, 33.

[95] Chapman. "Pope Honorius I." See also Hefele, *A History of the Councils of the Church*, Vol. V, 33: "These expressions. . . are, moreover, approved neither by the Holy Scriptures nor by the Synods; and they should be avoided, because their use produces new controversies."

the faith, condemned nothing, and defined nothing.[96] He merely agreed with Sergius's decision to not allow talk of either "one operation" or "two operations."

Of course, Sergius felt reassured by Honorius's approval. The patriarch and the emperor then worked together to compose a document, named *Ecthesis*, to enforce what they perceived to be the pope's instructions. That is, everyone was to "confess one will," while avoiding both the expressions "one operation" and "two operations."[97] From this grew the Monothelite controversy, which until then was not fully understood.

Honorius died before the *Ecthesis* was published in 640, so he did not have the opportunity to clarify his thought further. However, Severinus—Honorius's successor—refused to ratify the document.[98] Severinus would rule for only two months, but his successor John IV was also very active against Monothelitism.

Seeing that he had lost the support of the papacy, Emperor Heraclius blamed patriarch Sergius—who, in the meantime, had died—for the whole thing and disowned his own *Ecthesis* before he himself died in 641.[99] But Pyrrhus, who succeeded Sergius as patriarch of Constantinople, would keep pushing for Monothelitism, justifying himself with Honorius's allowances.

An act of apologetics was in order. And this is exactly what John IV set out to do. The pope sent a letter to Constans II, the new emperor, asking for the *Ecthesis* to be fully withdrawn. This document became known precisely as the *Apology for Honorius*. In this apology, John IV explains that both Sergius "of reverend memory" and Honorius "of blessed memory" only used the expression "one will" because they would not admit contrary wills:[100]

> The whole West is scandalized by our brother, the Patriarch Pyrrhus proclaiming, in his letters which are circulated in all directions, novelties which are contrary to the rule of faith, and

[96] Chapman. "Pope Honorius I."
[97] Chapman. *The Condemnation of Pope Honorius*, 24-25.
[98] Chapman. "Pope Honorius I."
[99] Chapman. *The Condemnation of Pope Honorius*, 29.
[100] Chapman. *The Condemnation of Pope Honorius*, 30.

> referring to our predecessor, Pope Honorius of blessed memory, as of his opinion, *which was entirely foreign to the mind of the Catholic Father*. . . The Patriarch Sergius communicated to the said Roman bishop that some maintained two *contrary wills* in Christ. . . In such wise our predecessor Honorius answered Sergius, that there were not in the Redeemer two *contrary wills*, *i.e.* also a will in the members, as He had assumed nothing of the sin of the first man. The Redeemer did indeed assume our nature, but not the fault. *Let, then, no unintelligent critic blame Honorius*, that he speaks only of the human and not also of the divine nature, but let him know that *he answered that concerning which the patriarch inquired. Where the wound is, there the healing is applied.*[101]

Another champion of orthodoxy, St. Maximus the Confessor, took a similar approach. When Pyrrhus asked Maximus how he could both try to defend Honorius and "two wills," the saint replied: "Who is the trustworthy interpreter of this letter, he who composed it in the name of Honorius, or those who spoke in Constantinople what was according to their own mind?" To which Pyrrhus replied: "He who composed it."[102] This is, interestingly, in accordance with our modern understanding. As we have seen in the last chapter, *Lumen Gentium* teaches that the pope's judgments are to be "sincerely adhered to, according to his manifest mind and will."[103] Therefore, if Honorius intended his teaching in an orthodox way, this is the way we should interpret it.

---

[101] Hefele, *A History of the Councils of the Church*, Vol. V, 52-53. John Chapman, whom we have quoted extensively until now, does not agree with John IV's defense. He calls it "very lame" (Chapman. *The Condemnation of Pope Honorius*, 30). However, even he agrees that Honorius did not intended to deny that Jesus had two wills, as in Chapman. "Pope Honorius I": "No doubt Honorius did not really intend to deny that there is in Christ a human will, the higher faculty; but he used words which could be interpreted in the sense of that heresy, and he did not recognize that the question was not about the unity of the Person Who wills, nor about the entire agreement of the Divine Will with the human faculty, but about the distinct existence of the human faculty as an integrant part of the Humanity of Christ."

[102] Hefele, *A History of the Councils of the Church*, Vol. V, 53.

[103] Vatican II. *Lumen Gentium*, 25.

We have already seen ample evidence that Honorius did indeed intend to teach in an orthodox way, though his wording was prone to misunderstanding. But Maximus brought forth another weighty argument in support of this thesis. The saint appealed to the testimony of Honorius's secretary, a certain Joannes Symponus. This person had drafted Honorius's letters, so he knew what the pope really meant when he asked him to write them. The secretary testified in writing that Honorius was answering Sergius's question, and therefore only meant that Jesus did not have two contradictory wills.[104]

Pyrrhus was desolated. The patriarch asked Maximus whether there was a way to save the memory of both Sergius and Honorius, who had acted out of ignorance. Maximus replied that the only way was to "keep silence as to their persons, yet to anathematize the heresy."[105] It seemed, for an instant, that Honorius's reputation might be salvaged after all.

Unfortunately, such was not meant to be. After wobbling a bit on the issue, Pyrrhus refused to recant the *Ecthesis*. He was deposed and replaced by a certain Paul, who also refused to confess "two wills." Paul agreed to withdraw the *Ecthesis*, but replaced it with another document, called *Typos*. The *Typos* no longer taught "one will," but still required that no one talk about "one operation" or "two operations."[106]

Here, we stumble upon a new obstacle to Honorius's defense. In his letter, Honorius confessed one will. John IV, Maximus, and Symponus were able to clarify Honorius's manifest mind and will on this subject. Since the pope's intentions were orthodox, that is how we should read his teachings. However, Honorius had also supported Sergius's decision to forbid any talk about "one operation" or "two operations." Here, we are no longer talking about a *doctrinal* matter (i.e., a teaching on faith and morals,) but about a *disciplinary* arrangement set up by Sergius and confirmed by Honorius.[107]

As we have seen in chapter 12, disciplinary decisions also enjoy some degree of divine assistance, though this assistance is much lesser than for magisterial pronouncements. Furthermore, unlike doctrine, disciplines do

---

[104] Hefele, *A History of the Councils of the Church*, Vol. V, 53-54.

[105] Chapman. *The Condemnation of Pope Honorius*, 34.

[106] Chapman. *The Condemnation of Pope Honorius*, 44-45.

[107] Chapman. *The Condemnation of Pope Honorius*, 17.

change across time and space, and can even contradict each other. In this case, Honorius had affirmed a discipline during a time when the Monothelite controversy was still in its inception. As the dispute grew and matured, it was obvious that this discipline needed to be rescinded, so that the orthodox understanding ("two wills") would not be silenced alongside the heretical one ("one will.")[108] This was understood by Honorius's successors, who did rescind the discipline. But the Monothelites clung rigidly to the previous discipline because it helped them fulfill their agenda, since now the popes had taken the other side of the dispute. Thanks to the Monothelites' stubbornness, Honorius's reputation had to be tarnished if orthodoxy was to survive.[109]

This went about for some time, even after all the major players in the dispute had died. To help heal the division, the new Emperor Constantine IV decided to convoke an ecumenical council. It was the sixth of such councils to be held, and also the third to be hosted at Constantinople. The proceedings were opened in 680 by the papal legates, who became the council's presidents, sitting in a place of honor next to the emperor.[110]

The Patriarch of Constantinople was named Macarius, and he followed on his Monothelite predecessors' footsteps. At the council, Macarius declares that he "did not publish new expressions, but what we received." It was, therefore, a fitting example for this book. Macarius then proceeds to list from whence he has received this "tradition." He mentioned the former patriarchs of Constantinople and some local synods, but he also appealed to "Honorius, who was Pope of old Rome."[111]

It was the time for the papal legates to make their move. They brought a long letter from Pope St. Agatho. In this letter, Agatho confirms the orthodox doctrine of the two wills, but he does not seem to disagree, in essence, with Honorius's intended meaning:

---

[108] Chapman. "Pope Honorius I": "No doubt it was still held at Rome that Honorius had not intended to teach 'one Will,' and was, therefore, not a positive heretic. But no one would deny that he recommended the negative course which the Typus enforced under severe penalties."

[109] Chapman. *The Condemnation of Pope Honorius*, 46-47.

[110] Chapman. *The Condemnation of Pope Honorius*, 73-74.

[111] Chapman. *The Condemnation of Pope Honorius*, 74-75.

> For we equally detest the blasphemy of division and of commixture. For when we confess two natures and two natural wills, and two natural operations in our one Lord Jesus Christ, *we do not assert that they are contrary or opposed one to the other* (*as those who err from the path of truth* and accuse the apostolic tradition of doing. Far be this impiety from the hearts of the faithful!), nor as though separated (per se separated) in two persons or subsistences, but we say that as the same our Lord Jesus Christ has two natures so also he has two natural wills and operations, to wit, the divine and the human.[112]

In other words, Agatho condemns the notion that Jesus had "two contradictory wills." He calls this idea, a "blasphemy of division and commixture." This was precisely what Honorius condemned, if we take his manifest mind and will on the subject. So, Honorius was indeed orthodox in his intended meaning. The remainder of Agatho's letter is a hymn to papal authority and reliability:

> [B]ecause the true confession thereof for which Peter was pronounced blessed by the Lord of all things, was revealed by the Father of heaven, for he received from the Redeemer of all himself, by three commendations, the duty of feeding the spiritual sheep of the Church; under whose protecting shield, *this Apostolic Church of his has never turned away from the path of truth in any direction of error, whose authority, as that of the Prince of all the Apostles, the whole Catholic Church*. . . which, it will be proved, by the grace of Almighty God, *has never erred from the path of the apostolic tradition, nor has she been depraved by yielding to heretical innovations*, but from the beginning she has received the Christian faith from her founders, the princes of the Apostles of Christ, and remains *undefiled unto the end*, according to the divine promise of the Lord and Saviour himself, which he uttered in the holy Gospels to the prince of his disciples: saying, "Peter, Peter, behold, Satan has desired to have you, that he might

---

[112] Constantinople III, "Session 4."

> sift you as wheat; but I have prayed for you, that (your) faith fail not. And when you are converted, strengthen your brethren."[113]

It is fascinating how Pope St. Agatho holds that the Church of Rome is "preserved ever immaculate" (see chapter 12), even while condemning a heresy supposedly espoused by one of his predecessors. It is obvious he saw no contradiction in what he was doing. If Agatho's letter, which secured the anathematization of Monothelitism, did not see in Honorius's episode a cause against the reliability of the papacy, then neither should we. The Council Fathers, in fact, did not relax this tension. Rather, they fully embraced it (see chapter 4).[114]

Though Agatho's letter might still have saved Honorius's reputation, the Monothelites would not go down alone. Macarius of Constantinople brought forward a package with some documents grounding his Monothelite views, including Honorius's letter to Sergius. This letter, for some reason, had not been presented to the council before, and the emperor was not even aware of its contents. It was now obvious that the only way to silence Macarius once and for all was to condemn Honorius's letter. This the council did, finally ending the controversy.

The Third Council of Constantinople decreed that "Honorius also, who was Pope of elder Rome, be with them [the Monothelites] cast out of the holy Church of God, and be anathematised with them, because we have found by his letter to Sergius that he followed his opinion in all things and

---

[113] Constantinople III, "Session 4."

[114] Chapman. "Pope Honorius I": "It is clear, then, that the council did not think that it stultified itself by asserting that Honorius was a heretic (in the above sense) and in the same breath accepting the letter of Agatho as being what it claimed to be, an authoritative exposition of the infallible faith of the Roman See." See also Hausam. "Historical Challenges to the Infallibility of the Church, Part Three": "While the Council Fathers and Pope Leo II are clear in condemning Honorius, yet, as I mentioned, they and subsequent Fathers, Councils, and Popes continue from this point on to affirm what they had affirmed before--the primacy, authority, and infallibility of the Apostolic See of Rome. At no point during the First Millennium is there ever, to my knowledge, any attempt by anybody to explain how these two positions can be harmonized. And yet these Fathers clearly did not see their affirmations as being in conflict. Therefore, whatever we say about Honorius or about papal reliability, if we are to be faithful in representing the position of these Fathers, we must not attempt to pit the one against the other."

confirmed his wicked dogma."[115] In the final acclamations, the Council Fathers sang "Anathema to. . . Honorius, the heretic," alongside Sergius, Pyrrhus, Paul, and Macarius.[116] Which was interesting, since the Council also took great pains to list all previous Christological controversies and how, in those disputes, the popes were always champions of orthodoxy. This they did so they could more easily appeal to Agatho's authority on this subject. Once again, they saw no conflict between all these statements.[117]

However, if the decree was to be binding, it needed be ratified by the pope. Agatho died in the meantime and was succeeded by Leo II. Leo would indeed confirm the council, but change the wording in a slight, but crucial way:

> And in like manner we anathematize the inventors of the new error, that is, Theodore, Bishop of Pharan, Sergius, Pyrrhus, Paul, and Peter, betrayers rather than leaders of the Church of Constantinople, and also *Honorius, who did not attempt to sanctify this Apostolic Church with the teaching of apostolic tradition, but by profane treachery permitted its purity to be polluted.*[118]

Please note how Leo separated Honorius's condemnation from that of the others listed as "inventors of the new error." Honorius is not anathematized for being a heretic, but for failing to sanctify the Church and permitting its purity to be polluted. In other words, he is not condemned for heresy, but for negligence. Leo is, in fact, even more explicit on this point, when he writes to the Spanish bishops: "With Honorius, who did not, as became the Apostolic authority, extinguish the flame of heretical teaching

---

[115] Chapman. *The Condemnation of Pope Honorius*, 90-92.

[116] Chapman. *The Condemnation of Pope Honorius*, 95.

[117] Chapman. *The Condemnation of Pope Honorius*, 99-103. This could also have been due to a certain ambiguity on the meaning of the word "heretic" back then. See Sheehan. *Apologetics and Catholic Doctrine*, 214: "It is, however, much disputed whether the Fathers of Constantinople intended to stigmatize Honorius as a heretic in the modern acceptation of the term. The word seems to have been applied in those days to anyone whose actions, apart from any positive teaching, was thought to favor heresy or schism."

[118] Chapman. *The Condemnation of Pope Honorius*, 114.

in its first beginning, but fostered it by his negligence."[119] This is, therefore, how we should understand the council's anathema.[120]

From that point onward, every pope up to the eleventh century had to take up an oath, anathematizing Honorius "because he assisted the base assertion of the heretics."[121] The next two ecumenical councils also anathematized Honorius, though the eighth council also formally declared that the Church of Rome had never erred.[122] Finally, Honorius was mentioned as a heretic in the lessons of the Roman Breviary for the feast of St. Leo II until the eighteenth century, when the name was omitted "as liable to cause misunderstanding"[123] (i.e., being used by anti-Catholic apologists).

So, where does this leave us? Obviously, Pope Honorius's letter cannot—as has been done before by Protestants and Gallicans—be used as an argument against papal infallibility, since Honorius did not infallibly define any doctrine.[124] Some Catholic apologists have tried to defend the opposite

---

[119] Chapman. "Pope Honorius I."

[120] See Sheehan. *Apologetics and Catholic Doctrine*, 214: "The decree of the Council of Constantinople must be regarded as condemnatory of the conduct of Honorius, not of his teachings as head of the Church. So much is clear from the words of Leo II, who explained that he had confirmed the decree, because Honorius had been negligent 'in extinguishing the rising flame of heresy.' The decree of a General Council is infallible only in the sense only in the sense that it is ratified by the Pope." John Chapman, whom we have quoted at length as an authority on Pope Honorius, believes it is not cogent to argue that Leo tried to salvage Honorius by changing the anathema. He goes so far as saying that, if this was Leo's intention, he was "mistaken." He argues instead that Catholics had viewed Honorius's letter as merely his personal opinion. This thesis, in my opinion, does not hold, for reasons which I am going to explain very briefly. Chapman also says that Leo's wording is actually more condemnatory of Honorius, since it speaks of "polluting." But my aim is to defend Honorius's magisterial reliability, not his person, for I hold to papal primacy, not papal impeccability (see chapter 12). See Chapman. *The Condemnation of Pope Honorius*, 114-115.

[121] Hausam. "Historical Challenges to the Infallibility of the Church, Part Three."

[122] Chapman. *The Condemnation of Pope Honorius*, 115.

[123] Chapman. *The Condemnation of Pope Honorius*, 116.

[124] Bishop Hefele, whom we have quoted as an authority on Pope Honorius, thought that his teaching was indeed infallible. However, John Chapman very cogently explains why that is not the case (see Chapman. *The Condemnation of Pope Honorius*, 16.) See also Sheehan. *Apologetics and Catholic Doctrine*, 214: "His case [Honorious's] does not yield no argument against Papal Infallibility. Honorius did not pronounce a definition ex cathedra, for he said expressly: 'It does not behoove

extreme: that Honorius's letters were not official, but only private letters to a fellow bishop expressing his personal opinion.[125] But this does not hold, since Honorius was answering a doctrinal question posed by Sergius. Furthermore, his letter had an impact in ecclesiastical affairs, being used as a foundation for Church discipline for decades. So, it was obviously seen as official. Nor can we argue that Honorius's letters are later forgeries—their authenticity is above suspicion.[126]

In my opinion, the way to untie these knots is to read the whole affair through the lens of a developed doctrine on papal magisterium, specifically the principles laid out in *Lumen Gentium*, the Doctrinal Commen-tary on the *Professio fidei*, and *Donum Veritatis*. Namely, we must make a distinction between two separate affirmations: doctrinal statements (teaching) and disciplinary decisions (practical implications.) Honorius did the former when he confessed "one will," and the latter when he confirmed Sergius's actions of not allowing the use of both "one will" and "two wills."

As far as doctrine goes, we know that a magisterial teaching must be read according to the pope's "manifest mind and will." John IV, Maximus the Confessor, and Symponus convincingly argue that Honorius's manifest mind and will when he confessed "one will" was not to teach Monothelitism, but to condemn the proposition that Jesus had two contradictory wills, something that St. Agatho also condemned in his acclaimed letter to the Third Council of Constantinople.

As regards discipline, we know that Honorius also meant well, for he wanted to avoid scandal. He was acting at a time when the Monothelite propositions had not yet fully crystallized. It was not yet clear at the time that they were dealing with a new heresy. But as the controversy raged on, this discipline became detrimental to the spread of orthodoxy, since it silenced orthodoxy alongside heresy. We have seen in the previous chapter that, though criticizing a discipline enjoining papal approval is dangerous, the faithful can try to change a discipline they see as imprudent, as long as they do not force the issue if such is obviously not the will of the pope. In

---

us to settle the question whether the number of operations in Christ was one or two.'"

[125] Chapman. *The Condemnation of Pope Honorius*, 114-115.

[126] Chapman. *The Condemnation of Pope Honorius*, 7. See also Hausam. "Historical Challenges to the Infallibility of the Church, Part Three."

this case, Honorius did not have time to reinforce or reverse anything. However, the discipline was overturned by both popes and council—who more than anything, have the authority to do so. Those who, appealing to a false tradition, refused to accept this disciplinary reversal were the ones who ended up being condemned as heretics.

The discipline itself contains no heresy. The most that we can say is that this discipline fostered heresy by defect. Honorius can, therefore, be condemned solely for negligence. Which is precisely what his anathema says, if we take into consideration the way it was ratified by Leo II. Therefore, Honorius does not cast shadow onto papal reliability in the least. This has, in fact, been the traditional understanding of the Church for centuries, until anti-Catholic apologists tried, for the first time, to drive a wedge between Honorius and Church's indefectibility to promote their own agendas.

Pope John XXII

The final case is that of Pope John XXII, the most oft quoted example besides Honorius. In 1316, a certain Jacques d'Euse was elected pope, and took for himself the name John, the twenty-second pontiff to select that name.

Were it not for the sad episode of his alleged heresy, John XXII would have been known as a fierce combatant of the so-called "Spirituals" or "Fraticelli," a rigorist outgrowth of the Franciscan order. The Fraticelli believed that they were the original Friars Minor and that adherence to the Franciscan rule of poverty was necessary for salvation. When John XXII tried to rein in on their radicalism, they refused to submit to him, instead claiming that he was not really pope, as he had abrogated the Rule of St. Francis, which, according to them, represented the Gospel pure and simple. The Fraticelli in all their iterations would end up being condemned as heretics.[127]

However, another controversy exploded during John XXII's pontificate. Before his election, John had written a theological work about the beatific vision, the divine encounter that souls experience in heaven. In this work, Jacques postulated that the souls of the departed would only be able

[127] Bihl. "Fraticelli."

to see this beatific vision *after* the final judgment, even if they were already pure (and therefore merited heaven) or purified (after finishing their atonement in purgatory.)[128]

After becoming pope, John XXII would advance this view in his sermons. On All Saints Day of 1331, and on the third Sunday of Advent the same year, John preached that the souls of the blessed departed would go to heaven but would not experience the beatific vision immediately. Rather, they would sleep until the final judgment, when they would be elevated to the beatific vision. His rationale was simple: the beatific vision is the ultimate reward of the blessed departed; as the supreme recompense, it cannot belong to the soul alone, nor to the body alone, but to the entirety of the person. Since the resurrection of the body will only occur at the final judgment, then it stood to reason that the blessed would only experience the beatific vision after being reunited with their glorified bodies.[129]

John would develop these ideas even further on the eve of the Epiphany in 1332, where he applied the same principle to the condemnation of the damned, to wit, that they would only experience the fires of hell after the final judgment. He justifies himself with the fact that demons can tempt us here on earth, something that would not be possible if they were confined to hell.[130]

The problem is that the opposite statement—that the blessed souls experience the beatific vision *immediately* after death or after being purified in purgatory—would become a dogma of faith. This is because the beatific vision is defined as "the *immediate* knowledge of God that the souls enjoy in heaven." It is called "vision" to distinguish it from the *mediate* knowledge of God which the human mind may attain in the present life.[131] Nowadays, the Catholic Church teaches that the blessed souls see the divine essence with an intuitive vision, and even face to face, without the mediation of any creature, even *before* taking up their bodies again in the general judgment.[132]

Some apologists have defended John XXII, correctly noting that he taught his opinion *before* the dogma of the immediate beatific vision had

---

[128] Kirsch. "Pope John XXII."

[129] Le Bachelet. "Benoit XII," 659-660.

[130] Le Bachelet. "Benoit XII," 661.

[131] Pace. "Beatific Vision."

[132] CCC, 1023.

been formally defined.[133] Heresy is the *obstinate* denial of some truth that must be believed with Catholic faith.[134] Obstinacy requires a firm subjective conviction in which one understands that one's opinions conflict with Catholic teaching. If there is no obstinacy, the person is not in heresy, but merely in error. It is hard to argue, therefore, that a Catholic can be a heretic before the dogma has been defined.[135] This is why we do not claim that Thomas Aquinas was a heretic in the thirteenth century, even if he did not confess the dogma of the Immaculate Conception, for this dogma would only be defined by Pius IX in 1854.

However, as accurate as this defense is, it is insufficient for the purpose of this book. My aim is not to prove that a given pope was not a formal heretic, but to prove the reliability of the magisterium. If Pope John XXII taught error in his capacity as successor of Peter and bound the faithful to what would become a heresy, then submitting to this pope would be following him into error and the "recognize and resist" logic would be justified. The case of John XXII becomes an especially attractive argument for traditionalists of this variant, since the pope's sermons created quite a commotion, with several theologians correcting the pope.[136] But is this really what happened?

---

[133] Le Bachelet. "Benoit XII," 669: "There is no heresy in the remarks of John XXII, since at the time of the controversy the point in question had not yet been sanctioned by the Church, neither by a formal definition nor by a belief that was in fact sufficiently clear and universal."

[134] CCC, 2089.

[135] Wilhelm. "Heresy": "Heresy thus willed is imputable to the subject and carries with it a varying degree of guilt; it is called formal, because to the material error it adds the informative element of 'freely willed.' Pertinacity, that is, obstinate adhesion to a particular tenet is required to make heresy formal. For as long as one remains willing to submit to the Church's decision he remains a Catholic Christian at heart and his wrong beliefs are only transient errors and fleeting opinions. . . Pertinacious adhesion to a doctrine contradictory to a point of faith clearly defined by the Church is heresy pure and simple, heresy in the first degree. But if the doctrine in question has not been expressly 'defined' or is not clearly proposed as an article of faith in the ordinary, authorized teaching of the Church, an opinion opposed to it is styled *sententia haeresi proxima*, that is, an opinion approaching heresy."

[136] Kwasniewski. "How to Properly Understand the Role of the Papacy": "But what happened when John XXII preached that? Did everybody just bow their heads and fold their hands and say, 'We have to accept that. We better start rewriting the catechism'? Did they say, 'Well, that's wrong, but out of respect, out of religious submission of intellect and will, we have to go along with what the Pope

First of all, we must ascertain whether John XXII taught this heresy magisterially. Of course, his theological work published *before* his election as pope does not enjoy retroactive magisterial authority and can be dismissed as mere opinion of a private theologian. But what about his sermons? Though they possess low magisterial weight, papal homilies do still enjoy a certain degree of ordinary magisterial authority.[137]

Yet, there is a detail that makes all the difference. As we have seen in chapter 12, submission of mind and will must be given to the pope's ordinary magisterium, but "according to his manifest mind and will."[138] Did John XXII made his mind and will manifest as to how his sermons were to be received? During his second sermon, the pontiff made it abundantly clear that he was not teaching infallibly. Rather, this was his personal opinion. He preached:

> If I am mistaken here, let the one who knows better correct me. This is how it seems to me, nothing else; unless someone shows me a contrary decision of the Church or an authoritative argument from Sacred Scripture that would express this matter more clearly than the above-cited authorities.[139]

In other words, even while preaching a homily, the pope is clear that he is merely expressing his opinion on this matter and inviting those who may disagree to come forward and correct him. This is obviously not authentic magisterial teaching, since this is defined as a "teachings on faith and morals, presented as true or at least sure."[140] While the pope did indeed advance his opinion, and his opinion was later deemed erroneous, his purpose was

---

was saying'? No, they opposed him. His theologians, Dominicans, Franciscan, they objected to him. They said, 'This is false. You have to recant this.'"

[137] See Peters, "A Non-Magisterial Magisterial Statement?": "Popes and bishops, addressing faith and morals, in public statements made during a constitutive part of a liturgy (see the definition of a 'homily' in Canon 767), are, I think, engaged in a magisterial act."

[138] Vatican II. *Lumen Gentium*, 25.

[139] Le Bachelet. "Benoit XII," 662, as translated of the original Latin by Gleize. "The Question of Papal Heresy."

[140] CDF. "Doctrinal Commentary on the *Professio fidei*," 10.

not to use his papal authority to teach that erroneous opinion, but to promote debate on this question.

And debate is precisely what ensued. As I said before, many theologians who held the more common view that souls attain immediate beatific vision after death started to disagree with the pope, sometimes even vigorously.[141] John XXII sent two envoys to the renowned University of Paris to stimulate more discussion there and to defend the pontiff's opinion. This stirred even more tumult, and the uproar eventually reached the French king's ears.[142]

King Philip IV, listening to his leading Parisian theologians, rejected the view of delayed beatific vision and even threatened to condemn one of the papal envoys as a heretic or promoter of heresy.[143] Some traditionalists of today argue that the king went as far as intimidating the pope with very strong language,[144] but we now know that this violent tone is not to be found in the original documents, and was rather imputed to them by later Gallican controversialists.[145] Either way, we now know that this is not a proper way to act towards the pope. If *Donum Veritatis* affirms that it is wrong to use the weight of public opinion to pressure the magisterium,[146] then abusing the secular power for the same reason is obviously also not justifiable.

To the king's demand, the pope replied with a very moderate and considerate letter. Since John had allowed freedom of discussion, the monarch should allow it too, until the Holy See would decide to settle the matter.[147] Philip then convoked a solemn assembly on December 19, 1333, gathering

---

141 Le Bachelet. "Benoit XII," 663-664.

142 Le Bachelet. "Benoit XII," 665-666.

143 Le Bachelet. "Benoit XII," 666.

144 Kwasniewski. "How to Properly Understand the Role of the Papacy": "There was a king who got involved, the king of France, who actually threatened the Pope and said, 'If you don't retract this, you better retract this or else.' I'm not really quite sure what he was threatening, but kings and emperors used to be kind of. . . sometimes they kept the Church on track, even as other times, they led off into weird directions. So, the point is that I think there was a healthier sense all around, prior to the 19th century." Personally, I do not think it was "healthy" when kings threatened popes in doctrinal matters.

145 Le Bachelet. "Benoit XII," 666.

146 CDF, *Donum Veritatis*, 39.

147 Le Bachelet. "Benoit XII," 666.

as many weighty names as he could get, including princes, bishops, abbots, magistrates, even the Patriarch of Jerusalem.[148] On January 2, 1334, they signed a joint letter subscribing to the doctrine of the immediate beatific vision, and requesting the pope to infallibly define the matter. Can this be used as a precedent to the many "corrections" we have seen in Francis's pontificate? Not at all. Let us see what they wrote:

> As to this question, where Your Holiness has shown so much knowledge and subtlety, by assembling for one of the parties more numerous and stronger authorities than any doctor appears to have brought up until now—all however, we were told, *in the form of an exposition, without determining or even affirming or firmly supporting anything*—we earnestly beg Your Beatitude, in all humility and respect, to deign to decide it, confirming by a definition the truth of the feeling in which the piety of the Christian people you govern has always maintained.[149]

The tenor of this letter clearly contrasts with the "corrections" against Pope Francis. The tone is respectful, and not in a lip service kind of way. Nowhere is the pope accused of teaching heresy, either implicitly or explicitly. Quite the contrary, he is said to have shown "much knowledge and subtlety" on this matter. Most importantly, and unlike the modern "corrections," the letter's authors accurately grasp what is up for discussion and open for further definition. They understood the pope's manifest mind and will.

Be that as it may, it does not really matter. The letter may have helped the pope confirm his course of action, but John had already reversed his ways even before the letter had been signed.[150] The Fraticelli—John XXII's heretical adversaries—were weaponizing the whole controversy to undermine his papacy's authority. If the pope was a heretic, then how could he be reliable on his decisions where he rebuked them? They went as far as

---

[148] Le Bachelet. "Benoit XII," 666.

[149] Le Bachelet. "Benoit XII," 666-667 (my translation from the original French).

[150] Le Bachelet. "Benoit XII," 667.

asking for the convocation of an ecumenical council to condemn the Holy Father! Fortunately, their efforts here came to naught.[151]

From this we can see that the perception of John XXII as a heretic came not from the theologians that contradicted him, but from heretics profiting from this case to advance their own agenda. This sad state of affairs would continue in later times, when Protestants, Gallicans, and now traditionalists, would use John XXII's case to justify dissent from their own popes.

In light of these events, John gathered a consistory of cardinals, prelates, and theologians on December 28, 1333, while the Parisian theologians were still meeting. The pontiff proclaimed that he wanted this topic to be discussed in depth, and for five days there were debates on the beatific vision with arguments pro and con. The conclusion: there is *immediate* beatific vision after death of a pure or purified soul.[152] Even before the Parisian letter's ink was dry, John had already accepted this conclusion, declaring:

> So that my intentions would not be misunderstood, and that no one would claim that we have thought or think anything contrary to the Holy Church or the orthodox faith, I have expressly said that, during the controversy about the beatific vision of the souls, all that we have said, argued, or proposed in our sermons and conferences, *we have argued and proposed with no intent to determine, decide, or believe* anything contrary to Holy Scripture or the orthodox faith, but only hold and believe what is according to Holy Scripture and the Catholic faith. If, by misfortune, you will find in these conferences and sermons ideas that are, or can be construed as, being in opposition with Holy Scripture and the orthodox faith, we say and affirm that such was not our intention, and we expressly revoke it, we renounce those points and will not defend them, both in the future and in the present.[153]

---

[151] Kirsch. "Pope John XXII."
[152] Le Bachelet. "Benoit XII," 667.
[153] Le Bachelet. "Benoit XII," 667-668.

On March 10, John sent a letter to King Philip, again reaffirming this.[154] Finally, on his deathbed in 1334, the pope solemnly confessed the immediate beatific vision before his cardinals. He then clarified: "If in any way we have said something else or have expressed ourselves otherwise on this matter, we said so while remaining attached to the Catholic faith. . . and while *speaking by way of exposition and discussion*; this is what we affirm, and *this is the sense in which everything must be taken*."[155] The historicity of this solemn retraction is indisputable.[156]

Since the beginning of this controversy, the pope was very clear and consistent. Never did he try to cover his theological view under St. Peter's mantle, but always expressed his opinion as a private teacher, and made that abundantly clear. Not only that, but he also always allowed free debate to shed light into this controversial point, so those who contradicted him never went beyond the boundaries of legitimate discussion. If we must submit to the pope's teachings according to his manifest mind and will, then this is how we should take this whole affair. John XXII was not teaching magisterially, so one cannot evoke this episode to question the magisterium's reliability. There was no magisterial pronouncement to begin with, infallible or otherwise.

The matter would be settled very quickly, though. Five weeks after his election as John's successor, Benedict XII preached a sermon wherein he taught that the blessed souls see God clearly and immediately after death. Two days later, he convoked a consistory with the theologians that had sided with John XXII on delayed beatific vision. There, Benedict explained his reasoning to them, so that they would accept the correct doctrine. The new pontiff then published his predecessor's deathbed confession in the form of a bull.[157] Finally, Benedict published his own papal document, titled *Benedictus Deus*, infallibly defining the doctrine of the immediate beatific vision. The controversy was now closed, and Benedict could now focus on combatting the true heretics, the rigorist Fraticelli.

---

[154] Le Bachelet. "Benoit XII," 668.
[155] Le Bachelet. "Benoit XII," 668.
[156] Le Bachelet. "Benoit XII," 668.
[157] Le Bachelet. "Benoit XII," 669.

Conclusion

Let us return to the allegorical story with which we started this book. Heresy had stolen Tradition's royal clothes and passed herself off as being the king's daughter. This way she deceived many city folk. Tradition, in the meantime, arrived at the city completely naked. Even as she cried that she was the rightful heir, no one seemed to believe her, except a handful of sensible people who were concerned that they may be misled by appearances and insult the real princess in the process. Tradition's explanations of how she came to be in that situation seemed convoluted, but were not impossible, or even implausible. So, how could the citizens know who the real Tradition was?

One of the townsfolk brought some parchments, bearing the annals of the city. There they found a physical description of princess Tradition. But this would not do. As I said before, Tradition and Heresy looked very much alike. The physical description in the annals could be applied to any of the contenders, depending on how one would interpret these passages. If only the scrolls could speak and point to the one they were referring to, it would be easy! But, though authoritative, they were not alive. They required interpretation from the readers. And the ones deceived by Heresy would read them in a way that would confirm their own perceptions.

The answer, then, was simple. If Tradition was the king's daughter, then they should bring her to the presence of the king. The monarch would definitely recognize his dearest offspring. However, when they arrived at the royal palace, they found out that the king was absent on a faraway campaign and would not return for quite some time. His Majesty had, however, given the keys of the kingdom to his prime minister, so that he would govern the country in his absence as his vicar.

The vicar also knew Tradition personally. He had met her at the court and in the palace's halls. So, he would certainly recognize her. Surely, as a human being, the vicar could have momentarily confused the princess with someone else, when seeing her from afar or from behind. But this would be only for a fleeting moment, and not have any consequence whatsoever on whether he could reliably recognize the king's daughter or not.

They brought Tradition to the vicar's presence. They also summoned Heresy for examination, forcibly dragging her from one of the houses where she was feasting. The vicar examined both their faces thoroughly and was not tricked by Heresy's stunning outfit. He knew Tradition in person. After judging, the vicar accurately pointed to the true Tradition. The soldiers stripped Heresy of her stolen clothes and returned them to their rightful owner. As for Heresy, they cast her outside the palace's gates, in the same shameful state as she had left Tradition by the lake.

However, Heresy was not finished with her con. When the citizens she had duped came to the palace to inquire on all the commotion, she cried that the vicar had allied himself with an impostor to stage a coup against the king. The vicar—she lied—had placed an innovation in the princess' throne and cast out the true Tradition, so he could rule as he saw fit, for the fake would never contradict him.

The people were outraged against the vicar, but in the end, there was nothing they could do. He was in the palace, commanding the armies and the nation. So, they covered Heresy with their finest garments and went out of the city walls. There, they created their own city and served the fake Tradition as the true princess, eagerly awaiting the day the king would return and punish both the impostor and the treacherous vicar. They waited a long time. One year. Nine years. Sixty years. But though they did not relent, the king never came to validate their actions. All they managed to do was to place themselves outside the protection of the city's walls. . .

***

At the end of this book, I hope to have shown the dangers of a private interpretation of tradition. It is true, heresy/heterodoxy is always an innovation. We should indeed be on guard against that, adhering instead to the tradition handed to us. But we must also be attentive to a dangerous pitfall. *Tradition can also be confused with an innovation.* In the first section of this book, I have explained that this can be done through four mechanisms: *aggiornamento*, *ressourcement*, doctrinal development, and *opposizione polare.*

Aggionarmento means that we express the perennial tradition in new ways, adapted to each culture and age, sometimes even getting rid of nonbinding traditions that should not be confused with tradition as the deposit of faith (see chapter 1). *Ressourcement* means that we may retrieve from the depths of history some traditional understanding that may, in the meantime, have been forgotten, and that may therefore be confused as a novel addition by those who are not acquainted with it (see chapter 2). Doctrinal development means that non-infallible and reformable teachings can be developed, always in continuity, never in contradiction, though sometimes this continuity may bear the appearance of contradiction (see chapter 3). And finally, *opposizione polare* means that sometimes orthodoxy holds a delicate tension between two polar opposites, and that relaxing such tension—as tempting as it is—is what eventually constitutes heresy (see chapter 4).

Not only can tradition be confused with novelty, but *heresy can also be confused with tradition*, especially if heresy is used as an easy solution against the apparent innovation of some traditional teaching. Historical precedent for this error is aplenty, and I have gathered examples going from Peter to Pius X (see section 2). Therefore, even if modern traditionalists uncritically accept this idea that one can resist the pope if he contradicts one's private interpretation of tradition, it is not prudent to do so. History proves it. Paraphrasing St. Cardinal Newman, I would dare say that to "be deep in history is to cease to be a traditionalist."[1]

Of course, the Church's hierarchy, namely popes and councils, are not the creators of tradition, but their servants. They cannot simply teach whatever they please. They are, nonetheless, tradition's authoritative interpreters (see chapter 12). In this sense—and contrary to a common traditionalist objection—we do not claim that whatever the pope says is true. We do, however, believe that this objective truth that exists independently of the pope, is reliably interpreted by him. We do not say that St. Peter created a new truth when he allowed the Gentiles to eat pork (see chapter 5). We do not say that the First Nicaean Council created a new truth when it introduced the new word *homoousios* into the creed (see chapter 6). What we do say in those instances is that those things are true in themselves, and the Church interpreted them accordingly and accurately. When we argue otherwise as regards the post-conciliar Church in general and Pope Francis in particular, we are applying to them a premise that we do not apply to the

[1] Newman, *Development of Christian Doctrine*, 8: "To be deep in history is to cease to be a Protestant."

pre-conciliar Church, to wit, that what they teach is not true. The way this is solved is by arguing that they are creating new "truths," whereas the apparent novelties of the pre-conciliar Church were just that: "apparent."

Since heresy can be confused with tradition, and since tradition can be confused with novelty, we cannot interpret traditional statements in a literalist or proof-texting fashion, detached from the *living* tradition of the *ecclesial community* (see chapter 1 and 10). The orthodox interpretation is always more nuanced than this, taking into consideration all the complexities in question. If previous pronouncements were to be interpreted "as is," in a literalist fashion, there would be no need for an interpreter. Tradition would be perspicuous, and so would scripture (see chapter 8), so the magisterium would be superfluous. But we have seen from historical precedent that this is not the case. The magisterium was needed in the past and continues to be needed still to this day.

Since tradition is not perspicuous, we need an interpreter. This interpreter must be *authoritative* (see chapter 12), and it must be *living*. Only a living tradition can interact with the controversies of the day and with all the intricacies and subtleties at play, taking into account the circumstances that produced those polemics to give an accurate answer. Words written in a piece of paper cannot do this, no matter how inerrant or authoritative they are. As the late Christian scholar Jaroslav Pelikan famously remarked:

> *Tradition is the living faith of the dead; traditionalism is the dead faith of the living.* Tradition lives in conversation with the past, while remembering where we are and when we are and that it is we who have to decide. Traditionalism supposes that nothing should ever be done for the first time, so all that is needed to solve any problem is to arrive at the supposedly unanimous testimony of this homogenized tradition.[2]

Pope Francis very often agrees with this statement, to the chagrin of many traditionalists. In fact, he has explicitly quoted it.[3] This is what he means when he says that the deposit of faith is not "a museum to view, nor just

[2] Pelikan. "Christianity as an Enfolding Circle."

[3] Francis, "Press Conference during the flight of return to Rome from Canada"

something to safeguard, but is a living spring from which the Church drinks, to satisfy the thirst of, and illuminate the deposit of life."[4] Faith, he says, "is not a lovely exhibition of artefacts from a distant past or a museum, but an ever-present event, an encounter with Christ that takes place in the here and now of our lives. So we cannot pass it on by simply repeating the same old things, but by communicating the newness of the Gospel. In this way, faith remains alive and has a future."[5]

Tradition is, therefore, a "guarantee of the future."[6] Not a "container of ashes," but a "living tree that grows, flourishes, and bears fruit."[7] Like a tree, tradition is "vertical,"[8] either growing deep roots or shooting its branches towards the sky. If tradition is "vertical," we must always look either up or down—and by doing so, move forward.[9] What we cannot do is step backwards.[10] This is why Francis criticizes those he calls "*indietristi*," an Italian term that roughly translates as "backwardists." He carefully distinguishes these backwardists from traditional-minded people, even if the former call themselves traditional.[11] Contrary to what traditionalists claim, Pope Francis has indeed seen through our history and intuited a—dare I say—very traditional danger, the same danger that this book warns about:

> *Opposed to this there is the fashion – in every age*, but in this age in the Church's life I consider it dangerous – that instead of drawing from the roots in order to move forward – meaning fine traditions – we "step back", not going up or down, but backwards. This "back-stepping" makes us a sect; it makes you "closed" and cuts off your horizons. *Those people call themselves guardians of traditions, but of dead traditions.* The true Catholic Christian and human tradition is what that fifth-century theologian [Saint Vincent of Lerins]

---

[4] Francis. "Introductory Remarks."

[5] Francis. "Address during the Apostolic Journey to Kazakhstan."

[6] Francis. "Address to the Participants in the International Conference."

[7] Francis, "Press Conference during the flight of return to Rome from Romania" (my translation from the original Italian).

[8] Francis. "Address during the Apostolic Journey to Kazakhstan."

[9] Francis. "Address to the Participants in the International Conference."

[10] Francis. "Address during the Apostolic Journey to Kazakhstan." See also Francis. "Address to the Participants in the International Conference."

[11] Francis. "Address during the Apostolic Journey to Kazakhstan."

> described as a constant growth: throughout history tradition grows, progresses: *ut annis consolidetur, dilatetur tempore, sublimetur aetate.* That is authentic tradition, which progresses with our children.[12]

So, how do we recognize true tradition? Again, we need a living, authoritative interpreter. This interpreter is the magisterium, and the faithful are bound to adhere to its pronouncements according to the level of authority of said pronouncements. However, even in the case of non-infallible magisterial teachings, we must show submission of mind and will according to the magisterial agents' intentions (see chapter 12). Theologians can present their concerns if they have them, but within the due limits placed by *Donum Veritatis.* And even in matters of governance and Church discipline, the magisterium enjoys some level of divine assistance, something that the individual faithful does not necessarily possess. The Catholic can try to respectfully change those disciplines, but he cannot force the magisterium if that is something the pope and council manifestly do not wish.

Nor can we evade this by taking recourse to the supposed heretical popes of the past. As we have seen in chapter 13, no pope has ever magisterially bound the Church to a heretical teaching. Popes may have been neglectful though, and unwittingly helped spread heresy and error. But they were never obdurate in doing so, and this situation was quickly reversed by subsequent magisterial agents, with equal authority—popes and ecumenical councils—if not by the pope in question himself. Be that as it may, all these episodes relate to a single doctrinal topic. There is no precedent for a pope to consistently spread heterodoxy in a plethora of different issues, or to be consistently wrong in doctrine and discipline. Nor would that be consistent with the traditional notion that the pope enjoys divine assistance in the integral part of his mission. Neither is there a precedent for a period of *sede vacante* greater than three years. Traditionalists of various stripes admit as such when they argue that we are living in unprecedented times.

But are we really living in such unprecedented times? Or is it more likely that traditionalists are falling for the age-old mistake of confusing tradition with innovation, and confusing heresy with tradition? There is

---

[12] Francis. "Address to the Participants in the International Conference."

certainly a weightier historical precedent for huge swathes of faithful Catholics rebelling against popes and councils on the basis of their erroneous personal interpretations of tradition, eventually severing their communion with the Catholic Church, the "pillar and foundation of truth,"[13] the "guarantor of unity,"[14] the "custodian of tradition,"[15] "preserved ever immaculate."

I beg my traditionalist readers to at least consider if this is a risk worth taking. Do not be too hasty to read only to refute, but please reflect on everything I have written and draw conclusions judiciously, thoughtfully, and prayerfully. Remember that the eternal fate of your souls is at stake. If the reader is willing to at least entertain the possibility that he may have not fully grasped the scope of the Church's tradition, he or she will be able to find a wealth of online apologetical resources explaining how the controversial teachings of Vatican II and Pope Francis can be fully reconciled with perennial tradition. Do not dismiss those who provide elucidations as "mental gymnasts" or the like. If someone has found an acceptable explanation, should this person not be heard before being dismissed alongside the magisterium? The contradictions are merely apparent, one must only be open to accept the explanations. A hermeneutic of continuity *is* possible but it must be done, not in our terms, but in the context of the *living* tradition. Otherwise, we are merely assuming a hermeneutic of rupture (with the magisterium and, therefore, with tradition) under the guise of a hermeneutic of continuity. A satanic snare indeed.

I would just like to conclude with Cardinal Newman's prescient words in his aptly named Essay in Aid of a Grammar of Assent. Though he is addressing the case of a Protestant convert, the lessons he poses can (and should) be taken into the heart of the modern traditionalist as well:

> A man is converted to the Catholic Church from his admiration of its religious system, and his disgust with Protestantism. That admiration remains; but, after a time, he leaves his new faith, perhaps returns to his old. The reason, if we may conjecture, may sometimes be this: he has never believed in the Church's

[13] 1 Tim 3:15.
[14] John Paul II, *Ut Unum Sint*, 88.
[15] Francis. *Traditionis Custodes.*

> infallibility; in her doctrinal truth he has believed, but in her infallibility, no. *He was asked, before he was received, whether he held all that the Church taught, he replied he did; but he understood the question to mean, whether he held those particular doctrines "which at that time the Church in matter of fact formally taught," whereas it really meant "whatever the Church then or at any future time should teach."* Thus, he never had the indispensable and elementary faith of a Catholic, and was simply no subject for reception into the fold of the Church. This being the case, when the Immaculate Conception is defined, *he feels that it is something more than he bargained for* when he became a Catholic, and accordingly he gives up his religious profession. *The world will say that he has lost his certitude of the divinity of the Catholic Faith, but he never had it.*[16]

***

We now turn to our old friend Thomas Lawson. With the help of Justin Peterson, Tom has gone through quite the spiritual journey. He has started to read more of Francis and Catholic Social Doctrine from the primary sources, not from commentaries from Catholic media. His hostility towards the Holy Father has certainly subsided. In fact, he has learned quite a lot from Francis and was even surprised by some of his spiritual insights, that forced him to consider things in ways he would never even have entertained otherwise. However, the mental framework he has acquired through years of traditionalist thinking is not easy to overcome. He still finds some of Francis's teachings strange, even alien to the way he perceives Catholicism. But nowadays, Tom does not assume—as he did before—that this is Francis's fault.

Still, Tom cannot bring himself to agree with the Holy Father on many things. *Traditionis Custodes*, for one. Though Tom finally acknowledges—something he would not even dare do before—that there are elements in traditionalist circles that merit Francis's strong response, he still has quite the fondness for the TLM. Since his parish no longer offers the pre-

[16] Newman, *An Essay in Aid of a Grammar of Assent*, 240.

conciliar liturgy, Tom felt compelled to drive tens of miles away from home to attend the nearest TLM, hosted by the SSPX.

It is Sunday. Time for mass. As he sits in the car, Tom is struck by a sudden memory. Not all *Novus Ordo* masses are irreverent! In fact, Tom was converted precisely when he attended the ordinary form of the Roman missal at his parish! It was only later that his traditionalist friends introduced him to the TLM. Could the *Novus Ordo* be invalid and, at the same time, have brought him to the Catholic faith? He reminisced that blessed moment when he felt Jesus's presence in the Eucharist. Yes. Yes, Christ was there as well, not just the TLM.

Thomas tries to remember the mass schedules. He calculates the driving time, given the distance he must travel. If he leaves now, he can attend both masses. He glances at the intersection in the horizon. To the left is the SSPX TLM, miles away from home. To the right is his parish, a few minutes away, and the post-Vatican II mass that cured him of his Protestant errors.

For a minute or two, Tom ponders on what to do. He closes his eyes. He prays on it. Finally, he makes his decision. He turns the ignition key. He has made his choice. . .

Bibliography

"A Beautiful Mystery: The History of the Society of St. Pius X" *General House*, https://fsspx.org/en/history-of-the-SSPX

Acta Apostolicae Sedis. Libreria Editrice Vaticana. Vatican.va.

Adeyemi, Seni. "6 Reasons Protestants and Roman Catholics can never unite." *Purely Presbyterian 1646*, July 29, 2016. https://purelypresbyterian.com/ 2016/07/29/6-reasons-protestants/

Agius, George. *Tradition and the Church*. Rockford: TAN Books and Publishers Inc., 2005.

Akin, Jimmy. "Peter in Galatians". *Catholic Answers*, May 1, 1998.

Alexander, Kenneth. "Vatican II Cannot Be Separated from Its 'Spirit.'" *One Peter Five*, April 20, 2020. https://onepeterfive.com/vatican-ii-spirit/

Allen, Elise. "Damage to 'miraculous crucifix' not as serious as reported, rector says." *Crux*, April 1, 2020. https://cruxnow.com/vatican/2020/04/damage-to-miraculous-crucifix-not-as-serious-as-reported-rector-says

Altieri, Christopher. "From What, Precisely, Are *Amoris Laetitia* 'Dissenters' Dissenting?" *Catholic World Report*, January 5, 2018. https://www.catholicworldreport.com/2018/01/05/from-what-precisely-are-amoris-laetitia-dissenters-dissenting/

Ambrose of Milan. *Commentary on Twelve Psalms of David.* https://www.catholicfaithandreason.org/st-ambrose-of-milan-333-397-ad.html

Apologistas Católicos. http://apologistascatolicos.com.br/index.php/vaticano-ii/

Arel, Dan. "Sorry Republicans, but Jesus was a Marxist," *Huffington Post*, October 3, 2014. https://www.huffpost.com/entry/sorry-republicans-but-jes_b_5916564/

Arendzen, John. "Docetae." *The Catholic Encyclopedia*. Vol. 5. New York: Robert Appleton Company, 1909. http://www.newadvent.org/cathen/05070c.htm

———. "Ebionites." *The Catholic Encyclopedia.* Vol. 5. New York: Robert Appleton Company, 1909. http://www.newadvent.org/cathen/05242c.htm

———. "Gnosticism." *The Catholic Encyclopedia.* Vol. 6. New York: Robert Appleton Company, 1909. https://www.newadvent.org/cathen/06592a.htm

Aristotle. *Metaphysics.* Santa Fe: Green Lion Press, 2002.

Armstrong, Dave. "Definitions: Radical Catholic Reactionaries vs. Mainstream 'Traditionalists.'" *Patheos Catholic*, December 3, 2012. https://www.patheos.com/blogs/davearmstrong/2012/12/definitions-radical-catholic-reactionaries-mainstream-traditionalists-and-supposed-neo-catholics.html

———. "Does Paul's Rebuke of Peter Disprove Papal Infallibility?" *National Catholic Register*, June 29, 2020.

———. "The Clearness, or 'Perspicuity,' of Sacred Scripture." *National Catholic Register*, November 17, 2017. https://www.ncregister.com/blog/the-clearness-or-perspicuity-of-sacred-scripture/

Artemi, Eirini. "Cyril of Alexandria's critique of the term THEOTOKOS by Nestorius of Constantinople." *Acta Theologica*, Vol. 32, no. 2, (Dec. 2012): suppl. Bloemfontein.

Aucone, Daniele. "Tomismo dialettico." *Domenicane.* https://www.dominicanes.it/predicazione/meditazioni/1407-tomismo-dialettico.html

Augustine of Hippo. *On the New Testament*, Sermon LXXII, as quoted in http://www.clerus.org/bibliaclerusonline/en/index.htm

———. *On the Trinity.* Book II. https://www.newadvent.org/fathers/130102.htm

Bacchus, Francis. "Three Chapters." *The Catholic Encyclopedia.* Vol. 14. New York: Robert Appleton Company, 1912. http://www.newadvent.org/cathen/14707b.htm

Backler, Katherine. "Cardinal Sarah reiterates ad orientem comments and urges priests to carry out 'liturgical examination of conscience.'" *The Tablet*, August 24, 2016. https://www.thetablet.co.uk/news/6037/cardinal-sarah-reiterates-ad-orientem-comments-and-urges-priests-to-carry-out-liturgical-examination-of-conscience/

Bainvel, Jean. "Tradition and the Living Magisterium." *The Catholic Encyclopedia*, Vol. 5. New York: Robert Appleton Company, 1909. https://www.newadvent.org/cathen/15006b.htm

Baker, Todd. *Exodus from Rome: A Biblical and Historical Critique of Roman Catholicism*, Vol. 1. Bloomington: iUniverse LLC, 2014, 103.

Barbour, Hugh. "We're not a 'Religion of the Book'", *Catholic Answers*, November 17, 2018. https://www.catholic.com/magazine/online-edition/ were-not-a-religion-of-the-book

Barnes, Timothy. "The Capitulation of Liberius and Hilary of Poitiers." *Phoenix*, Vol. 46, No. 3 (Autumn, 1992): 256-265.

Barnett, S.J. "Where was your Church before Luther? Claims for the Antiquity of Protestantism Examined." *Church History*, Vol. 68, No. 1 (Mar. 1999): 14-41.

Barry, William. "Arianism." *The Catholic Encyclopedia.* Vol. 1. New York: Robert Appleton Company, 1907. http://www.newadvent.org/cathen/01707c.htm

Beatrice, Pier Franco. "The word 'homoousios' from Hellenism to Christianity." *Church History*, Vol. 71, No. 2, (Jun. 2002): 243-272.

Bellarmine, Robert. *On the Roman Pontiff: In Five Books (De Controversiis).* Translated by Ryan Grant. Post Falls: Mediatrix Press, 2017.

Belloc, Hilaire. *The Great Heresies.* Immortal, 2018.

Benedict XV. *Ad Beatissimi Apostolorum*, Libreria Editrice Vaticana, 1914. Vatican.va.

Benedict XVI. "Address to the General Assembly of the Italian Episcopal Conference." Libreria Editrice Vaticana, 2012. Vatican.va

———. *Africae Munus*, Libreria Editrice Vaticana, 2011. Vatican.va

———. *Declaratio*, February 10, 2013. Vatican.va.

———. "Farewell Address to the Eminent Cardinals present in Rome." February 28, 2013. Vatican.va.

———. "General Audience." May 3, 2006. Vatican.va.

———. *Homily of the Mass for the Possession of the Chair of the Bishop of Rome.* Libreria Editrice Vaticana, 2005. Vatican.va

———. *Introduction to Christianity.* 2nd ed. San Francisco: Communio, 2004.

———. *Jesus of Nazareth: from the Baptism in the Jordan to the Transfiguration.* New York: Doubleday Broadway Publishing Group, 2007.

———. *Jesus of Nazareth: Holy Week: from the Entrance into Jerusalem to the Resurrection*. San Francisco: Ignatius Press, 2011.

———. "Letter of His Holiness Pope Benedict XVI to the Bishops of the Catholic Church concerning the remission of the excommunication of the four Bishops consecrated by Archbishop Lefebvre." Libreria Editrice Vaticana, 2009. Vatican.va

———. "Letter of His Holiness Pope Benedict XVI to the Bishops of the Catholic Church on the occasion of the publication of the Apostolic Letter 'Motu Proprio Data' *Summorum Pontificum* on the use of the Roman Liturgy prior to the Reform of 1970." Libreria Editrice Vaticana, 2007. Vatican.va

———. *Summorum Pontificum*. Libreria Editrice Vaticana, 2007. Vatican.va.

Benedictine Monks of Solesmes. *Papal Teachings: The Church*. Translated by Mother O'Gorman. Boston: St. Paul Editions, 1980.

Benedictow, Ole. "The Black Death: The Greatest Catastrophe Ever." *History Today*, Vol 55, Issue 3 (March 2005). https://tinyurl.com/bdhnpwsx

Benigni, Umberto. "Ultramontanism." *The Catholic Encyclopedia*. Vol. 15. New York: Robert Appleton Company, 1912. http://www.newadvent.org/cathen/15125a.htm

Bennet, Rod. *Four Witnesses: The Early Church in her own words*. San Francisco: Ignatius Press, 2002.

Bergsman, John, and Scott Hahn. "Noah's nakedness and the curse of Canaan". *Journal of Biblical Literature*, Vol. 124, No. 1 (Spring 2005): 25-40.

Berry, Sylvester. *The Church of Christ: An Apologetical and Dogmatic Treatise*. Eugene: Wipf and Stock, 1955.

Bettenson, Henry. *Documents of the Christian Church*. Vol 2. Oxford: Oxford University Press, 1963.

Bickerton, Dominica. "The Development of a Theology of Tradition: Basil's On The Holy Spirit and Yves Congar's Tradition and Traditions." *Theology Graduate Theses* (Summer 2020): 14.

Bihl, Michael. "Fraticelli." *The Catholic Encyclopedia*. Vol. 6. New York: Robert Appleton Company, 1909. http://www.newadvent.org/cathen/06244b.htm

Bishops of the Pastoral Region of Buenos Aires. "Criterios básicos para la aplicación del capítulo VIII de '*Amoris laetitia*'. Texto de los Obispos de la Región de Buenos Aires (Argentina)." *Vida Nueva*, September 21, 2016. https://www.vidanuevadigital.com/documento/criterios-basicos-para-la-aplicacion-del-capitulo-viii-de-amoris-laetitia-texto-de-los-obispos-de-la-region-de-buenos-aires-argentina/

Blackburn, Jim. "Does papal infallibility mean the pope is perfect or inerrant?" *Catholic Answers*, September 18, 2020. https://www.catholic.com/qa/does-papal-infallibility-mean-the-pope-is-perfect-or-inerrant

Blackman, Daniel. "Cardinal Sarah Promotes Advent Launch of 'Ad Orientem' Liturgical Renewal." *National Catholic Register*, July 6, 2016. https://www.ncregister.com/news/cardinal-sarah-promotes-advent-launch-of-ad-orientem-liturgical-renewal

Blumenthal, Uta-Renate. "Gregorian Reform". *Encyclopedia Britannica*, September 23, 2011. https://www.britannica.com/event/Gregorian-Reform.

Borghesi, Massimo. "I Maestri di Papa Francesco". *Vita e Pensiero Plus+*, March 31, 2018 https://rivista.vitaepensiero.it/news-vp-plus-i-maestri-di-papa-francesco-4902.html

———. *The Mind of Pope Francis: Jorge Mario Bergoglio's Intellectual Journey*. Collegeville: Liturgical Press Academy, 2018.

Borto, Pawel. "From an Apology for Catholicism to Theological Modernism: The Principle of Development in Alfred Loisy's Thought." *Verbum Vitae*, Vol. 40, No. 2 (2022): 501-513.

Brother André Marie [pseud.]. "*Amoris Laetitia* and the 'Authentic Magisterium.'" *Catholicism.Org* (blog), December 5, 2017. https://catholicism.org/amoris-laetitia-authentic-magisterium.html.

Broussard, "Paul's Rebuke and Peter's Infallibility." *Catholic Answers Focus*, May 20, 2020

Burke, Raymond. "'*Amoris Laetitia*' and the Constant Teaching and Practice of the Church." *National Catholic Register*, April 12, 2016. https://www.ncregister.com/news/amoris-laetitia-and-the-constant-teaching-and-practice-of-the-church

———. "Interview With Cardinal Burke… (Part 2) Discriminating Mercy: Defending Christ And His Church With True Love," by Don Fier. *The Wanderer*, August 14, 2017. https://tinyurl.com/5n96bbmn

Burke, Ronald. "Loisy's Faith: Landshift in Catholic Thought." *The Journal of Religion*, Vol. 60, No. 2 (Apr. 1980): 138-164

Buttiglione, Rocco. *Risposte Amichevoli Ai Critici Di Amoris Laetitia.* Milano: Edizioni Ares, 2017.

Buscemi, Georges, Robert Cassidy, Thomas Crean, Matteo d'Amico, Nick Donnelly, Maria Guarini, Robert Hickson et al. "Open Letter to the Bishops of the Catholic Church," April 30, 2019. https://www.documentcloud.org/ documents/5983408-Open-Letter-to-the-Bishops-of-the-Catholic.html

Campbell, Thomas. "Pope St. Anicetus." *The Catholic Encyclopedia.* Vol. 1. New York: Robert Appleton Company, 1907. http://www.newadvent.org/cathen/01514a.htm

Catholic Church, ed. *Catechism of the Catholic Church.* Libreria Editrice Vaticana, 1993. Vatican.va.

Catholic News Agency. "Full Text of Pope Francis' in-Flight Press Conference from Abu Dhabi," February 5, 2019. https://www.catholicnewsagency.com/ news/40492/full-text-of-pope-francis-in-flight-press-conference-from-abu-dhabi/

———. "Pope St. Victor I." https://www.catholicnewsagency.com/ saint/st-victor-i-pope-527

Catholic News Service. "Vatican rejects Cardinal Sarah's ad orientem appeal." *Catholic Herald*, July 12, 2016. https://catholic-herald.co.uk/vatican-rejects-cardinal-sarahs-ad-orientem-appeal/

Chapman, John. "Council of Ephesus." *The Catholic Encyclopedia.* Vol. 5. New York: Robert Appleton Company, 1909. http://www.newadvent.org/cathen/05491a.htm

———. "Monophysites and Monophysitism." *The Catholic Encyclopedia.* Vol. 10. New York: Robert Appleton Company, 1911. http://www.newadvent.org/ cathen/10489b.htm

———. "Pope Honorius I." *The Catholic Encyclopedia.* Vol. 7. New York: Robert Appleton Company, 1910. http://www.newadvent.org/ cathen/07452b.htm

———. "Pope Liberius." *The Catholic Encyclopedia.* Vol. 9. New York: Robert Appleton Company, 1910. http://www.newadvent.org/ cathen/09217a.htm

———. *Studies on the Early Papacy.* Jackson: Ex Fontibus Company, 2012.

———. *The Condemnation of Pope Honorius*. London: Catholic Truth Society, 1907.

———. "The Contested Letters of Pope Liberius." *Revue Bénédictine*, Vol. 27, Issue 1-4 (1910): 172-203.

Chapman, Michael. "Catholic Scholar: 'Pope Francis Has Created Enough Confusion' 'So People Now Can Ignore 'Moral Teachings.'" *CNSNews*, March 6, 2018. https://www.cnsnews.com/blog/michael-w-chapman/catholic-scholar-pope-francis-has-created-enough-confusion-so-people-now-can

Chapp, Larry, Sean Domencic, Marc Barnes, Rodney Howsare, David Oatney, Tom Gourlay, Oscar Paniagua, et al. *Manifesto of the New Traditionalism.* December 22, 2021. https://gaudiumetspes22.com/ blog/a-manifesto-of-the-new-traditionalism

Chemnitz, Martin. *Examination of the Council of Trent, Part I.* St. Louis: Concordia Publishing House, 1971 (Kindle edition).

Chesterton, Gilbert. *St. Thomas Aquinas.* New York: Dover Publications, 2009.

———. *The Everlasting Man.* New York: Dover Publications, 2007.

Chrysostom, John, *De Lazaro Concio.*

———. *Homily 16 on Matthew*, as quoted in https://www.newadvent.org/fathers/200116.htm

Congar, Yves. *Chrétiens en dialogue: contributions catholiques à l'oecuménisme.* Paris: Éditions du CERF, 1964.

———. *La Tradition et la vie de l'Eglise.* Paris: Les Édition du CERF, 1984.

———. *True and False Reform in the Church.* Minnesota: Liturgical Press, 2011.

Congregation for the Doctrine of the Faith. "Doctrinal Commentary on the Concluding Formula of the *Professio Fidei*." June 29, 1998. Vatican.va.

———. "Instruction *Donum Veritatis* on the Ecclesial Vocation of the Theologian," December 29, 1975. Vatican.va.

———. "Letter to the Bishops regarding the new revision of number 2267 of the Catechism of the Catholic Church on the death penalty, from the Congregation for the Doctrine of the Faith," August 2, 2018. Vatican.va.

———. "The Primacy of the Successor of Peter in the Mystery of the Church," November 18, 1998. Vatican.va.

Connell, Gerald. "Pope Francis: There will be no 'the reform of the reform' of the liturgy." *America Magazine*, December 6, 2016. https://www.americamagazine.org/faith/2016/12/06/pope-francis-there-will-be-no-reform-reform-liturgy

Constance. "Session 13," February 15, 1415, as quoted in https://www.papalencyclicals.net/ councils/ecum16.htm

Constantinople III. "Session 4." November 15, 680, as quoted in *New Advent*. https://www.newadvent.org/fathers/3813.htm

Corbellini, Vital. "A Participação de Atanásio no Concílio de Nicéia e a sua defesa do Homooúsios." *Teocomunicação*, Vol. 37, No 157 (Set. 2007): 396-408.

Cornwell, Michelle. "Cardinal Sarah to conduct study into Ordinary and Extraordinary Mass forms." *The Tablet*, July 6, 2016. https://www.thetablet.co.uk/news/5799/cardinal-sarah-to-conduct-study-into-ordinary-and-extraordinary-mass-forms

Cowdrey, Herbert. "Pope Gregory VII and the liturgy." *Journal of Theological Studies*, *NS*, Vol. 55, Pt. 1 (April 2004): 55-83.

Crary, David. "Vatican warns US bishops over get-tough Communion." *AP News*, May 10, 2021. https://tinyurl.com/2ad5kfxr

Cristescu, Vasile. "The Expression of True Faith by the First Ecumenical Council of Nicaea." *European Journal of Science and Theology*, Vol. 8, No.1 (March 2012): 105-121.

Cronin, Eoin. "Abandoning Apostolic Celibacy would be a mistake." *Crisis Magazine*, November 4, 2019. https://www.crisismagazine.com/2019/abandoning-apostolic-celibacy-would-be-a-mistake

Crowe, Brandon. "What did Jesus mean when He said 'Not an Iota not a Dot, will pass from the Law until all is accomplished'?" *Ligonier*, November 12, 2016. https://www.ligonier.org/learn/articles/what-did-jesus-mean-when-he-said-not-iota-not-dot-will-pass-law-until-all-accomplished

Currie, Chuck. "Currie: Here's why I'm a pro-choice pastor." *The Portland Tribune*, October 20, 2021. https://pamplinmedia.com/pt/10-opinion/ 525286-419878-currie-heres-why-im-a-pro-choice-pastor

Curtis, Ken. "Whatever Happened to the Twelve Apostles?" *Christianity.com*, April 28, 2010. https://www.christianity.com/church/ church-history/timeline/1-300/whatever-happened-to-the-twelve-apostles-11629558.html

Daneshmand, Justin. "When Heresy was Orthodox—Quartodecimanism as a Brief Case Study." *Centre for the Study of Christian Origins*, March 30, 2018. http://www.christianorigins.div.ed.ac.uk/2018/03/30/when-heresy-was-orthodox-quartodecimanism-as-a-brief-case-study/

Darantière, Karen. "Traditionis Custodes: Guardians of tradition or betrayers of tradition?" *LifeSiteNews*, July 20, 2021. https://www.lifesitenews.com/opinion/traditionis-custodes-guardians-of-tradition-or-betrayers-of-tradition/

Darras, Joseph-Epiphane. *General History of the Catholic Church: From the Commencement of the Christian Era Until the Present Time.* Vol. 1. New York: P. O'Shea Publisher, 1866.

Daud, Maria. "Miraculous crucifix from 1522 plague moved to St. Peter's for pope's 'Urbi et Orbi' blessing." *Aleteia.* March 26, 2020. https://aleteia.org/2020/03/26/miraculous-crucifix-from-1522-plague-moved-to-st-peters-for-popes-urbi-et-orbi-blessing/

Davies, Lizzy. "Pope Francis declares: 'I would like to see a church that is poor and is for the poor'." *The Guardian*, March 16, 2013. https://www.theguardian.com/world/2013/mar/16/pope-francis-church-poverty

Davis, Charlotte. "Classicism and the Renaissance: The Rebirth of Antiquity in Europe." *The Collector*, November 10, 2019. https://www.thecollector.com/classicism-and-the-renaissance-the-rebirth-of-antiquity-in-europe/

de Mattei, Roberto. Pius IX, translated by John Laughland. Herefordshire: Gracewing, 2004.

de Sousa, Raymond. "Father Raymond J. de Souza on the Pope: The Holy Father takes his leave." *National Post*, February 12, 2013. https://nationalpost.com/opinion/father-raymond-j-de-souza-on-the-pope-the-holy-father-takes-his-leave/

Dégert, Antoine. "Gallicanism." *The Catholic Encyclopedia.* Vol. 6. New York: Robert Appleton Company, 1909. http://www.newadvent.org/ cathen/06351a.htm

Deines, Roland. "Can the 'Real' Jesus be identified with the Historical Jesus? A Review of the Pope's Challenge to Biblical Scholarship and the Various Reactions it provoked." *Didaskalia* XXXIX, I (March 2012): 11-46.

Derksen, Mario. "Apostasy in Abu Dhabi: Francis says God wills Diversity of Religions" *Novus Ordo Watch*, February 4, 2019. https://novusordowatch.org/2019/02/apostasy-francis-diversity-of-religions/

———. "Can a Heretical Pope be Deposed? St. Robert Bellarmine refutes the Anti-Sedevacantists." *Novus Ordo Watch*, June 8, 2015. https://novusordowatch.org/2015/06/can-heretical-pope-be-deposed/

———. "No, Catholics Can't 'Recognize and Resist': Response to One Peter Five" *Novus Ordo Watch*, December 13, 2021. https://novusordowatch.org/2021/12/no-recognize-resist-sammons-one-peter-five/

———. "Ratzinger, Hegel, and '*Summorum Pontificum*'" *Novus Ordo Watch*, June 6, 2017. https://novusordowatch.org/2017/06/ratzinger-hegel-summorum-pontificum/

———. "White Smoke, Anti-Pope: A Response to Rev. Brian Harrison" *Novus Ordo Watch*, March 2, 2017. https://novusordowatch.org/2017/03/white-smoke-anti-pope/

Dobbs, Kenneth. "Taking the Tradpill." *One Peter Five*, May 4, 2020. https://onepeterfive.com/tradpill/

Dougherty, Michael. "Pope Francis is a humble man, but a terrible choice." *National Post*, March 16, 2013. https://nationalpost.com/opinion/michael-brendan-dougherty-pope-francis-is-a-humble-man-but-a-terrible-choice

———. "Roma Locuta Est, deal with it." *National Review*, October 28, 2019. https://www.nationalreview.com/2019/10/roma-locuta-est-deal-with-it/

Douthat, Ross. "The Plot to Change Catholicism." *The New York Times*. October 17, 2015. https://www.nytimes.com/2015/10/18/opinion/sunday/the-plot-to-change-catholicism.html

———. *To Change the Church: Pope Francis and the Future of Catholicism*. New York: Simon & Schuster Paperbacks, 2018.

Dreher, Rod. "The Catholics Left Out In The Cold." *The American Conservative*, November 10, 2013. https://www.theamericanconservative.com/the-catholics-left-out-in-the-cold/

Editors of the Encyclopaedia Britannica. "Gregorian Chant." *Encyclopedia Britannica*, March 9, 2007. https://www.britannica.com/topic/Sabellianism

———. "Hussite." *Encyclopedia Britannica*, July 20, 1998. https://www.britannica.com/topic/Hussite/

———. "Sabellianism" *Encyclopedia Britannica*, July 20, 1998. https://www.britannica.com/topic/Sabellianism

———. "Saint Victor I." *Encyclopedia Britannica*, Feb 13. 2022, https://www.britannica.com/biography/Saint-Victor-I

Eli, Bradley. "Cardinals decry the misuse of the synod to revolutionize the Church." *Church Militant*, September 27, 2019. https://www.churchmilitant.com/news/article/using-pan-amazon-synod-for-revolution

———. "Vatican 2022 Synod on Synodality" *Church Militant*, March 9, 2020. https://www.churchmilitant.com/news/article/vatican-2022-synod-on-synodality

Fahey, Paul. "The Living Bridge to LGBT Catholics." *Where Peter Is*. January 15, 2020. https://wherepeteris.com/the-living-bridge-to-lgbt-catholics/

Farrow, Mary. "Pope Francis Signs Peace Declaration on 'Human Fraternity' with Grand Imam." *Catholic News Agency*, February 4, 2019. https://www.catholicnewsagency.com/news/40483/pope-francis-signs-peace-declaration-on-human-fraternity-with-grand-imam.

Fastiggi, Robert. "*Amoris Laetitia* and the Magisterium: Interview with Dr. Robert Fastiggi," by Pedro Gabriel. *The City and the World*, September 21, 2022. https://thecityandtheworld.com/interview-with-dr-fastiggi/

Fellay, Bernard. "Interview with Bishop Bernard Fellay: The Society of St. Pius X and the Doctrinal Preamble." *Documentation Information Catholiques Internationales*, November 28, 2011. https://tinyurl.com/2mnpv2a6

Ferrara, Christopher. "*Amoris Laetitia*: Anatomy of a Pontifical Debacle" *The Remnant Newspaper*, April 18, 2016. https://remnantnewspaper.com/web/index.php/articles/item/ 2464-amoris-laetitia-anatomy-of-a-pontifical-debacle

———. "Can the Church ban Capital Punishment?" *Crisis Magazine*, December 2, 2011. https://www.crisismagazine.com/2011/can-the-church-ban-capital-punishment

Ferré, Alberto. "La Chiesa, popolo tra i popoli," in Ferré, Alberto. *Il risorgimento cattolico latinoamericano*. Bologna: La Nuova Agape, 1983.

Feser, Edward. "Capital punishment should not end (UPDATED)." *Edward Feser* (blog), March 7, 2015. http://edwardfeser.blogspot.com/2015/ 03/capital-punishment-should-not-end.html

———. "Papal Fallibility." *Edward Feser* (blog), November 21, 2015. http://edwardfeser.blogspot.com/2015/11/papal-fallibility.html

———. "The Church permits criticism of popes under certain circumstances." *Edward Feser* (blog), May 20, 2018. http://edwardfeser.blogspot.com/2015/03/capital-punishment-should-not-end.html

Florence. "Session 11," February 4, 1442, as quoted in https://www.papalencyclicals.net/councils/ecum17.htm

Flynn, Gabriel, and Paul Murray. *Ressourcement, a Movement for Renewal in Twentieth-Century Theology*. New York: Oxford University Press, 2012.

Fortescue, Adrian. "Liturgy." *The Catholic Encyclopedia*. Vol. 9. New York: Robert Appleton Company, 1910. http://www.newadvent.org/cathen/09306a.htm

———. "The Roman Rite." The Catholic Encyclopedia. Vol. 13. New York: Robert Appleton Company, 1912. http://www.newadvent.org/cathen/13155a.htm

Francis. "Address of His Holiness in the Meeting with Bishops, Priests, Deacons, Consecrated Persons, Seminarians and Pastoral Workers during the Apostolic Journey to Kazakhstan." September 15, 2022. Vatican.va.

———. "Address of His Holiness to the Participants in the International Conference: 'Lines of Development of the Global Compact on Education,' promoted by the Congregation for Catholic Education (of Institutes of Studies.)" June 1, 2022. Vatican.va.

———. *Amoris Laetitia*. Libreria Editrice Vaticana, 2016. Vatican.va.

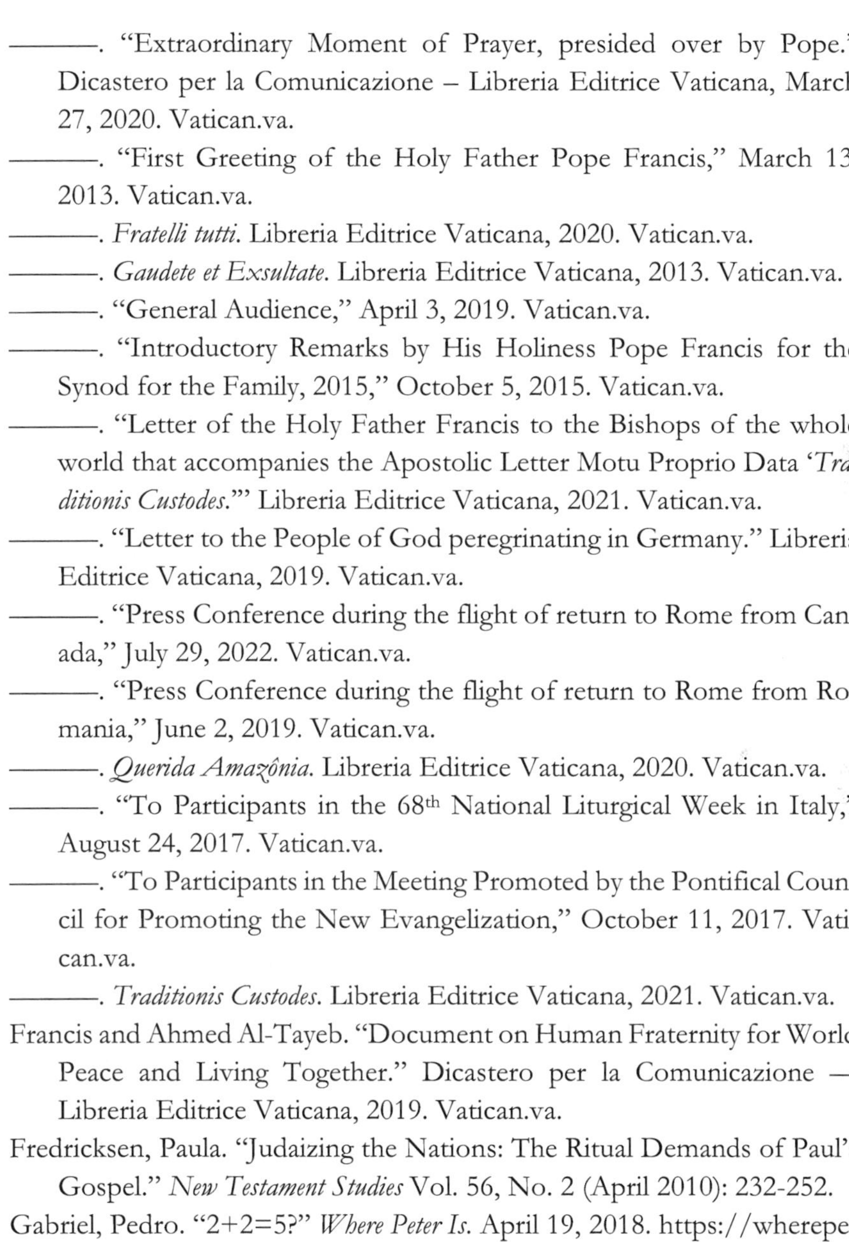

———. "Extraordinary Moment of Prayer, presided over by Pope." Dicastero per la Comunicazione – Libreria Editrice Vaticana, March 27, 2020. Vatican.va.

———. "First Greeting of the Holy Father Pope Francis," March 13, 2013. Vatican.va.

———. *Fratelli tutti*. Libreria Editrice Vaticana, 2020. Vatican.va.

———. *Gaudete et Exsultate*. Libreria Editrice Vaticana, 2013. Vatican.va.

———. "General Audience," April 3, 2019. Vatican.va.

———. "Introductory Remarks by His Holiness Pope Francis for the Synod for the Family, 2015," October 5, 2015. Vatican.va.

———. "Letter of the Holy Father Francis to the Bishops of the whole world that accompanies the Apostolic Letter Motu Proprio Data '*Traditionis Custodes*.'" Libreria Editrice Vaticana, 2021. Vatican.va.

———. "Letter to the People of God peregrinating in Germany." Libreria Editrice Vaticana, 2019. Vatican.va.

———. "Press Conference during the flight of return to Rome from Canada," July 29, 2022. Vatican.va.

———. "Press Conference during the flight of return to Rome from Romania," June 2, 2019. Vatican.va.

———. *Querida Amazônia*. Libreria Editrice Vaticana, 2020. Vatican.va.

———. "To Participants in the 68th National Liturgical Week in Italy," August 24, 2017. Vatican.va.

———. "To Participants in the Meeting Promoted by the Pontifical Council for Promoting the New Evangelization," October 11, 2017. Vatican.va.

———. *Traditionis Custodes*. Libreria Editrice Vaticana, 2021. Vatican.va.

Francis and Ahmed Al-Tayeb. "Document on Human Fraternity for World Peace and Living Together." Dicastero per la Comunicazione — Libreria Editrice Vaticana, 2019. Vatican.va.

Fredricksen, Paula. "Judaizing the Nations: The Ritual Demands of Paul's Gospel." *New Testament Studies* Vol. 56, No. 2 (April 2010): 232-252.

Gabriel, Pedro. "2+2=5?" *Where Peter Is*. April 19, 2018. https://wherepeteris.com/225-2/

———. "Death Penalty—continuity or hardness of heart?" *Where Peter Is*, September 24, 2018. https://wherepeteris.com/death-penalty-continuity-or-hardness-of-heart/

———. "Death penalty—the Gen 9:6 objection." *Where Peter Is*, June 19, 2019. https://wherepeteris.com/death-penalty-the-gen-96-objection/

———. "Following Christ, but Not His Vicar." *Where Peter Is*, July 9, 2019 https://wherepeteris.com/following-christ-but-not-his-vicar/

———. "*Fratelli tutti* – Francis's most traditional document?" *Where Peter Is*, October 29, 2020. https://wherepeteris.com/fratelli-tutti-franciss-most-traditional-document/

———. "Is *Fratelli Tutti* a 'leftist' encyclical?" *Where Peter Is*, December 2, 2020. https://wherepeteris.com/is-fratelli-tutti-a-leftist-encyclical/

———. "Married priests and Querida Amazônia: my thoughts" *Where Peter Is*, February 17, 2020. https://wherepeteris.com/married-priests-and-querida-amazonia-my-thoughts/

———. "Our Lady of the Amazon: Pray for us" *Where Peter Is*, October 13, 2019. https://wherepeteris.com/our-lady-of-the-amazon-pray-for-us/

———. "Our Lady of the Amazon: solving the contradictions" *Where Peter Is*, October 25, 2019. https://wherepeteris.com/our-lady-of-the-amazon-solving-the-contradictions/

———. "Paganism in the Vatican? Hermeneutic of Suspicion at its peak." *Where Peter Is*, October 6, 2019. https://wherepeteris.com/paganism-in-the-vatican-hermeneutic-of-suspicion-at-its-peak/

———. "Pluralism and the will of God… is there another way to look at it?" *Where Peter Is*, March 12, 2019. https://wherepeteris.com/pluralism-and-the-will-of-god-is-there-another-way-to-look-at-it/

———. "Pope Francis and apostates: is this the communion of saints?" *Where Peter Is*, February 4, 2022. https://wherepeteris.com/the-flight-of-the-doctrinal-butterfly/

———. "Pope Francis, Pro-Life Champion." *Where Peter Is*, April 25, 2018. https://wherepeteris.com/pope-francis-pro-life-champion/

———. "Showing mercy towards traditionalists." *Where Peter Is*, April 11, 2019. https://wherepeteris.com/showing-mercy-towards-traditionalists/

———. "Sola Traditio." *Where Peter Is*, February 8, 2018. https://wherepeteris.com/sola-traditio/

———. "The Crucified Church: Tensions with the flavor of the Gospel." *Where Peter Is*, February 10, 2020.

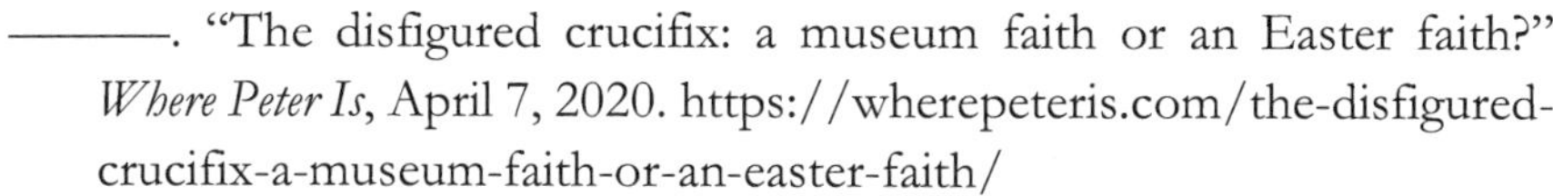

———. "The disfigured crucifix: a museum faith or an Easter faith?" *Where Peter Is*, April 7, 2020. https://wherepeteris.com/the-disfigured-crucifix-a-museum-faith-or-an-easter-faith/

———. "The Flight of the Doctrinal Butterfly." *Where Peter Is*, June 30, 2021. https://wherepeteris.com/the-flight-of-the-doctrinal-butterfly/

———. "The infallibly erring Pope." *Where Peter Is*, January 3, 2020. https://wherepeteris.com/the-infallibly-erring-pope/

———. *The Orthodoxy of Amoris Laetitia.* Eugene: Wipf and Stock, 2022.

———. "The Perspicuity of Tradition." *Where Peter Is*, March 28, 2021. https://wherepeteris.com/the-perspicuity-of-tradition/

———. "*Urbi et Orbi*: Meeting the real Pope Francis." *Where Peter Is*, March 30, 2020. https://wherepeteris.com/urbi-et-orbi-meeting-the-real-pope-francis/

———. "Vatican II and 'Weaponized Ambiguity.'" *Where Peter Is*, October 1, 2020. https://wherepeteris.com/vatican-ii-and-weaponized-ambiguity/

———. "Was Pope Benedict Forced to Resign?" *Where Peter Is*, February 28, 2018. https://wherepeteris.com/was-pope-benedict-forced-to-resign/

Gagliarducci, Andrea. "*Humanae Vitae* Needs No Update, Commission Chair Says." *Catholic News Agency*, May 23, 2018. https://www.catholicnewsagency.com/news/38475/humanae-vitae-needs-no-update-commission-chair-says

Gasper, Phil. "Jesus the Revolutionary?" *The Socialist Worker*, December 13, 2011. https://socialistworker.org/2011/12/14/jesus-the-revolutionary

Giansoldati, Franca. "Danneggiato il crocifisso 'miracoloso': troppa pioggia durante la preghiera del Papa." *Il Messaggero*, March 28, 2020. https://www.ilmessaggero.it/vaticano/papa_francesco_crocifisso_danneggiato_san_marcello_miracolo_pioggia_restauro_preghiera-5138660.html

Giunta, Eric. "Where Peter Isn't, Part I: When Popes are Infallible, and when they are not." *Laboravi Sustinens*, February 23, 2021. https://ericsgiunta.wordpress.com/2021/02/23/where-peter-isnt-part-i-when-popes-are-infallible-and-when-they-are-not/

Gleize, Jean-Michel. "The Question of Papal Heresy—Part 2." *SSPX*, February 14, 2017. https://sspx.org/en/news-events/news/question-papal-heresy-part-2

———. "The State of Necessity". *SiSiNoNo*, No. 84, January 2009.

Gloria.tv. "Cross Crumbles - Coronavirus Continues." March 30, 2020. https://gloria.tv/post/8oeFDUv2tEd74AZPemCAbpaY1

———. "Viganò: Not Even The Most Optimistic Freemason Would Have Dreamed Francis' Papacy," November 22, 2019. https://gloria.tv/post/ZAR2rh2u3K3b36obpsjknTw1i/

Gracida, René. "What next?" *Abyssus Abyssum Invocat*, February 4, 2019. https://abyssum.org/2019/02/04/what-next/

Gregg, Samuel. "*Fratelli Tutti* is a familiar mixture of dubious claims, strawmen, genuine insights." *Catholic World Report*, October 5, 2020. https://www.catholicworldreport.com/2020/10/05/fratelli-tutti-is-a-mixture-of-dubious-claims-strawmen-genuine-insights/

Gregory XVI. *Mirari Vos*, 1832. https://www.papalencyclicals.net/Greg16/g16mirar.htm

Griffin, Patrick. "Rites." *The Catholic Encyclopedia.* Vol. 13. New York: Robert Appleton Company, 1912. http://www.newadvent.org/cathen/13064b.htm

Griffith, Susan. "Apostolic Authority and the 'Incident at Antioch': Chrysostom on Galatians 2:11-14." *Studia Patristica*, Vol. XCVI, (Jan. 2017): 117-126.

Groen, Basilius. "The Interplay of Hebrew, Greek and Latin in Christian Worship during the First Millenium: some views." *Ökumenisches Forum*, Issue 40-41, (2018-2019): 39-62.

Grondin, Charles. "Why Did Jesus Condemn the Practice of Corban?" *Catholic Answers*, July 14, 2022. https://www.catholic.com/qa/why-did-jesus-condemn-the-practice-of-corban

Guarino, Thomas. "Pope Francis and St. Vincent of Lérins." *First Things*, August 16, 2022. https://www.firstthings.com/web-exclusives/2022/08/ pope-francis-and-st-vincent-of-lrins

———. *The Disputed Teachings of Vatican II: Continuity and Reversal in Catholic Doctrine.* Grand Rapids: William B. Eerdmans, 2018.

Guilbert, George. "Harnack, Loisy, and the Gospel." *The Biblical World*, Vol 40, No 2 (Aug 1912): 92-96.

Gurian, Waldemar. "Lamennais." *The Review of Politics*, Vol. 9, No. 2 (Apr 1947): 205-229.

Hall, Kennedy. "'Prayers answered': Catholics denied Mass during COVID lockdowns establish new Latin Mass Chapel." *LifeSiteNews*, October 19, 2021. https://www.lifesitenews.com/news/prayers-answers-catholics-denied-mass-during-covid-lockdowns-establish-new-latin-mass-chapel/

Hanna, Erin. "On holiest of days, Pope slams women's ordination supporters." *Women's Ordination Conference*, April 5, 2012. https://www.womensordination.org/2012/04/on-holiest-of-days-pope-slams-womens-ordination-supporters/

Hardon, John. *Catholic Dictionary: An Abridged and Updated Edition of the Modern Catholic Dictionary*. New York: Image, 2013.

Harris, R. Laird. *Fundamental Protestant Doctrines*. Wilmington: Bible Presbyterian Press, 1949.

Harrison, Brian. "Vatican II's Declaration on Religious Liberty." *Catholic Answers*, July 1, 2015. https://www.catholic.com/magazine/print-edition/ vatican-iis-declaration-on-religious-liberty

Hausam, Mark. "Historical Challenges to the Infallibility of the Church, Part Three: Pope Honorius." *The Christian Freethinker*, July 30, 2019. http://freethoughtforchrist.blogspot.com/search/label/Pope%20Honorius/

———. "Historical Challenges to the Infallibility of the Church, Part Two: Pope Liberius." *The Christian Freethinker*, July 27, 2019. http://freethoughtforchrist. blogspot.com/search/label/Pope%20Liberius

———. "Was Pope Vigilius a heretic?" *Where Peter Is*, August 14, 2019. https://wherepeteris.com/was-pope-vigilius-a-heretic/

Hay, Jennifer. "Did the Early Christians subscribe to Sola Scriptura?" *Catholic Answers*, April 1, 2009. https://www.catholic.com/magazine/print-edition/did-the-early-christians-subscribe-to-sola-scriptura

Hefele, Joseph. *A History of the Councils of the Church from the Original Documents*, Vol. IV. Translated by William Clark. Edinburgh: T & T Clark, 1895.

———. *A History of the Councils of the Church from the Original Documents*, Vol. V. Translated by William Clark. Edinburgh: T & T Clark, 1896.

Henderson, Alan. "According to a 19th century legend, the Truth and the Lie meet one day." *Medium*, January 1, 2020. https://medium.com/@mistywindow/according-to-a-19th-century-legend-the-truth-and-the-lie-meet-one-day-b318378935f4

Henley, Jon. "Italy records lowest coronavirus death toll for a week." *The Guardian*, April 1, 2020. https://www.theguardian.com/world/2020/apr/01/italy-extends-lockdown-amid-signs-coronavirus-infection-rate-is-easing

Hickson, Maike. "Bp. Schneider: Pope Must Formally Correct Statement That God Wills False Religions." *LifeSiteNews*, May 8, 2019. https://www.lifesitenews.com/news/bp-schneider-pope-must-formally-correct-statement-that-god-wills-false-religions/

Hilary of Poitiers. *On the Trinity*. Book V, as quoted in https://www.newadvent.org/fathers/330205.htm

Hillerbrand, Hans. "Martin Luther." *Encyclopedia Britannica*, July 20, 1998. https://www.britannica.com/biography/Martin-Luther

Hindson, Ed, and Dan Mitchell. *The Popular Encyclopedia of Church History*. Eugene: Harvest House Publishers, 2013.

Hirsch, Emil, Kaufmann Kohler, Joseph Jacobs, Aaron Friedenwald, Isaac Broydé. "Circumcision." *The Jewish Encyclopedia*, New York: Funk & Wagnalls, 1901—1906. https://www.jewishencyclopedia.com/articles/4391-circumcision

Hoakley. "Too Real: the narrative paintings of Jean-Léon Gérôme, 7." *The Eclectic Light Company*, August 16, 2018. https://eclecticlight.co/2018/08/16/too-real-the-narrative-paintings-of-jean-leon-gerome-7/

Holmes, Jeremy. "On non-infallible teachings of the Magisterium and the meaning of '*obsequium religiosum*,'" *Catholic World Report*, December 30, 2017. https://www.catholicworldreport.com/2017/12/30/on-non-infallible-teachings-of-the-magisterium-and-the-meaning-of-obsequium-religiosum/

Horn, Trent. "'Prudential Judgment,' and Voting Q+A." *Catholic Answers*, September 24, 2020.

"How Constantine's Victory at The Milvian Bridge let to the spread of Christianity" *History Hit*, October 28, 2016. https://tinyurl.com/2p9yan4a/

Howard, Thomas. *The Pope and the Professor: Pius IX, Ignaz von Dollinger, and the Quandary of the Modern Age.* Oxford: Oxford University Press, 2017.

Huddleston, Gilbert. "Pope St. Gregory I ('the Great')." *The Catholic Encyclopedia.* Vol. 6. New York: Robert Appleton Company, 1909. http://www.newadvent.org/cathen/06780a.htm/

Hughes, Joseph. "Utraquism." *The Catholic Encyclopedia.* Vol. 15. New York: Robert Appleton Company, 1912. http://www.newadvent.org/cathen/15244b.htm/

Ickert, Scott. "Catholic Controversialist Theology and 'Sola Scriptura:' the case of Jacob van Hoogstraten." *The Catholic Historical Review*, Vol. 74, No. 1 (Jan 1988): 13-33.

Ignatius of Antioch. "Epistle to the Romans." https://www.newadvent.org/fathers/0107.htm

———. "Epistle to the Smyrnaeans", as quoted in Bennet, Rod. *Four Witnesses: The Early Church in her own words.* San Francisco: Ignatius Press, 2002.

Irenaeus of Lyons. *Against Heresies*, Book III. https://www.newadvent.org/fathers/0103303.htm

Instituto Nacional de Estatística. *Censos 2011 Resultados Definitivos—Portugal.* Lisbon, 2012.

Ivereigh, Austen. *The Wounded Shepherd.* New York: Henry Holt and Co., 2019.

Jenner, Henry. "Gallican Rite." *The Catholic Encyclopedia.* Vol. 6. New York: Robert Appleton Company, 1909. http://www.newadvent.org/cathen/06357a.htm

———. "Mozarabic Rite." *The Catholic Encyclopedia.* Vol. 10. New York: Robert Appleton Company, 1911. http://www.newadvent.org/cathen/10611a.htm

"Jesus was a capitalist - not a socialist." *Reclaiming America for Jesus Christ.* December 20, 2010. http://reclaimamericaforchrist.org/2010/12/20/jesus-was-a-capitalist-not-a-socialist/

John, Duke of Saxony, George, Margrave of Brandenburg, Ernest, Duke of Lueneberg, Philip, Landgrave of Hesse, John Frederick, Duke of Saxony, Francis, Duke of Lueneburg, Wolfgang, Prince of Anhalt, et al. *Augsburg Confessions.* 1530. https://bookofconcord.org/augsburg-confession/

John Paul II. "Eucharistic Celebration at Trans World Dome, St. Louis." January, 27, 1999. Vatican.va.

———. *Familiaris Consortio.* Libreria Editrice Vaticana, 1981. Vatican.va.

———. *Ut Unum Sint.* Libreria Editrice Vaticana, 1995. Vatican.va.

John XXIII. "Discorso del Santo Padre nella Solenne Apertura del Concilio Ecumenico Vaticano II." October 11, 1962. Vatican.va.

Johnson, Samuel. *The Absolute Impossibility of Transubstantiation Demonstrated.* London: The Sun, 1688; Ann Arbor: Early English Books Online Text Creation Partnership, 2022. https://tinyurl.com/3kahymw5/

Jong, Jonathan. "On receiving communion in one kind." *St. Mary Magdalen School of Theology.* March 11, 2020. https://www.theschooloftheology.org/posts/essay/communion-in-one-kind/

Joseph, Peter. "The Catholic Magisterium." *The Catholic Answer*, September/October 1998.

Joy, John. "Capital Punishment and the Infallibility of the Church" *Dialogos Institute*, October 27, 2017. https://dialogos-institute.org/blog/wordpress/capital-punishment-and-the-infallibility-of-the-church-john-p-joy/

———. "Disputed Questions on Papal Infallibility—Part 1." *One Peter Five*, August 5, 2022. https://onepeterfive.com/disputed-questions-on-papal-infallibility-part-1/

Kaiser, Denis. "Leo the Great on the Supremacy of the Bishop of Rome." *Andrews University Seminary Student Journal* Vol. 1, No. 2 (2015): 73-89.

Keating, Joseph. "Christianity." *The Catholic Encyclopedia.* Vol. 3. New York: Robert Appleton Company, 1908. http://www.newadvent.org/cathen/03712a.htm

Kirby, Sarah. "7 Persistent Myths About Henri de Lubac's Theology," *Church Life Journal*, March 23, 2023. https://tinyurl.com/yr34x5n4

Kirsch, Johann. "Pope John XXII." *The Catholic Encyclopedia.* Vol. 8. New York: Robert Appleton Company, 1910. http://www.newadvent.org/cathen/08431a.htm

———. "Pope St. Hormisdas." *The Catholic Encyclopedia.* Vol. 7. New York: Robert Appleton Company, 1910. http://www.newadvent.org/cathen/07470a.htm

———. "Pope St. Victor I." *The Catholic Encyclopedia.* Vol. 15. New York: Robert Appleton Company, 1912. http://www.newadvent.org/cathen/15408a.htm

———. "Pope Vigilius." *The Catholic Encyclopedia.* Vol. 15. New York: Robert Appleton Company, 1912. http://www.newadvent.org/cathen/15427b.htm

Kovach, Tony. "An Interactive Detective Story." *Catholic Answers*, July 1, 1999. https://www.catholic.com/magazine/print-edition/an-interactive-detective-story

Kwasniewski, Peter. *From Benedict's Peace to Francis's War.* Brooklyn: Angelico Press, 2021.

———. "How Protestants, Orthodox, Magisterialists and Traditionalists differ on the Three Pillars of Christianity." *One Peter Five*, May 26, 2022. https://onepeterfive.com/how-protestants-orthodox-magisterialists-and-traditionalists-differ-on-the-three-pillars-of-christianity/

———. "How to Properly Understand the Role of the Papacy (Guest: Dr. Peter Kwasniewski)" by Eric Sammons. *Crisis Magazine*, August 19, 2022. https://www.crisismagazine.com/podcast/how-to-properly-understand-the-role-of-the-papacy-guest-dr-peter-kwasniewski

———. "My Journey from Ultramontanism to Catholicism." *Catholic Family News blog*, February 21, 2021. https://catholicfamilynews.com/blog/2021/02/04/my-journey-from-ultramontanism-to-catholicism/

———. "Pius X Condemns Modernism: Relevant Then, Relevant Now." *One Peter Five*, September 18, 2018. https://onepeterfive.com/pius-modernism-relevant/

———. "What does it mean to be a 'traditional Catholic? Aren't all Catholics traditional?" *Rorate Caeli*, February 22, 2012. https://rorate-caeli.blogspot.com/2012/01/who-is-traditionalist.html?m=1

La Bachelet. "Benoit XII." *Dictionnaire de Théologie Catholique. Tome Deuxième.* 13th Edition. Paris: Letouzey et Ané Editeurs, 1910, 653-669.

Lambe, Patrick. "Biblical Criticism and Censorship in Ancien Régime France: the Case of Richard Simon." *The Harvard Theological Review*, Vol. 78, No. 1/2 (Jan-Apr. 1985): 149-177.

Lawler, Phil. "Pope's new encyclical ignores previous social teaching." *Catholic Culture*, October 8, 2020. https://www.catholicculture.org/commentary/popes-new-encyclical-ignores-previous-social-teaching/

———. "The Liturgical Edsel." *Catholic Culture*, December 22, 2021. https://www.catholicculture.org/commentary/liturgical-edsel-11085/

———. "This Disastrous Papacy." *Catholic Culture*, March 1, 2017. https://www.catholicculture.org/commentary/this-disastrous-papacy/

———. "*Traditionis Custodes*: a needless extension of papal power." *Catholic Culture*, February 17, 2022. https://www.catholicculture.org/commentary/traditionis-custodes-needless-extension-papal-power/

Lee, Brendan. "Coronavirus and Communion: Sharing is not always caring." *Newcastle Herald*, July 1, 2021. https://www.newcastleherald.com.au/story/6660207/coronavirus-and-communion-sharing-is-not-always-caring/

Leo XIII. *Aeterni Patris*, Libreria Editrice Vaticana, 1879. Vatican.va.

———. *Sapientiae Christianae*. Libreria Editrice Vaticana, 1890. Vatican.va.

Levy, Ian. "Interpreting the Intention of Christ: Roman Responses to Bohemian Utraquism from Constance to Basel," in *Europe After Wyclif*, edited by Patrick Hornbeck and Michael Van Dussen, New York: Fordham University Press, 2017, 173-195.

Lewis, Mike. "A Myth that won't die." *Mike Lewis Extra*, September 30, 2021. https://mikelewis.substack.com/p/a-myth-that-wont-die

———. "Getting it Half-right: Sedes and SSPX." *Where Peter Is*, March 21, 2019. https://wherepeteris.com/getting-it-half-right-sedes-and-sspx/

———. "Perspective on the China / Vatican deal." *Where Peter Is*, September 30, 2018. https://wherepeteris.com/perspective-on-the-china-vatican-deal/

———. "Simply Inadmissible." *Where Peter Is*, May 22, 2020. https://wherepeteris.com/simply-inadmissible/

Loader, William. *Jesus' Attitude Towards the Law: A Study of the Gospels*. Michigan: William B. Eerdman's Publishing Company, 2002.

Lopes, Antonino. *The Popes. The Lives of the Pontiffs throughout 2000 Years of History*. Rome: Futura Edizione, 2005.

Lossky, Vladimir. *In the Image and Likeness of God.* New York: St. Vladimir's Seminary Press, 1974.

Luther, Martin. *The Babylonian Captivity of the Church, 1520—the Annotated Luther Study Edition,* edited by Paul Robinson. Minneapolis: Fortress Press, 2016.

Luther, Martin, Justus Jonas, John Bugenhagen, Caspar Creutziger, Niclas Ambsdorf, George Spalatin, Philip Melanchthon, et al. *Smalcald Articles.* 1537. https://bookofconcord.org/smalcald-articles/

MacErlean, Andrew. "Motu Proprio." *The Catholic Encyclopedia*, Vol. 10. New York: Robert Appleton, 1911. https://www.newadvent.org/cathen/10602a.htm/

Mallett, Mark. "On Vatican Funkiness." *The Now Word* (blog), October 22, 2019 https://www.markmallett.com/blog/2019/10/22/on-vatican-funkiness/

Mares, Courtney. "Amazon Synod: Ecological ritual performed in Vatican gardens for pope's tree planting ceremony." *Catholic News Agency*, October 4, 2019. https://www.catholicnewsagency.com/news/42454/amazon-synod-ecological-ritual-performed-in-vatican-gardens-for-popes-tree-planting-ceremony

Marinou-Boura, Theoni. "The term Mother of God in the Church Fathers and writers." *Pemptousia*, September 5, 2016. https://pemptousia.com/2016/09/the-term-mother-of-god-in-the-church-fathers-and-writers/

Marshall, Taylor. "182: Red Pilled on Pope Francis with Patrick Coffin, Dr Taylor Marshall and Timothy Gordon [Podcast]." *Chartable* podcast, 01:33:36. https://chartable.com/podcasts/taylor-marshall-catholic-show/episodes/27325875-182-red-pilled-on-pope-francis-with-patrick-coffin-dr-taylor-marshall-and-timothy-gordon-podcast/

———. *The Crucified Rabbi: Judaism & the Origins of Catholic Christianity.* Dallas: Saint John Press, 2009.

Martini, Stefano. "La malinconia come luogo della criticità della condizione umana." Lecture for the Istituto di Cultura Italo-Tedesco, 2010. https://irp-cdn.multiscreensite.com/c6e448df/files/uploaded/2011_Romano_Guardini.pdf

Martins, Nuno. *Introdução à Teologia.* Lisbon, Universidade Católica Editora, 2003.

Massey, Michael. "Sedevacantism is Modern Day Luciferianism." *One Peter Five*, December 2, 2019. https://onepeterfive.com/sedevacantism-luciferianism/

Mathews, Shailer. "The Council at Jerusalem." *The Biblical World*, Vol. 33, No. 5 (May 1909): 337-342.

Mathison, Keith. "Solo scriptura—the difference a vowel makes." *Modern Reformation*, Vol. 16, No. 2 (March/April 2007): 25-29.

McCown, Chester. "Alfred Loisy: Unfaltering Critic." *The Journal of Religion*, Vol. 22, No. 1 (Jan. 1942): 20-38.

McCusker, Matthew. "Key doctrinal errors and ambiguities of Amoris Laetitia." *Rome Life Forum*, May 6, 2016.

———. "The almost unbelievable account of how the Synod on the family was almost hijacked by an anti-family agenda." *LifeSiteNews*, June 24, 2015. https://www.lifesitenews.com/opinion/the-almost-unbelievable-account-of-how-the-synod-on-the-family-was-almost-h/

McGuckin, John. *St. Cyril of Alexandria and the Christological controversy*. Leiden: E.J. Brill, 1994.

Mews, Constant. "Gregory the Great, the Rule of Benedict and Roman liturgy: the evolution of a legend." *Journal of Medieval History*, Vol. 37, No. 2 (2011): 125-144.

Miller, Peter. "A Brief Defense of Traditionalism." *Seattle Catholic,* December 21, 2001. https://www.seattlecatholic.com/article_20011221_A_Brief_Defense_of_Traditionalism.html

Milles, Brian. "A Hegelian Papacy?" *One Peter Five*, October 23, 2014. https://onepeterfive.com/a-hegelian-papacy/

Mirus, Jeffrey. "Pope St. Pius V and *Quo Primum*: Did the Pope Intend to Bind His Successors from Changing the Tridentine Mass?" *EWTN*, 1996. https://tinyurl.com/ypvtveaw/

Modello, Geoffrey. "Hegelianism." *The Catholic Encyclopedia*, Vol. 5. New York: Robert Appleton Company, 1909. https://www.newadvent.org/cathen/07192a.htm

Mohrmann, Christine. "How Latin Came to Be the Language of Early Christendom." *Studies: An Irish Quarterly Review*, Vol. 40, No. 159 (Sep. 1951): 277-288.

Montagna, Diane. "Exclusive: Bishop Schneider Wins Clarification on 'Diversity of Religions' from Pope Francis, Brands Abuse Summit a

'Failure.'" *LifeSiteNews*, March 7, 2019. https://www.lifesitenews.com/news/bishop-schneider-extracts-clarification-on-diversity-of-religions-from-pope-francis-brands-abuse-summit-a-failure/

Morrisey, F.G. "Apostolic Exhortation." *New Catholic Encyclopedia*, 2nd Edition, Vol. 1. Washington, DC: Catholic University of America, 2003, 585–86.

Moss, Candida. "Hubristic Specialists: Catholic Responses to Higher Biblical Criticism," *Studies in the Bible and Antiquity* Vol. 8, Article 4 (2016): 32-44.

Mullin, Robert. *A Short World History of Christianity*. Louisville: Westminster John Knox Press, 2008.

Nash, Tom. "A Primer on Biblical Typology." *Catholic Answers*. https://www.catholic.com/qa/a-primer-on-biblical-typology/

———. "Who are the Twelve Apostles, and what happened to them?" *Catholic Answers*. https://www.catholic.com/qa/were-all-twelve-apostles-martyred/

Nestorius. "Reply to Cyril of Alexandria's Second Letter," as quoted in *Early Church Texts*. https://earlychurchtexts.com/public/nestorius_second_letter_to_cyril.htm

———. "Third Letter of Nestorius to Celestine of Rome." Translated by Mark DelCogliano. Tertullian.org. https://www.tertullian.org/fathers/nestorius_two_letters_01.htm

New Catholic [pseudo.], "The Horror" *Rorate Caeli*, March 13, 2013. https://rorate-caeli.blogspot.com/2013/03/the-horror-buenos-aires-journalist.html

New World Encyclopedia contributors. "Scholasticism." *New World Encyclopedia*, https://www.newworldencyclopedia.org/p/index.php?title=Scholasticism&oldid=1026539

Newman, John Henry. *An Essay in Aid of a Grammar of Assent*. London: Burns, Oates, & Co., 1874.

———. *An Essay on the Development of Christian Doctrine*. 6th Edition. Notre Dame: University of Notre Dame Press, 1989.

Noll, Mark. "Martin Luther and the Concept of 'True' Church." *The Evangelical Quarterly*, Vol. 50, No. 2 (Apr.-June 1978): 79-85.

Oestreicher, Paul. "Was Jesus gay? Probably." *The Guardian*, April 20, 2012. https://www.theguardian.com/commentisfree/belief/2012/apr/20/was-jesus-gay-probably/

O'Neill, Taylor. "A Defense of Ultramontanism Contra Gallicanism." *Church Life Journal*, October 12, 2018. https://churchlifejournal.nd.edu/articles/a-defense-of-ultramontanism-contra-gallicanism/

O'Malley, John. *Trent: What happened at the Council.* Cambridge: Belknap Press, An Imprint of Harvard University Press, 2013.

———. *Vatican I: the Council and the making of the Ultramontane Church.* Cambridge: Belknap Press, An Imprint of Harvard University Press, 2018.

———. *What Happened at Vatican II.* Cambridge: Belknap Press, An Imprint of Harvard University Press, 2010.

Ott, Ludwig. *Fundamentals of Catholic Dogma.* Baronius Press, 2018.

Pace, Edward. "Beatific Vision." *The Catholic Encyclopedia.* Vol. 2. New York: Robert Appleton Company, 1907. http://www.newadvent.org/cathen/02364a.htm

Pakaluk, Michael. "Cardinal Dulles's Dubia." *First Things*, August 6, 2018. https://www.firstthings.com/web-exclusives/2018/08/cardinal-dulless-dubia/

Pauck, Wilhelm. "Adolf von Harnack". *Encyclopedia Britannica*, June 6, 2022, https://www.britannica.com/biography/Adolf-von-Harnack

Paul VI. *Evangelii Nuntiandi.* Libreria Editrice Vaticana, 1975. Vatican.va.

———. "General Audience" January 12, 1966. Vatican.va.

———. "General Audience" January 19, 1972. Vatican.va.

Pelikan, Jaroslav. "Christianity as an Enfolding Circle [Conversation with Jaroslav Pelikan]" by Joseph Carey. *U.S. News & World Report.* Vol. 106, no. 25 (June 26, 1989): 57

Pelletier, Rodney. "Self-described Catholics abandoning true teachings". *Church Militant*, June 14, 2021. https://www.churchmilitant.com/news/article/deserting-doctrine/

Pentin, Edward. "Cardinal Burke on *Amoris Laetitia Dubia*: 'Tremendous Division' Warrants Action." *National Catholic Register*, November 15, 2016. https://www.ncregister.com/news/cardinal-burke-on-amoris-laetitia-dubia-tremendous-division-warrants-action/

———. "Full Text and Explanatory Notes of Cardinals' Questions on '*Amoris Laetitia*.'" *National Catholic Register*, November 14, 2016.

https://www.ncregister.com/blog/full-text-and-explanatory-notes-of-cardinals-questions-on-amoris-laetitia/

Peters, Edward. "A Non-Magisterial Magisterial Statement?" *In the Light of the Law* (blog), December 15, 2015. https://canonlawblog.wordpress.com/2015/12/15/a-non-magisterial-magisterial-statement/

Pettegrew, Larry. "The Perspicuity of Scripture." *TMSJ*, Vol 15, No. 2 (Fall 2004): 209-225.

Phips, William. "Did Jesus marry?" *The New York Times*, January 20, 1971.

Pié-Ninot, Salvador. "L'Ultima Parola." *L'Osservatore Romano*, March 17, 2017.

Pius IX. *Quartus Supra*, 1873. https://www.papalencyclicals.net/pius09/p9quartu.htm

———. *Syllabus of Errors*, 1864. https://www.papalencyclicals.net/pius09/p9syll.htm

———. *Tuas Libenter.* December 21, 1863. Vatican.va.

Pius V. *Quo Primum*, 1570. https://www.papalencyclicals.net/pius05/p5quopri.htm

Pius X. "Discorso del Santo Padre Pio X ai Sacerdoti dell'Unione Apostolica in Occasione del Cinquantesimo Anniversario della Fondazione," November 18, 1912. Vatican.va.

———. *Il Fermo Proposito.* Libreria Editrice Vaticana, 1905. Vatican.va.

———. *Pascendi Dominici Gregis*, Libreria Editrice Vaticana, 1907. Vatican.va.

———. *The Oath against Modernism*, https://www.papalencyclicals.net/pius10/p10moath.htm

Pius XI. *Casti Connubii.* Libreria Editrice Vaticana, 1930. Vatican.va.

Pius XII. "A los Participantes en el I Congreso Internacional de Histopatología del Sistema Nervioso." September 14, 1952. Vatican.va.

———. *Divino Afflante Spiritu.* Libreria Editrice Vaticana, 1943. Vatican.va.

———. *Humani Generis.* Libreria Editrice Vaticana, 1950. Vatican.va.

———. *Mystici Corporis Christi.* Libreria Editrice Vaticana, 1943. Vatican.va.

Pontifical Council for Justice and Peace. *Compendio de la Doctrina Social de la Iglesia.* Libreria Editrice Vaticana, 2004. Vatican.va.

"Portuguese Black Pudding (Morcela) Recipe", *Portuguese Recipes*, April 16, 2016. https://portugueserecipes.ca/recipe/274/1/Portuguese-Black-Pudding--Morcela-?r=1

Price, Richard, and Mary Whitby. *Chalcedon in Context.* Liverpool: Liverpool University Press, 2009.

"A Portuguese favorite: Arroz de cabidela recipe", *Taste Porto.* https://tasteporto.com/typical-portuguese-food-recipe-arroz-de-cabidela/

Ramis, Gabriel. "Liturgical Families in the West," in *Introduction to the Liturgy*, edited by Anscar Chupungco, Minnesota: Liturgical Press, 1997, 25-29.

Ratzinger, Joseph. "Mass '*Pro Eligendo Romano Pontifice*': Homily of Card. Joseph Ratzinger." April 18, 2005. Vatican.va.

———. *Principles of Catholic Theology. Building Stones for a Fundamental Theology.* San Francisco: Ignatius Press, 1987.

———. "Relativism: The Central Problem for Faith Today." *EWTN Global Catholic Television Network*, May 1996. https://www.ewtn.com/catholicism/library/relativism-the-central-problem-for-faith-today-2470/

———. "Worthiness to Receive Holy Communion: General Principles." *EWTN Global Catholic Television Network*. https://www.ewtn.com/ catholicism/library/worthiness-to-receive-holy-communion-general-principles-2153/

Reno, Russell. "Questioning the Shutdown." *First Things*, March 20, 2020. https://www.firstthings.com/web-exclusives/2020/03/questioning-the-shutdown/

Rosner, Brian. *Paul and the Law: Keeping the Commandments of God.* Illinois: InterVarsity Press, 2013.

Rutler, George. "Pope Francis' new comments on the death penalty are incoherent and dangerous." Catholic World Report, December 18, 2018. https://www.catholicworldreport.com/2018/12/18/pope-francis-new-comments-on-the-death-penalty-are-incoherent-and-dangerous/

Sammons, Eric. "Can Catholics 'Recognize and Resist'?" *One Peter Five*, December 13, 2021. https://onepeterfive.com/can-catholics-recognize-and-resist/

Sauvage, George. "Traditionalism." *The Catholic Encyclopedia.* Vol. 15. New York: Robert Appleton Company, 1912. http://www.newadvent.org/cathen/15013a.htm

Savelle, Charles. "A Reexamination of the Prohibitions in Acts 15". *Bibliotheca Sacra*, 161 (October-December 2004): 449-68.

Schaff, Philip. *Nicene and Post-Nicene Fathers*, Series II, Vol. 14. Grand Rapids: Christian Classics Ethereal Library.

Schatz, Klaus. *Papal Primacy: From Its Origins to the Present.* Minnesota: The Liturgical Press, 1990.

Schatz, Klaus. Vaticanum I, 1869-1870. Paderborn: Verlag Ferdinand Schöningh, 1992.

Schiffer, Kathy. "Dulia and Hyperdulia: Do Catholics really worship Mary?" *National Catholic Register*, December 10, 2020. https://www.ncregister.com/blog/dulia-hyperdulia-and-mary/

Schneider, Athanasius. "On the question of a heretical pope." *Gloria Dei*, March 28, 2019. https://www.gloriadei.io/on-the-question-of-a-heretical-pope/

Schnitker, Sarah, and Robert Emmons "Hegel's Thesis-Antithesis-Synthesis Model." In: Runehov, Anne, and Lluis Oviedo. *Encyclopedia of Sciences and Religions.* Springer: Dordrecht, 2013.

Sheehan, Michael. *Apologetics and Catholic Doctrine.* Edited by Peter Joseph. London: Baronius, 2009.

Sheed, Frank. *Theology for Beginners.* London: Sheed and Ward, 1960.

Sheridan, Edward. "A Note on Mr. Blanshard." Thought: Fordham University Quarterly, 1950, Vol. 25, Issue 4, 692-695.

Skeel, David, and Tremper Longman. "The Mosaic Law in Christian Perspective." *University of Pennsylvania Law School Public Law and Legal Theory Research Paper Series*, Research Paper No. 11-25 (August 2, 2011): 1-21.

Skojec, Steve. "Smashing Traditions: The Vatican War Machine is Back." *One Peter Five*, January 21, 2016. https://onepeterfive.com/smashing-traditions-the-vatican-war-machine-is-back/

———. "The Hermeneutic of Ambiguity." *One Peter Five*, November 17, 2014. https://onepeterfive.com/hermeneutic-ambiguity/

Smith, Scott. "Friends Don't Let Friends Accidentally Dogmatize the Extreme Opinion of Albert Pighius." *Reduced Culpability*, October 30, 2021. https://reducedculpability.blog/2021/10/30/friends-dont-let-friends-accidentally-dogmatize-the-extreme-opinion-of-albert-pighius/

Solimeo, Luiz. "Fratelli Tutti: A Socialist-Utopian, Ecumenical-Interreligious Encyclical." *The American Society for the defense of Tradition, Family, and Property* (blog), October 29, 2020. https://www.tfp.org/ fratelli-tutti-a-socialist-utopian-ecumenical-interreligious-encyclical/

Sommer, Benjamim. *The Bodies of God and the World of Ancient Israel.* New York: Cambridge University Press, 2009.

Soro, Mar. *The Church of the East: Apostolic & Orthodox*. San Jose: Adiabene Publications, 2007.

Sparks, Matthew. "*Sub Utraque Specie*: *a Reformed Argument for Communion under both kinds.*" Paper presented in Partial Fulfillment of the Requirements for ST5250-Ecclesiology and Sacraments. Reformed Seminary, 2020.

Spencer, Robert. "The Truth about Pope Honorius." *Catholic Answers*, September 1, 1994. https://www.catholic.com/magazine/print-edition/the-truth-about-pope-honorius/

Spinka, Matthew, and Frantisek Bartos. "Jan Hus." *Encyclopedia Britannica*, July 20, 1998. https://www.britannica.com/biography/Jan-Hus

Stern, Jay. "Jesus' Citation of Dt 6,5 and Lv 19,18 in the light of Jewish Tradition." *The Catholic Biblical Quarterly*, Vol. 28, No. 3 (July 1966): 312-316.

Strand, Kenneth. "John as Quartodeciman: A Reappraisal." *Journal of Biblical Literature*, Vol. 84, No. 3 (Sep. 1965): 251-258.

———. "Sunday Easter and Quartodecimanism in the Early Christian Church." *Andrews University Seminary Studies*, Vol. 28, No. 2 (Summer 1990): 127-13.

Strickland, Joseph, Henry Gracida, Robert Mutsaerts, Athanasius Schneider, James Altman, Heinz-Lothar Barth, Donna Bethell et al. "*The teaching of the Catholic faith on the reception of the Holy Eucharist.*" https://www.lifesitenews.com/wp-content/uploads/2022/09/The-teaching-of-the-Catholic-faith-on-the-reception-of-the-Holy-Eucharist.pdf

Swidler, Leonard. *Jesus was a Feminist: What the Gospels reveal about His Revolutionary Perspective.* Plymouth: Sheed and Ward, 2007.

Tanner, J. Paul. "Apostate Jerusalem as Babylon the Great: Another Look at Revelation 17-18." Paper presented at *ETS SW Regional Conference, Fort Worth, Texas, March 31, 2017.*

Tawfike, Mina. "The Mother of God: Theotokos—Reevaluation of the term." *Diss. Alexandria School of Theology*, 2011. http://tinyurl.com/2cn92pt4/

"The 21 Ecumenical Councils." *New Advent.* https://www.newadvent.org/library/almanac_14388a.htm

The Italian Insider. "Ratzinger comes to defence of Pope Francis." March 13, 2018. http://www.italianinsider.it/?q=node/6505/

Thiessen, Matthew. "Abolishers of the Law in Early Judaism and Matthew 5,17-20." *Biblica* Vol. 93, No. 4 (2012): 543-556.

Thomson, Judith. "A Defense of Abortion". *Philosophy & Public Affairs*, Vol. 1, No. 1 (Fall 1971): 39-54.

Toner, Patrick. "Communion under Both Kinds." *The Catholic Encyclopedia.* Vol. 4. New York: Robert Appleton Company, 1908. http://www.newadvent.org/cathen/04175a.htm

Tossati, Marco. "The Amazon Synod: a Trojan Horse to destroy Priestly Celibacy?" *One Peter Five*, March 29, 2019. https://onepeterfive.com/amazon-synod-celibacy/

"Tradition." *Merriam-Webster.com.* 2022. https://www.merriam-webster.com

Travers, Patrick. "*Amoris Laetitia* and Canon 915: A Merciful Return to the 'Letter of the Law.'" Pts. 1 and 2. *Periodica de Re Canonica*, Vol. 107, No. 1 (2018): 297–326; No. 3 (2018): 367–418.

Trent. "4th Session," April 8, 1546, as quoted by http://www.thecounciloftrent.com/

Turner, William. "Scholasticism." *The Catholic Encyclopedia*, Vol. 5. New York: Robert Appleton Company, 1909. https://www.newadvent.org/cathen/13548a.htm

Urbano, Arthur. "Clothes and the Man: How popes communicate through clothing." *America Magazine*, May 13, 2013. https://www.americamagazine.org/issue/clothes-and-man/

Vale, Gillian, Sarah Davis, Susan Lambeth, Steven Schapiro. "Acquisition of a socially learned tool use sequence in chimpanzees: Implications for cumulative culture." *Evolution and Human Behavior* Vol. 38, Issue 5 (September, 2017): 635–44.

van den Aardweg, Gerard, Claude Barthe, Philip Beattie, Jehan de Belleville, Robert Brucciani, Mario Caponnetto, Robert Cassidy, et al. "*Correctio Filialis de Haeresibus Propagatis.*" July 16, 2017. https://www.correctiofilialis.org/

van der Breggen. "Acorns and oak trees . . . and abortion." *Apologia*, October 2, 2008. http://apologiabyhendrikvanderbreggen.blogspot.com/2008/10/ acorns-and-oak-treesand-abortion.html

Vatican I. "Dogmatic Constitution on the Catholic Faith: *Dei Filius*," April 24, 1870. https://www.papalencyclicals.net/councils/ecum20.htm

———. "Dogmatic Constitution on the Church of Christ: *Pastor Aeternus*," July 18, 1870. https://www.papalencyclicals.net/councils/ecum20.htm

Vatican II. *Dei Verbum*, November 18, 1965. Vatican.va.

———. *Dignitatis Humanae.* December 7, 1965. Vatican.va.

———. *Gaudium et Spes.* December 7, 1965. Vatican.va.

———. *Gravissimum educationis.* October 28, 1965. Vatican.va.

———. *Lumen Gentium.* November 21, 1964. Vatican.va.

———. *Optatam totius.* October 28, 1965. Vatican.va.

Vatican News. "Pope Francis-Feast of Saint Francis 2019-10-04." *YouTube* video, 01:13:00. October 4, 2019. https://www.youtube.com/watch?v=1wioisaIU2I/

Vennari, "Modernism in a Nutshell—Religions must change with the times" as seen in *Reject Modernism*, December 5, 2013. https://rejectmodernism.com/2013/12/05/modernism-in-a-nutshell/

Vere, Peter. "A Canonical History of the Lefebvrite Schism." *MA thesis*, Saint Paul University, 1999. https://www.catholicculture.org/culture/library/view.cfm?recnum=1392

Vermeersch, Arthur. "Modernism." *The Catholic Encyclopedia*, Vol. 10. New York: Robert Appleton, 1911

Vilijoen, Francois. "Jesus' Teaching on the 'Torah' in the Sermon on the Mount." *Neotestamentica* Vol. 40, No. 1 (2006): 135-155.

Vincent of Lérins. *Commonitorium.* Edited by Philip Schaff and Henry Wace. Translated by C.A. Heurtley. From *Nicene and Post-Nicene Fathers,*

Second Series. Buffalo: Christian Literature, 1894. http://www.newadvent.org/fathers/3506.htm

Visser, Jan. "The Old Catholic churches of the Union of Utrecht." *International Journal for the Study of the Christian Church*, Vol. 3, No. 1 (2003): 68-84.

Vones, Ludwig. "The Substitution of the Hispanic Rite by the Roman Rite in the Kingdoms of the Iberian Peninsula," in *Hispania Vetus: Musical-Liturgical Manuscripts from Visigothic Origins to the Franco-Roman Transition (9th-12th centuries)*. Edited by Susana Zapke, Bilbao: Fundación BBVA, 2007.

Voter's Guide for Serious Catholics. San Diego: Catholic Answers Action, 2006.

Waldstein, Michael. "Historical-Critical Scripture Studies and the Catholic Faith." *EWTN Global Catholic Television Network*, https://www.ewtn.com/catholicism/library/historicalcritical-scripture-studies-and-the-catholic-faith-12336/

Wedig, Mark. "Reception of the Eucharist Under Two Species." *Pastoral Liturgy*, November 27, 2010. http://www.pastoralliturgy.org/resources/0705ReceptionEucharistTwoSpecies.php

Weigel, George. "Caritas in Veritate in Gold and Red." *National Review*, July 7, 2009. https://www.nationalreview.com/2009/07/caritas-veritate-gold-and-red-george-weigel/

Wells, Christopher. "Pope announces extraordinary *Urbi et Orbi* blessing." *Vatican News*, March 22, 2020. https://www.vaticannews.va/en/pope/news/2020-03/pope-calls-for-christians-to-unite-in-prayer-for-end-to-pandemic.html

Westminster Assembly of Divines. *Westminster Confession of Faith*. 1646, as quoted by http://files1.wts.edu/uploads/pdf/about/WCF_30.pdf

White, Clare. "A clump of cells. What it is and what it isn't." *Medium*. February 4. 2018. https://medium.com/@ClaireJWhite/a-clump-of-cells-71071af908d9

Wilhelm, Joseph. "Heresy." *The Catholic Encyclopedia*. Vol. 7. New York: Robert Appleton Company, 1910. http://www.newadvent.org/cathen/07256b.htm

———. "Jan Hus." *The Catholic Encyclopedia*. Vol. 7. New York: Robert Appleton Company, 1910. http://www.newadvent.org/cathen/07584b.htm

Winfield, Nicole. "Pope's Amazon synod proposes married priests, female leaders." *Associated Press*, October 27, 2019. https://tinyurl.com/5n7p35te/

———. "Pope reverses Benedict, reimposes restrictions on Latin Mass." *Associated Press*, July 16, 2021. https://tinyurl.com/5b3yu3hs/

Ybarra, Eric. "Pope Victor I (189-98) & the Roman Primacy – Critical Analysis." *Eric Ybarra* (blog), January 13, 2017. https://tinyurl.com/23a3tsc4/

Appendices

List of Popes[1]

No.	Name (Birth name)	Pontificate	Highlights
1.	St. Peter (Simon Bar-Jonah)	33-67	Was the first pope, chosen by Jesus Christ Himself. Settled the Judaizer controversy at the Council of Jerusalem. Was corrected by St. Paul when, in his private capacity, he contradicted what he had decreed at the council.
2.	St. Linus	67-76	Was the first successor of Peter
10.	St. Pius I	140-155	Excommunicated Marcion.
11.	St. Anicetus	155-166	Met with St. Polycarp of Smyrna and allowed liturgical diversity as regards to the date of Easter celebration.
14.	St. Victor I	189-199	Was the first pope to use Latin in Church official documents and possibly even the liturgy. Excommunicated the Quartodecimans.
16.	St. Callixtus I	217-222	Excommunicated Sabellius
25.	St. Dionysius	259-268	Resolved the controversy between Bishop Dionysius of Alexandria and some Christians (probably Sabellians) accusing him of not professing the *homoousios*.
33.	St. Sylvester I	314-335	Was pope at the time of Emperor Constantine's death.
36.	Liberius	352-366	Was one of the allegedly heretical popes, purported to have signed a Semi-Arian statement under duress.
43.	St. Celestine I	422-432	Helped St. Cyril of Alexandria condemn Nestorius.

[1] Data from Lopes. *The Popes.* Only the popes mentioned in this book are listed. Only the highlights mentioned in this book are stated. St.—saint. Bld.—Blessed. Vb.—Venerable.

44.	St. Sixtus III	432-440	Continued the campaign against Nestorianism.
45.	St. Leo the Great	440-461	Contributed a tome to the Council of Chalcedon, thereby aiding in the condemnation of Monophysitism. Consolidated the universal authority of the bishop of Rome by calling himself "heir to Peter" and "vicar of Peter." Composed the oldest extant liturgical book of the Roman rite. Went outside Rome's walls to plead with Attila the Hun to spare the city.
49.	St. Gelasius I	492-496	Composed the Gelasian sacramentary, with a Roman rite containing a mix of Roman and Gallican elements.
52.	St. Hormisdas	514-523	Composed the Formula of Hormisdas, declaring the Catholic religion to be preserved ever immaculate in the Roman see, and demanded his fellow bishops to sign this formula to heal a schism.
59.	Vigilius	537-555	Was one of the allegedly heretical popes, having refused to condemn the Nestorian Three Chapters, but eventually changed his mind. Ratified the decrees of the Second Council of Constantinople, condemning the Three Chapters.
64.	St. Gregory the Great	590-604	Reformed the liturgy, crystallizing the Roman rite. Established the Gregorian chant.
70.	Honorius I	625-638	Was one of the allegedly heretical popes, since he confessed that Jesus did not have two opposing wills in a way that could be misconstrued as Monothelite, having also allowed Monothelite heresy to spread through negligence.

71.	Severinus	640	Refused to ratify the Monothelite *Ecthesis*.
72.	John IV	640-642	Tried to quell the ascension of Monothelitism. Wrote an apology for Pope Honorius.
79.	St. Agatho	678-681	Wrote a letter to the Third Council of Constantinople, extolling the reliability of the papacy, thereby aiding in the condemnation of Monothelitism.
80.	St. Leo II	682-683	Ratified the decrees of the Third Council of Constantinople, thereby securing the condemnation of Monothelitism, but also changing the anathematization of Honorius from "heresy" to "negligence."
95.	Adrian I	772-795	Helped Charlemagne implement the Roman rite in the Frankish empire.
122.	John X	914-928	Approved the Mozarabic rite.
156.	Alexander II (Anselmo da Baggio)	1061-1073	Tried to suppress the Mozarabic rite at first, but relented after the local synod of Mantua declared it free from error.
157.	St. Gregory VII (Hildebrando di Soana)	1073-1085	Implemented the so-called Gregorian reforms, aimed at curbing clerical immorality and corruption. Suppressed the Mozarabic rite. Excommunicated the Holy Roman Emperor Henry IV, thereby strengthening the papacy's secular power.
171.	Lucius III (Ubaldo Allucignoli)	1181-1185	Condemned the Waldensians and the Cathars.
193.	Boniface VIII (Benedetto Caetani)	1294-1303	Infallibly defined, in his bull *Unam Sanctam*, that Christ and His Vicar constitute one sole head, and that outside the Church there is no salvation.
196.	John XXII (Jacques d'Euse)	1316-1334	Condemned the Fraticelli as heretics. Was one of the allegedly heretical popes, since he held, for a time,

			erroneous beliefs on the beatific vision, though he did not preach them magisterially, only by way of allowing discussion.
197.	Benedict XII (Jacques Fournier)	1334-1342	Defined the dogma of the immediate beatific vision in the bull *Benedictus Deus.*
210.	Pius II (Enea Piccolomini)	1458-1464	Reversed the Council of Basel's concessions for Utraquist practices.
217.	Leo X (Giovanni dei Medici)	1513-1521	Condemned Luther with the bull *Exsurge Domini.*
225.	St. Pius V (Antonio Ghisleri)	1566-1572	Implemented the decisions of the Council of Trent, meant to counter the Protestant Reformation. Promulgated a version of the Roman missal according to Trent's directives, which would become known as the TLM.
227.	Sixtus V (Felice Peretti)	1585-1590	Praised scholastic theology.
240.	Bld. Innocent XI (Benedetto Odescalchi)	1676-1689	Clashed with the authority of King Louis XIV of France, prompting the 1681 Assembly of Clergy that would crystallize Gallicanism.
241.	Alexander VIII (Pietro Ottoboni)	1689-1691	Published the bull *Inter Multiplices*, nullifying the 1681 declaration of the French clergy
254.	Gregory XVI (Bartolomeo Cappellari)	1831-1846	Condemned the indifferentist ecumenical movement of his day in the encyclical *Mirari Vos.* Condemned Lamennais's liberalism in the encyclical *Singulari Nos.*
255.	Bld. Pius IX (Giovanni Mastai-Ferretti)	1846-1878	Promoted the Ultramontane movement. Defined the dogma of the immaculate conception in the bull *Ineffabilis Deus.* Promulgated the Syllabus of Errors. Introduced the concept of "ordinary magisterium" into the official papal lexicon. Defended Pope Liberius in the encyclical *Quartus Supra.* Convoked the First Vatican Council.

			Lost the Papal States.
256.	Leo XIII (Vincenzo Pecci)	1878-1903	Kickstarted Church Social Doctrine with the publication of the encyclical *Rerum Novarum*, condemning Communism and asserting private property rights. Fomented the neo-scholastic movement and the revival of St. Thomas Aquinas's theology in his encyclical *Aeterni Patris*. Asked for the faithful's obedience, not only to the infallible magisterium, but to the ordinary magisterium in his encyclical *Sapientiae Christianae*.
257.	St. Pius X (Giuseppe Sarto)	1903-1914	Condemned and effectively quelled the Modernist movement through the publication of the encyclical *Pascendi Dominici Gregis*. Implemented and called for liturgical reforms.
258.	Benedict XV (Giacomo della Chiesa)	1914-1922	Formulated the principle "old things, but in a new way."
259.	Pius XI (Achille Ratti)	1922-1939	Asked for the faithful's obedience, not only to the infallible magisterium, but to the ordinary magisterium in his encyclical *Casti Connubii*.
260.	Vb. Pius XII (Eugenio Pacelli)	1939-1958	Guided the Church through World War 2. Spoke favourably of the historical-critical method in his encyclical *Divino Afflante Spiritu*. Clarified that papal encyclicals belong to the ordinary magisterium in his encyclical *Humani Generis*. Explained that one cannot follow Christ without following His Vicar, in the encyclical *Mystici Corporis Christi*. Tried to quell the *ressourcement* movement.
261.	St. John XXIII (Angelo Roncalli)	1958-1963	Promulgated a new edition of the Roman missal (the last one before Vatican II). Convoked the Second Vatican Council.

			Developed the concept of *aggiornamento* and "signs of the times."
262.	St. Paul VI (Giovanni Montini)	1963-1978	Implemented the Second Vatican Council, namely the liturgical reforms requested by it. Published the exhortation *Evangelii Nuntiandi*, about evangelization in our times.
264.	St. John Paul II (Karol Wojtyla)	1978-2005	Published a new Catechism of the Catholic Church, still in effect today. Campaigned for a worldwide abolition of the death penalty. Allowed communion only for the divorced and remarried couples that agreed to live as "brother and sister" in the exhortation *Familiaris Consortio.*
265.	Benedict XVI (Joseph Ratzinger)	2005-2013	Promoted a "hermeneutic of continuity" towards Vatican II, as opposed to a "hermeneutic of rupture." Tried to curb the "dictatorship of relativism" of modern times. Campaigned for the abolition of the death penalty worldwide, just like his predecessor. Promulgated *Summorum Pontificum*, allowing a greater freedom in the celebration of the pre-conciliar edition of the Roman missal. Was the first pope to voluntarily resign in 718 years.
266.	Francis (Jorge Bergoglio)	2013-Present	Tried to implement a model of Church governance modelled after the concept of synodality. Allowed communion for divorced and remarried people with mitigating circumstances diminishing subjective culpability in his exhortation *Amoris Laetitia.* Continued his predecessors' diplomatic deals with China. Taught that the death penalty was now to be considered morally inadmissible.

			Signed the Abu Dhabi Joint Declaration with the Grand Imam of Al Azhar, Ahmed Al-Tayeb, marking a new stage of cooperation between Catholicism and Islam. Convoked a synod to promote the evangelization of the Pan-Amazon region and to defend the rights of the indigenous peoples. Shepherded the Church through the COVID-19 pandemic, namely through his famous extraordinary *Urbi et Orbi* address Published the social encyclical *Fratelli tutti*, about human fraternity. Published the apostolic letter *Desiderio desideravi* on the liturgy. Promulgated *Traditionis Custodes*, restricting the 1962 edition of the Roman missal.

List of Councils[2]

<table>
<tr><th>No.</th><th>Name</th><th>Date</th><th>Major highlights</th></tr>
<tr><td>Apost.</td><td>Council of Jerusalem</td><td>49</td><td>Condemned the Judaizer heresy, allowing Gentiles to eat from unclean meats and to not be circumcised.</td></tr>
<tr><td>1.</td><td>First Council of Nicaea</td><td>325</td><td>Promulgated the Nicene creed.
Defined the consubstantiality of the Son with the Father (homoousios).
Condemned Arianism.
Condemned Quartodecimanism.</td></tr>
<tr><td>2.</td><td>First Council of Constantinople</td><td>381</td><td>Added the clauses relative to the Holy Spirit to the Nicene creed.</td></tr>
<tr><td>3.</td><td>Council of Ephesus</td><td>431</td><td>Condemned Nestorianism.
Endorsed the term Theotokos.</td></tr>
<tr><td>4.</td><td>Council of Chalcedon</td><td>451</td><td>Condemned the heresy of Monophysitism.</td></tr>
<tr><td>5.</td><td>Second Council of Constantinople</td><td>553</td><td>Condemned the Nestorian Three Chapters.</td></tr>
<tr><td>6.</td><td>Third Council of Constantinople</td><td>680-681</td><td>Condemned the heresy of Monothelitism.</td></tr>
<tr><td>9.</td><td>First Lateran Council</td><td>1123</td><td rowspan="2">Implemented reforms in ecclesiastical discipline, aimed at curbing clerical corruption. Instituted mandatory clerical celibacy. Prohibited clerical investiture by kings and princes.</td></tr>
<tr><td>10.</td><td>Second Lateran Council</td><td>1139</td></tr>
<tr><td>16.</td><td>Council of Constance</td><td>1414-1418</td><td>Ended the Great Schism of the West.
Condemned Hussism and the necessity of Utraquism.</td></tr>
<tr><td>17.</td><td>Council of Basel-Ferrara-Florence</td><td>1431-1439</td><td>Allowed the Utraquists to commune in both kinds, as long as they acknowledged the doctrine of concomitance.
Allowed eating meat of strangled animals and blood.
Hinted at papal supremacy, which would be developed later on.</td></tr>
</table>

[2] Data from "The 21 Ecumenical Councils." *New Advent.* Only the ecumenical councils mentioned in this book are listed. Though the Council of Jerusalem is not considered an ecumenical council, I have decided to list it here due to its importance for this book. Local councils are not listed. Only the highlights mentioned in this book are stated. Apost. —Apostolic.

19.	Council of Trent	1545-1563	Defined the dogmas of transubstantiation and concomitance. Condemned Protestantism. Instituted ecclesial reforms. Laid out the principles for the Counter-Reformation. Requested a liturgical reform, subsequently carried out by Pope St. Pius V. Reaffirmed Constance's condemnation of the necessity of Utraquism.
20.	First Vatican Council	1869-1870	Defined the dogmas of papal supremacy and papal infallibility. Condemned Gallicanism. Condemned Traditionalism.
21.	Second Vatican Council	1962-1965	Promoted a more dialogical approach towards the modern world. Developed Catholic teaching on ecumenism and interreligious dialogue, and also Church-state relations. Requested a liturgical reform, subsequently carried out by Pope St. Paul VI. Rehabilitated the *ressourcement* theologians.

List of Heresies[3]

Name	Heresiarch	Major tenets	Condemnation (date)
Arianism	Arius	The Son is a creature and, therefore, not coeternal with the Father.	First Council of Nicaea (325)
Catharism	Unknown	There are two gods: the good God of the New Testament, and the evil demiurge of the Old Testament (*see Marcionism*). The Eucharist, purgatory, and prayers to the saints or for the dead are false teachings. Procreation is evil.	Bull *Ad abolendam* by Pope Lucius III (1184)
Docetism	Unknown	Jesus was only divine, not human, and His body was merely an illusion.	Epistle to the Smyrnaeans by St. Ignatius of Antioch (ca. 110)
Ebionism	Unknown	Jesus was merely a prophet, chosen by God because He was righteous in following the law. Christians should, therefore, also follow the whole of Mosaic law.	*Against Heresies* by St. Irenaeus of Lyons (ca. 180)
Eutychianism	Eutyches	*See Monophysitism*	

[3] Only the heresies mentioned in this book are listed.

Febronianism	Bishop von Hontheim (Justinius Febronius)	*German version of Gallicanism*	
Fraticelli heresy	Angelo da Clareno	Following the Franciscan rule of poverty is necessary for salvation. The Church was a corrupt entity, and the pope had no jurisdiction over their rule.	Bull *Sancta Romana Ecclesia* by John XXII (1317)
Gallicanism	Several	Papal primacy is limited by the temporal power of French kings, by the authority of ecumenical councils, by the consent of French bishops, and by the canons and customs of the local French churches.	Dogmatic Constitution *Pastor Aeternus*, by the First Vatican Council (1870)
Gnosticism	Several	*Heterogeneous group linked by the following common beliefs*: 1) salvation comes from knowledge (gnosis); 2) matter is a deterioration of spirit; 3) the ultimate end is freeing oneself from matter and returning to the God-spirit.	*Against Heresies* by St. Irenaeus of Lyons (ca. 180)
Hussism	Jan Huss	There should be freedom of preaching. Clerics should not own property, and	Council of Constance (1415)

		Church property should be expropriated. *See also Utraquism*	
Josephism	Joseph II	*Austrian version of Gallicanism*	
Judaizer heresy	Unknown	Gentile converts to Christianity must follow all the precepts of the Mosaic law, including circumcision.	Council of Jerusalem (ca. 49)
Lollardism	John Wycliffe	The Eucharist undergoes consubstantiation, not transubstantiation. The sacrament of Confession is blasphemous. Clerical celibacy and prayers for the individual dead are not advisable.	Council of Constance (1415)
Marcionism	Marcion	The benevolent God of the New Testament that sent Jesus Christ as a savior is not the same as the malevolent creator God of the Old Testament.	Marcion's excommunication by Pope St. Pius I (ca. 144)
Modernism	Alfred Loisy	The Church must adapt her dogmas do the modern world.	Encyclical *Pascendi Dominici Gregis* by Pope St. Pius X (1907)
Monophysitism	Eutyches	Jesus had only one nature, the human nature having been absorbed into the divine nature	Council of Chalcedon (451)
Monothelitism	Sergius Pyrrhus	Jesus has only one will, instead of a	Third Council of Constantinople (681)

		human will and a divine will	
Nestorianism	Nestorius	Jesus had distinct human and divine hypostases, therefore the term *Theotokos* is incorrect	Council of Ephesus (431)
Protestantism	Martin Luther Ulrich Zwingli John Calvin	*Heterogeneous group linked by the beliefs in* sola fide *("faith alone,")* sola gratia *("grace alone,") and* sola scriptura *("scripture alone.") They also believe (in general) that certain Catholic doctrines like the veneration of saints, carving of statues of the saints, and purgatory are unscriptural and thus, false.*	Bull *Exsurge Domine* by Pope Leo X (1520) Council of Trent (1545-1563)
Quartodecimanism	Polycrates of Ephesus	The most traditional practice is for Easter to be celebrated on the same date as the Jewish Passover.	Polycrates's excommunication by Pope St. Victor I (180-190s) First Council of Nicaea (325)
Sabellianism	Sabellius	The Trinity consists in three operations or modes, instead of three distinct persons.	Sabellius's excommunication by Pope St. Callixtus I (ca. 220)
Semi-Arianism	George of Laodicea Eustathius of Sebaste	Father and Son are not of the same substance (*homoousios*) but of similar substances (*homoiousios*).	Writings by St. Athanasius of Alexandria (350-370s)

Taboritism	Petr Hromadka	*Radical branch of Utraquism, which rejected the doctrine of concomitance and the concessions given by the Council of Basel.*	Council of Trent (1545-1563)
Traditionalism	Felicité de Lamennais	Before trusting in reason, one must take a leap of faith, blindly believing in "general reason" (the common agreement of all).	Dogmatic Constitution *Dei Filius*, by the First Vatican Council (1870)
Utraquism	Jan Huss Jacob of Mies	The laity must receive communion under both species, both bread and wine.	Council of Constance (1415) Council of Trent (1545-1563)
Waldensianism	Peter Waldo	There is a need to live in apostolic poverty that supersedes the prerogatives of the local bishops.	Bull *Ad abolendam* by Pope Lucius III (1184)

Index

S

Printed in Great Britain
by Amazon